AMERICAN DIABETES
ASSOCIATION

THE AMERICAN DIETETIC
ASSOCIATION

The New Family Cookbook

for People with Diabetes

SIMON & SCHUSTER

SIMON & SCHUSTER
Rockefeller Center
1230 Avenue of the Americas
New York, NY 10020

Copyright © 1999 by the American Diabetes Association
and The American Dietetic Association
All rights reserved,
including the right of reproduction
in whole or in part in any form.
SIMON & SCHUSTER and colophon are
registered trademarks of Simon & Schuster Inc.
Designed by Edith Fowler
Manufactured in the United States of America

10   9   8   7   6   5   4   3   2

Library of Congress Cataloging-in-Publication Data

The new family cookbook for people with diabetes /
American Diabetes Association ; The American
Dietetic Association.
     p.   cm.
   Includes index.
   1. Diabetes—Diet therapy Recipes.   I. American
Diabetes Association.   II. American Dietetic
Association.
RC662.N49   1999
641.5'6314—dc21   99-27030   CIP
ISBN 0-684-82660-7

American Diabetes Association and
The American Dietetic Association gratefully acknowledge the following contributors:

Recipe Alterations and Testing:
Mary Abbott Hess, MS, RD

Nutrition Analysis and Exchange Calculations:
Madelyn L. Wheeler, MS, RD, CDE

Recipe Headnote Writer:
Kerry Neville, MS, RD

Managing Editor:
Raeanne Sarazen, RD

Contents

Foreword

THE BEST COOKBOOKS help us create delicious meals that appeal to our senses of sight, smell, and taste. If you get the added bonus of meals that are also healthful and nutritious, you have found a treasure of a cookbook indeed. If you have special health or dietary concerns, the search for such a cookbook can be frustrating. *The New Family Cookbook for People with Diabetes* offers you both good food and good health.

The recipes were developed for people with diabetes by The American Dietetic Association and the American Diabetes Association in their Family Cookbooks, volumes I, II, III, and IV. We've chosen the best recipes from these volumes and updated them using the newest and healthiest ingredients available. In addition, *The New Family Cookbook for People with Diabetes* incorporates the most recent nutrition recommendations for people with diabetes. These recommendations are designed to improve the health of persons with diabetes.

The recipes in this book help you and your family take the right steps toward good eating and good health. To help you take the mystery out of healthful eating, nutrient information and exchange values are provided per serving for each recipe.

We have learned a great deal about food and the nutrition it provides. This book translates our learning into practical solutions you can use as you plan and prepare your meals each day.

LINDA B. HAAS, PHC, RN, CDE
President,
Health Care & Education
American Diabetes Association

ANN M. COULSTON, MS, RD, FADA
President,
The American Dietetic Association

Introduction

FOOD GIVES US ENERGY and provides essential nutrients for good health, but eating food is also something we enjoy and look forward to. It's hard to imagine breaks at work, a trip to the movies, watching sports, and gathering together for holidays, birthdays, or picnics without our favorite foods!

When you (or a family member) is diagnosed with diabetes, you may have concerns and questions about your eating habits and whether or not you can eat your favorite foods.

Having diabetes does not mean giving them up entirely, but you may need to eat some foods less often or in smaller amounts and you may need to buy or make more healthful versions of some of the foods you enjoy.

Remember: the food that is good for you is the same food that is good for people without diabetes. You won't need to spend more time in the kitchen chopping, mixing, and preparing special meals. Your family and friends can enjoy the same healthful foods that you are eating and enjoying. Take a look through this book—you're sure to find some family favorites.

The recipes in the cookbook are easy to prepare, and the ingredients are readily available in supermarkets or well-stocked grocery stores. Whether you love to cook or are just learning how, this book can help you manage your diabetes.

ABOUT THE RECIPES

The 400 recipes in this book are the best of the best from the Family Cookbook series, volumes I to IV, published by the American Diabetes Association and The American Dietetic Association. To create the most delicious and healthful dishes, the recipes chosen for this collection were revised, updated, and taste-tested to make sure they are consistent with the latest diabetes recommendations and make the best use of new food products available in the marketplace today.

The updates and changes to the recipes include the following:

• Recipes use new lower-fat ingredients whenever possible.

Most Americans eat too much fat, which can contribute to the development of diabetes, heart disease, cancer, and obesity. In this book, the ingredient chosen for a recipe is the lowest-fat product that could be used to create a dish with the best taste and texture. For example, each recipe that uses salad dressing, mayonnaise, or sour cream was tested with light, low-fat, and fat-free variations. If you want to eat foods with a minimal amount of fat, you can use fat-free products in recipes that call for the low-fat versions. The texture and taste of the dish may change but the recipe will still taste fine. Remember, however, that fat-free does not mean carbohydrate-free or calorie-free.

• Recipes use unsaturated fats whenever possible.

Monounsaturated fats (olive or canola oil) and polyunsaturated fats (sunflower and other vegetable oils) are better for your heart than saturated fats (butter or meat fats). Eating too much saturated fat, as well as cholesterol, can increase your risk of cardiovascular disease. To further lower the cholesterol in the recipes, use egg substitutes or egg whites instead of whole eggs.

• Most recipes use sugar instead of sugar substitutes.

Recent nutrition guidelines for diabetes management allow sugar as part of a healthful eating plan. Sugar has the same effect on blood glucose levels as other carbohydrates, such as rice or potatoes. But keep in mind that sugar doesn't contain the nutrients (vitamins, minerals, and fiber) that are in other carbohydrate-rich foods like rice and potatoes. That's the main reason to eat only small amounts of sugar. Foods containing sugar count as part of the total amount of carbohydrate in your eating plan. For blood glucose control, the *amount* of carbohydrate you eat is more important than the *source* of carbohydrate.

• In recipes with more than 400 mg of sodium, the amount of sodium is set in **bold type** and there is an arrow ▶ pointing to the sodium line.

Eating too much sodium may contribute to high blood pressure in sodium-sensitive individuals. Table salt is the most common form of sodium in our diets. However, many foods contain sodium. Sometimes you can taste it, as in pickles and bacon. Other times you cannot. There is "hidden" sodium in many foods, such as cheese, salad dressing, tomato sauce, and canned foods. If you need to reduce the amount of sodium you eat, omit the salt from a recipe and/or use low-sodium versions of canned foods, such as vegetables, broths, and sauces. To boost the flavor of the dish, experiment with herbs or spices. Not everyone should use salt substitutes. Check with your doctor or dietitian before using them.

• Recipes provide a choice of fresh or dried herbs.

You may like the flavor of garden-fresh herbs that you buy at the supermarket or grow at home. Or you may like the convenience of dried herbs. Whichever you prefer, the amounts for both forms are listed in the recipes.

• Each recipe has a new nutrient analysis and the latest diabetes exchange information.

The recipe nutrient and exchange information is for one serving. Measure your serving size the first time you make a recipe. Portion size is an important factor in controlling your weight and blood glucose level. As time goes on, you'll develop an ability to estimate portion size visually without measuring and weighing.

NUTRIENT ANALYSIS

Each recipe includes a complete nutrient analysis with the same nutrient information you find on the Nutrition Facts label on food packages. When a recipe lists a choice of ingredients, the first choice was used for the nutrient analysis. The analysis does not include optional ingredients and garnishes.

EXCHANGE INFORMATION

Each recipe provides the most up-to-date exchange information for people who use an individualized meal plan based on exchanges. (The exchange lists are in the Appendix.) Exchange lists are foods listed together because they are alike. Each serving of a food has about the same amount of carbohydrate, protein, fat, and calories as the other foods on that list.

If you use the exchange information in the recipes, it will be helpful for you to know the following:

- Only whole or half exchanges are listed, not smaller fractions such as quarters.

- Foods from the carbohydrate group (starch, fruit, milk, and other carbohydrate exchanges) may be interchanged. Each exchange group contains about 15 grams of carbohydrate.

- If a recipe is a "free food," it has no more than 20 calories and no more than 5 grams of carbohydrate per serving.

- If you eat 1 or 2 exchange servings of vegetables at a meal, you do not need to count them as part of your meal plan. However, if you eat 3 or more servings of vegetables at a meal, you will need to count the exchanges.

- If beans, peas, or lentils are the main ingredient in a recipe, the exchange information may include *starch* and *very lean meat* to help plan vegetarian meals. If the recipe contains beans, peas, or lentils as one of the many ingredients, they are included as a starch only.

- If more than half of the fat in a recipe is one type of fat, the exchange listing provides the specific type of fat (monounsaturated fat, polyunsaturated fat, or saturated fat). This does not affect the amount of total fat or calories, but it can help you identify the predominant type of fat used in the recipe.

WHAT IS DIABETES?

Your body produces glucose from the foods you eat and uses this glucose as fuel. Glucose travels around your body in the bloodstream, but it has to get into your cells before you can use it. Insulin, a hormone made by the pancreas, is the key that opens the door and lets glucose into the cells. People who have diabetes either do not make enough insulin or cannot use the insulin that they make. Therefore, the glucose cannot get into their cells, so their blood glucose levels increase. Untreated diabetes causes great thirst, frequent urination, blurred vision, weakness, sudden weight loss, fatigue, and irritability.

If your diabetes is not discovered or is not managed properly, the high blood glucose levels damage body tissues and blood vessels over time. This is why people with diabetes are more likely to have heart and blood vessel disease, and kidney, eye, and nerve damage. If you keep your blood glucose levels close to normal, you can avoid many of these complications. Therefore, it is important for you to learn how food, activity, and medications affect your blood glucose level and what you can do to manage it.

Presently, about 16 million people in the United States have diabetes, but more than 5 million of them don't know it. About 625,000 people a year are diagnosed with diabetes. You are more likely to develop diabetes if you are overweight, inactive, 45 years of age or older, or have a relative with diabetes. Also, people of African-American, Hispanic-American, Native-American, Asian-American, and Pacific Island backgrounds are especially at risk. Women who have had a baby that weighed more than 9 pounds also have a higher risk of developing diabetes later in life.

People with type 1 diabetes do not produce any insulin, and need insulin injections. If you have type 1 diabetes, you need to coordinate your insulin with what you eat, when you eat, and your physical activity. Your insulin injections and meals are planned so that the insulin is available when you need to get glucose from your bloodstream into your cells. This helps you keep your blood glucose levels close to normal and prevent the damage that results from high blood glucose levels.

People with type 2 diabetes may make some insulin but cannot use it properly. Many people with type 2 diabetes can keep their blood glucose levels close to normal by eating healthful food choices and getting daily exercise. Some people with type 2 diabetes need to take pills to help their bodies use more of the insulin they make. Others take another kind of pill that slows carbohydrate absorption so that glucose does not surge into their blood after a meal. And some people with type 2 diabetes need insulin injections to keep their blood glucose levels near normal.

MANAGING DIABETES

So far there is no cure for diabetes. But you can manage your diabetes so you prevent long-term complications and feel well day-to-day. The management of diabetes involves three things:

- food
- exercise
- medication

Generally speaking, food raises your blood glucose level; exercise and medication lower it. You need to balance these three to keep your blood glucose level close to normal.

FOOD

You can make a difference in your blood glucose control through your food choices. You do not need special foods. In fact, the foods that are good for you are good for everyone. However, it's important to eat about the same amount of food at the same time each day. Regardless of the level of your blood glucose, avoid skipping meals or snacks, as this may lead to large swings in blood glucose levels.

Your dietitian will take into consideration your age, life-style, activity level, food preferences, and health goals to determine your calorie, carbohydrate, protein, and fat needs. Your dietitian can then translate your nutrient needs into a meal plan to get the right balance among your food, medication, and exercise. Also, your dietitian can help you prepare for times when you are sick or for emergencies when you can't eat healthful foods, or can't eat them at the right time. It's always a good idea to visit your dietitian any time your schedule changes or when you have a life change, such as going off to college, starting a new job, having a baby, or retiring, or whenever your meal plan isn't working for you.

Remember, the more information you provide about what you eat and what you are willing to change, the better your dietitian can tailor your meal plan, and the more likely you are to follow it.

EXERCISE

Your body uses insulin more efficiently when you exercise, whether or not you have diabetes. That's why people with type 2 diabetes can sometimes manage their blood glucose levels with just food and exercise. Also, if you take insulin or diabetes pills, you may need a lower dose if you start to exercise regularly. Exercise also makes your heart healthier. This is important because people with diabetes are more likely to get heart disease.

You don't have to jog or take an aerobics class every day. Start slowly and do whatever type of exercise you enjoy, such as walking, dancing, or swimming. You could start by walking for 5 minutes each day and work up to 30 minutes a day by making your walk 5 minutes longer each week. The important thing is to do something each day, for a total of 30 minutes of activity. Your body works best when you use it.

MEDICATION

Your diabetes care team, which includes your doctor and dietitian, will decide whether you need insulin and/or diabetes pills. If you need either one, they will teach you how and when to take them and how to balance the medication with your food and exercise.

Your diabetes care team will show you how to test your blood glucose level. They will also help you learn to adjust your food, exercise, and medication to keep your blood glucose level close to normal throughout the day.

MEAL PLANNING

An individualized meal plan is one of the most important tools for managing your diabetes. Your meal plan will serve as a guide to help you know what to eat, when to eat, and how much to eat at each meal or snack.

There are several meal-planning approaches your dietitian may recommend. The most common "tools" are based on: the Diabetes Food Guide Pyramid, exchange lists, and counting grams of carbohydrate. These help you eat similar amounts of carbohydrate, fat, protein, and/or calories at the same times each day. Your meal plan will also help you learn about foods and how their nutrient content affects your blood glucose and lipid levels. A registered dietitian can help decide which tool will work best for you.

THE DIABETES FOOD GUIDE PYRAMID

The Diabetes Food Guide Pyramid, which is based on the Dietary Guidelines for Americans as well as the Food Guide Pyramid, tells you about the food groups and how many servings to eat from each food group each day. Even if you don't remember the exact number of servings from each group, the size of the pyramid blocks used to represent each group reminds you how much to eat from that food group.

The bottom level shows the foods you should eat most of every day—grains, beans, and starchy vegetables (6 or more servings). The next level up shows that you should choose plenty of vegetables (3 to 5 servings) and fruits (2 to 4 servings). Be sure to measure your fruit serving sizes. If you eat large servings of fruit, you may eat too much carbohydrate and your blood glucose level may increase too much. Eating foods from these three groups, which are at the base of the pyramid, is the foundation of a healthful meal plan.

Moving up the pyramid, milk and yogurt (2 to 3 servings) and meat and others (2 to 3 servings) are represented by smaller blocks. These foods are important for good health too, but in moderate amounts. Choose low-fat or fat-free milk and yogurt for calcium and other vitamins and minerals without too much fat. Choose lean meats, poultry without the skin, seafood, and dry beans and peas for iron and other vitamins and minerals without too much saturated fat and cholesterol.

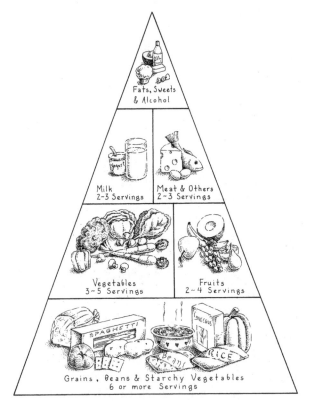

The Diabetes Food Guide Pyramid

At the very top of the pyramid, fats, sweets, and alcohol are represented by a small triangle. This group includes oil, butter, margarine, salad dressing, mayonnaise, doughnuts, cookies, cakes, chips, and alcoholic beverages. Your dietitian can show you how to use the new low-fat or fat-free alternatives to many of these foods.

Don't try to follow all the guidelines at once. Make one change at a time, such as eating more vegetables or drinking fat-free milk. When this change becomes part of your eating habits, make another change. After a while your new, more healthful eating habits will improve your blood glucose control, cholesterol level, weight, and overall health. The good news is that The Diabetes Food Guide Pyramid illustrates a healthful eating plan for everyone, so your family and friends can follow it too.

EXCHANGE LISTS

The exchange lists meal-planning approach has been used since 1950 and has been updated several times. The most recent exchange lists have many more choices on the food lists to make your meal plan more flexible. The exchange lists divide foods into three main groups: Carbohydrate, Meat and Meat Substitutes, and Fat. Every food on a list contains about the same amount of carbohydrate, protein, and fat in the serving size listed. So you can substitute or "exchange" one food on a list for another food on the same list. (See page 480 for the exchange lists.)

The Carbohydrate Group has five lists: starch, fruit, milk, other carbohydrates, and vegetables. Foods from the starch list, fruit list, milk list, and other carbohydrates list all contain 60 to 90 calories and 12 to 15 grams of carbohydrate in one serving, whereas the vegetable list contains 25 calories and 5 grams of carbohydrate. Therefore, these foods can be exchanged for one another occasionally. For example, if you are at a restaurant and fruit is not available, you may choose an extra serving of bread instead. The other carbohydrates list includes desserts and snack foods. If you use a lot of these foods in your meal plan, you may not get all the nutrients you need. But you can enjoy an occasional serving of these foods to replace a starch, fruit, or milk in your meal plan and still keep your diabetes under good control.

The Meat and Meat Substitutes group has four lists of meats and other protein foods: very lean, lean, medium-fat, and high-fat meats. One serving of each of these foods contains 7 grams of protein and no carbohydrate. The fat content varies from 0 to 1 gram for very lean meat and meat substitutes to 8 grams for high-fat meat and meat substitutes.

Foods in the Fat group are divided into three types: monounsaturated, polyunsaturated, and saturated. Monounsaturated and polyunsaturated fats are more heart-healthy than saturated fats, but all three types contain 5 grams of fat, no carbohydrate, and 45 calories per serving.

The exchanges also include a list of Free Foods—one serving of these foods does not provide enough calories or carbohydrate to be counted in your meal plan. However, as with all foods within an exchange list, it's important to check the serving size.

Some Nutrition Facts labels on food packages (see page 20), such as breakfast cereals and frozen entrées, provide exchange information as well as nutrient information.

You and your dietitian can design a meal plan that lists how many exchanges you should have from each list at each meal or snack. You can choose which foods on the lists to eat and check the appropriate serving size. For many people with diabetes, this is a preferred meal-planning approach. Like the Diabetes Food Guide Pyramid, a meal plan based on exchanges can help you to control your blood glucose, cholesterol level, and weight, and to eat a healthful diet. All the recipes in this cookbook provide exchange information.

CARBOHYDRATE COUNTING

Carbohydrate counting is a sophisticated meal-planning approach that can offer a lot of flexibility. This approach is based on the main influencer of blood glucose—grams of carbohydrate in foods. Your dietitian will develop a meal plan that indicates the amount of carbohydrate to be eaten at meals and snacks. If you know how much carbohydrate you are eating, you have a good idea of what your blood glucose level will be.

Carbohydrates are found in starches and sugars. Foods that contain carbohydrate include:
- breads, crackers, and cereals
- pasta, rice, and grains
- vegetables
- milk and yogurt
- fruit and juice
- sugar, honey, syrup, and molasses

All sugars are carbohydrates. Sugars are added to foods such as baked goods and frozen desserts and are present naturally in foods such as milk and fruit. If you look at the Nutrition Facts labels on some unsweetened foods, such as unsweetened yogurt, you will see sugars listed because of the natural sugar (lactose) from the milk. The Nutrition

Facts label gives one value for the total amount of natural and added sugar in a food. However, keep in mind that all carbohydrate turns into blood glucose sooner or later. The *kinds* or sources of carbohydrate are less important than the *total amount* of carbohydrate.

If you use carbohydrate counting as a meal-planning approach, you and your dietitian will decide on a "target" amount of carbohydrate that you should eat at each meal and snack. The amount of carbohydrate will be balanced with your physical activity and medication to keep your blood glucose level close to normal.

When your meal plan is based on carbohydrate counting, it is important that you eat the same amount of carbohydrate at the same time each day. You don't have to eat the same foods, just foods with the same amount of carbohydrate. You can use Nutrition Facts labels, exchange lists, nutrient value tables, or pocket counters to help determine how many grams of carbohydrate various foods contain. Also, the recipes in this cookbook provide the amount of carbohydrate per serving. This is extremely helpful if you are using carbohydrate counting as your meal-planning approach.

SERVING SIZES

Whichever meal-planning tool you use, it's vital that you learn about serving sizes. You may be working very hard at eating the right foods at the right time, but if you eat too much or too little, your blood glucose level will be too high or too low.

How do you know if your serving is the right size? Start by measuring your food with measuring cups, measuring spoons, or a food scale. Don't trust your eyes to estimate a serving size until you've had some practice. For at least a week, measure and weigh everything you eat. You will know whether your meal plan is working by measuring your blood glucose level one to two hours after you eat. Judging by the results, you and your dietitian can make the necessary changes to your meal plan.

Even when you have been following your meal plan for a long time, it's a good idea to measure your servings occasionally to make sure your estimates are correct. You may be able to use mental pictures or visual cues to help you eat the right serving sizes. For example, you may know that 1 cup of milk fills your glass to a certain point or that a 3-ounce serving of meat is about the same size as a deck of cards.

READING FOOD LABELS

It is easy to buy healthful bread, plain rice and pasta, fruits, and vegetables. But with other foods it can be hard to know which are most healthful and which will fit best into your meal plan. The Nutrition Facts label found on food packages can help you decide which foods to buy and how they will fit into your meal plan.

The first thing you should check on the Nutrition Facts label is the serving size. Make sure that this is the amount you usually eat. If you eat twice as much, you will get double the calories and other nutrients shown on the Nutrition Facts label. If you use exchange lists, remember that the serving size on the food label may be different from that in the exchange lists. For example, the serving size for orange juice is 8 fluid ounces on a Nutrition Facts label and 4 fluid ounces (½ cup) in the exchange lists. So an 8-fluid-ounce juice box would be listed on the label as one serving, but you would need to count it as 2 fruit exchanges. The label also tells you the number of servings per container, which can help you serve the appropriate amount.

Nutrition Facts

Serving Size ½ cup (114 g)
Servings Per Container 4

Amount Per Serving

Calories 260 Calories From Fat 120

	% Daily Value*
Total Fat 13 g	20%
Saturated Fat 5 g	25%
Cholesterol 30 mg	10%
Sodium 660 mg	28%
Total Carbohydrate 31 g	10%
Dietary Fiber 0 g	0%
Sugars 5 g	
Protein 5 g	

Vitamin A 4%	•	Vitamin C 2%
Calcium 15%	•	Iron 4%

*Percent Daily Values are based on a 2,000 calorie diet. Your daily values may be higher or lower depending on your calorie needs:

	Calories:	2,000	2,500
Total Fat	Less than	65 g	80 g
Sat Fat	Less than	20 g	25 g
Cholesterol	Less than	300 mg	300 mg
Sodium	Less than	2,400 mg	2,400 mg
Total Carbohydrate		300 g	375 g
Dietary Fiber		25 g	30 g

Calories per gram:
Fat 9 • Carbohydrate 4 • Protein 4

The next section tells you about the calories, fat, cholesterol, sodium, carbohydrate, and protein in one serving of the food. The total number of calories in a serving and the number of calories that come from fat are listed first. For fat, saturated fat, cholesterol, sodium, total carbohydrate, and dietary fiber the actual amount (grams or milligrams) and the Percent Daily Value are listed. If your meal plan is based on counting grams of carbohydrate, grams of fat, or calories, you will find this information very helpful.

The Percent Daily Value shows how much of your daily allowance for that nutrient one serving of the food provides, based on someone eating 2,000 calories per day. If you eat fewer than 2,000 calories per day, the food would provide a greater percentage of your daily allowance for each nutrient; if you eat more than 2,000 calories per day, the food would provide a smaller percentage of your daily allowance. Your dietitian can help you figure out your own daily values in grams and percentages for your calorie level. The Percent Daily Value helps you see how the food can fit into a healthful eating plan. If you eat a food that provides a large percentage of the Daily Value for fat, try to balance it with foods that provide a lower percentage of the Daily Value at the same meal or later in the day.

For vitamin A, vitamin C, calcium, and iron, the Nutrition Facts panel lists only the Percent Daily Value. These percentages can help you find foods that are good sources of each of these nutrients.

The Nutrition Facts label also has an ingredient list. The ingredient list details exactly what is present in a product. Ingredients are listed in order of weight, with the largest amount listed first and the smallest amount listed last. For example, if the first ingredient in a breakfast cereal is sugar and the second ingredient is the grain, the cereal is probably high in sugar.

Using the food label should be part of your strategy for healthful eating. Your dietitian can help you practice using food labels to make the best decisions about what to buy.

BON APPÉTIT!

You may feel that you have to think very hard about what you eat. But with time, you will find it easier to make healthful food choices. This cookbook is a tool you and your family can use to make it easier to prepare and eat foods that help you manage your diabetes, and your overall health. Set the table, relax, and enjoy your meal.

IN ADDITION

For customized answers to your food and nutrition questions, call the Consumer Nutrition Hot Line of The American Dietetic Association's National Center for Nutrition and Dietetics at 900-CALL-AN-RD (900-225-5267). To listen to recorded messages in English or Spanish, or to obtain a referral to an RD in your area, call 800-366-1655. Visit The American Dietetic Association's Web site at www.eatright.org.

For general information about diabetes, call the American Diabetes Association at 800-DIABETES (800-342-2383). A free packet of information about diabetes is available upon request. Also, if you are interested in ordering other American Diabetes Association books, or would like to receive a free catalogue of books, call 800-232-6733. Visit the American Diabetes Association's Web site at www.diabetes.org.

1

BREAKFAST AND BRUNCH: EGG DISHES, PANCAKES, WAFFLES, AND FRENCH TOAST

Whether you're searching for an on-the-run weekday morning meal or an entrée to enjoy leisurely with family and friends, you'll find a recipe here to fit the bill. Eggs, waffles, pancakes—all of your favorites are included. More breakfast treats can be found in Breads, Biscuits, and Muffins, chapter 2.

EGGS

Eggs will always be part of the good old American breakfast, and are a good, lean source of protein. For many years, eggs had a bad reputation because of their cholesterol content. But even people following a low-cholesterol diet can enjoy up to 3 eggs per week.

Once you reach your "three egg" limit, you can still enjoy eggs, just in a slightly different form. Egg substitutes or plain egg whites can be used in place of whole eggs in almost all recipes. As a rule of thumb, 2 egg whites or ¼ cup of egg substitute equals one whole egg. Look for egg substitute in the frozen foods section of your market. It keeps indefinitely, so pick up a package to have on hand.

If you purchase whole eggs, store them in the refrigerator in the original cartons, not in the egg holder on your refrigerator door. Strong-smelling foods have aromas that can easily penetrate porous eggshells, and the carton helps block out some of the odor. You can store whole eggs up to 1 month in the refrigerator. Discard any eggs that are unclean, cracked, broken, leaking, or show discolored interiors.

Be sure to cook eggs thoroughly to destroy salmonella, a type of bacteria that can contaminate eggs and poultry. Cook eggs to a minimum temperature of 165°F. Scrambled eggs, omelets, and frittatas should be cooked until they are thick and no visible liquid egg remains; basic egg dishes should have completely set (not runny) whites and yolks.

Try our versions of favorite egg dishes like Scrambled Eggs with Ham, Vegetable Frittata, Spinach Quiche, and Cheese Soufflé. With their terrific taste and great texture, all you'll miss are fat and calories. And if you use egg substitute instead of whole eggs, you'll cut out the cholesterol, too.

SPANISH OMELET

Add a little spice to your Sunday morning with this tempting entrée. An exception to the general rule of cooking eggs over low heat, omelets should be cooked quickly at a higher temperature. A good omelet should have a creamy middle and be tender and firm on the outside. It takes a bit of experience to make a good omelet, but practicing the technique is fun and omelets are delicious even when they aren't perfect.

1 omelet (2 servings)

1 teaspoon margarine
2 tablespoons chopped green bell pepper
2 tablespoons chopped onion
2 tablespoons chopped celery
One 8-ounce can tomato sauce
1 teaspoon Worcestershire sauce
4 large eggs
½ teaspoon salt
Pinch of freshly ground pepper

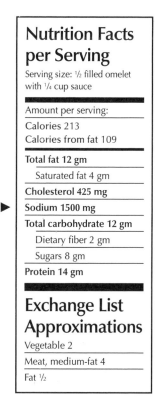

Nutrition Facts per Serving

Serving size: ½ filled omelet with ¼ cup sauce

Amount per serving:

Calories 213
Calories from fat 109

Total fat 12 gm
  Saturated fat 4 gm
Cholesterol 425 mg
Sodium 1500 mg
Total carbohydrate 12 gm
  Dietary fiber 2 gm
  Sugars 8 gm
Protein 14 gm

Exchange List Approximations

Vegetable 2
Meat, medium-fat 4
Fat ½

1. Melt the margarine in a small nonstick skillet. Add the green pepper, onion, and celery, and cook 4 minutes, or until tender. Add the tomato and Worcestershire sauces. Simmer 5 to 7 minutes. Keep warm on low heat.
2. In a small bowl, beat the eggs, 2 tablespoons water, salt, and pepper with a fork.
3. Pour the egg mixture into a second skillet sprayed with nonstick pan spray. Cook on medium heat without stirring. The outer edges may be lifted to allow uncooked egg to flow under when the pan is tilted.
4. When the eggs are light brown on the bottom and the top is almost firm, spoon ½ cup sauce over half the omelet. With a spatula, fold the other side of the omelet over to cover the sauce.
5. Cut the omelet in half; lift separately from the pan or tilt the skillet to roll the omelet halves onto serving plates. Spoon half the remaining sauce over each serving.

SCRAMBLED EGGS WITH HAM

This is such a quick and easy egg dish that there's no need to wait for the weekend to treat yourself. To save time in the morning, chop and prepare all of the ingredients the night before, or buy frozen chopped pepper and onion to keep on hand. If you're concerned about cholesterol, use egg whites or egg substitute instead of whole eggs.

4 servings

6 large eggs
2 tablespoons water or fat-free milk
1 green onion with green top, finely
     chopped
½ teaspoon salt
Pinch of pepper
1 teaspoon margarine
½ cup (about 2 ounces) diced cooked
     ham
¼ cup chopped green bell pepper

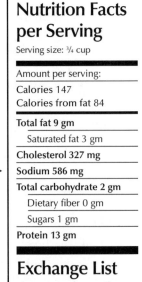

Nutrition Facts per Serving

Serving size: ¾ cup

Amount per serving:

Calories 147
Calories from fat 84

Total fat 9 gm
  Saturated fat 3 gm
Cholesterol 327 mg
Sodium 586 mg
Total carbohydrate 2 gm
  Dietary fiber 0 gm
  Sugars 1 gm
Protein 13 gm

Exchange List Approximation

Meat, medium-fat 2

1.   Beat the eggs in a bowl. Add the water or milk, green onion, salt, and pepper.
2.   Melt the margarine in a nonstick skillet. Sauté the ham and green pepper 1 to 2 minutes. Add the egg mixture. Cook, stirring gently, until the eggs are cooked through but still moist. Serve hot.

GARDEN PIE

Bring a taste of the garden indoors with this savory fresh vegetable pie. It's quick and easy to make, and you can decrease the fat content even more if you use a low-fat biscuit mix. Try a slice of pie accompanied by a fresh green salad for a light evening meal or lunch.

1 pie (6 servings)

2 cups thinly sliced peeled zucchini
1½ cups seeded and diced fresh
    tomatoes
½ cup chopped onion
½ cup grated Parmesan cheese
¼ teaspoon freshly ground pepper
1½ cups fat-free milk
¾ cup biscuit mix (Bisquick-type)
3 large eggs

Nutrition Facts per Serving	
Serving size: 1 slice	
Amount per serving:	
Calories 180	
Calories from fat 66	
Total fat 7 gm	
Saturated fat 3 gm	
Cholesterol 113 mg	
Sodium 397 mg	
Total carbohydrate 19 gm	
Dietary fiber 2 gm	
Sugars 7 gm	
Protein 10 gm	

Exchange List Approximations

Starch 1	
Vegetable 1	
Meat, medium-fat 1	

1.   Preheat the oven to 400°F. Prepare a 9-inch glass or ceramic pie plate with nonstick pan spray.
2.   Layer the zucchini, tomatoes, and onion in the pie plate. Sprinkle the Parmesan cheese and pepper evenly over the vegetables.
3.   Combine the milk, biscuit mix, and eggs. Beat until smooth, about 1 minute; pour over the vegetables.
4.   Bake about 30 minutes. Let set 5 minutes before cutting into 6 equal wedges.

SPINACH QUICHE

A quiche makes an excellent entrée for brunch or a light lunch. This filling is especially tasty, loaded with spinach and green onions and seasoned to perfection. You can use a refrigerated ready-to-bake pie crust instead of making your own if you prefer. Just begin the recipe at Step 2.

1 quiche (6 servings)

CRUST

1½ cups sifted all-purpose flour
½ teaspoon salt
½ cup margarine, cut in pieces

FILLING

One 10-ounce package frozen chopped
    spinach
4 large eggs
One 12-ounce can fat-free evaporated
    milk
4 green onions with green tops, thinly
    sliced
½ teaspoon dry mustard
½ teaspoon salt
⅛ teaspoon pepper
½ cup grated Parmesan cheese

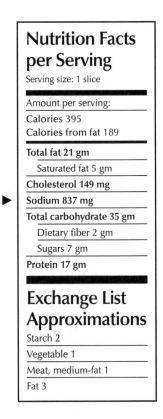

**Nutrition Facts
per Serving**

Serving size: 1 slice

Amount per serving:

Calories 395
Calories from fat 189

Total fat 21 gm
   Saturated fat 5 gm

Cholesterol 149 mg

Sodium 837 mg

Total carbohydrate 35 gm
   Dietary fiber 2 gm
   Sugars 7 gm

Protein 17 gm

**Exchange List
Approximations**

Starch 2

Vegetable 1

Meat, medium-fat 1

Fat 3

1.   For the crust, combine the flour, salt, and margarine with a pastry blender or in the bowl of a food processor and process a few seconds until the mixture has the texture of soft bread crumbs. Sprinkle 3 tablespoons ice water over the dough. Process a few seconds until the dough starts to form a ball. (If the dough is too dry, add another 1 tablespoon ice water.) Wrap the dough in wax paper or a plastic bag and chill 1 hour.

2.   Preheat the oven to 400°F. Remove the dough from the refrigerator and roll into a circle on a lightly floured board or between sheets of wax paper. Fit the dough into a 9-inch pie pan; flute the rim. Prick the crust with the tines of a fork about 8 times. Bake 10 minutes, or until the shell is lightly browned. Remove from the oven and cool.

3.   For the filling, cook the spinach according to the package directions until tender. Drain thoroughly and pat dry with paper towels.

4.   Beat the eggs; add the spinach and all the remaining ingredients except the cheese.

5.   Pour the filling into the crust. Sprinkle the top of the quiche with cheese.

6.   Bake at 400°F for 30 to 35 minutes, or until a knife inserted in the center comes out clean. Remove from oven; let stand 10 minutes before cutting into 6 equal wedges.

VEGETABLE FRITTATA

Frittatas are to the Italians what omelets are to the French. Unlike in an omelet, the filling in a frittata is mixed with the eggs and the entire blend is cooked slowly in a skillet until set. You can serve a whole frittata as an entrée or half portions as side dishes or appetizers. Frittatas are just as delicious chilled or at room temperature as they are hot.

1 frittata (4 servings)

1 teaspoon margarine
1 small onion, thinly sliced
1 small red bell pepper, sliced into
    thin strips
1 boiled red potato, peeled, sliced
1 cup broccoli florets
1/4 cup (1 ounce) shredded light Swiss
    cheese such as Jarlsberg or
    Lorraine
3 whole large eggs, lightly beaten
3 egg whites, lightly beaten
1/4 teaspoon salt
1/8 teaspoon freshly ground pepper
Pinch of paprika

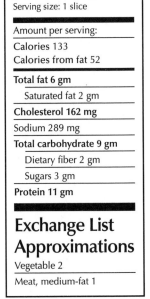

Nutrition Facts per Serving

Serving size: 1 slice

Amount per serving:

Calories 133
Calories from fat 52

Total fat 6 gm
  Saturated fat 2 gm
Cholesterol 162 mg
Sodium 289 mg
Total carbohydrate 9 gm
  Dietary fiber 2 gm
  Sugars 3 gm
Protein 11 gm

Exchange List Approximations

Vegetable 2
Meat, medium-fat 1

1.   Preheat the oven to 450°F.
2.   Put the margarine in an 8-inch pie plate or quiche pan; place in the oven to melt. Arrange the onion slices on the margarine; cook in the hot oven for 5 minutes.
3.   Remove the pan from the oven; arrange the red pepper, potato, and broccoli on top of the onion. Sprinkle on the cheese.
4.   In a medium bowl, combine the whole eggs, egg whites, salt, and pepper; pour over the cheese mixture. Sprinkle with paprika. Bake for 12 to 15 minutes, or until the eggs are set in the middle. Slice into 4 equal portions and serve hot or cooled to room temperature.

CRUSTLESS ZUCCHINI QUICHE

Here's a great way to use up all that leftover zucchini from your garden. With only 4 grams of fat per slice, and the tempting combination of zucchini and cheese, you'll forget that the crust is missing.

1 quiche (6 servings)

²/₃ cup chopped onion
1 teaspoon margarine
2 cups ¼-inch slices zucchini
3 large eggs
²/₃ cup fat-free evaporated milk
½ teaspoon salt
⅛ teaspoon freshly ground pepper
Pinch of nutmeg
²/₃ cup shredded reduced-fat Monterey
    Jack cheese or reduced-fat Colby-
    Jack, or a combination
Pinch of paprika

Nutrition Facts per Serving

Serving size: 1 slice

Amount per serving:

Calories 101
Calories from fat 40

Total fat 4 gm
  Saturated fat 2 gm
Cholesterol 112 mg
Sodium 322 mg
Total carbohydrate 7 gm
  Dietary fiber 1 gm
  Sugars 5 gm
Protein 8 gm

Exchange List Approximations

Vegetable 1
Meat, medium-fat 1

1. Preheat the oven to 350°F. Prepare an 8-inch glass pie plate with nonstick pan spray.
2. In a large skillet, sauté the onion in the margarine for 2 to 3 minutes; add the zucchini and sauté for 5 minutes. Put the zucchini mixture in the pie plate.
3. Beat the eggs with the milk, salt, pepper, and nutmeg. Pour the egg mixture over the zucchini mixture and top with the cheese and paprika.
4. Bake for about 45 minutes, or until the edges are brown and the eggs are set in the center. Let cool at least 5 minutes before slicing in 6 equal wedges. Serve hot or at room temperature.

CHEESE SOUFFLÉ

Baked soufflés are light, airy mixtures that begin with a thick, egg-yolk–based sauce that's folded into beaten egg whites. We used low-fat Cheddar cheese in this recipe, but other cheeses such as low-fat Swiss, Colby, or Monterey Jack can be used instead. Baked soufflés are very fragile and must be served immediately after removal from the oven. A special soufflé dish—a round dish with high straight sides—is a must for helping the soufflé to rise properly. They're widely available in houseware stores.

1 soufflé (6 servings)

¼ cup (½ stick) margarine
¼ cup all-purpose flour
1 cup fat-free evaporated milk
1 cup (4 ounces) shredded reduced-fat
    Cheddar cheese
2 basil leaves, chopped, or ¼ teaspoon
    dried basil or oregano
Pinch of cayenne pepper
2 large egg yolks
5 large egg whites, beaten stiff but not dry

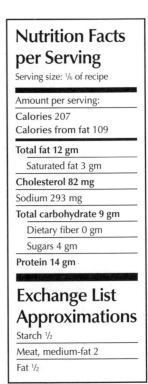

**Nutrition Facts
per Serving**

Serving size: ⅙ of recipe

Amount per serving:

Calories 207
Calories from fat 109

Total fat 12 gm
   Saturated fat 3 gm
Cholesterol 82 mg
Sodium 293 mg
Total carbohydrate 9 gm
   Dietary fiber 0 gm
   Sugars 4 gm
Protein 14 gm

**Exchange List
Approximations**

Starch ½
Meat, medium-fat 2
Fat ½

1. Preheat oven to 400°F. Prepare a 2-quart soufflé dish with nonstick pan spray.
2. Melt the margarine over low heat in a medium saucepan; add the flour, stirring until smooth. Cook for 1 minute, stirring constantly. Gradually add the evaporated milk; cook over medium heat, stirring constantly, until the mixture is thick and bubbly. Add the cheese and seasonings; stir until the cheese melts.
3. Lightly beat the egg yolks in a small bowl. Gradually stir in ¼ of the hot cheese mixture. Add the egg yolk mixture to the cheese sauce in the saucepan. Gently fold in the beaten egg whites.
4. Pour the mixture into the prepared soufflé dish. Bake for 30 minutes, or until puffed and golden. Serve immediately.

PANCAKES, WAFFLES, AND FRENCH TOAST

We've revamped all of the dishes so they're lower in fat and calories compared to their full-fat counterparts, so go ahead and enjoy. Baked Orange French Toast, Northwest Berry Puff, and Whole Wheat Blueberry Rice Pancakes are just a few examples of the breakfast delights we've included.

Most of the pancake, waffle, and French toast recipes in this chapter contain sugar, either as an ingredient in the recipe or as a topping. Thanks to the recent revision of the nutrition guidelines for people with diabetes, sugar may be used as part of a healthful eating plan. You simply need to count foods containing sugar as part of the total carbohydrate you're allowed. We've made it easy for you, providing a complete breakdown of exchanges and carbohydrate counts in all of our recipes. If you're concerned about cholesterol, remember that you can use egg substitute or egg whites in place of whole eggs in any of these recipes.

PANCAKES

Although known by many names—flapjacks, griddle cakes, hotcakes—pancakes are always a homey treat. Pancake batter should be lumpy, so be careful not to overmix or you'll end up with tough cakes. For variety, add ½ cup of blueberries or 1 small banana, thinly sliced; then sprinkle a handful of fruit on top for a pretty garnish and serve with light pancake syrup or real maple syrup. Remember to count carbohydrate values for the syrup and/or any added fruit.

8 pancakes (4 servings)

1¼ cups all-purpose flour
1 tablespoon baking powder
2 teaspoons sugar
½ teaspoon salt
1 large egg, beaten, or ¼ cup
    egg substitute
1 cup fat-free milk
2 tablespoons canola or corn oil

1. Sift together the flour, baking powder, sugar, and salt in a large bowl.
2. Combine the egg, milk, and oil in a small bowl and add to the dry ingredients. Stir only until the dry ingredients are moistened. (The batter will be lumpy.)
3. Preheat a large skillet or griddle and spray when hot with nonstick pan spray. Pour about ¼ cup batter for each pancake on the hot griddle or skillet. Cook about 3 minutes, until bubbles form on the top and the edges are dry. Turn and cook about 2 minutes more.

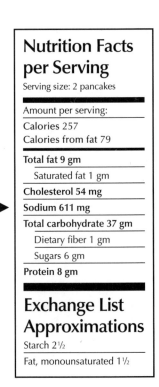

Nutrition Facts per Serving

Serving size: 2 pancakes

Amount per serving:

Calories 257
Calories from fat 79

Total fat 9 gm
  Saturated fat 1 gm
Cholesterol 54 mg
Sodium 611 mg
Total carbohydrate 37 gm
  Dietary fiber 1 gm
  Sugars 6 gm
Protein 8 gm

Exchange List Approximations

Starch 2½

Fat, monounsaturated 1½

SAVORY PANCAKE PUFF

Beautifully puffed and golden brown, this savory pancake is delicious and perfect for showing off at a Sunday brunch. Serve with lean turkey sausages and Tropical Fruit Cup (page 439) or Ambrosia (page 440).

1 pancake puff (4 servings)

½ cup finely chopped onion
1 tablespoon margarine
1 tablespoon chopped fresh rosemary,
     or 1 teaspoon crushed dried
     rosemary
¾ cup fat-free milk
⅓ cup all-purpose flour
¼ teaspoon salt
2 large eggs, or ½ cup egg substitute

1. Preheat the oven to 400°F. Spray a 10-inch glass pie pan with nonstick pan spray.
2. In a small skillet, sauté the onion in the margarine for 3 minutes. Stir in the rosemary; cook 1 minute more.
3. Combine the milk, flour, salt, and eggs in a blender or food processor and blend until smooth. Add the onion mixture; blend 5 seconds more. Pour into the prepared pie pan.
4. Bake until puffed and golden brown, about 25 to 30 minutes. Cut into 4 equal slices; serve warm.

Nutrition Facts per Serving

Serving size: ¼ pancake

Amount per serving:

Calories 127
Calories from fat 50

Total fat 6 gm
  Saturated fat 1 gm
Cholesterol 107 mg
Sodium 235 mg
Total carbohydrate 13 gm
  Dietary fiber 1 gm
  Sugars 4 gm
Protein 6 gm

Exchange List Approximations

Starch 1

Fat 1

WHOLE WHEAT BLUEBERRY RICE PANCAKES WITH MAPLE TOPPING

These pancakes include an unexpected ingredient—rice—that adds great texture and body to the batter. Served hot with a special maple topping, they're sure to become a weekend staple at your house.

12 pancakes (6 servings)

PANCAKES

³/₄ cup fresh or thawed frozen
    blueberries
¹/₂ cup plus 1 tablespoon all-purpose
    flour
¹/₂ cup whole wheat flour
3 tablespoons sugar
¹/₂ teaspoon baking soda
¹/₄ teaspoon salt
1 cup cooked rice, chilled
1 cup low-fat (1 percent fat) buttermilk
¹/₂ cup fat-free milk
2 tablespoons margarine, melted
1 teaspoon pure vanilla extract
2 large egg whites, beaten stiff

MAPLE TOPPING

¹/₄ cup unsalted margarine, at room
    temperature
1 teaspoon honey
¹/₂ teaspoon imitation maple flavoring
¹/₄ teaspoon pure vanilla extract

Nutrition Facts per Serving
Serving size: 2 pancakes plus 2 teaspoons maple topping
Amount per serving:
Calories 280
Calories from fat 109
Total fat 12 gm
Saturated fat 2 gm
Cholesterol 2 mg
Sodium 320 mg
Total carbohydrate 37 gm
Dietary fiber 2 gm
Sugars 12 gm
Protein 7 gm

Exchange List Approximations

Starch	2
Fruit	¹/₂
Fat	2

1. In a medium bowl, toss the blueberries with 1 tablespoon of the all-purpose flour to coat. Set aside.

2. Combine the remaining all-purpose and whole wheat flours, the sugar, baking soda, and salt in a large bowl; mix well. Add the rice, buttermilk, fat-free milk, melted margarine, and vanilla; mix just until the dry ingredients are moistened. Fold in the beaten egg whites, then the blueberries.

3. Combine all the ingredients for the maple topping in a small bowl and reserve.

4. Prepare a griddle or large nonstick skillet with nonstick pan spray; heat until hot. Pour about ¼ cup batter for each pancake on the hot griddle or skillet. Cook about 3 minutes, until bubbles form and the edges are dry. The bottom should be light brown. Turn and cook about 2 minutes more. Serve with maple topping.

WHOLE WHEAT YOGURT PANCAKES

Hearty pancakes like these taste best when spread with 100 percent fruit preserves or orange marmalade. Just check the labels of toppings and add in the appropriate exchanges. Pancakes can be frozen and kept up to 3 months, so make a few extra to keep on hand when you need a quick breakfast. To store, cool the pancakes first, slide squares of wax paper between them, and place the stack in a freezer-proof container. To reheat frozen pancakes, arrange them in a single layer on a baking sheet and bake at 325°F for about 8 to 9 minutes, or until heated through.

12 pancakes (4 servings)

1 cup whole wheat flour
1 tablespoon sugar
1 teaspoon baking powder
½ teaspoon baking soda
⅛ teaspoon salt
1 large egg, or ¼ cup egg substitute
½ cup plain low-fat yogurt
1 cup low-fat (1 percent fat) buttermilk

1. Combine the flour, sugar, baking powder, baking soda, and salt in a large bowl.
2. Beat the egg with the yogurt in a medium bowl; add the buttermilk. Add to the dry ingredients; mix just until the dry ingredients are moistened. (The batter will be lumpy.)
3. Prepare a hot griddle or large nonstick skillet with nonstick pan spray. Pour in about ¼ cup batter for each pancake. Cook about 3 minutes, until bubbles form on top and the edges are dry. The bottom should be light brown. Turn and cook about 2 minutes more.

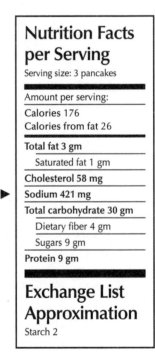

Nutrition Facts per Serving

Serving size: 3 pancakes

Amount per serving:

Calories 176
Calories from fat 26

Total fat 3 gm
  Saturated fat 1 gm
Cholesterol 58 mg
Sodium 421 mg
Total carbohydrate 30 gm
  Dietary fiber 4 gm
  Sugars 9 gm
Protein 9 gm

Exchange List Approximation

Starch 2

FLUFFY HIGH-FIBER, LOW-FAT PANCAKES

Wheat flour, miller's bran, and rolled oats pack a powerful fiber punch in this recipe, and lend a delightful texture too; low-fat buttermilk adds a rich, tangy flavor. If you don't have buttermilk on hand, you can substitute 1 cup of 1 percent milk with 1 tablespoon of lemon juice added. Let the mixture sit for a few minutes to thicken before adding to the oats and bran.

8 pancakes (4 servings)

1 cup low-fat (1 percent fat) buttermilk
½ cup quick-cooking rolled oats
⅔ cup miller's bran (unprocessed, uncooked wheat bran)
1 large egg, or ¼ cup egg substitute
¼ cup whole wheat flour
2 teaspoons sugar
¾ teaspoon baking soda
¼ teaspoon salt

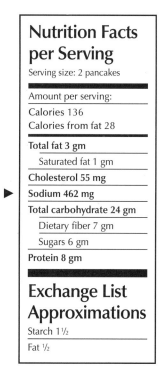

Nutrition Facts per Serving

Serving size: 2 pancakes

Amount per serving:

Calories 136
Calories from fat 28

Total fat 3 gm
  Saturated fat 1 gm
Cholesterol 55 mg
Sodium 462 mg
Total carbohydrate 24 gm
  Dietary fiber 7 gm
  Sugars 6 gm
Protein 8 gm

Exchange List Approximations

Starch 1½

Fat ½

1.   Combine the buttermilk, oats, and bran in a large bowl. Let stand 5 minutes. Add the egg and beat until blended.
2.   In a small bowl, mix the whole wheat flour, sugar, baking soda, and salt until blended. Add to the bran mixture and blend until all the flour is moistened.
3.   Prepare a hot skillet or griddle with nonstick pan spray. Pour in about ¼ cup batter for each pancake. Cook about 3 minutes, or until bubbles form on the top and the edges are dry. Turn and cook the pancakes about 2 minutes more.

BAKED APPLE PANCAKE

Puffed, brown, and crusty on the outside, eggy-soft in the middle, and topped with caramelized brown sugar and cinnamon apples, this pancake is simply a slice of heaven. For a sumptuous brunch, serve with lean turkey sausages or Canadian bacon, freshly squeezed orange juice, and a mix of cantaloupe and honeydew melon balls.

1 pancake (6 servings)

PANCAKE

1 cup fat-free milk
³/₄ cup all-purpose flour
2 large egg whites
1 large whole egg
¹/₂ teaspoon baking powder
2 tablespoons sugar
2 tablespoons margarine, melted
2 teaspoons pure vanilla extract
1 teaspoon grated lemon zest

TOPPING

1 large tart apple, peeled, cored, and
thinly sliced
2 tablespoons brown sugar
2 teaspoons fresh lemon juice
¹/₂ teaspoon cinnamon

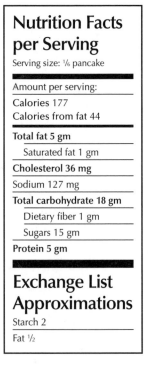

Nutrition Facts per Serving

Serving size: ¹/₆ pancake

Amount per serving:

Calories 177
Calories from fat 44

Total fat 5 gm
  Saturated fat 1 gm
Cholesterol 36 mg
Sodium 127 mg
Total carbohydrate 18 gm
  Dietary fiber 1 gm
  Sugars 15 gm
Protein 5 gm

Exchange List Approximations

Starch 2
Fat ¹/₂

1. Preheat the oven to 400°F. Spray a 10-inch ovenproof skillet with nonstick pan spray.
2. Combine all the pancake ingredients in blender or food processor; blend until smooth.
3. Pour into the prepared skillet; bake for 20 to 25 minutes or until puffed and browned.
4. Meanwhile, spray a small skillet with nonstick pan spray. Add the apple slices, brown sugar, lemon juice, and cinnamon. Sauté over low heat until the apples are softened and slightly caramelized, about 10 minutes.
5. Spoon over the pancake. Cut the pancake into 6 servings and serve immediately.

NORTHWEST BERRY PUFF

A delicious breakfast treat your whole family will enjoy! This fun pancake puffs way over the top of the pan and is garnished with heaps of berries and a dusting of powdered sugar. Beautiful to look at and scrumptious to eat.

1 pancake (6 servings)

2 large whole eggs
1 large egg white
½ cup fat-free milk
½ cup all-purpose flour
1 tablespoon granulated sugar
⅛ teaspoon salt
2 cups fresh raspberries, blackberries,
     boysenberries, blueberries,
     strawberries, or a combination
1 tablespoon powdered sugar

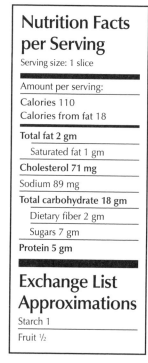

Nutrition Facts per Serving

Serving size: 1 slice

Amount per serving:

Calories 110
Calories from fat 18

Total fat 2 gm
   Saturated fat 1 gm
Cholesterol 71 mg
Sodium 89 mg
Total carbohydrate 18 gm
   Dietary fiber 2 gm
   Sugars 7 gm
Protein 5 gm

Exchange List Approximations

Starch 1
Fruit ½

1. Heat the oven to 450°F. Prepare a 10-inch ovenproof skillet or glass pie pan with non-stick pan spray.

2. Beat the eggs and egg white in a medium bowl. Whisk in the milk. Slowly whisk in the flour, sugar, and salt. Pour into the prepared skillet and bake 15 minutes. Reduce the heat to 350°F and bake 10 minutes more, or until the batter is puffed and brown. Remove from the oven and slide the puff onto a serving plate.

3. Cover with fruit (if strawberries are used, slice large berries in bite-size pieces); sift powdered sugar over the pancake. Cut the puff into 6 equal wedges.

RICOTTA-FILLED BLINTZES

These blintzes are wonderful as a dessert or for a sweet Sunday brunch treat. Unfilled crêpes can be wrapped securely and frozen for up to 3 months, or refrigerated for 2 days, and filled crêpes may be chilled up to 24 hours before baking. If filled and chilled, increase the baking time for the blintzes to 20 minutes.

12 filled crêpes (6 servings)

CRÊPES

³/₄ cup all-purpose flour
³/₄ cup fat-free milk
2 large egg whites, or ¹/₂ cup egg
    substitute
1 tablespoon margarine, melted

FILLING

One 15-ounce container low-fat ricotta
    cheese
2 tablespoons powdered sugar or
    chocolate-flavored powdered
    sugar
1¹/₂ teaspoons pure vanilla extract
¹/₃ cup strawberry or raspberry jam

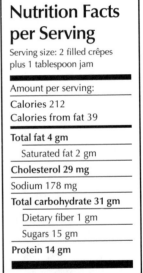

Nutrition Facts per Serving

Serving size: 2 filled crêpes plus 1 tablespoon jam

Amount per serving:

Calories 212
Calories from fat 39

Total fat 4 gm
  Saturated fat 2 gm
Cholesterol 29 mg
Sodium 178 mg
Total carbohydrate 31 gm
  Dietary fiber 1 gm
  Sugars 15 gm
Protein 14 gm

Exchange List Approximations

Starch 1
Other carbohydrate 1
Meat, lean 1

1. Combine the flour, milk, egg whites, and margarine in a food processor or blender. Process until smooth. Refrigerate up to 8 hours. Stir or shake before using.
2. Heat a 5- or 6-inch nonstick crêpe pan or small nonstick skillet over medium heat. Spray with nonstick pan spray.
3. Pour about 3 tablespoons of batter (use a ¹/₄ cup dry measuring cup about ³/₄ full) into the hot pan, tilting to spread the batter evenly. Cook until the bottom of the crêpe is lightly browned; turn and cook 30 seconds more.
4. Remove each crêpe to a sheet of wax paper and repeat the process until all the batter is used. You should have 12 crêpes.

5. Preheat the oven to 350°F. Prepare a 9 x 13-inch baking dish with nonstick pan spray.

6. For the filling, combine the cheese, sugar, and vanilla in a food processor or blender. Process until smooth.

7. Spoon 2 heaping tablespoons of filling down the center of each crêpe. Roll up; place seam side down in the baking dish. Cover with foil.

8. Bake the crêpes for 15 to 18 minutes, or until heated through. Serve warm with jam.

BASIC CRÊPES

Making crêpes takes a little practice, but once you get the hang of it, they're great fun to do. The trick is to pour off any excess batter—you want just a very thin layer of batter on the bottom of the pan. Fill these paper-thin yet sturdy pancakes with sweet or savory mixtures: cheese, poultry, vegetables, jams, or fruits. Whichever filling you select, be sure to add in the appropriate exchanges. If the crêpes are to be served as a dessert or with a fruit sauce, mix 1 tablespoon of sugar into the batter (which adds 1 more gram of carbohydrate per serving). For savory crêpes, add 1 tablespoon of fresh minced herbs to the batter.

24 crêpes (12 servings)

3 large eggs, or ¾ cup egg substitute
⅛ teaspoon salt
1½ cups all-purpose flour
1½ cups fat-free milk
2 tablespoons canola or corn oil

1. Combine the eggs and salt in a medium bowl. Add the flour alternately with the milk, beating until smooth after each addition. Add the oil and mix well.
2. Cover and refrigerate the batter for at least 1 hour.
3. Prepare a small nonstick skillet with non-stick pan spray. For each crêpe, pour 2 table-spoons batter into the skillet; turn the skillet to coat the surface evenly with a very thin layer of batter. Heat the skillet until moderately hot and cook the crêpes over medium heat until the bottom of the crêpe is lightly browned and the edges lift easily from the side of the pan. Turn and brown the other side 15 to 30 seconds. This side will be browned only in spots.

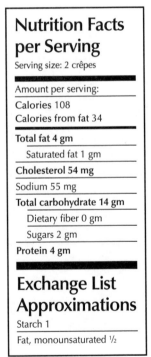

**Nutrition Facts
per Serving**

Serving size: 2 crêpes

Amount per serving:

Calories 108
Calories from fat 34

Total fat 4 gm
  Saturated fat 1 gm
Cholesterol 54 mg
Sodium 55 mg
Total carbohydrate 14 gm
  Dietary fiber 0 gm
  Sugars 2 gm
Protein 4 gm

**Exchange List
Approximations**

Starch 1

Fat, monounsaturated ½

WAFFLES

Waffle batters are usually richer than pancake batters and so yield a crispier product. Separating the egg whites from the yolks, as recommended in this recipe, also helps to make the waffles lighter.

8 waffles (8 servings)

1¾ cups all-purpose flour
1 tablespoon baking powder
½ teaspoon salt
2 large eggs, separated
1¼ cups fat-free milk
⅓ cup canola or corn oil

1. Preheat a waffle iron.
2. Sift the flour, baking powder, and salt into a large bowl.
3. Combine the egg yolks, milk, and oil in a small bowl; stir into the dry ingredients.
4. In a small bowl, beat the egg whites until stiff; fold into the batter.
5. Spray the hot waffle iron with nonstick pan spray. Pour in the batter, using a scant ½ cup per waffle. Bake until the waffles are crisp and brown.

Nutrition Facts per Serving

Serving size: 1 waffle

Amount per serving:

Calories 217
Calories from fat 99

Total fat 11 gm
  Saturated fat 1 gm
Cholesterol 54 mg
Sodium 227 mg
Total carbohydrate 24 gm
  Dietary fiber 1 gm
  Sugars 2 gm
Protein 6 gm

Exchange List Approximations

Starch 1½

Fat, monounsaturated 2

FRENCH TOAST

Nothing beats the taste of French toast on a lazy Sunday morning. Dry bread (try thick cuts of French bread or challah) is best to use because if the bread is fresh it absorbs too much of the egg and milk mixture. Leave the slices out overnight to stale, or use day-old bread. Top French toast with light pancake syrup, unsweetened applesauce, fresh berries, 100 percent fruit preserves, or warm fruit compote. Just remember to count in the carbohydrate exchange values for whichever topping and amount you use.

4 slices (2 servings)

2 large eggs, slightly beaten, or ½ cup
    egg substitute
½ cup fat-free milk
⅛ teaspoon salt
4 slices day-old white bread or
    sourdough bread
1 tablespoon margarine

1.   Mix the eggs, milk, and salt in a pie pan. Dip the bread in the egg mixture to coat on both sides, letting the bread soak up all the egg mixture.
2.   Melt the margarine in a large nonstick skillet over medium heat.
3.   Brown both sides of each piece of bread in the skillet. Serve immediately with your choice of topping.

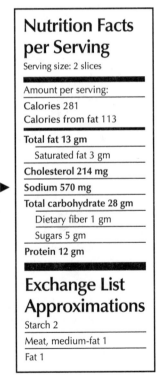

Nutrition Facts per Serving

Serving size: 2 slices

Amount per serving:

Calories 281
Calories from fat 113

Total fat 13 gm
    Saturated fat 3 gm
Cholesterol 214 mg
Sodium 570 mg
Total carbohydrate 28 gm
    Dietary fiber 1 gm
    Sugars 5 gm
Protein 12 gm

Exchange List Approximations

Starch 2

Meat, medium-fat 1

Fat 1

BAKED ORANGE FRENCH TOAST

This orange-flavored version of French toast is baked instead of fried, resulting in a crispier product that has just a smidgen of fat. Best of all, baking the French toast means you can cook enough for the entire family at once. You can even prepare this recipe ahead of time and keep the pan, covered with plastic wrap, in the refrigerator overnight. Just pop it into the oven (without the plastic wrap) when the alarm goes off, and about 25 minutes later—a scrumptious breakfast!

6 slices (3 servings)

1/4 cup fresh orange juice
2 large large egg whites
1/2 teaspoon pure vanilla extract
6 slices day-old French bread,
　　　cut 1 inch thick
1 tablespoon powdered sugar
1 medium orange, peeled and cut into 6
　　　wedges

1. Preheat the oven to 350°F. Prepare a cookie sheet with nonstick pan spray.
2. Beat the orange juice, egg whites, and vanilla together in a large bowl. Dip the bread slices on both sides and place them on the prepared cookie sheet. Spoon any remaining juice mixture over the slices.
3. Bake for 15 to 17 minutes, or until golden brown, turning once after 8 minutes.
4. Serve hot, sprinkled with powdered sugar and garnished with orange wedges.

Nutrition Facts per Serving

Serving size: 2 slices with 2 orange wedges

Amount per serving:

Calories 185
Calories from fat 17

Total fat 2 gm
　Saturated fat 0 gm
Cholesterol 1 mg
Sodium 306 mg
Total carbohydrate 35 gm
　Dietary fiber 2 gm
　Sugars 10 gm
Protein 7 gm

Exchange List Approximations

Starch 2

Fruit 1/2

2

BREADS, BISCUITS, AND MUFFINS

Nothing beats the taste or aroma of homemade baked goods. Orange Cranberry Bread, Blueberry Banana Loaf, Fresh Peach Muffins, and Buttermilk Biscuits are just a sampling of the wonderful recipes we've created in this chapter. Try them for breakfast, as a snack, or even for dessert.

Most of the recipes contain sugar as an ingredient, which can affect blood glucose levels. But as long as you include their total carbohydrate contribution in your meal plan, there's no reason you can't enjoy their great taste.

Breads are an important source of B vitamins, minerals, and starches. Foods made from whole grains, like whole wheat flour, are also good sources of fiber. Experts recommend a fiber intake of 20 to 35 grams per day for all Americans, including people with diabetes. However, most people get only about 11 grams per day.

In the following recipes, we've kept saturated fat and cholesterol down by using oils and margarine in place of butter, and have decreased the total fat by using fat-free milk in place of whole milk or cream whenever possible. We've also tried to boost the fiber content of some of your favorites by using whole wheat flour or adding bran, oats, nuts, fruits, and vegetables where possible.

While breads, muffins, and biscuits by themselves can be low in fat, toppings like butter or margarine, depending on the amount used, can virtually double the fat content of an item. Opt for low-fat spreads like fruit butters, chutney, jam, reduced-fat margarine, or fat-free or reduced-fat cream cheese instead. Just remember to count whichever topping you choose into your meal plan.

QUICK BREADS AND MUFFINS

All quick breads can be made into muffins, and vice versa. Both are leavened with eggs and baking powder and/or baking soda, and take just minutes to prepare. Combining the wet and dry ingredients is also a quick process, because overmixing results in a coarse-textured, low-rising bread, or muffins filled with air tunnels. Mix the batter just until moist—it should be lumpy, not smooth. Any small lumps will disappear during baking.

When adding dried fruit, such as raisins, to breads and muffins, toss them first very lightly with flour so they don't all sink to the bottom of the batter. Use nonstick sprays instead of shortening or butter to grease loaf pans and muffin tins; paper cup liners are another option for muffins. Bake quick breads and muffins in the center of a preheated oven. Quick breads are ready when the loaf pulls away from the sides of the pan, or when a toothpick inserted into the bread or muffin comes out clean. Cracks are typical in quick breads, and there's nothing you can do to prevent them.

Remove the baked muffins from the pans immediately and cool on wire racks. Loaves should cool in the pans for 5 minutes, then be transferred to racks to finish cooling, or they'll steam and get soggy on the bottom. Make sure you cool loaves thoroughly for several hours before slicing them; they won't crumble as easily.

BISCUITS AND SCONES

Biscuits and scones are traditionally quite high in fat. We've adapted some favorite recipes to decrease unwanted fat but still retain the tender, light texture. When cutting out biscuits with a cookie cutter, push straight down into the dough. If you twist the cutter as you push down, you'll get lopsided biscuits. For crusty sides, arrange biscuits 1 inch apart on cookie sheets. For tender sides, place them close together in a shallow baking pan. Remove biscuits and scones from the pans immediately after baking and let them cool slightly on wire racks.

RAISIN BREAD

Nothing beats the warm smell of a freshly baked loaf of bread, always a favorite at breakfast or as a snack. Indulge in a slice of this hearty raisin bread, spread with just a touch of margarine or jam. (Be sure to add in the appropriate exchange for the spread you choose.)

1 loaf (18 slices)

2¾ cups all-purpose flour
3½ teaspoons baking powder
¼ cup sugar
1½ teaspoons salt
1¼ cups fat-free evaporated milk
⅓ cup margarine, melted
2 large eggs, or ½ cup egg substitute
2 teaspoons grated orange zest
½ cup chopped raisins

Nutrition Facts per Serving

Serving size: 1 thick slice

Amount per serving:

Calories 131
Calories from fat 22

Total fat 2 gm
　Saturated fat 1 gm
Cholesterol 24 mg
Sodium 319 mg
Total carbohydrate 23 gm
　Dietary fiber 1 gm
　Sugars 7 gm
Protein 4 gm

Exchange List Approximation

Starch 1½

1.   Preheat the oven to 350°F. Prepare a 9 x 5-inch loaf pan with nonstick pan spray.
2.   Sift the flour, baking powder, sugar, and salt into a large bowl.
3.   Mix the milk, margarine, eggs, and orange zest in a medium bowl. Add to the dry ingredients. Mix until just blended; stir in the raisins. Pour into the prepared pan and bake for 1¼ hours.
4.   Cool on a wire rack at room temperature at least 1½ hours before slicing into 18 slices.

ONION CHEESE BREAD

This savory bread is more like a biscuit than a bread. It's so delicious served warm, you don't even need any butter. The bread is simple to make, too, because no rising is needed. Just mix the batter and pop it into the oven.

1 loaf (8 wedges)

½ cup chopped onion
4 teaspoons margarine
1½ cups biscuit mix
1 large egg, beaten, or ¼ cup
    egg substitute
½ cup fat-free milk
¾ cup (about 3 ounces) grated reduced-
    fat Cheddar cheese
1 teaspoon poppy seeds (optional)

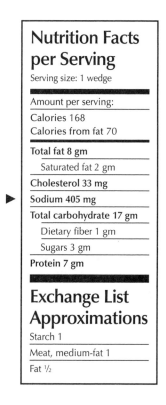

Nutrition Facts per Serving

Serving size: 1 wedge

Amount per serving:

Calories 168
Calories from fat 70

Total fat 8 gm
   Saturated fat 2 gm
Cholesterol 33 mg
Sodium 405 mg
Total carbohydrate 17 gm
   Dietary fiber 1 gm
   Sugars 3 gm
Protein 7 gm

Exchange List Approximations

Starch 1

Meat, medium-fat 1

Fat ½

1. Preheat the oven to 400°F. Prepare an 8-inch-diameter round cake pan with nonstick pan spray.
2. In a small nonstick skillet, sauté the onion in 2 teaspoons of the margarine until tender.
3. Put the biscuit mix in a medium bowl.
4. Combine the egg and milk in a small bowl; add to the biscuit mix and stir to combine. Add the onion and half the cheese. Mix quickly. Spread the dough evenly in the prepared baking pan.
5. Melt the remaining 2 teaspoons margarine and brush over the bread. Sprinkle the top with the remaining cheese, and the poppy seeds if desired.
6. Bake 20 to 25 minutes, or until the bread is firm and light brown. Cut into 8 equal wedges. Serve warm.

IRISH SODA BREAD

Caraway seeds and currants add an interesting texture and a bit of sweetness to this traditional soda bread recipe. Since soda bread is low in fat and quite dense in texture, it doesn't keep very long. Serve it warm from the oven and freeze the leftovers.

1 loaf (16 wedges)

2 cups plus 2 tablespoons all-purpose
    flour
2 teaspoons baking soda
2 teaspoons sugar
1 teaspoon salt
2 tablespoons margarine
¹/₂ cup dried currants
1 tablespoon grated orange zest
2 teaspoons caraway seeds (optional)
³/₄ cup fat-free milk
1 tablespoon vinegar

Nutrition Facts per Serving
Serving size: 1 thin wedge
Amount per serving:
Calories 98
Calories from fat 14
Total fat 2 gm
Saturated fat 0 gm
Cholesterol 0 mg
Sodium 327 mg
Total carbohydrate 18 gm
Dietary fiber 1 gm
Sugars 5 gm
Protein 2 gm

Exchange List Approximations

Starch 1

Fat ¹/₂

1. Preheat the oven to 375°F. Prepare an 8-inch-diameter round cake pan with nonstick pan spray.

2. Sift 2 cups of the flour, the baking soda, sugar, and salt into a large bowl.

3. Cut in the margarine with a pastry blender until the mixture resembles coarse cornmeal. Add the currants, orange zest, and caraway seeds if desired. Set aside.

4. Combine the milk and vinegar; add ¹/₂ of the milk mixture to the dry ingredients. Blend quickly. Add the remaining milk mixture and stir only until blended.

5. Turn the dough onto a surface sprinkled with remaining 2 tablespoons flour. Knead about 10 times and shape into a round loaf. Place in the prepared pan.

6. Bake for 30 to 35 minutes. Remove from the oven and cool on a wire rack. Cut into 16 thin wedges.

APPLESAUCE NUT BREAD

Perfect for breakfast or with an afternoon cup of tea, this quick bread is a snap to make. The applesauce helps keep the bread moist and the cinnamon, cloves, and raisins enhance its natural sweetness and great apple flavor.

1 loaf (18 slices)

1 large egg, slightly beaten, or ¼ cup
    egg substitute
1 cup unsweetened applesauce
½ cup canola or corn oil
½ cup sugar
½ cup raisins
½ cup chopped walnuts
1¾ cups all-purpose flour
2 teaspoons baking powder
½ teaspoon salt
1½ teaspoons cinnamon
½ teaspoon ground cloves

1. Preheat the oven to 350°F. Prepare a 9 x 5-inch loaf pan with nonstick pan spray.
2. In a large bowl, combine the egg, applesauce, oil, sugar, raisins, and walnuts; mix well.
3. Sift the flour, baking powder, salt, cinnamon, and cloves in a medium bowl and add to the applesauce mixture; mix well.
4. Pour the batter into the prepared pan. Bake for 1 hour. Cool 10 minutes on a wire rack before removing from the pan. When cool, cut into 18 slices.

Nutrition Facts per Serving
Serving size: ½-inch slice
Amount per serving:
Calories 165
Calories from fat 79
Total fat 9 gm
Saturated fat 1 gm
Cholesterol 12 mg
Sodium 110 mg
Total carbohydrate 21 gm
Dietary fiber 1 gm
Sugars 10 gm
Protein 2 gm

Exchange List Approximations
Starch 1
Fruit ½
Fat, monounsaturated 1½

BLUEBERRY BANANA LOAF

Looking for a way to use up ripe bananas? Banana bread certainly fills the bill, but most recipes are loaded with fat. We've slimmed down our version by cutting back on the margarine and we added whole wheat flour, rolled oats, and blueberries for texture and color. For a unique-looking loaf, bake the bread in a coffee can. Fill the can about ¾ full to allow for expansion of the dough, and reduce the baking time by 5 to 8 minutes.

1 loaf (16 slices)

1 cup whole wheat flour
¾ cup all-purpose flour
1 teaspoon baking soda
½ teaspoon cinnamon
¼ teaspoon salt
½ cup quick-cooking rolled oats
3 tablespoons margarine
⅓ cup sugar
1 large egg, or ¼ cup egg substitute
1 cup mashed ripe bananas (about
        2 whole bananas)
1 tablespoon fresh lemon juice
1 cup (about 4 ounces) fresh or thawed
        frozen blueberries

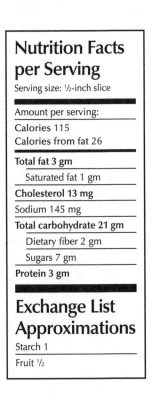

**Nutrition Facts
per Serving**

Serving size: ½-inch slice

Amount per serving:

Calories 115
Calories from fat 26

Total fat 3 gm
    Saturated fat 1 gm
Cholesterol 13 mg
Sodium 145 mg
Total carbohydrate 21 gm
    Dietary fiber 2 gm
    Sugars 7 gm
Protein 3 gm

**Exchange List
Approximations**

Starch 1
Fruit ½

1.   Preheat the oven to 350°F. Spray an 8½ x 4½-inch loaf pan with nonstick pan spray.
2.   Combine both flours, the baking soda, cinnamon, and salt in a large bowl. Stir in the oats.
3.   Cream the margarine and sugar in the large bowl of an electric mixer. Beat in the egg; add the bananas and lemon juice. Stir until blended.
4.   Add the dry ingredients and mix just until moistened. Gently fold in the blueberries.
5.   Pour the batter into the loaf pan and bake for about 1 hour, until an inserted toothpick comes out clean.
6.   Let the bread cool in the pan for 10 minutes; turn it out onto a wire rack to cool completely. Wrap and refrigerate several hours before cutting into 16 slices.

CORN BREAD

Corn bread is the perfect accompaniment to hearty stews, chili, and casseroles. The yellow cornmeal called for in this recipe makes a tender, soft bread, but you can experiment with other grades of cornmeal if you like, for variety.

12 servings

1 cup yellow cornmeal
1 cup sifted all-purpose flour
1 tablespoon baking powder
$\frac{1}{2}$ teaspoon salt
$\frac{3}{4}$ cup fat-free milk
2 large eggs, slightly beaten, or $\frac{1}{2}$ cup
    egg substitute
3 tablespoons canola or corn oil

Nutrition Facts per Serving
Serving size: 2¼-inch square
Amount per serving:
Calories 130
Calories from fat 42
Total fat 5 gm
Saturated fat 1 gm
Cholesterol 36 mg
Sodium 207 mg
Total carbohydrate 18 gm
Dietary fiber 1 gm
Sugars 1 gm
Protein 4 gm

Exchange List Approximations

Starch 1

Fat, monounsaturated 1

1. Preheat the oven to 425°F. Spray a 9-inch-square pan with nonstick pan spray.
2. Combine the cornmeal, flour, baking powder, and salt in a large bowl. Combine the milk, eggs, and oil in a small bowl, add to the dry ingredients, and blend well.
3. Pour into the prepared baking pan. Bake for 20 to 25 minutes, until an inserted toothpick comes out clean. Remove from the oven and turn out of the pan onto a rack. Cool slightly before cutting. Cut into 12 equal portions. Serve warm.

SOUTHERN CORN BREAD

Baking this traditional Southern corn bread in a preheated, greased cast-iron pan will give a crisp, dark crust. For Mexican corn bread, add 2 tablespoons chopped green chiles or 3 tablespoons drained salsa to the batter. Neither addition will change the exchange values.

8 servings

1 cup yellow cornmeal
2 tablespoons all-purpose flour
1 teaspoon baking powder
1/2 teaspoon baking soda
1/4 teaspoon salt
1 cup low-fat (1 percent fat) buttermilk
    or soured fat-free milk (add 1
    tablespoon lemon juice to 1 cup
    fat-free milk)
1 large egg, or 1/4 cup egg substitute
1 tablespoon vegetable shortening or
    margarine

Nutrition Facts per Serving
Serving size: 1 wedge
Amount per serving:
Calories 109
Calories from fat 28
Total fat 3 gm
Saturated fat 1 gm
Cholesterol 28 mg
Sodium 237 mg
Total carbohydrate 17 gm
Dietary fiber 1 gm
Sugars 2 gm
Protein 3 gm

Exchange List Approximations

Starch 1

Fat 1/2

1. Combine the cornmeal, flour, baking powder, baking soda, and salt in a medium bowl.
2. Add the milk and egg and stir until blended. Set aside 30 minutes to soften the cornmeal.
3. Preheat the oven to 425°F. Place the shortening in an 8-inch ovenproof skillet (preferably cast-iron) or cake pan. Put the skillet or pan in the hot oven. When the shortening is very hot, add it to batter and mix well. Immediately pour the batter into the skillet or pan.
4. Bake for 20 to 25 minutes, until the bread is firm and lightly browned around the edges. Cool 5 to 10 minutes. Cut into 8 equal wedges and serve warm.

ORANGE CRANBERRY BREAD

Deliciously sweet and slightly tart, orange cranberry bread is always a winner. This recipe goes one better by cutting the fat but not the taste. Fresh cranberries keep for about a month, but you can freeze them, too, for up to a year. There's no need to defrost frozen cranberries before using them in a recipe; just add them to the batter frozen.

1 loaf (18 slices)

2 cups all-purpose flour
½ cup sugar
½ teaspoon baking soda
½ teaspoon salt
1 medium orange
2 teaspoons margarine, melted
1 large egg, beaten, or ¼ cup egg
    substitute
1 teaspoon pure vanilla extract
1 cup fresh or frozen cranberries,
    coarsely chopped
½ cup chopped walnuts

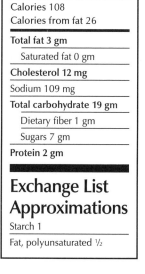

Nutrition Facts per Serving

Serving size: ½-inch slice

Amount per serving:

Calories 108
Calories from fat 26

Total fat 3 gm
   Saturated fat 0 gm
Cholesterol 12 mg
Sodium 109 mg
Total carbohydrate 19 gm
   Dietary fiber 1 gm
   Sugars 7 gm
Protein 2 gm

Exchange List Approximations

Starch 1

Fat, polyunsaturated ½

1. Preheat the oven to 350°F. Cut aluminum foil to fit the bottom of a 9 x 5-inch loaf pan and spray the sides of the pan with nonstick pan spray.

2. Sift the flour, sugar, baking soda, and salt together in a large bowl.

3. Grate the zest from the orange and set aside. Cut the orange in half and squeeze the juice into a measuring cup. Add the grated zest and melted margarine to the juice and add enough hot water to make 1 cup.

4. Stir the liquids into the dry ingredients. Add the egg, vanilla, cranberries, and walnuts; stir to mix.

5. Pour the batter into the prepared pan and bake for 1 hour, or until a toothpick inserted in the top of the loaf comes out clean. Cool in the pan on a wire rack.

6. If time permits, let stand overnight for easy slicing. Cut the loaf into 18 slices.

ZUCCHINI LEMON BREAD

When your summer garden is overflowing with zucchini, try this good-for-you recipe. Zucchini has a mild taste and is very versatile, harmonizing well with the flavors of the other ingredients. To help trim fat, we decreased the amount of nuts and oil traditionally used in zucchini bread recipes.

1 loaf (18 slices)

1 cup all-purpose flour
¹⁄₂ cup whole wheat flour
¹⁄₂ cup sugar
1¹⁄₂ teaspoons baking powder
1 teaspoon salt
¹⁄₂ teaspoon baking soda
1 cup packed shredded peeled zucchini
¹⁄₃ cup chopped walnuts
¹⁄₂ teaspoon grated lemon zest
¹⁄₂ teaspoon cinnamon
¹⁄₂ cup fat-free milk
¹⁄₃ cup canola or corn oil
2 large eggs, or ¹⁄₂ cup egg substitute

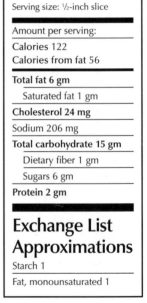

Nutrition Facts per Serving

Serving size: ¹⁄₂-inch slice

Amount per serving:

Calories 122
Calories from fat 56

Total fat 6 gm
    Saturated fat 1 gm
Cholesterol 24 mg
Sodium 206 mg
Total carbohydrate 15 gm
    Dietary fiber 1 gm
    Sugars 6 gm
Protein 2 gm

Exchange List Approximations

Starch 1

Fat, monounsaturated 1

1.   Preheat the oven to 350°F. Prepare a 9 x 5-inch loaf pan with nonstick pan spray.

2.   Combine the flours, sugar, baking powder, salt, and baking soda in a large bowl. Stir in zucchini, walnuts, lemon zest, and cinnamon.

3.   Combine the milk, oil, and eggs; add to the dry ingredients and mix until the dry ingredients are moistened. Spread evenly in the prepared pan.

4.   Bake 50 to 60 minutes, or until a toothpick inserted in the center comes out clean.

5.   Let the bread stand in the pan for 5 minutes; turn the loaf out onto a wire cooling rack. When cool, cut in 18 slices.

BAKING POWDER BISCUITS

Piping hot biscuits fresh out of the oven are irresistible. The problem is that most biscuits are packed with hidden fat. This recipe solves that dilemma, offering just 4 grams of fat per biscuit. Try mixing in 1 tablespoon chopped fresh or 1 teaspoon dried herbs like thyme, tarragon, or chives to add pizzazz. Small herbed biscuits make lovely sandwiches when split and filled with thin slices of smoked turkey, ham, or a scoop of chicken salad. Be sure to add the appropriate exchanges for any fillings.

12 biscuits (12 servings)

2 cups plus 1 tablespoon all-purpose
    flour
1 tablespoon baking powder
1 teaspoon salt
1/4 cup margarine or vegetable
    shortening
1/4 cup fat-free milk

Nutrition Facts per Serving
Serving size: 1 biscuit
Amount per serving:
Calories 120 Calories from fat 36
Total fat 4 gm
Saturated fat 1 gm
Cholesterol 0 mg
Sodium 337 mg
Total carbohydrate 18 gm
Dietary fiber 1 gm
Sugars 1 gm
Protein 3 gm

Exchange List Approximations

Starch 1

Fat 1

1.   Preheat the oven to 450°F.
2.   Mix 2 cups of the flour, the baking powder, and salt in a large bowl. Cut in the margarine with a pastry blender until the mixture resembles coarse crumbs. Add the milk and stir to mix.
3.   Turn the dough onto a surface floured with the remaining 1 tablespoon flour. Knead a few times, just enough to mix thoroughly. Roll the dough to a thickness of 1/2 inch; cut into biscuits with a 2-inch cutter. Reroll the scraps and use all the dough.
4.   Place the biscuits on an ungreased baking sheet. Bake 12 to 15 minutes until firm and light brown.

BUTTERMILK BISCUITS

These biscuits are lighter and airier than baking powder biscuits and come out of the oven puffed and golden brown. Buttermilk adds a distinctive flavor and helps make very tender dough.

9 biscuits (9 servings)

1 cup plus 1 tablespoon all-purpose flour
1 teaspoon baking powder
1/2 teaspoon baking soda
1/4 teaspoon salt
1/4 cup vegetable shortening or
     margarine
1/3 cup plus 2 tablespoons low-fat
     (1 percent fat) buttermilk

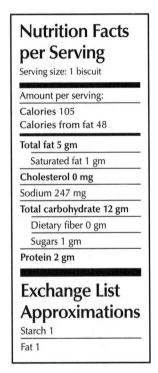

Nutrition Facts per Serving

Serving size: 1 biscuit

Amount per serving:

Calories 105
Calories from fat 48

Total fat 5 gm
  Saturated fat 1 gm
Cholesterol 0 mg
Sodium 247 mg
Total carbohydrate 12 gm
  Dietary fiber 0 gm
  Sugars 1 gm
Protein 2 gm

Exchange List Approximations

Starch 1

Fat 1

1. Preheat the oven to 425°F. Prepare a cookie sheet with nonstick pan spray.
2. Combine 1 cup of the flour, the baking powder, baking soda, and salt in a medium bowl. Cut in the shortening with a pastry blender until the mixture resembles coarse crumbs. Stir in the buttermilk to get a stiff dough.
3. Roll or pat out the dough on a board floured with the remaining 1 tablespoon flour to 1/2-inch thickness. Cut 2-inch rounds and place the biscuits 1 inch apart on the prepared cookie sheet. Use all the dough, but do not roll it out more than twice or you'll toughen it.
4. Bake for 8 to 10 minutes, or until puffed and golden. Serve hot or warm.

SCONES

Scones are great for breakfast, snacks, and of course for afternoon tea. In England, scones are traditionally served with jam or clotted cream and berries. Top yours with 100 percent fruit spread or a bit of light cream cheese and strawberries. Just be sure to add in the appropriate exchange value for whichever topping you choose. Raisins or currants are used in this recipe, but you can substitute an equal amount of other dried fruits like apricots, cherries, or cranberries, if you prefer.

16 scones (16 servings)

3 tablespoons margarine
2 cups plus 2 tablespoons all-purpose
    flour
1 tablespoon sugar
1½ teaspoons baking powder
½ teaspoon baking soda
¼ teaspoon salt
½ cup fat-free milk
¼ cup dark raisins or dried currants
1 teaspoon grated orange zest

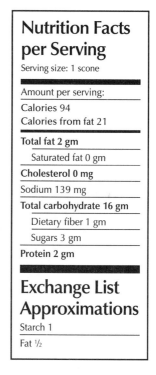

Nutrition Facts per Serving

Serving size: 1 scone

Amount per serving:

Calories 94
Calories from fat 21

Total fat 2 gm
   Saturated fat 0 gm
Cholesterol 0 mg
Sodium 139 mg
Total carbohydrate 16 gm
   Dietary fiber 1 gm
   Sugars 3 gm
Protein 2 gm

Exchange List Approximations

Starch 1
Fat ½

1. Preheat the oven to 450°F. Spray a cookie sheet with a generous amount of butter-flavored nonstick pan spray.

2. In a food processor or large bowl using a pastry blender, cut the margarine into 2 cups of the flour until the mixture resembles coarse crumbs. Add the sugar, baking powder, baking soda, and salt. Stir or process just until blended. Add the milk; stir or process just until the dry ingredients are moistened. Stir in the raisins and orange zest.

3. Gather the dough into a ball and roll out on a board lightly floured with the remaining 2 tablespoons flour to a thickness of ½ inch. Cut into rounds using a 2½-inch cookie cutter, or slice with a knife into 16 triangles. Place on the prepared cookie sheet.

4. Bake for 7 to 10 minutes, or until the scones are lightly browned. Serve warm.

CHEESE AND BASIL SCONES

Parmesan and Romano cheeses are lower in fat than most cheeses, and a little bit goes a long way in adding flavor to these savory scones. The buttermilk adds richness to the recipe, allowing us to reduce the fat even more. Use fresh (not dried) basil if you can—fresh herbs have a flavor that dried herbs just can't match.

12 scones (12 servings)

2 cups plus 1 tablespoon all-purpose
    flour
¼ cup (1 ounce) freshly grated
    Parmesan or Romano cheese
2 tablespoons chopped fresh basil,
    or 2 teaspoons dried basil
2 teaspoons baking powder
½ teaspoon baking soda
¼ teaspoon freshly ground pepper
⅔ cup low-fat (1 percent fat) buttermilk
3 tablespoons extra virgin olive oil
1 tablespoon beaten egg, or 1
    tablespoon egg substitute

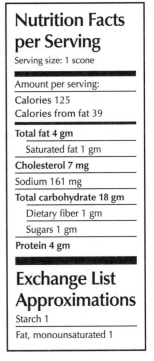

Nutrition Facts per Serving

Serving size: 1 scone

Amount per serving:

Calories 125
Calories from fat 39

Total fat 4 gm
  Saturated fat 1 gm
Cholesterol 7 mg
Sodium 161 mg
Total carbohydrate 18 gm
  Dietary fiber 1 gm
  Sugars 1 gm
Protein 4 gm

Exchange List Approximations

Starch 1
Fat, monounsaturated 1

1. Preheat the oven to 450°F. Spray a cookie sheet with a generous amount of nonstick pan spray.
2. Combine 2 cups of the flour, the cheese, basil, baking powder, baking soda, and pepper in a medium bowl.
3. Add the buttermilk and oil; mix only until the dry ingredients are moistened. Divide the dough into 2 balls. Knead each ball gently 3 times on a surface floured with the remaining 1 tablespoon flour.
4. Pat the dough into 2 circles, each 7 to 8 inches in diameter, on the prepared cookie sheet. With a sharp knife, score each disk ¼ inch deep into 6 wedges; do not cut through.
5. Brush the tops of the dough rounds with egg to glaze. Bake 10 to 12 minutes, or until golden brown. Cut each disk into 6 wedges while hot. Serve the scones warm or at room temperature.

BRAN MUFFINS

These moist, fiber-rich muffins are a delicious way to greet the morning. When preparing the batter, stir the ingredients just until blended. If you overbeat, the muffins will come out tough and chewy. For added flavor and texture, you could toss 1 cup of raisins or currants into the batter (and add ½ fruit exchange per serving) if you wish.

12 muffins (12 servings)

1 large egg, or ¼ cup egg substitute
¼ cup sugar
1¾ cups fat-free milk
1½ tablespoons margarine, melted
2 cups bran cereal (shredded type, not
      bran flakes)
1 cup all-purpose flour
1 tablespoon baking powder
½ teaspoon salt

Nutrition Facts per Serving
Serving size: 1 muffin
Amount per serving:
Calories 112
Calories from fat 21
Total fat 2 gm
Saturated fat 1 gm
Cholesterol 18 mg
Sodium 322 mg
Total carbohydrate 22 gm
Dietary fiber 4 gm
Sugars 8 gm
Protein 4 gm

Exchange List Approximation
Starch 1½

1. Preheat the oven to 400°F. Prepare a 12-cup muffin tin with nonstick pan spray or line the muffin cups with paper liners.

2. Beat the egg in a medium bowl. Add the sugar, milk, and margarine; beat well. Stir in the bran. Allow to stand 2 minutes for the bran to soften.

3. Sift the dry ingredients together into a small bowl; add to the bran mixture. Stir just until blended.

4. Divide the batter among the 12 muffin cups; each will be about ⅔ full.

5. Bake 20 to 25 minutes, until a toothpick inserted in the center of a muffin comes out clean.

ORANGE CURRANT OAT BRAN MUFFINS

Oat bran is a terrific source of soluble fiber in the diet and may help lower blood cholesterol levels. The currants, orange juice, buttermilk, and orange zest add richness, sweetness, and zip to this recipe without adding too much fat. For mini-muffins, use 24 small muffin cups for the regular tins and reduce the baking time to 12 to 15 minutes.

12 muffins (12 servings)

1 cup uncooked oat bran
1 cup all-purpose flour
$1/4$ cup sugar
1 tablespoon baking powder
$1/2$ teaspoon baking soda
$1/2$ teaspoon cinnamon
$1/4$ teaspoon salt
$1/2$ cup dried currants or golden raisins
2 large egg whites
3 tablespoons margarine, melted
$1/4$ cup fresh orange juice
$3/4$ cup low-fat (1 percent fat) buttermilk
1 teaspoon grated orange zest

Nutrition Facts per Serving
Serving size: 1 muffin
Amount per serving:
Calories 141
Calories from fat 33
Total fat 4 gm
Saturated fat 1 gm
Cholesterol 1 mg
Sodium 252 mg
Total carbohydrate 23 gm
Dietary fiber 2 gm
Sugars 11 gm
Protein 4 gm

Exchange List Approximations
Starch 1½
Fat ½

1. Preheat the oven to 375°F. Line a 12-cup muffin tin with paper liners.

2. Combine the oat bran, flour, sugar, baking powder, baking soda, cinnamon, and salt in a medium bowl. Stir in the currants.

3. Beat the egg whites with a whisk in a small bowl. Whisk in the margarine, then the orange juice, buttermilk, and orange zest. Add to the dry ingredients; mix just until the dry ingredients are moistened.

4. Divide the batter among the 12 muffin cups. Bake 20 to 25 minutes, or until a toothpick inserted in the center of a muffin comes out clean.

NORTHERN-STYLE DOUBLE CORN MUFFINS

Whole corn kernels add a nice texture and enhance the moist and tender crumb of this recipe. It's doubtful you'll have leftovers, but you can freeze extra muffins for up to 3 months. These muffins are a terrific accompaniment to soups like Vegetable Chowder (page 103) or New England Fish Chowder (page 122).

12 muffins (12 servings)

1 cup yellow or white cornmeal
½ cup all-purpose flour
1 tablespoon sugar
2 teaspoons baking powder
½ teaspoon baking soda
1 cup (4 ounces) fresh corn kernels or
        thawed frozen corn kernels
1 cup low-fat (1 percent fat) buttermilk
1 large egg, beaten, or ¼ cup egg
        substitute
2 tablespoons margarine, melted

1.   Preheat the oven to 400°F. Line a 12-cup muffin tin with paper liners.
2.   Combine the cornmeal, flour, sugar, baking powder, and baking soda in a medium bowl. Stir in the corn. Add the buttermilk, egg, and margarine; mix just until the dry ingredients are moistened.
3.   Divide the batter to fill 12 muffin cups; each will be about ¾ full.
4.   Bake 15 minutes, or until a toothpick inserted in the center of a muffin comes out clean. Serve warm.

Nutrition Facts per Serving

Serving size: 1 muffin

Amount per serving:

Calories 108
Calories from fat 25

Total fat 3 gm
    Saturated fat 1 gm
Cholesterol 18 mg
Sodium 163 mg
Total carbohydrate 18 gm
    Dietary fiber 1 gm
    Sugars 2 gm
Protein 3 gm

Exchange List Approximations

Starch 1
Fat ½

FRESH PEACH MUFFINS

These muffins are a peach of a treat and bursting with summer flavor. For the sweetest taste, look for peaches that smell fragrant and yield to slight pressure. (Avoid those that are hard, green, or have any bruises and soft spots.) To speed the ripening of peaches, place them in a paper bag with an apple and pierce several holes in the bag with the tip of a knife. They should ripen in a day or so.

12 muffins (12 servings)

1 cup peeled, chopped fresh ripe
    peaches
1 teaspoon fresh lemon juice
1 cup all-purpose flour
1 cup whole wheat flour
¼ cup sugar
1 tablespoon baking powder
½ teaspoon mace
¼ teaspoon salt
1 large egg, or ¼ cup egg substitute
¼ cup canola or corn oil
1 cup fat-free milk

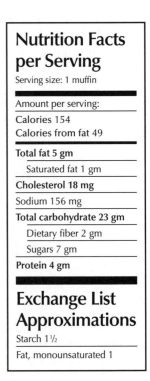

Nutrition Facts per Serving

Serving size: 1 muffin

Amount per serving:

Calories 154
Calories from fat 49

Total fat 5 gm
   Saturated fat 1 gm

Cholesterol 18 mg

Sodium 156 mg

Total carbohydrate 23 gm
   Dietary fiber 2 gm
   Sugars 7 gm

Protein 4 gm

Exchange List Approximations

Starch 1½

Fat, monounsaturated 1

1. Preheat the oven to 400°F. Prepare a 12-cup muffin pan with nonstick pan spray or line the muffin cups with paper liners.
2. Combine the peaches and lemon juice in a small bowl. Stir to mix; set aside.
3. In a large bowl, combine the flours, sugar, baking powder, mace, and salt; mix thoroughly.
4. Beat the egg, oil, and milk together in a small bowl. Add to the dry ingredients and stir until the flour is moistened.
5. Fold in the peaches. Divide batter among the muffin cups; each will be about ⅔ full.
6. Bake about 25 minutes, or until a toothpick inserted in the center of a muffin comes out clean. Remove the muffins from the pan immediately to avoid sticking.

MATZO MEAL POPOVERS

Eggs are the only leavening ingredient in popovers, so they are best served hot out of the oven. Crisp on the outside and soft, moist, and hollow in the center, they're a treat for any occasion. For savory popovers, add a bit of cheese or herbs to the dough. Or for a taste of sweetness, top plain popovers with a little jam or marmalade. One tablespoon of jam or marmalade adds 1 fruit exchange.

12 popovers (12 servings)

½ cup canola or corn oil
1 cup matzo meal
2 tablespoons sugar
½ teaspoon salt
4 large eggs

1. Preheat the oven to 400°F. Prepare a 12-cup muffin tin with a generous amount of nonstick pan spray.
2. In a medium saucepan, bring 1 cup water and the oil to a rapid boil. Remove from the heat; add the matzo meal, sugar, and salt and mix well. Add the eggs one at a time, beating after each addition.
3. Divide the batter among the muffin cups. Bake for 15 minutes; reduce the heat to 375°F and bake 45 minutes longer, until the popovers are puffed and brown.

Nutrition Facts per Serving

Serving size: 1 popover

Amount per serving:

Calories 159
Calories from fat 101

Total fat 11 gm	
Saturated fat 1 gm	
Cholesterol 71 mg	
Sodium 118 mg	
Total carbohydrate 11 gm	
Dietary fiber 0 gm	
Sugars 2 gm	
Protein 3 gm	

Exchange List Approximations

Starch 1

Fat, monounsaturated 2

3

APPETIZERS, DIPS, AND SPREADS

Whatever you call them—canapés, crudités, dips, spreads, nibbles, hors d'oeuvres—they're all considered appetizers. Since hors d'oeuvres are often the downfall of those trying to watch fat and calories, we offer recipes in this chapter that keep nutrition as well as taste in mind.

Appetizers are generally intended to subdue hunger pangs and tease the appetite, not provide a meal, so keep serving sizes small. At parties, offer both hot and cold varieties of appetizers in a mix of shapes, color, flavors, and textures. Many appetizers make great casual snacks, too.

Crudités—crisp raw or quickly blanched vegetables—are always a winner, whether the setting is formal or casual. We've included a number of reduced-fat dips to accompany the crudités, including Hummus, Spicy Artichoke Dip, Creamy Three-Onion Dip, and Cheddar Cheese Dip. Low-fat or fat-free versions of mayonnaise, sour cream, yogurt, and buttermilk are the base ingredients for many of these dips. In addition to serving the dips as an accompaniment to vegetables, try them with low-fat chips or crackers, pretzels, or even as sandwich fillings.

When selecting vegetables to accompany the dip, choose a variety of colors and textures. Occasionally, vegetables are left whole, but more often they are cut, peeled, or in some way prepared as finger food. The list that follows shows which vegetables can be left raw and which should be blanched.

RAW	*BLANCHED*
Jicama sticks	Sugar snap peas
Peeled baby carrots	Broccoli and cauliflower florets
Turnip sticks	Asparagus spears
Radishes	Green beans
Celery	
Whole baby squash	
Yellow squash or zucchini rounds	
White mushrooms	
Cherry tomatoes	
Fennel	
Cucumber sticks	
Red, yellow, and green bell pepper slices	
Endive and radicchio leaves	

To blanch crudités, bring a large pot of water to a boil. Have a bowl of ice-cold water ready. Place the vegetables in a sieve or the strainer section of a pasta pot and immerse in the boiling water for 2 or 3 minutes, or just long enough to barely soften the vegetable, fix the color, and intensify the flavor. Immediately place the vegetables in the bowl of ice-cold water to stop the cooking.

For parties, estimate about ¼ to ⅓ pound of vegetables per person. Arrange the vegetables decoratively on a platter or in a basket lined with a pretty napkin, and trim the perimeter with fresh herbs or lettuce leaves, if desired. Make sure all the vegetables are fresh and unblemished, crisp, and well washed before serving them. Be creative: hollow out some vegetables to act as containers; small heads of red cabbage, brightly colored peppers, or round squash make good "bowls."

You, your family, and guests will enjoy tidbits like Baby Corn in Jalapeño Vinaigrette, Picante Potato Skins, Salmon Mousse, Honey-Mustard Chicken Wings, Italian Pita Crisps, and Miniature Crab Puffs. We've worked hard to reduce fat and calories in these recipes—so much so that you won't realize what's missing! Whether you're planning a special party or just relaxing with friends to watch a football game, you're sure to find the right appetizer to suit the occasion in the following pages.

MINIATURE CRAB PUFFS

Mini cream puff shells, here filled with tasty crab salad, are luxurious party fare, and fortunately they require far less time and skill to make than their decorative appearance would indicate. An economical alternative to expensive real crab is surimi—imitation crab made from fish—which is sold at fish markets and in seafood departments at supermarkets.

16 puffs (8 servings)

PUFF SHELLS

4 tablespoons (½ stick) unsalted
    margarine
⅛ teaspoon salt
½ cup all-purpose flour
2 large eggs

FILLING

One 6½-ounce can crabmeat, drained
    and flaked, or 6 ounces crabmeat,
    fresh or frozen, flaked
1 green onion with green top, thinly
    sliced, or 2 tablespoons chopped
    chives
2 tablespoons chopped pimiento or red
    bell pepper
2 tablespoons light mayonnaise
1 clove garlic, minced

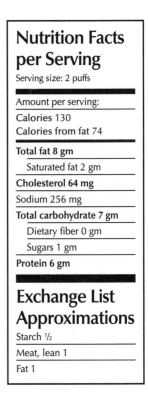

Nutrition Facts per Serving

Serving size: 2 puffs

Amount per serving:

Calories 130
Calories from fat 74

Total fat 8 gm
  Saturated fat 2 gm

Cholesterol 64 mg

Sodium 256 mg

Total carbohydrate 7 gm
  Dietary fiber 0 gm
  Sugars 1 gm

Protein 6 gm

Exchange List Approximations

Starch ½

Meat, lean 1

Fat 1

1. Preheat the oven to 425°F. In a 1-quart saucepan, bring ½ cup water, the margarine, and salt to a boil.

2. Add all the flour, vigorously stirring over medium heat until the dough leaves the sides of the pan and forms a ball.

3. Remove from heat; allow the dough to cool for 5 minutes. Beat in the eggs 1 at a time.

4. Drop rounded teaspoonfuls of batter onto an ungreased cookie sheet. Bake for 10 minutes; reduce the heat to 350°F. Continue baking 17 to 20 minutes longer, or until the puffs are golden brown. Cool on a wire rack.

5.   Slice a thin cap off the top of each puff; remove the doughy inside. (Puffs and tops may be kept up to 2 days in an airtight container.)

6.   Combine all the filling ingredients and mix well. Immediately before serving, fill the puffs and replace the caps.

MUSHROOM PÂTÉ

Cultivated white mushrooms (champignons) work very well in this recipe, but for a deeper, earthier flavor, you might want to try fresh shiitakes. To prepare champignons, simply cut off and discard the stem ends and wipe the mushrooms clean with a damp cloth. Because shiitake stems are very tough, they should be discarded or reserved for use in stock. Serve the pâté as an hors d'oeuvre with crackers or thinly sliced French bread, stuff it into small puff shells (page 70), or substitute low-fat or fat-free ricotta cheese for the mayonnaise and use the pâté as filling for crêpes (page 44).

1 cup (8 servings)

1 tablespoon unsalted margarine
8 ounces fresh mushrooms, cleaned and
     finely chopped
1/2 cup finely chopped onion
1 teaspoon Worcestershire sauce
1 teaspoon fresh lemon juice
1/4 teaspoon salt
1/8 teaspoon freshly ground pepper
2 tablespoons light mayonnaise

1. In a medium skillet over medium heat, melt the margarine. Add the mushrooms and onion; cook until lightly browned.

2. Stir in the Worcestershire sauce, lemon juice, salt, and pepper. Cook until the liquid has evaporated, about 15 minutes, stirring often.

3. Cool. Stir in the mayonnaise. Pack the warm pâté in a bowl or mold sprayed with nonstick pan spray. Cover tightly and chill at least 2 hours. Invert and tap the bottom to unmold.

Nutrition Facts per Serving

Serving size: 2 tablespoons

Amount per serving:

Calories 35
Calories from fat 24

Total fat 3 gm
   Saturated fat 0 gm
Cholesterol 2 mg
Sodium 107 mg
Total carbohydrate 2 gm
   Dietary fiber 1 gm
   Sugars 1 gm
Protein 1 gm

Exchange List Approximation

Fat 1/2

POLENTA CANAPÉS

Polenta, or cooked cornmeal, is a staple in Northern Italy, where it is served in a number of creative ways as a first course or as an accompaniment to roasts and stews. Just after it has finished cooking, and while it is still soft and creamy, polenta is often accompanied by a savory sauce or by grilled mushrooms or other vegetables. When it cools, polenta becomes firm and can be cut into shapes, combined with other ingredients, and reheated—as in this recipe.

16 canapés (8 servings)

One 13- to 14-ounce can reduced-
    sodium chicken broth, or
    2 cups Homemade Chicken
    Broth (page 101)
½ cup yellow cornmeal
¼ teaspoon salt
1 tablespoon olive oil
4 marinated artichoke hearts, drained
    and quartered
3 slices (about 3 ounces) part-skim
    mozzarella cheese, cut into
    32 very thin strips

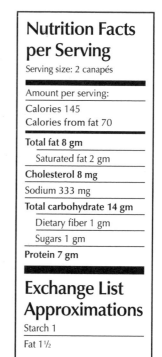

Nutrition Facts per Serving

Serving size: 2 canapés

Amount per serving:

Calories 145
Calories from fat 70

Total fat 8 gm
  Saturated fat 2 gm
Cholesterol 8 mg
Sodium 333 mg
Total carbohydrate 14 gm
  Dietary fiber 1 gm
  Sugars 1 gm
Protein 7 gm

Exchange List Approximations

Starch 1
Fat 1½

1.   Combine 1 cup water, the broth, cornmeal, and salt in a saucepan. Bring to a boil, stirring constantly. Simmer over low heat 10 to 12 minutes, or until thickened, stirring frequently. Stir in the oil.

2.   Spray an 8-inch-square dish or pan with nonstick pan spray. Pour the batter into the pan and chill until firm.

3.   Cut the polenta into 16 squares, each 2 x 2 inches. Place the squares on a jelly roll pan or cookie sheet. Place an artichoke heart quarter on each square. Crisscross 2 strips of cheese over each artichoke heart, forming an X. Preheat the broiler.

4.   Broil 5 to 6 inches from the heat until the cheese is melted and the polenta is heated through, about 3 minutes.

CRUNCHY SNACK MIX

Keep these tangy nibbles on hand for snacks, for party appetizers, or as part of a brown-bag lunch. Once the mix is prepared, measure it into ½-cup portions and store in paper cups or small plastic bags; that way you won't have to guess later on how much mix goes into each serving.

4 cups (8 servings)

2 tablespoons margarine
½ teaspoon seasoned salt
2 teaspoons Worcestershire sauce
1 cup unsweetened oven-toasted rice
    cereal, such as Rice Chex or
    Crispix
1½ cups unsweetened oven-toasted
    wheat cereal, such as Wheat Chex
1 cup (1 ounce, or about 90) thin pretzel
    sticks
½ cup (1 ounce, or about 32) reduced-
    fat tiny cheese crackers

1. Preheat the oven to 250°F. Melt the margarine in a shallow baking pan; stir in the salt and Worcestershire sauce.
2. Add the cereals, pretzels, and crackers. Stir to coat the pieces with margarine.
3. Bake 45 minutes, stirring every 15 minutes. Spread on paper towels to cool. Store in an airtight container.

Nutrition Facts per Serving

Serving size: ½ cup

Amount per serving:

Calories 85
Calories from fat 17

Total fat 2 gm
    Saturated fat 0 gm
Cholesterol 0 mg
Sodium 301 mg
Total carbohydrate 16 gm
    Dietary fiber 1 gm
    Sugars 1 gm
Protein 2 gm

Exchange List Approximation

Starch 1

ITALIAN PITA CRISPS

Sparked with garlic, basil, and Parmesan cheese, these zesty crisps are excellent with dips, soups, or salads. You may find it convenient to keep a package or two of frozen pita breads, preferably made with whole wheat flour for extra fiber, in the freezer. The breads will defrost in minutes at room temperature, and the pita crisps can be made in just 15 minutes.

32 appetizers (8 servings)

2 pitas, each about 6 inches in diameter
1 tablespoon olive oil
1 clove garlic, finely minced
1/4 teaspoon dried basil or oregano
2 teaspoons grated Parmesan cheese

1. Preheat the oven to 350°F. Spray 1 or 2 cookie sheets with nonstick pan spray. Cut each pita into 8 wedges; split each wedge to separate the halves. Arrange in a single layer on the cookie sheet(s).
2. Mix the olive oil and garlic. Brush over the pita sections; sprinkle with basil and cheese.
3. Bake 8 to 10 minutes, or until lightly browned and crisp. Serve hot, or cool and store in an airtight container.

Nutrition Facts per Serving
Serving size: 4 crisps
Amount per serving:
Calories 59
Calories from fat 18
Total fat 2 gm
Saturated fat 0 gm
Cholesterol 0 mg
Sodium 88 mg
Total carbohydrate 8 gm
Dietary fiber 0 gm
Sugars 0 gm
Protein 2 gm

Exchange List Approximations
Starch 1/2
Fat, monounsaturated 1/2

DEVILED EGGS

Horseradish and mustard add zing to this perennial favorite, beloved by adults and children alike. Serve the eggs as a first course or part of a buffet, or as one of the elements of an antipasto platter.

4 servings

4 large hard-cooked eggs
1 tablespoon plus 1 teaspoon fat-free
    mayonnaise
2 teaspoons prepared mustard
1 teaspoon drained prepared
    horseradish
$^1/_2$ teaspoon anchovy paste (optional)
$^1/_4$ teaspoon salt
Pinch of freshly ground pepper
Pinch of paprika, or 8 small sprigs parsley

1. Slice the eggs in half lengthwise. Remove the yolks and mash in a small bowl with a fork.
2. Add the mayonnaise, mustard, horseradish, anchovy paste if desired, salt, and pepper to the yolks. Mix well until smooth.
3. Fill the egg halves with the yolk mixture. Garnish each with paprika or parsley sprigs.

Nutrition Facts per Serving

Serving size: 2 halves

Amount per serving:

Calories 80
Calories from fat 46

Total fat 5 gm
    Saturated fat 2 gm
Cholesterol 213 mg
Sodium 276 mg*
Total carbohydrate 2 gm
    Dietary fiber 0 gm
    Sugars 1 gm
Protein 6 gm

Exchange List Approximation

Meat, medium-fat 1

* *If optional anchovy paste is used, sodium per serving is 308 mg.*

CAPONATA

Here's a classic recipe for the rich vegetable stew that is traditionally served cold or at room temperature as a first course or sandwich spread, or hot as a side dish. Try to find the large salted capers (rinse and drain them before using), available in specialty foods stores and some supermarkets; these add authentic southern Italian flavor, as do fruity olive oil and olive oil–flavored spray.

3 cups (6 servings)

1 pound eggplant, peeled and cubed
1 teaspoon salt
1 tablespoon olive oil
1 medium onion, thinly sliced
1 large clove garlic, minced
One 8-ounce can diced tomatoes, with
    liquid
½ cup thinly sliced celery
½ cup diced yellow or green bell
    pepper
2 tablespoons sliced pimiento-stuffed
    green olives
1 teaspoon drained capers
2 teaspoons sugar
2 tablespoons red wine vinegar
3 large fresh basil leaves, shredded,
    or 1 teaspoon dried basil

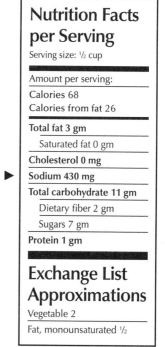

Nutrition Facts per Serving

Serving size: ½ cup

Amount per serving:

Calories 68
Calories from fat 26

Total fat 3 gm
  Saturated fat 0 gm
Cholesterol 0 mg
Sodium 430 mg
Total carbohydrate 11 gm
  Dietary fiber 2 gm
  Sugars 7 gm
Protein 1 gm

Exchange List Approximations

Vegetable 2
Fat, monounsaturated ½

1.   Sprinkle the eggplant cubes with salt and place in a colander to drain for 1 hour. Pat dry with paper towels.

2.   Spray a large skillet with olive oil–flavored nonstick pan spray and add half the olive oil. Sauté the eggplant over medium heat until tender, about 5 minutes. Remove and set aside.

3.   Heat the remaining oil in the same skillet. Sauté the onion and garlic until tender, about 5 minutes.

4.   Stir in the remaining ingredients except the basil. Cover; simmer over low heat for 30 minutes, stirring occasionally.

5.   Stir in the reserved eggplant and the basil and cook uncovered for 5 to 10 minutes, or until most of the liquid is absorbed.

BABY CORN IN JALAPEÑO VINAIGRETTE

In this piquant Mexican-style appetizer, a spicy vinaigrette adds sparkle to mild-flavored baby corn. The dish can be prepared up to three days in advance.

8 servings

One 15-ounce can or two 7-ounce jars
      whole baby corn cobs, rinsed
      and drained
¼ cup chopped cilantro
¼ cup red or white wine vinegar
2 tablespoons olive oil
1 small jalapeño pepper, seeded and
      minced

1. Combine all the ingredients in a glass dish; refrigerate, covered, and marinate at least 2 hours or overnight. (The mixture may be refrigerated up to 3 days.)

2. Drain the corn before serving chilled or at room temperature.

Nutrition Facts per Serving	
Serving size: about 4 pieces	
Amount per serving:	
Calories 27	
Calories from fat 15	
Total fat 2 gm	
Saturated fat 0 gm	
Cholesterol 0 mg	
Sodium 5 mg	
Total carbohydrate 3 gm	
Dietary fiber 1 gm	
Sugars 2 gm	
Protein 1 gm	

Exchange List Approximation

Vegetable 1

CUCUMBER CUPS WITH HORSERADISH

Cucumber, cream cheese, and horseradish are combined in a refreshing mouthful, a welcome addition to a vegetable hors d'oeuvre tray that might also include Baby Corn in Jalapeño Vinaigrette (page 78), Greek-Style Marinated Mushrooms (page 80), Caponata (page 77), and Italian Pita Crisps (page 75).

18 appetizers (9 servings)

2 ounces reduced-fat cream cheese
　　　(Neufchâtel), at room
　　　temperature
2 tablespoons light or fat-free
　　　mayonnaise
1 tablespoon drained prepared
　　　horseradish
1 large peeled cucumber (about 12
　　　ounces), preferably seedless
18 small parsley or dill sprigs

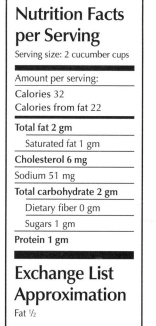

Nutrition Facts per Serving

Serving size: 2 cucumber cups

Amount per serving:

Calories 32
Calories from fat 22

Total fat 2 gm
　　Saturated fat 1 gm
Cholesterol 6 mg
Sodium 51 mg
Total carbohydrate 2 gm
　　Dietary fiber 0 gm
　　Sugars 1 gm
Protein 1 gm

Exchange List Approximation

Fat ½

1.　Combine the cream cheese, mayonnaise, and horseradish; chill at least 30 minutes.

2.　Score the cucumber lengthwise with the tines of a fork. Cut the cucumber crosswise into ½-inch slices, making 18. Using a melon baller or ½ teaspoon measuring spoon, scoop out a small hollow on the straight side. Do not cut all the way through.

3.　Transfer the cream cheese mixture to a pastry bag fitted with a fluted tip. Pipe the cheese mixture into the cucumber cups. (Use a small spoon if a pastry bag is not available.) Garnish the tops of the cups with parsley or dill sprigs.

GREEK-STYLE MARINATED MUSHROOMS

Vegetables cooked à la grecque—that is, simmered in a garlicky vinaigrette made with fruity olive oil, good-quality wine vinegar, and coriander seeds—are a traditional French first course. They are usually served at room temperature, often over lettuce or mixed greens. The mushrooms can be served with toothpicks as an hors d'oeuvre or with other salads as a first course.

3⅓ cups (10 servings)

3 cloves garlic, minced
⅓ cup extra virgin olive oil
¼ cup red wine vinegar
1 tablespoon whole coriander seeds
½ teaspoon dried thyme
½ teaspoon dried oregano
¼ teaspoon freshly ground pepper
1½ pounds small to medium
        mushrooms, cleaned,
        stems trimmed flat

1. In a large sauté pan, sauté the garlic in the oil for 2 minutes. Add the remaining ingredients except the mushrooms; bring to a simmer.
2. Add the mushrooms; cover and simmer over low heat for 5 minutes, or until the mushrooms are tender, stirring occasionally.
3. Put the mixture in a glass bowl or jar. Cover and refrigerate 1 to 4 days. Drain off and discard the marinade before serving.

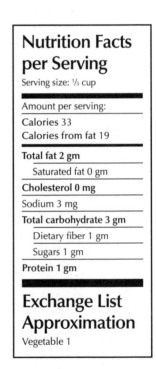

Nutrition Facts per Serving

Serving size: ⅓ cup

Amount per serving:

Calories 33
Calories from fat 19

Total fat 2 gm
  Saturated fat 0 gm
Cholesterol 0 mg
Sodium 3 mg
Total carbohydrate 3 gm
  Dietary fiber 1 gm
  Sugars 1 gm
Protein 1 gm

Exchange List Approximation

Vegetable 1

PICANTE POTATO SKINS

For a milder flavor, use Monterey Jack cheese without jalapeños. To increase the spice quotient, use a hot salsa. The skins are mouthwateringly good at any time of year, but they are especially delicious during the fall and winter. Bake the potatoes any time within two days of serving, then complete the final preparation while the oven is preheating.

12 potato skins (6 servings)

3 baking potatoes (about 1 pound total)
3 tablespoons prepared salsa or picante
    sauce
1 tablespoon margarine, melted
³/₄ cup (3 ounces) shredded reduced-fat
    Monterey Jack cheese with
    jalapeños

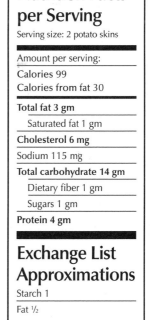

**Nutrition Facts
per Serving**

Serving size: 2 potato skins

Amount per serving:

Calories 99
Calories from fat 30

Total fat 3 gm
  Saturated fat 1 gm
Cholesterol 6 mg
Sodium 115 mg
Total carbohydrate 14 gm
  Dietary fiber 1 gm
  Sugars 1 gm
Protein 4 gm

**Exchange List
Approximations**

Starch 1

Fat ½

1. Preheat the oven to 400°F. Do not bake the potatoes in a microwave for this recipe, because the skins will become too soft. Prepare a cookie sheet with nonstick pan spray.
2. Wash the potatoes and poke them with a fork or the tip of a knife in several places. Bake the potatoes 1 hour, or until tender; cool.
3. Cut the potatoes in half lengthwise. Carefully scoop out the pulp, leaving ¼-inch-thick shells. (Reserve the pulp for another use.) Cut each shell in half lengthwise; place on a cookie sheet.
4. Combine the salsa and margarine; brush over the insides of shells. Bake until crisp, about 15 minutes.
5. Sprinkle the skins with cheese; return to the oven for 5 minutes or until the cheese is melted. Serve warm.

SALMON MOUSSE

Salmon mousse is to first courses what chocolate mousse is to desserts: creamy, richly flavored, and sumptuous. Pale pink slices of mousse nestled in lettuce leaves are an elegant beginning for a dinner party. The mousse, served as the main course of a light spring supper, can be accompanied by a yogurt-dill sauce and steamed asparagus and new potatoes. Just be sure to include the appropriate exchange or carbohydrate values for any additions.

6 servings

1 pound salmon fillet or salmon steaks,
    skin and bones removed
3 large egg whites
1 tablespoon chopped fresh dill, or
    1 teaspoon dried dill weed
½ teaspoon salt
⅛ teaspoon white pepper
1 cup fat-free evaporated milk, very cold
6 dill sprigs (optional, for garnish)

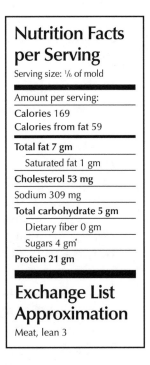

Nutrition Facts per Serving

Serving size: ⅙ of mold

Amount per serving:

Calories 169
Calories from fat 59

Total fat 7 gm
  Saturated fat 1 gm
Cholesterol 53 mg
Sodium 309 mg
Total carbohydrate 5 gm
  Dietary fiber 0 gm
  Sugars 4 gm
Protein 21 gm

Exchange List Approximation

Meat, lean 3

1. Preheat the oven to 350°F. Spray a 3-cup ring mold with nonstick pan spray.
2. Purée the fish in a food processor. Add the egg whites, dill, salt, and pepper. With the machine running, pour in the milk through the feed tube. Process just until blended.
3. Pour the mixture into the prepared mold; cover with wax paper. Set the mold in a pan containing about 1 inch of hot water. Bake for 20 to 25 minutes, or until firm to the touch. Unmold, slice into 6 equal portions, and serve hot, at room temperature, or chilled. Garnish with dill sprigs if desired.

SANTA FE SHRIMP

This is a pretty appetizer—pink shrimp and green herbs set off against flecks of red pimiento—and a good make-ahead dish for a cocktail buffet or served on a plate and passed around as finger food. Cooked bay scallops, or sea scallops cut into two or three pieces, can be substituted for the shrimp.

Approximately 30 shrimp (6 servings)

1 pound (about 30) cooked shrimp,
    peeled, tails left on
¼ cup fresh lime juice
3 tablespoons olive oil
2 cloves garlic, minced
4 green onions with green tops,
    chopped
1 small jalapeño pepper, seeds removed,
    jalapeño finely chopped
2 tablespoons chopped roasted red
    pepper or pimiento
3 tablespoons chopped fresh cilantro
6 large leaves Boston or red leaf lettuce

Nutrition Facts per Serving
Serving size: ⅙ recipe (about 5 shrimp)
Amount per serving:
Calories 122
Calories from fat 43
Total fat 5 gm
Saturated fat 1 gm
Cholesterol 114 mg
Sodium 125 mg
Total carbohydrate 4 gm
Dietary fiber 1 gm
Sugars 2 gm
Protein 16 gm

Exchange List Approximation

Meat, lean 2

1.   Place the shrimp in a glass bowl or zip-top bag.

2.   Combine all the other ingredients except the lettuce in a small bowl; pour over the shrimp. Toss well to cover all surfaces of the shrimp. Refrigerate at least 1 hour to marinate, turning every 30 minutes.

3.   Lift the shrimp, with onion and pepper bits, from the marinade with a slotted spoon. Discard the marinade. Serve the shrimp on lettuce leaves.

BUFFALO-STYLE CHICKEN WINGS

You can adjust the spiciness of these juicy wings by increasing or decreasing the hot pepper sauce and cayenne. The wings are welcome party fare, traditionally served with celery sticks and Blue Cheese Dip (page 88).

24 wing sections (6 servings)

2 pounds chicken wings (about 12)
3 tablespoons unsalted margarine,
    melted
2 tablespoons hot pepper sauce
1/4 teaspoon salt
1/8 teaspoon cayenne pepper (optional)

Nutrition Facts per Serving	
Serving size: 4 wing sections	
Amount per serving:	
Calories 223	
Calories from fat 145	
Total fat 16 gm	
Saturated fat 4 gm	
Cholesterol 57 mg	
Sodium 152 mg	
Total carbohydrate 0 gm	
Dietary fiber 0 gm	
Sugars 0 gm	
Protein 18 gm	

Exchange List Approximation
Meat, medium-fat 3

1. Preheat the oven to 325°F. Prepare a rimmed cookie sheet or jelly roll pan with nonstick pan spray.
2. Split the wings at each joint; discard the tips or reserve them for soup. Place the wings on the prepared pan and bake for 30 minutes. Discard the fat and juices.
3. Combine the margarine, hot pepper sauce, salt, and cayenne pepper (if you like). Place wings in a bowl or jar. Pour 2/3 of the margarine mixture over the wings; reserve the remaining mixture. Cover the wings and refrigerate at least 3 hours or overnight. Turn several times.
4. Before serving, broil the wings 3 to 4 inches from the heat for 5 to 6 minutes on each side, turning, until brown and crisp; brush often with the reserved marinade. Brush with the reserved margarine mixture before serving.

HONEY-MUSTARD CHICKEN WINGS

Chicken wings deliver a lot of flavor for a relatively low price. A chicken drumette is the meaty drumstick section of the wing, and drumettes can ordinarily be purchased frozen. If they are not available, buy 2 pounds of whole chicken wings and cut each into 3 segments. Use the 2 meaty sections for this recipe and reserve the tips for stock.

8 servings (16 drumettes)

2 tablespoons spicy brown mustard or
      prepared mustard with
      horseradish
1 tablespoon plus 1 teaspoon honey
$1/3$ cup plain dry bread crumbs
$1\frac{1}{2}$ pounds chicken wing drumettes
      (about 16 pieces)
$1/4$ teaspoon Hungarian paprika,
      preferably hot (optional)

1. Preheat the oven to 375°F. Spray a cookie sheet with nonstick spray.
2. Combine the mustard and honey in a small bowl. Place the bread crumbs in a separate shallow bowl. Brush each wing section with the mustard mixture. Roll each in bread crumbs; shake off the excess.
3. Place the wings on the cookie sheet and sprinkle with paprika, if desired. Bake the wings 30 minutes, or until crisp. Serve warm.

Nutrition Facts per Serving

Serving size: 2 drumettes

Amount per serving:

Calories 129
Calories from fat 63

Total fat 7 gm
   Saturated fat 2 gm
Cholesterol 29 mg
Sodium 113 mg
Total carbohydrate 6 gm
   Dietary fiber 0 gm
   Sugars 3 gm
Protein 10 gm

Exchange List Approximations

Starch $1/2$

Meat, medium-fat 1

BLACK BEAN AND CILANTRO SPREAD

Full flavored, rich in fiber, and with a preparation time of about 5 minutes, this spread will become one of your standbys. Try it with Italian Pita Crisps (page 75) or use it as spread for roasted vegetables or grilled meat sandwiches. It's a natural filling for burritos and tacos, too.

1¼ cups (10 servings)

One 15- or 16-ounce can black beans,
    rinsed and drained
2 teaspoons fresh lime juice
1 teaspoon olive oil
¼ to ½ teaspoon hot pepper sauce
¼ cup fresh cilantro leaves
2 tablespoons finely diced red onion

1. Purée the beans, lime juice, oil, and pepper sauce in a food processor or blender, scraping down the sides once or twice.
2. Add the cilantro. Process just until the leaves are coarsely chopped and well mixed. Stir in the red onion.
3. Serve at room temperature. (If chilled, the mixture will be difficult to spread.)

Nutrition Facts per Serving

Serving size: 2 tablespoons

Amount per serving:

Calories 44
Calories from fat 5

Total fat 1 gm
    Saturated fat 0 gm
Cholesterol 0 mg
Sodium 53 mg
Total carbohydrate 7 gm
    Dietary fiber 3 gm
    Sugars 1 gm
Protein 3 gm

Exchange List Approximation

Starch ½

SPICY ARTICHOKE DIP

Canned artichokes are a useful pantry item, easy to add to an antipasto platter or to transform into marinated salad with chunked white mushrooms and a sharp vinaigrette. Here the artichokes are made into a tangy dip which can accompany crudités, crackers, or Italian Pita Crisps (page 75).

1 cup (8 servings)

One 14-ounce can artichoke hearts,
    drained
One 4-ounce can chopped green chiles,
    drained
2 tablespoons light mayonnaise
1 tablespoon fresh lemon juice
1 teaspoon olive oil
1/4 teaspoon hot pepper sauce

1.   Combine all the ingredients in a food processor or blender. Blend until almost smooth.

2.   Heat the mixture in a medium saucepan for 5 minutes over low heat, or until hot, or bake in a small casserole at 350°F for 15 minutes. Serve warm.

Nutrition Facts per Serving
Serving size: 2 tablespoons
Amount per serving:
Calories 30
Calories from fat 17
Total fat 2 gm
Saturated fat 0 gm
Cholesterol 2 mg
Sodium 178 mg
Total carbohydrate 3 gm
Dietary fiber 1 gm
Sugars 1 gm
Protein 1 gm

Exchange List Approximation

Vegetable 1

BLUE CHEESE DIP

A superb dip for vegetables, sliced tart apples, quartered pears, crackers, and chips, this is also the preferred sauce for Buffalo-Style Chicken Wings (page 84).

1 cup (8 servings)

½ cup low-fat cottage cheese
¼ cup plain low-fat yogurt
1 tablespoon chopped onion
½ cup (2 ounces) crumbled blue cheese
¼ teaspoon salt
¼ teaspoon Worcestershire sauce
4 drops hot pepper sauce

1.   Purée the cottage cheese, yogurt, and onion in a food processor or blender.
2.   Stir in the remaining ingredients. Refrigerate at least 1 hour for the flavors to blend.

Nutrition Facts per Serving

Serving size: 2 tablespoons

Amount per serving:

Calories 40
Calories from fat 20

Total fat 2 gm
  Saturated fat 1 gm

Cholesterol 7 mg

Sodium 237 mg

Total carbohydrate 1 gm
  Dietary fiber 0 gm
  Sugars 1 gm

Protein 4 gm

Exchange List Approximation

Meat, lean 1

CHEDDAR CHEESE DIP

Cauliflower, broccoli, celery, fennel, or other crisp raw vegetables will bring out the forthright flavor of Cheddar in this dip. Try it with sliced apples and pears, as well as with chips and crackers.

1½ cups (8 servings)

½ cup (2 ounces) shredded reduced-fat
     Cheddar cheese
¾ cup plain low-fat yogurt
¼ teaspoon freshly ground pepper
½ teaspoon salt
2 tablespoons minced fresh parsley

1.   Combine all the ingredients; mix well.
2.   Chill several hours for flavors to blend.

Nutrition Facts per Serving
Serving size: 3 tablespoons
Amount per serving:
Calories 34
Calories from fat 12
Total fat 1 gm
Saturated fat 1 gm
Cholesterol 6 mg
Sodium 202 mg
Total carbohydrate 2 gm
Dietary fiber 0 gm
Sugars 2 gm
Protein 3 gm

Exchange List Approximation

Meat, lean ½

CHILE CON QUESO

This mildly spiced combination of chiles, tomatoes, and cheese can be served with baked or low-fat tortilla or nacho chips, or Italian Pita Crisps (page 75). Or spoon it over baked potatoes, chick-peas, or kidney beans.

1 cup (8 servings)

½ cup chopped onion
1 large clove garlic, minced
One 4-ounce can chopped green chiles,
        drained
1 cup canned diced tomatoes, drained
⅛ teaspoon salt
1½ cups (about 6 ounces) shredded
        reduced-fat Monterey Jack
        cheese, Cheddar cheese, or a
        combination

1.   Spray a 2-quart saucepan with nonstick pan spray. Sauté the onion and garlic until soft, about 3 to 4 minutes.
2.   Stir in the chiles, tomatoes, and salt; simmer 10 minutes. Add the cheese, stirring until it is just melted. Serve warm.

Nutrition Facts per Serving
Serving size: 2 tablespoons
Amount per serving:
Calories 60
Calories from fat 24
Total fat 3 gm
Saturated fat 2 gm
Cholesterol 10 mg
Sodium 218 mg
Total carbohydrate 3 gm
Dietary fiber 1 gm
Sugars 2 gm
Protein 6 gm

Exchange List Approximation

Meat, lean 1

MINTED CUCUMBER DIP

Fresh mint, now available year-round, gives this low-calorie dip its characteristic bright flavor. Serve the dip in a hollowed-out vegetable as the centerpiece of a platter of crudités. Leftover dip can be transformed into a creamy salad dressing by adding a little olive oil and vinegar.

1½ cups (8 servings)

One 8-ounce carton plain low-fat yogurt
⅓ cup finely chopped peeled cucumber
2 tablespoons grated onion
1 tablespoon chopped fresh mint, or
      1 teaspoon dried mint leaves
1 teaspoon sugar
1 hollowed-out bell pepper, squash,
      or red cabbage (as serving
      container)
Fresh mint sprigs (optional, for garnish)

1. Combine the yogurt, cucumber, onion, mint, and sugar. Refrigerate at least 1 hour for the flavors to blend.
2. Place the dip in a hollowed-out pepper, squash, or red cabbage. Garnish with mint sprigs if desired.

Nutrition Facts per Serving
Serving size: 3 tablespoons
Amount per serving:
Calories 21
Calories from fat 4
Total fat 0 gm
Saturated fat 0 gm
Cholesterol 2 mg
Sodium 20 mg
Total carbohydrate 3 gm
Dietary fiber 0 gm
Sugars 3 gm
Protein 2 gm

Exchange List Approximation
Vegetable 1

HORSERADISH DIP

A delicious complement to raw and blanched vegetables, this dip can be thinned with a little fresh lemon juice or water and used as a sauce for Salmon Mousse (page 82) or for cold poached salmon or other fish. Fennel, cucumbers, celery, endive spears, and cherry tomatoes have a special affinity for this combination of flavors.

1 cup (8 servings)

One 8-ounce carton plain low-fat yogurt
1 tablespoon light mayonnaise
1 tablespoon prepared horseradish

1.   Combine all the ingredients; mix well.
2.   Refrigerate, covered, at least 1 hour for the flavors to blend.

**Nutrition Facts
per Serving**

Serving size: 2 tablespoons

Amount per serving:

Calories 24
Calories from fat 9

Total fat 1 gm
   Saturated fat 0 gm
Cholesterol 3 mg
Sodium 36 mg
Total carbohydrate 2 gm
   Dietary fiber 0 gm
   Sugars 2 gm
Protein 2 gm

**Exchange List
Approximation**

Fat ½

GUACAMOLE

Guacamole is a good accompaniment for highly seasoned Mexican dishes and is an essential component of many burritos and tacos. Use this basic version as a dip for baked or low-fat tortilla chips or Italian Pita Crisps (page 75). For a spicy dip, add hot pepper sauce, salsa, picante sauce, chili powder, and chopped green chiles. For more authentic flavor, substitute lime juice for lemon juice and add chopped fresh cilantro. None of these additions affects nutrient content or exchange values.

¾ cup (6 servings)

1 ripe medium-sized avocado (about
    8 ounces), peeled, cut in half,
    pit removed
1 tablespoon fresh lemon juice
1 tablespoon finely chopped green
    onion
2 tablespoons diced tomato, fresh
    or canned
¼ teaspoon salt

1. Place the avocado halves in a bowl; add the lemon juice and mash with a fork.
2. Add the onion, tomato, and salt; mix lightly. Cover tightly and use as soon as possible, as the dip will darken if exposed to air.

Nutrition Facts per Serving
Serving size: 2 tablespoons
Amount per serving:
Calories 57
Calories from fat 48
Total fat 5 gm
Saturated fat 1 gm
Cholesterol 0 mg
Sodium 101 mg
Total carbohydrate 3 gm
Dietary fiber 2 gm
Sugars 0 gm
Protein 1 gm

Exchange List Approximation

Fat, monounsaturated 1

SPICY VEGETABLE DIP

This crunchy dip with the subtle flavor of lemon zest can be made in minutes from ingredients on hand. Serve with carrot, celery, or fennel sticks, red or green bell pepper strips, radishes, blanched cauliflower or broccoli, and other crisp vegetables.

1½ cups (12 servings)

One 8-ounce carton plain low-fat yogurt
¼ cup chili sauce
1 tablespoon prepared horseradish
1 teaspoon grated lemon zest
1 teaspoon salt
2 tablespoons minced celery
1 tablespoon minced green bell pepper
1 tablespoon minced green onion

1. Combine all the ingredients; mix well.
2. Refrigerate for several hours for the flavors to blend.

Nutrition Facts per Serving
Serving size: 2 tablespoons
Amount per serving:
Calories 18
Calories from fat 3
Total fat 0 gm
Saturated fat 0 gm
Cholesterol 2 mg
Sodium 276 mg
Total carbohydrate 3 gm
Dietary fiber 0 gm
Sugars 2 gm
Protein 1 gm

Exchange List Approximation

Free Food

SPINACH DIP

This mild, herby vegetable dip is especially delicious with sweet sliced jicama, endive spears, carrot sticks, and trimmed stalks of celery, or serve it with Italian Pita Crisps (page 75) or Italian bread.

2¹⁄₂ cups (16 servings)

One 10-ounce package frozen chopped
      spinach, thawed and drained
¹⁄₂ cup light or fat-free mayonnaise
One 8-ounce carton plain low-fat yogurt
¹⁄₄ cup chopped fresh parsley, or
      2 tablespoons dried parsley flakes
¹⁄₄ cup finely chopped onion
2 teaspoons snipped fresh dill, or
      ¹⁄₂ teaspoon dill weed
¹⁄₄ teaspoon salt

1.   Pat the spinach with paper towels to remove excess liquid. Combine with the remaining ingredients.

2.   Cover and refrigerate at least 1 hour for the flavors to blend.

Nutrition Facts per Serving
Serving size: 2¹⁄₂ tablespoons
Amount per serving:
Calories 39
Calories from fat 23
Total fat 3 gm
Saturated fat 0 gm
Cholesterol 4 mg
Sodium 114 mg
Total carbohydrate 2 gm
Dietary fiber 0 gm
Sugars 2 gm
Protein 1 gm

Exchange List Approximations

Vegetable 1

Fat, polyunsaturated ¹⁄₂

HUMMUS

Chick-peas, with their nutty flavor and grainy texture, are very high in dietary fiber, carbohydrates, and protein. Puréed with sesame seed paste, lemon juice, and spices, they make a classic spread that can be served alone with Italian Pita Crisps (page 75) or used as part of a Middle Eastern *mezze* appetizer platter with other regional specialties such as Tabbouleh (page 162), stuffed grape leaves, peperoncini, and black oil-cured olives. Chopped raw vegetables and hummus are a natural combination for a pita pocket sandwich. Crudités of choice are bell peppers, celery, and blanched green beans. If you like the flavor of raw garlic (and some do), add an extra clove or more to the chick-peas.

1½ cups (6 servings)

One 15-ounce can chick-peas (garbanzo
     beans), drained, or 1¾ cups
     cooked chick-peas
2 tablespoons tahini (sesame seed paste)
2 tablespoons fresh lemon juice
1 clove garlic
½ teaspoon ground coriander
¼ teaspoon cumin
2 dashes hot pepper sauce
1½ teaspoons sesame seeds, toasted
     (optional)

1. Place all the ingredients except the sesame seeds in blender or food processor. Blend until smooth.

2. Garnish with sesame seeds if desired.

Nutrition Facts per Serving

Serving size: ¼ cup

Amount per serving:

Calories 103
Calories from fat 34

Total fat 4 gm
   Saturated fat 0 gm

Cholesterol 0 mg

Sodium 70 mg

Total carbohydrate 14 gm
   Dietary fiber 3 gm
   Sugars 2 gm

Protein 5 gm

Exchange List Approximations

Starch 1

Fat ½

TEX-MEX BEAN DIP

This is a hearty dip, good with baked or low-fat tortilla chips, or used as one of the elements of a burrito or taco sandwich. Crisp, distinctively flavored crudités taste best with this dip, such as radishes, jicama, or celery.

2½ cups (about 12 servings)

1 clove garlic, minced
1 tablespoon olive oil
One 16-ounce can pinto beans, rinsed
    and drained
⅓ cup prepared salsa or picante sauce
1 teaspoon chili powder
1 teaspoon ground cumin
2 green onions with green tops,
    thinly sliced
¼ cup chopped cilantro
½ teaspoon salt

1. Sauté the garlic in the oil in a medium saucepan until soft, about 3 minutes. Add the beans and mash them coarsely with a wooden spoon. Add the salsa, chili powder, and cumin; heat through.

2. Stir in the green onions, cilantro, and salt; stir well, adding a tablespoon or two of water if the mixture is too thick. Serve warm.

Nutrition Facts per Serving

Serving size:
About 3 tablespoons

Amount per serving:

Calories 49
Calories from fat 12

Total fat 1 gm
    Saturated fat 0 gm
Cholesterol 0 mg
Sodium 70 mg
Total carbohydrate 7 gm
    Dietary fiber 2 gm
    Sugars 1 gm
Protein 2 gm

Exchange List Approximation

Starch ½

CREAMY THREE-ONION DIP

In this variation on an old favorite, onion soup dip, we add just enough soup mix to lift the onion flavor but not so much that we overwhelm it. Use the dip as a topping for mashed potatoes or noodles, or serve with mild-tasting vegetables, such as zucchini, cherry tomatoes, blanched sugar snap peas, and endive spears.

1 cup (8 servings)

1 cup light sour cream
2 green onions with green tops,
    finely chopped
2 tablespoons finely chopped red onion
1 tablespoon dry onion soup mix

1.   Combine all the ingredients; mix well.
2.   Chill at least 2 hours for the flavors to blend.

Nutrition Facts per Serving

Serving size: 2 tablespoons

Amount per serving:

Calories 36
Calories from fat 22

Total fat 2 gm
   Saturated fat 2 gm
Cholesterol 10 mg
Sodium 123 mg
Total carbohydrate 3 gm
   Dietary fiber 0 gm
   Sugars 2 gm
Protein 1 gm

Exchange List Approximation

Fat, saturated ½

4

SOUPS

Hot or chilled, creamy or broth, spicy or fruity, hearty or puréed—soups can be used in many ways. They're simple, versatile, and equally at home as an appetizer or the main dish.

Homemade broth adds a rich flavor base to soups and sauces that canned varieties just can't match. Make a batch over the weekend and freeze it in quantities you'll use later: 4-cup containers if you're planning to use it as a base for soups, or in convenient ice cube trays for use in sauces. When making broth, don't add salt unless you're planning to serve it as a first course. Homemade broth is used as a base ingredient in many recipes, and adding salt when the broth is simmering concentrates its flavor, resulting in a too-salty final product.

Although homemade is definitely preferred, canned broth will suffice in a jam. Just be sure to buy low-sodium canned broth, since regular canned broth is notoriously high in sodium. If you have a few spare minutes, you can "fix up" canned broth by simmering it with an onion wedge, celery stalk, sprigs of parsley, a bay leaf, and garlic to help improve the flavor.

Almost all soups can be made in advance. Many actually improve with age, since time gives the flavors a chance to mingle. Soup also freezes well, so make an extra big batch and freeze leftovers. Be sure to use top-quality, fresh ingredients in your soup. Although soup is a good way to use up leftover meat or vegetables, don't make it a "dumping ground" for older produce that should be discarded instead. If you plan to add salt to the soup, wait until the end of the cooking time so it doesn't become overly salty as it cooks. It's best to taste the soup toward the end of cooking and then season to taste. Soups kept in the refrigerator or in the freezer may need to be diluted a bit and reseasoned before serving.

Defatting soup is very easy and can save you a significant amount of fat and calories. To defat, simply cool the soup, place the pot in the refrigerator to chill, and lift or spoon off the fat that rises and congeals at the top of the pot. Don't remove the fat until you're ready to serve the soup, though—the layer of fat acts as a seal and helps preserve it. If time is short, you can also use a quick defatting method: toss a few ice cubes into the soup, which makes the fat rise and congeal around the ice; then spoon out the fat. While this is a timesaving method, keep in mind that it may dilute the broth slightly.

Be creative and dress up plain soups with interesting garnishes. Some specific ideas are included with the recipes in this chapter, but play around with other ingredients, too. A sprinkle of fresh herbs, a dusting of grated cheese, a dollop of low-fat sour cream or fat-free plain yogurt, a thin slice of lemon, toasted croutons or garlic bread slices, or a scattering of diced fresh vegetables can greatly enhance a soup's appearance and flavor. Just remember to add the appropriate exchange value or carbohydrate count for whatever garnish you choose.

Most soups are a combination of many ingredients, like meats, grains or noodles, and vegetables. To help you determine how they fit into your meal plan, we've included both the grams of carbohydrate provided and their exchange values.

There's nothing like the heavenly aroma of soup as it simmers on the stove. Try a hearty soup like New England Fish Chowder, Chicken Soup with Lime and Cilantro, or Greek Lentil Soup for dinner tonight. If you're in the mood for vegetables, Tuscan Vegetable Soup with Orzo, Mushroom Barley Soup, or Wisconsin Beer-Onion Soup hits the spot. And on a hot summer night, chilled soups such as Cold Roasted Red Pepper Soup, Gazpacho, and Chilled Dutch Apple Soup are a refreshing delight.

HOMEMADE CHICKEN BROTH

Grandma was right—nothing beats the taste or versatility of homemade chicken broth. Chicken broth is often used as a base ingredient in many recipes, including soups, stews, and sauces, so don't add salt unless you're planning to serve it as a broth-type soup. Freeze in handy 1-cup containers or ice cube trays to use as needed in recipes.

2 quarts (8 servings)

3 pounds chicken backs, necks, and/or
      wings, or 1 whole chicken, cut
      in pieces
3 medium onions, coarsely chopped
2 medium carrots, coarsely chopped
2 ribs celery, coarsely chopped, or
      1 small leek, washed and
      chopped
8 whole peppercorns
½ cup parsley sprigs
2 bay leaves

1. Combine 3 quarts (12 cups) of water with all the ingredients in a Dutch oven or stockpot. Bring to a boil. Reduce the heat and simmer uncovered for 2 hours, skimming the foam as it collects on the surface.

2. Strain, pressing hard on the solids. Discard the solids. (If using a whole chicken, save the cooked chicken for another use.) Chill the stock until the fat is solid on top. Discard the fat. Store the soup, covered and refrigerated, up to 1 week, or freeze up to 6 months.

Nutrition Facts per Serving
Serving size: 1 cup
Amount per serving:
Calories 24   Calories from fat 22
Total fat 2 gm
Saturated fat 1 gm
Cholesterol 0 mg
Sodium 112 mg
Total carbohydrate 2 gm
Dietary fiber 0 gm
Sugars 1 gm
Protein 3 gm
Exchange List Approximation
Meat, lean ½

VEGETABLE BROTH

Vegetable broth should be as intensely and richly flavored as its meat or chicken counterpart. Use it to replace chicken or beef broth in vegetarian and other recipes, or to add flavor to steamed vegetables. Add salt, as desired, when serving as soup. To help retain nutrients, don't peel the vegetables before adding them to the pot, just scrub them thoroughly to remove dirt and sand. Most of the nutrients are found right under the skin, and are lost if the vegetables are peeled.

5 cups (10 servings)

3 medium carrots, coarsely chopped
2 medium onions, coarsely chopped
2 large ribs celery with leaves, coarsely
    chopped
1 medium tomato, chopped
$1/2$ cup parsley sprigs
1 bay leaf
$1/2$ teaspoon black peppercorns

1.   Combine 1 quart of water with all the ingredients in a large saucepan. Cover and heat to a boil, then reduce the heat and simmer 30 to 45 minutes.

2.   Strain, pressing on the solids. Discard the solids. Store the broth, covered and refrigerated, up to 3 days, or freeze for up to 6 months.

Nutrition Facts per Serving

Serving size: $1/2$ cup

Amount per serving:

Calories 7
Calories from fat 0

Total fat 0 gm
    Saturated fat 0 gm
Cholesterol 0 mg
Sodium 7 mg
Total carbohydrate 2 gm
    Dietary fiber 0 gm
    Sugars 1 gm
Protein 0 gm

Exchange List Approximation

Free food

VEGETABLE CHOWDER

Savor this hearty chowder, jam-packed with vegetables, when Old Man Winter is howling outside. Fat-free evaporated milk and reduced-fat cheese lend flavor, creaminess, and body without a lot of fat.

2 quarts (8 servings)

1 tablespoon olive oil
3 medium zucchini (1 pound), diced
$\frac{1}{2}$ cup chopped onion
2 tablespoons chopped fresh parsley
3 tablespoons all-purpose flour
2$\frac{1}{2}$ cups homemade Vegetable Broth
      (page 102) or canned reduced-
      sodium vegetable broth
1 teaspoon fresh lemon juice
$\frac{1}{2}$ teaspoon freshly ground pepper
1 cup frozen whole-kernel corn, or
      1 cup canned corn, drained
One 16-ounce can diced tomatoes,
      including juice
1 tablespoon snipped fresh basil leaves,
      or $\frac{1}{2}$ teaspoon dried basil
One 12-ounce can fat-free evaporated
      milk
1 cup (about 4 ounces) reduced-fat
      cubed American or light
      processed cheese

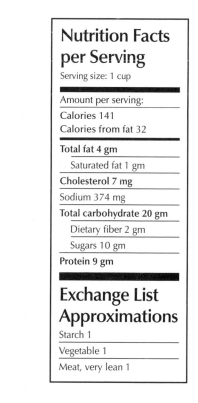

Nutrition Facts per Serving

Serving size: 1 cup

Amount per serving:

Calories 141
Calories from fat 32

Total fat 4 gm
  Saturated fat 1 gm

Cholesterol 7 mg

Sodium 374 mg

Total carbohydrate 20 gm
  Dietary fiber 2 gm
  Sugars 10 gm

Protein 9 gm

Exchange List Approximations

Starch 1

Vegetable 1

Meat, very lean 1

1. Heat the olive oil in a large saucepan. Add the zucchini, onion, and parsley. Cook for about 6 minutes, stirring occasionally.

2. Add the flour and stir until blended. Add the broth, lemon juice, and pepper. Stir while heating to a boil.

3. Add the corn, tomatoes with liquid, and basil; bring to a boil, stirring to prevent scorching.

4. Add the evaporated milk and heat just to boiling. Add the cheese; stir just until melted. Do not boil.

TUSCAN VEGETABLE SOUP WITH ORZO

This satisfying soup is a meal in itself, chock-full of sunny vegetables and orzo, a rice-shaped pasta. Add a warm, crusty loaf of peasant bread with a side of roasted garlic spread and Caesar Salad (page 130) to complete the meal.

7 cups (7 servings)

2 teaspoons olive oil
1 large onion, coarsely chopped
2 cloves garlic, minced
8 ounces mushrooms, sliced
1 cup dry white wine
1½ cups Homemade Chicken Broth
      (page 101) or Vegetable Broth
      (page 102), or canned reduced-
      sodium chicken broth
¼ teaspoon salt (optional)
¼ teaspoon freshly ground pepper
1 large zucchini, diced
1 large yellow squash, diced
½ cup (3 ounces) uncooked orzo
¼ cup chopped fresh basil, marjoram,
      oregano, or Italian parsley leaves,
      or 1 teaspoon dried basil plus
      1 teaspoon crushed marjoram
¼ cup (1 ounce) freshly grated
      Parmesan cheese

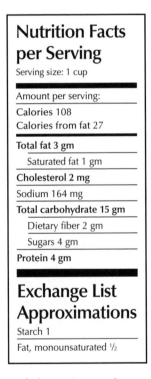

Nutrition Facts per Serving

Serving size: 1 cup

Amount per serving:

Calories 108
Calories from fat 27

Total fat 3 gm
  Saturated fat 1 gm

Cholesterol 2 mg

Sodium 164 mg

Total carbohydrate 15 gm
  Dietary fiber 2 gm
  Sugars 4 gm

Protein 4 gm

Exchange List Approximations

Starch 1

Fat, monounsaturated ½

1. Heat the oil in a large saucepan or Dutch oven; sauté the onion and garlic over medium heat until tender, about 4 minutes. Add the mushrooms; sauté 2 minutes.

2. Add the wine, broth, 2 cups water, salt if desired, and pepper; bring to a boil. Reduce the heat; cover and simmer 10 minutes. Add the two types of squash and the orzo; cover and simmer until the pasta and squash are tender, about 10 to 15 minutes.

3. Remove from the heat; stir in the herbs. Sprinkle with cheese at serving time.

MUSHROOM BARLEY SOUP

This soup takes just under 30 minutes to prepare and is wonderful as a light lunch entrée or dinner appetizer. Barley adds a mild nutty flavor and is a popular ingredient in soups or as a grain side dish. Try wild mushrooms in place of the regular white button variety, if desired.

1 quart (4 servings)

¾ cup chopped onion
1 tablespoon margarine
8 ounces mushrooms, sliced
2 tablespoons all-purpose flour
2 cups Homemade Chicken Broth
      (page 101) or canned reduced-
      sodium chicken broth
1 cup fat-free evaporated milk
¼ cup quick-cooking pearl barley
½ teaspoon salt (optional)
¼ teaspoon freshly ground pepper
1 tablespoon dry sherry
2 tablespoons chopped fresh parsley

Nutrition Facts per Serving
Serving size: 1 cup
Amount per serving:
Calories 162
Calories from fat 40
Total fat 4 gm
Saturated fat 1 gm
Cholesterol 2 mg
Sodium 157 mg*
Total carbohydrate 24 gm
Dietary fiber 2 gm
Sugars 9 gm
Protein 9 gm

Exchange List Approximations
Starch 1½
Fat 1

* If optional salt is used, sodium is 447 mg per serving.

1. Sauté the onion in the margarine in a skillet or medium pot about 5 minutes. Add the mushrooms; cook 5 to 8 minutes longer, until the mushrooms are lightly browned.

2. Sprinkle the vegetables with flour; cook 1 minute. Add the broth, evaporated milk, barley, salt if desired, and pepper. Cover and simmer until the barley is tender, about 12 minutes, stirring occasionally. Stir in the sherry and parsley just before serving.

POTATO SOUP

A substantial potato soup with a delicate chive accent that will warm you inside and out. Try Yukon Gold potatoes, with their rich texture and pretty golden color, instead of all-purpose potatoes, for an even creamier soup.

5 cups (5 servings)

2 medium potatoes (12 ounces total),
        peeled and diced
1/2 cup finely chopped onion
2 cups Homemade Chicken Broth
        (page 101) or canned reduced-
        sodium chicken broth
1 teaspoon salt
1/4 teaspoon celery seed
1/8 teaspoon freshly ground pepper
2 cups fat-free milk
1 tablespoon minced chives or minced
        green onion tops

Nutrition Facts per Serving
Serving size: 1 cup
Amount per serving:
Calories 94
Calories from fat 9
Total fat 1 gm
Saturated fat 0 gm
Cholesterol 2 mg
Sodium 556 mg
Total carbohydrate 17 gm
Dietary fiber 1 gm
Sugars 7 gm
Protein 6 gm

Exchange List Approximation

Starch 1

1.   Put all the ingredients except the milk and chives in a saucepan. Simmer, covered, until the potatoes are tender, about 15 minutes. Stir well to break up some of the diced potatoes.

2.   Add the milk; simmer, uncovered, 5 minutes.

3.   At serving time, sprinkle chives over the soup.

PUMPKIN SOUP

Pumpkin soup is always a fall favorite. This yellow-orange soup gets its sweetness not only from sugar but from cloves or nutmeg as well. It's the perfect start to a holiday meal, and so easy to make. If you're feeling especially festive, serve the soup in small, hollowed-out pumpkins.

5 cups (5 servings)

2 teaspoons margarine
¾ cup chopped onion
One 16-ounce can pumpkin purée
          (*not* pumpkin pie filling)
2 cups Homemade Chicken Broth
          (page 101) or canned reduced-
          sodium chicken broth
2 teaspoons sugar
½ teaspoon salt
⅛ teaspoon ground cloves or ground
          nutmeg
1 cup fat-free milk

Nutrition Facts per Serving
Serving size: 1 cup
Amount per serving:
Calories 89
Calories from fat 24
Total fat 3 gm
Saturated fat 1 gm
Cholesterol 1 mg
Sodium 318 mg
Total carbohydrate 15 gm
Dietary fiber 3 gm
Sugars 9 gm
Protein 4 gm

Exchange List Approximation

Starch 1

1.   Melt the margarine in a medium saucepan. Sauté the onion until softened, about 5 minutes.

2.   Add the pumpkin, broth, sugar, salt, and cloves; stir to mix well. Bring to a boil; reduce the heat and simmer for 15 minutes.

3.   Purée until smooth in a blender or food processor. Return to the saucepan.

4.   Add the milk; heat thoroughly but do not boil. Serve at once.

SPICY TOMATO BOUILLON

This soup requires just five simple ingredients, most of which you probably already have in your kitchen. Worcestershire and horseradish sauces add a nice spiciness without being overpowering. For a heartier soup, add ⅓ cup cooked rice to each bowl and ladle the soup on top. This will add 1 starch exchange or 15 grams of carbohydrate per serving.

3 cups (3 servings)

1¾ cups tomato juice
One 10¾-ounce can condensed
      beef broth
2 teaspoons lemon juice
1 teaspoon Worcestershire sauce
1 teaspoon prepared horseradish

1. Combine all the ingredients in a medium saucepan.
2. Simmer for approximately 10 minutes. Serve hot.

Nutrition Facts per Serving
Serving size: 1 cup
Amount per serving:
Calories 38
Calories from fat 4
Total fat 0 gm
Saturated fat 0 gm
Cholesterol 0 mg
Sodium 375 mg
Total carbohydrate 7 gm
Dietary fiber 1 gm
Sugars 5 gm
Protein 3 gm

Exchange List Approximation
Vegetable 2

CREAM OF CAULIFLOWER SOUP

This soup can easily be transformed into a "cream of any vegetable" soup simply by using the same quantity of other vegetables in place of the cauliflower and broccoli. For example, try spinach with chopped carrots or mushrooms. The Swiss or Jarlsberg cheese (a mild, Swisslike cheese) adds a bit of nutty flavor and creaminess.

6 cups (6 servings)

One 10-ounce package frozen
      cauliflower, or 10 ounces fresh
      cauliflower florets
One 10³/₄-ounce can condensed chicken
      broth
¹/₂ teaspoon mace
One 10-ounce package frozen chopped
      broccoli, or 10 ounces fresh
      broccoli florets
¹/₂ teaspoon mustard seed
¹/₂ teaspoon dried dill weed
¹/₃ cup chopped onion
2 tablespoons margarine
2 tablespoons all-purpose flour
¹/₂ teaspoon salt
¹/₈ teaspoon freshly ground pepper
      or white pepper
3³/₄ cups fat-free milk
1 cup (about 4 ounces) shredded light
      Swiss or Jarlsberg cheese

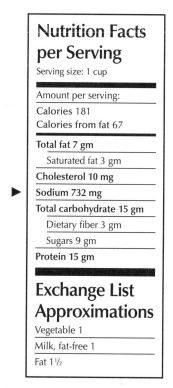

Nutrition Facts per Serving

Serving size: 1 cup

Amount per serving:

Calories 181
Calories from fat 67

Total fat 7 gm
  Saturated fat 3 gm
Cholesterol 10 mg
Sodium 732 mg
Total carbohydrate 15 gm
  Dietary fiber 3 gm
  Sugars 9 gm
Protein 15 gm

Exchange List Approximations

Vegetable 1
Milk, fat-free 1
Fat 1¹/₂

1. Cook the cauliflower in ¹/₂ cup of the broth for 5 to 8 minutes, or until tender, in a medium saucepan. Purée the cauliflower and pan liquid in a food processor or blender with the mace until smooth.

2. Cook the broccoli, covered, in the remaining broth with the mustard seed and dill weed for about 8 minutes, or until tender.

3. In a skillet, sauté the onion in the margarine until tender, about 5 minutes. Add the flour, salt, and pepper. Add the milk; cook, stirring, until the sauce thickens.

4. Add the cauliflower, broccoli, and cheese. Cook and stir until the soup is just heated through and the cheese is melted. Do not boil.

WISCONSIN BEER-ONION SOUP

We've slimmed down this American football favorite but still kept its trademark taste. The soup is traditionally laden with fat, but this version offers a mere 5 grams per bowl. Topped with a cheesy crouton and full of sweet caramelized onions, it's sure to score a touchdown with your family and friends.

7 cups (7 servings)

1 tablespoon margarine
3 medium yellow onions (about
        1 pound), thinly sliced
3 tablespoons all-purpose flour
¼ teaspoon freshly grated nutmeg
1 quart reduced-sodium beef broth
One 12-ounce bottle or can beer
7 slices French bread, each 2 inches in
        diameter and ½ inch thick
2 teaspoons olive oil
½ cup (about 2 ounces) shredded
        reduced-fat sharp Cheddar cheese

Nutrition Facts per Serving	
Serving size: 1 cup	
Amount per serving:	
Calories 124	
Calories from fat 43	
Total fat 5 gm	
Saturated fat 1 gm	
Cholesterol 4 mg	
Sodium 466 mg	
Total carbohydrate 14 gm	
Dietary fiber 1 gm	
Sugars 5 gm	
Protein 7 gm	

Exchange List Approximations

Starch 1

Fat, monounsaturated 1

1. Melt the margarine in a large saucepan. Sauté the onions over low heat until golden and very tender, about 15 minutes, stirring frequently. Sprinkle with flour and nutmeg; cook 1 minute.

2. Stir in the broth and beer; bring to a boil. Reduce the heat and simmer uncovered 25 minutes, stirring occasionally.

3. While the soup is simmering, make the croutons. Brush the bread lightly with oil and broil or toast until crisp.

4. Ladle the soup into bowls; top each with 1 crouton. Sprinkle the cheese on top of the soup and croutons.

BLACK BEAN SOUP

Whether you prefer it smooth or chunky, if you're a black bean soup fan, you'll love the spicy taste of this recipe. To make a smoother soup, purée half of the cooked soup and return it to the pot. Mix well to blend, and reheat. Top with a cool dollop of nonfat yogurt or nonfat sour cream to temper the heat (1 tablespoon is a free food exchange).

2 quarts (8 servings)

1 pound dried black beans
1 tablespoon salt
2 tablespoons olive oil
3 medium onions, chopped
1 cup chopped green bell pepper
1 clove garlic, minced
1 teaspoon ground cumin
1 teaspoon dried oregano
1 teaspoon dry mustard
1 tablespoon fresh lemon juice
2 green onions with green tops,
　　　chopped, for garnish

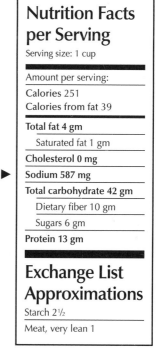

Nutrition Facts per Serving

Serving size: 1 cup

Amount per serving:

Calories 251
Calories from fat 39

Total fat 4 gm
　Saturated fat 1 gm
Cholesterol 0 mg
Sodium 587 mg
Total carbohydrate 42 gm
　Dietary fiber 10 gm
　Sugars 6 gm
Protein 13 gm

Exchange List Approximations

Starch 2½

Meat, very lean 1

1. Rinse and presoak the beans in water to cover overnight, or use the quick-cook method on the package. Drain.
2. Put 2 quarts of water, the soaked beans, and salt in a large pot and bring to a boil; cover and simmer on low heat for 2 hours.
3. Heat the oil in a skillet; add the onions and sauté about 5 minutes. Add the green pepper and sauté 5 minutes longer.
4. Add the onion mixture and all the remaining ingredients except the green onion garnish to the beans; simmer 1 hour more, stirring occasionally.
5. Top with chopped green onions at serving time.

GREEK LENTIL SOUP

This lentil soup is a meal in itself. For a pretty presentation, serve it in small hollowed bread bowls. Add a Greek Salad (page 140) or Fresh Spinach Salad (page 149) to complete the meal.

2 quarts (8 servings)

1¼ cups (about ½ pound) lentils
1 cup chopped onions
2 tablespoons olive oil
2 cloves garlic, crushed
1¼ teaspoons salt
¼ teaspoon freshly ground pepper
One 16-ounce can diced tomatoes,
        including liquid
1 bay leaf
1 teaspoon dried oregano
½ lemon, cut into very thin slices

Nutrition Facts per Serving
Serving size: 1 cup
Amount per serving:
Calories 153
Calories from fat 35
Total fat 4 gm
Saturated fat 1 gm
Cholesterol 0 mg
Sodium 459 mg
Total carbohydrate 22 gm
Dietary fiber 10 gm
Sugars 5 gm
Protein 9 gm

Exchange List Approximations

Starch 1½

Meat, very lean 1

1.   Wash the lentils and remove the stones, if any; drain well.

2.   Combine the lentils with 1 quart cold water, the onions, oil, garlic, salt, and pepper in a large saucepan. Bring to a boil. Add the tomatoes with their liquid, the bay leaf, and oregano. Lower the heat; cover and simmer 45 minutes, or until the lentils are tender.

3.   Before serving, remove and discard the bay leaf. Serve the soup hot, garnished with floating lemon slices.

MINESTRONE

Minestrone is a classic Italian soup brimming with a colorful rainbow of vegetables. As with many other soups, it's even better served the second day, when the flavors have had a chance to mingle.

6¹/₂ cups (about 6 servings)

1 tablespoon olive oil
2 cloves garlic, minced
¹/₂ cup chopped onion
1 medium carrot, thinly sliced
1 small zucchini, chopped
¹/₂ cup chopped celery
Two 13- to 14-ounce cans reduced-
    sodium beef broth
One 15-ounce can Italian-style stewed
    tomatoes, including juice
1 cup shredded cabbage
¹/₂ cup canned cannellini beans or other
    white beans, drained
1 teaspoon dried oregano
1 teaspoon salt
¹/₂ teaspoon coarsely ground pepper
³/₄ cup thawed frozen Italian green
    beans, or ³/₄ cup fresh green
    beans cut in 1-inch lengths
¹/₃ cup uncooked elbow macaroni
2 tablespoons freshly grated Parmesan
    cheese (optional)

Nutrition Facts per Serving
Serving size: About 1 cup
Amount per serving:
Calories 115 Calories from fat 26
Total fat 3 gm
Saturated fat 0 gm
Cholesterol 0 mg
Sodium 785 mg
Total carbohydrate 19 gm
Dietary fiber 3 gm
Sugars 5 gm
Protein 5 gm

Exchange List Approximations

Starch 1
Vegetable 1
Fat, monounsaturated ¹/₂

1. Heat the olive oil in a large pot, add garlic and onion, and sauté 5 minutes over medium heat until the onion is soft; add the carrot, zucchini, and celery and sauté 3 to 5 minutes longer.

2. Add the broth, 1¹/₂ cups water, the tomatoes with their liquid, the cabbage, white beans, oregano, salt, and pepper. Bring to a boil; reduce the heat and simmer 30 minutes.

3. Stir in the green beans and macaroni; simmer 10 to 15 minutes more. Taste and adjust the seasonings.

4. When serving, sprinkle 1 teaspoon grated Parmesan cheese over each bowl of soup, if desired.

HEARTY SPLIT PEA SOUP

Make this soup the next time you have a leftover ham bone. It adds a robust smoky flavor that enhances the taste of the many vegetables included in the soup, especially the peas. If you prefer a smooth (not chunky) consistency, purée the cooked soup in batches in a blender before serving.

2 quarts (8 servings)

1 tablespoon margarine
1 large carrot, chopped
½ cup chopped onion
¾ cup chopped celery with leaves
2 cups split peas
1 ham bone or small smoked ham hock
2 tablespoons chopped fresh parsley, or
     1 tablespoon dried parsley flakes
2 teaspoons salt
1 teaspoon dried basil
½ teaspoon ground allspice
½ teaspoon dried thyme
1 bay leaf
2 cups packed chopped raw spinach
     leaves
1 cup thawed frozen green peas

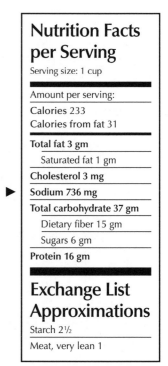

Nutrition Facts per Serving

Serving size: 1 cup

Amount per serving:

Calories 233
Calories from fat 31

Total fat 3 gm
  Saturated fat 1 gm

Cholesterol 3 mg

Sodium 736 mg

Total carbohydrate 37 gm
  Dietary fiber 15 gm
  Sugars 6 gm

Protein 16 gm

Exchange List Approximations

Starch 2½

Meat, very lean 1

1. Melt the margarine in a large pot. Add the carrot, onion, and celery and sauté over low heat until tender, about 10 minutes.

2. Add 6 cups water and the remaining ingredients except the spinach and green peas. Bring to a boil; cover and simmer 30 minutes.

3. Add the spinach and peas. Simmer 15 minutes more. Remove the ham bone or hock and the bay leaf before serving.

VICHYSSOISE

Vichyssoise is a potato and leek soup that's delightfully French and delicious. It's traditionally served chilled, but you can also serve it hot, if desired. Chilling this soup sometimes mutes its flavor, so if you decide to serve vichyssoise cold, taste it just before serving and adjust the seasoning as necessary.

9 cups (9 servings)

2 large leeks, well washed and thinly
    sliced, white parts only
2 large or 3 medium potatoes, peeled
    and sliced
6 cups Homemade Chicken Broth
    (page 101) or canned reduced-
    sodium chicken broth
1 cup fat-free evaporated milk
$\frac{1}{2}$ teaspoon salt
$\frac{1}{4}$ teaspoon white pepper
1 tablespoon minced chives, or
    1 tablespoon minced green
    onion tops, for garnish

1. In a large saucepan, combine the leeks, potatoes, and broth. Cook, covered, over medium heat until the vegetables are tender, about 30 minutes.
2. Purée through a food mill, food processor, or in a blender in batches, until smooth. Chill.
3. Stir in the evaporated skim milk, salt, and pepper. Garnish the soup with chives at serving time.

Nutrition Facts per Serving

Serving size: 1 cup

Amount per serving:

Calories 83
Calories from fat 15

Total fat 2 gm
  Saturated fat 1 gm

Cholesterol 1 mg

Sodium 235 mg

Total carbohydrate 15 gm
  Dietary fiber 2 gm
  Sugars 4 gm

Protein 5 gm

Exchange List Approximation

Starch 1

GAZPACHO

Serve this Spanish soup chilled in frosty mugs or in bright bowls. Its cool, refreshing flavor is the perfect way to enjoy the dog days of summer. Use the sweetest, juiciest tomatoes you can find. If they're fresh from the vine, all the better. Allow the soup to chill for at least an hour before serving, then adjust the seasonings to taste.

1 quart (4 servings)

4 medium tomatoes, quartered
1 small cucumber, peeled and sliced
½ medium onion, sliced
2 ribs celery, quartered
½ green bell pepper, cored, seeded,
      and sliced
½ cup cold water or ½ cup vegetable
      juice cocktail
1 tablespoon plus 1 teaspoon wine
      vinegar
1 tablespoon olive oil
1 clove garlic, minced
1 teaspoon salt
¼ teaspoon freshly ground pepper
2 tablespoons plain or garlic croutons

Nutrition Facts per Serving

Serving size: 1 cup

Amount per serving:

Calories 87
Calories from fat 37

Total fat 4 gm
  Saturated fat 1 gm
Cholesterol 0 mg
Sodium 621 mg
Total carbohydrate 13 gm
  Dietary fiber 3 gm
  Sugars 8 gm
Protein 2 gm

Exchange List Approximations

Vegetable 2

Fat, monounsaturated 1

1.   Core and seed 1 tomato. Chop fine; set aside.

2.   Combine all the remaining ingredients except the croutons in a blender or food processor. Blend only a few seconds, until the vegetables are finely chopped and well mixed. The soup should not be smooth.

3.   Add the reserved chopped tomato; chill.

4.   Serve very cold, topped with croutons.

CREAMY CARROT SOUP

This soup is packed with vitamin A, a nutrient that's important in maintaining good vision and healthy skin, hair, teeth, and bones. Use very sweet carrots for the best flavor. (If the carrots are rather bland, use a sweet potato in place of the white potato listed in the ingredients.) You can make this soup ahead of time and freeze it for up to 3 months, but don't add the buttermilk or garnish. When ready to use, thaw, stir well, add the buttermilk, and garnish just prior to serving.

1¹/₂ quarts (6 servings)

1 tablespoon margarine
5 medium carrots, thinly sliced
1 small onion, chopped
2 cups Homemade Chicken Broth
      (page 101), or canned reduced-
      sodium chicken broth)
1 large red bell pepper, cored, seeded,
      and chopped
1 medium potato, peeled and chopped
¹/₂ teaspoon hot pepper sauce
2 cups low-fat (1 percent) buttermilk
2 tablespoons chopped chives, or 1
      green onion with green top,
      chopped, for garnish

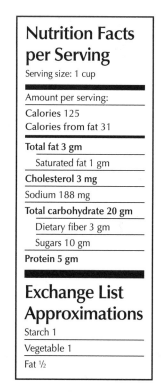

Nutrition Facts per Serving

Serving size: 1 cup

Amount per serving:

Calories 125
Calories from fat 31

Total fat 3 gm
  Saturated fat 1 gm
Cholesterol 3 mg
Sodium 188 mg
Total carbohydrate 20 gm
  Dietary fiber 3 gm
  Sugars 10 gm
Protein 5 gm

Exchange List Approximations

Starch 1
Vegetable 1
Fat ¹/₂

1. Melt the margarine in a large saucepan; add the carrots and onion; sauté over medium heat for 8 to 10 minutes.
2. Add the broth, red pepper, potato, and pepper sauce. Bring to a boil; reduce the heat. Cover and simmer 25 minutes, or until the vegetables are tender.
3. Transfer the soup to a food processor in batches. Process until very smooth. (The mixture will be thick.) Chill at least 4 hours or overnight.
4. Just before serving, stir in the buttermilk and mix well. Serve the soup chilled, garnished with chives.

COLD BUTTERNUT SQUASH SOUP

A velvety smooth first course that's made sweet by the squash and caramelized onions, this soup can be served either chilled or hot. To serve hot, stir in the buttermilk and heat through, but don't boil. To make a simple meal special, serve the soup along with crusty French bread and a salad of bitter greens tossed with Balsamic Vinaigrette dressing (page 176), toasted walnuts, and small chunks of blue cheese.

7 cups (7 servings)

1 tablespoon margarine
1½ cups chopped onion
1¾ pounds butternut or acorn squash,
      peeled, seeded, and cut into
      1-inch pieces
2 cups Homemade Chicken Broth
      (page 101), or canned reduced-
      sodium chicken broth
¼ teaspoon freshly grated nutmeg
1¾ cups low-fat (1 percent) buttermilk
Pinch of freshly grated nutmeg

1. Melt the margarine in a large saucepan over medium heat. Sauté the onion until soft, about 5 minutes.

2. Add the squash, broth, and 1 cup water. Cover and simmer until the squash is very tender, about 25 minutes.

3. Transfer in batches to a food processor or blender and purée until smooth. Stir in the nutmeg. Chill until cold.

4. Just before serving, stir in the buttermilk; garnish with freshly grated nutmeg.

Nutrition Facts per Serving
Serving size: 1 cup
Amount per serving:
Calories 90
Calories from fat 26
Total fat 3 gm
Saturated fat 1 gm
Cholesterol 2 mg
Sodium 113 mg
Total carbohydrate 15 gm
Dietary fiber 3 gm
Sugars 8 gm
Protein 4 gm

Exchange List Approximations

Starch 1

Fat ½

COLD ROASTED RED PEPPER SOUP

Roasting the peppers before adding them to this soup produces an intense and complex flavor with no added fat. You can either use bottled red peppers or roast your own. The roasting process is quite simple; refer to the Roasted Red Pepper and Goat Cheese Salad recipe on page 150 for specific instructions.

1 quart (4 servings)

¹/₂ cup chopped onion
1 teaspoon olive oil
2 to 3 red bell peppers (1 pound),
    roasted, peeled, seeded,
    and chopped)
3¹/₄ cups Homemade Chicken Broth
    (page 101) or canned reduced-
    sodium chicken broth
¹/₂ cup plain low-fat yogurt
¹/₂ teaspoon salt
4 sprigs fresh basil (optional)

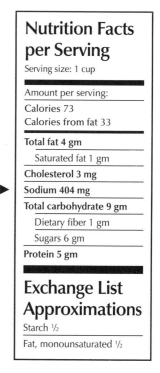

Nutrition Facts per Serving

Serving size: 1 cup

Amount per serving:

Calories 73
Calories from fat 33

Total fat 4 gm
    Saturated fat 1 gm
Cholesterol 3 mg
Sodium 404 mg
Total carbohydrate 9 gm
    Dietary fiber 1 gm
    Sugars 6 gm
Protein 5 gm

Exchange List Approximations

Starch ¹/₂

Fat, monounsaturated ¹/₂

1. Sauté the onion in the olive oil in a medium saucepan.
2. Add the peppers and broth; simmer for 15 minutes. Purée in a blender or food processor until smooth.
3. Cool; stir in the yogurt and salt; chill well.
4. At serving time, garnish the soup with fresh basil sprigs, if desired.

CHILLED CURRIED TOMATO SOUP

This chilled soup is a snap to make and very refreshing on a hot summer day. Curry adds a warm, spicy flavor to an otherwise ordinary tomato soup, and a bit of fresh mint is just the right flourish.

1 quart (4 servings)

One 28-ounce can crushed plum
    tomatoes in tomato sauce
1⅓ cups Homemade Chicken Broth
    (page 101), or canned reduced-
    sodium chicken broth
1 tablespoon brown sugar
2 teaspoons curry powder
One 8-ounce carton plain low-fat yogurt
2 tablespoons chopped fresh mint leaves

1. Combine the tomatoes and sauce, the broth, sugar, and curry powder in a medium saucepan. Simmer, uncovered, 10 minutes; cool to room temperature.

2. Purée in a food processor or blender. Strain to remove any seeds. Transfer to a large bowl; whisk in the yogurt. Chill until cold.

3. Sprinkle with chopped mint before serving.

Nutrition Facts per Serving

Serving size: 1 cup

Amount per serving:

Calories 137
Calories from fat 20

Total fat 2 gm
    Saturated fat 1 gm

Cholesterol 5 mg

Sodium 630 mg

Total carbohydrate 24 gm
    Dietary fiber 4 gm
    Sugars 17 gm

Protein 7 gm

Exchange List Approximations

Starch 1½

Vegetable 1

CHILLED DUTCH APPLE SOUP

Granny Smith apples lend a crisp tartness, balancing the sweetness of the other ingredients in this soup. Raisins are another unexpected and pleasant addition, contributing both flavor and texture.

1 quart (4 servings)

3 tart cooking apples (1 pound total),
      peeled, cored, cut into eighths
1 small cinnamon stick
¼ cup sugar
1½ teaspoons fresh lemon juice
½ teaspoon grated lemon zest
Pinch of cardamom
2 teaspoons cornstarch
¼ cup sauterne or dry sherry
2 tablespoons dark seedless raisins

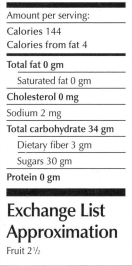

Nutrition Facts per Serving

Serving size: 1 cup

Amount per serving:

Calories 144
Calories from fat 4

Total fat 0 gm
  Saturated fat 0 gm

Cholesterol 0 mg

Sodium 2 mg

Total carbohydrate 34 gm
  Dietary fiber 3 gm
  Sugars 30 gm

Protein 0 gm

Exchange List Approximation

Fruit 2½

1. Combine the apples with 3½ cups water, the cinnamon stick, sugar, lemon juice, lemon zest, and cardamom; bring to a boil. Mix the cornstarch with 2 teaspoons water; add. Simmer 15 minutes, until the apples are fork-tender.

2. Lift out the apples with a slotted spoon and purée them (without liquid) in a food processor or blender. Discard the cinnamon stick.

3. Return the puréed apples to the pot. Stir in the wine and raisins; cook for 3 more minutes. Chill before serving.

NEW ENGLAND FISH CHOWDER

Use any mild-flavored fresh or defrosted frozen fish fillets for this rich chowder. Both ocean perch and frozen cod are good economical choices. We used fat-free evaporated milk instead of cream to help trim fat and calories.

1 quart (4 servings)

2 slices bacon, chopped
1/2 cup chopped onion
1 small potato, peeled and diced
1/4 cup chopped celery
8 ounces white fish fillets, cut in 1/2-inch
    pieces
One 12-ounce can fat-free evaporated
    milk
1/2 teaspoon salt
1/8 teaspoon freshly ground pepper
    to taste
1 tablespoon chopped fresh parsley

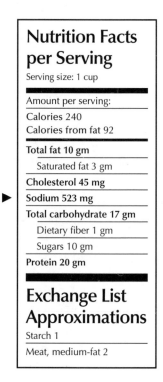

Nutrition Facts per Serving

Serving size: 1 cup

Amount per serving:

Calories 240
Calories from fat 92

Total fat 10 gm
  Saturated fat 3 gm
Cholesterol 45 mg
Sodium 523 mg
Total carbohydrate 17 gm
  Dietary fiber 1 gm
  Sugars 10 gm
Protein 20 gm

Exchange List Approximations

Starch 1

Meat, medium-fat 2

1.   Cook the bacon until limp in a medium saucepan. Add the onion and cook over medium heat until it is slightly browned.
2.   Add 1 1/4 cups water, the potato, and celery. Cook over low heat about 10 to 12 minutes, until the potato is partially tender.
3.   Add the fish. Continue cooking a few minutes, until the fish can be flaked with a fork.
4.   Add the evaporated milk, salt, and pepper; heat through. Sprinkle with parsley at serving time.

OYSTER STEW

Oyster stew is a coastal favorite and tastes best when fresh-shucked oysters are used. Look for them in the seafood department of your supermarket. Shucked oysters should be packed in a clear, not milky-colored liquid (which could indicate that they're past their prime). Canned oysters with liquid can also be substituted, if necessary. Serve the stew with its namesake accompaniment—small, round oyster crackers (24 oyster crackers equals 1 starch exchange or 15 grams of carbohydrate).

1 quart (4 servings)

2 tablespoons margarine
2 tablespoons all-purpose flour
2 cups fat-free milk
1 teaspoon Worcestershire sauce
¾ teaspoon salt
Dash of hot pepper sauce
2 cups shucked oysters, undrained
1 tablespoon minced fresh parsley

1.   Melt the margarine in a medium-sized pot. Remove from the heat.
2.   Gradually add the flour, mixing until smooth. Add the milk, stirring constantly with a whisk. Heat over low heat; continue whisking until the liquid thickens to the consistency of a thin white sauce.
3.   Add the Worcestershire sauce, salt, and hot pepper sauce.
4.   In a separate small pot, simmer the oysters in their own juice just until the edges curl. Add the oysters and juice to the sauce.
5.   Heat through but do not boil or the oysters will toughen. Serve hot, garnished with minced parsley.

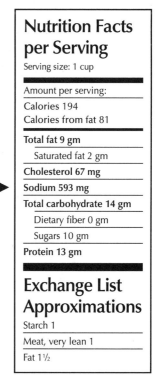

Nutrition Facts per Serving

Serving size: 1 cup

Amount per serving:

Calories 194
Calories from fat 81

Total fat 9 gm
  Saturated fat 2 gm

Cholesterol 67 mg

Sodium 593 mg

Total carbohydrate 14 gm
  Dietary fiber 0 gm
  Sugars 10 gm

Protein 13 gm

Exchange List Approximations

Starch 1

Meat, very lean 1

Fat 1½

TURKEY OR CHICKEN GUMBO

A favorite in New Orleans, gumbo is a Creole specialty. Slaves brought okra to America's South many years ago, and it's become a key ingredient in many dishes; in fact, most southern cooks will tell you that it's just not gumbo without okra. When cooked, okra yields a viscous substance that helps thicken and add flavor to the dish.

2 quarts (8 servings)

1 roast turkey carcass, or the bones and
    some meat from 1 whole chicken
1 teaspoon salt
1 tablespoon margarine
1 cup sliced fresh or defrosted frozen
    okra
1 cup sliced celery
1/2 cup chopped onion
1/4 cup diced green bell pepper
2 cloves garlic, minced
2 tablespoons all-purpose flour
One 16-ounce can tomatoes in tomato
    sauce
1/4 cup uncooked rice
2 tablespoons chopped fresh parsley
1/4 teaspoon ground cumin
1/4 teaspoon freshly ground pepper
1/4 teaspoon hot pepper sauce
1/4 teaspoon dried thyme

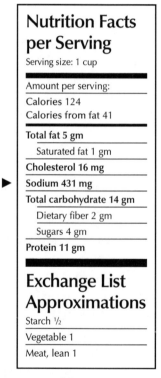

Nutrition Facts per Serving

Serving size: 1 cup

Amount per serving:

Calories 124
Calories from fat 41

Total fat 5 gm
  Saturated fat 1 gm
Cholesterol 16 mg
Sodium 431 mg
Total carbohydrate 14 gm
  Dietary fiber 2 gm
  Sugars 4 gm
Protein 11 gm

Exchange List Approximations

Starch 1/2
Vegetable 1
Meat, lean 1

1. Place the turkey or chicken carcass in a large pot; add any uncooked parts (neck, back, wings). Cover with water (about 2 quarts). Add salt and simmer, uncovered, over low heat about 2 hours, removing any foam that rises to the surface.

2. Pour the broth into a large container and chill. Skim off the fat. Remove the meat from the bones and reserve. (There should be at least 6 cups of broth and 1 cup of cooked turkey or chicken.)

3.   Melt the margarine in a large pot. Add the okra and sauté until it starts to brown, about 5 minutes. Add the celery, onion, green pepper, and garlic. Sprinkle the vegetables with flour. Stir until blended and starting to brown.

4.   Add the tomatoes and liquid. Stir, breaking the tomatoes into pieces; cook until the mixture begins to thicken.

5.   Add 1½ quarts of broth, the rice, parsley, cumin, pepper, pepper sauce, and thyme. Simmer 30 minutes. Add 1 cup of cooked poultry and heat 5 minutes more.

CHICKEN SOUP WITH LIME AND CILANTRO

This sophisticated soup has very few ingredients and takes no time at all to prepare. Lime and cilantro add a taste that's straight from Mexico and really spices up traditional chicken soup flavor.

5 cups (5 servings)

1 quart Homemade Chicken Broth
    (page 101), or canned reduced-
    sodium chicken broth
1 whole chicken breast, skinned, boned,
    and split, or 2 skinless, boneless
    breast halves (about ¾ pound)
3 tablespoons fresh lime juice
¼ cup coarsely chopped cilantro leaves

1. Bring the broth to a simmer in a large saucepan. Add the chicken; cover and simmer over low heat until it is just cooked through, about 8 to 10 minutes.
2. Remove and shred the chicken. Return it to the broth; add the lime juice and bring the soup to a boil. Ladle into soup bowls; sprinkle with cilantro.

Nutrition Facts per Serving	
Serving size: 1 cup	
Amount per serving:	
Calories 102	
Calories from fat 33	
Total fat 4 gm	
Saturated fat 1 gm	
Cholesterol 41 mg	
Sodium 126 mg	
Total carbohydrate 2 gm	
Dietary fiber 0 gm	
Sugars 1 gm	
Protein 18 gm	

Exchange List Approximation

Meat, lean 2

QUICK FRANK AND CORN CHOWDER

Cream-style corn and fat-free franks star as the main ingredients in this kid-approved soup. It's ideal for a weeknight meal when you don't have time to fuss.

1 quart (4 servings)

Two 97% fat-free frankfurters (about
      3 ounces), halved lengthwise
      and thinly sliced
$1/2$ cup chopped green bell pepper
$1/2$ cup chopped onion
One 17-ounce can cream-style corn
1 cup fat-free milk
1 cup (4 ounces) shredded reduced-fat
      Cheddar cheese

1.   Prepare a medium saucepan with nonstick pan spray; sauté the franks, green pepper, and onion until the onion is tender, about 5 minutes.

2.   Add the remaining ingredients; stir until the cheese melts. Do not boil. Serve hot.

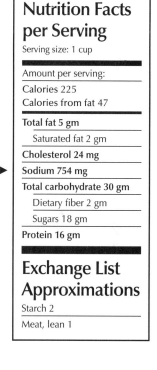

Nutrition Facts per Serving

Serving size: 1 cup

Amount per serving:

Calories 225
Calories from fat 47

Total fat 5 gm
   Saturated fat 2 gm

Cholesterol 24 mg

Sodium 754 mg

Total carbohydrate 30 gm
   Dietary fiber 2 gm
   Sugars 18 gm

Protein 16 gm

Exchange List Approximations

Starch 2

Meat, lean 1

5
SALADS AND SALAD DRESSINGS

Salads are versatile dishes. They can be used as an entrée, appetizer, side dish, or even dessert. In addition to greens, which we traditionally associate with salads, pasta, vegetables, fish and poultry, rice, beans, grains, and fruits serve as wonderful bases for salads.

GREEN SALADS

When you are making a green salad, there are many different kinds of greens you can use in addition to the old standby, iceberg lettuce. Spicy arugula, buttery Bibb, hearty romaine, ruffled red leaf, and spinach are just a few of the many possibilities.

Buy greens that are crisp and fresh and avoid those with bruised yellowish or brown leaves. Don't wash lettuce until you're ready to use it. It keeps longer if stored in plastic bags left slightly open, or in special vegetable bags that have airholes. When ready to serve, wash the leaves thoroughly and pat them dry, or use a salad spinner.

Dress salads just before serving. You get a better, more evenly distributed flavor when you toss the salad and dressing together rather than serving the dressing separately. The amount of dressing used is critical—too much drowns and wilts the greens, but not enough can leave the greens unseasoned.

OTHER SALADS

Some of the more unusual salads in this chapter use pasta, grains, and beans as the main ingredient instead of greens. Couscous Spinach Salad, Quinoa-Vegetable Salad, and Greek Chick-pea Salad are a sampling of the delicious recipes you'll find here. Herring Supreme, Curried Chicken Salad, and Tuscan Tuna and White Bean Salad showcase fish and chicken as scrumptious bases. And vegetables and fruits take center stage in salad recipes like Fresh Mushroom Salad Mimosa, New Potato and Green Bean Salad, Avocado and Grapefruit Salad with Sherry Vinaigrette, and Apple-Cabbage Slaw.

SALAD DRESSINGS

Dressings are often the nutritional downfall of salads. In regular green salads, as much as 200 calories may come from the dressing. And in other salads where grains, beans, vegetables, or fruits are the base, dressings can also compromise nutritional benefits with added fat. Although there are a plethora of low-fat and fat-free bottled salad dressings on the market nowadays that help solve the fat dilemma, their taste leaves something to be desired and they can be quite high in sodium. Homemade salad dressings have a taste that bottled just can't match, and they're actually quite easy to make. We've adapted some American favorites like Blue Cheese, Vinaigrette, and Thousand Island dressings to cut fat and calories but not taste. Dressings used in the nonlettuce salads have also been modified, using just a touch of flavorful oils, like olive or walnut; interesting vinegars, like balsamic and raspberry; low-fat dairy products like buttermilk or low-fat or fat-free yogurt; low-fat mayonnaise; and lots of herbs and spices to enhance flavor.

When we select oils for dressings, olive oil and canola are our two top picks. Both are rich in monounsaturated fatty acids. Monounsaturated fats may help reduce blood cholesterol levels more than other types of fats and are better for your heart. However, it's important to remember that all oils are still 100 percent fat and have about 120 calories per tablespoon, no matter how "heart healthy" they may be. Unsaturated, particularly monounsaturated, oils should be used whenever possible in place of other fats and oils in recipes, but *not* in addition.

CAESAR SALAD

This is an ideal first course: crisp romaine tossed with a sprightly dressing enlivened by garlic, anchovy paste, Worcestershire sauce, and lemon juice. To transform the salad into an entrée, add sliced grilled boneless chicken breasts and strips of raw or roasted red pepper for color. Either way, serve the salad with crusty bread. Be sure to add the appropriate exchanges or carbohydrate counts for any additional ingredients.

About 9 cups (6 servings)

1 large head romaine lettuce
¼ cup extra virgin olive oil
2 cloves garlic
½ cup rye, whole wheat, or sourdough
        croutons
1½ teaspoons anchovy paste
1 large egg *(see Note)*
1 teaspoon Worcestershire sauce
1 small lemon, juiced
¼ cup freshly grated Parmesan cheese
Pinch of freshly ground pepper

Nutrition Facts per Serving
Serving size: 1½ cups
Amount per serving:
Calories 138
Calories from fat 102
Total fat 11 gm
Saturated fat 2 gm
Cholesterol 40 mg
Sodium 170 mg
Total carbohydrate 5 gm
Dietary fiber 2 gm
Sugars 1 gm
Protein 5 gm

Exchange List Approximations

Vegetable 1

Fat, monounsaturated 2½

1. Rinse the lettuce leaves under cold running water, wrap in paper towels, and refrigerate at least 20 minutes.
2. Heat 1 teaspoon of the olive oil in a small skillet. Mince 1 garlic clove; add to the oil and cook for 1 minute. Add the croutons; toss to mix. Cook over medium heat until lightly toasted. Set aside.
3. Finely mince the remaining clove of garlic and put it in a salad bowl; add the anchovy paste, egg, Worcestershire sauce, and lemon juice. Beat well with a whisk and then slowly whisk in the remaining olive oil.
4. Tear the lettuce leaves into large bite-size pieces. Put in the salad bowl and add the Parmesan cheese and pepper. Toss to coat the greens with dressing. Top with croutons and serve immediately.

Note: The use of raw eggs carries the risk of salmonella. No recipe using raw eggs should be served to the very young, the very old, or anyone with a compromised immune system.

CARROT SALAD WITH DILL

This salad, jam-packed with vitamin A, will keep well for at least a day in the refrigerator. It's a good prepare-ahead side dish, or may be used as one of several salads on the buffet table. Carrots, because of their distinctive flavor, are delicious seasoned with diverse herbs and spices. To vary the flavor here, substitute raspberry vinegar for sherry or champagne vinegar, and use chopped fresh tarragon instead of dill.

3 cups (6 servings)

1 pound carrots (about 7), peeled and
      thinly sliced
½ cup finely chopped red or Spanish
      onion
1½ tablespoons canola or corn oil
1 tablespoon sherry or champagne
      vinegar
1 tablespoon chopped fresh dill, or
      1 teaspoon dried dill weed
½ teaspoon sugar
½ teaspoon salt
¼ teaspoon freshly ground pepper

Nutrition Facts per Serving
Serving size: ½ cup
Amount per serving:
Calories 73
Calories from fat 33
Total fat 4 gm
Saturated fat 0 gm
Cholesterol 0 mg
Sodium 246 mg
Total carbohydrate 10 gm
Dietary fiber 3 gm
Sugars 5 gm
Protein 1 gm

Exchange List Approximations

Vegetable 2

Fat, monounsaturated ½

1.   Cook the carrots in boiling water or in a steamer until crisp-tender, about 4 minutes. Rinse with cold water; drain well.

2.   Combine the carrots and onion in a medium bowl.

3.   Combine the oil, vinegar, dill, sugar, salt, and pepper in a small bowl; mix well. Toss with carrot mixture. Chill before serving.

COBB SALAD WITH LOUIS DRESSING

A tangy, creamy dressing heightens the flavors and textures of crisp, tender lettuces, smooth avocado, crisp bacon, and meaty chicken in this classic chopped salad, which you can serve as an appetizer or main course. Although the dressing can be made a day in advance, and the individual salad ingredients (except the avocado, which will darken) can be prepared early on the day the dish is being served, the salad itself should be assembled only at the last moment so that each ingredient retains as much of its individual character as possible. Both avocado and tomato are excellent sources of potassium, and tomatoes are notably high in vitamin A.

4 servings

SALAD

3 cups torn iceberg lettuce
3 cups torn red leaf lettuce
1 large hard-cooked egg, chopped
1 whole boneless, skinless chicken breast,
      cooked and cut into small cubes
      (about 1 cup cubed chicken)
4 strips bacon, cooked crisp and crumbled
1 small ripe avocado, cubed
1/2 cup chopped red onion
2 ripe small tomatoes or plum tomatoes,
      seeded and chopped

LOUIS DRESSING (MAKES 3/4 CUP)

3/4 cup plain low-fat yogurt
4 teaspoons chili sauce
1 tablespoon chopped fresh parsley, or
      1 teaspoon dried parsley flakes
1 clove garlic, minced
1/4 teaspoon salt
1/8 teaspoon freshly ground pepper
2 to 4 drops hot pepper sauce

Nutrition Facts per Serving
Serving size: About 1 1/2 cups salad plus 3 tablespoons dressing
Amount per serving:
Calories 247 Calories from fat 111
Total fat 12 gm
Saturated fat 3 gm
Cholesterol 98 mg
Sodium 408 mg
Total carbohydrate 14 gm
Dietary fiber 5 gm
Sugars 8 gm
Protein 22 gm

Exchange List Approximations
Vegetable 3
Meat, medium-fat 2
Fat, monounsaturated 1/2

1.   Line a large, flat bowl with mixed lettuces.

2.   Arrange all the other salad ingredients in rows on top of the lettuce.

3.   Combine the dressing ingredients; mix well. Serve the dressing alongside the salad.

CAULIFLOWER SALAD

Although cauliflower is often thought of as a cold-weather vegetable, it is at its most flavorful when it is just picked and sold at local farm stands in mid- to late summer. You can serve this creamy-crunchy salad as a first course, nestled in lettuce leaves and accompanied by Italian Pita Crisps (page 75). For a main course, arrange the salad on a platter with greens, tomato wedges, scallions, black olives, and radishes, and increase the portion amount. If you make these additions, add the appropriate exchange values or carbohydrate counts into your meal plan.

3½ cups (7 servings)

2 cups bite-size pieces cauliflower
3 large hard-cooked eggs, chopped
1 cup chopped celery
½ cup chopped green bell pepper
One 4-ounce jar pimientos, drained and
    minced
⅓ cup low-fat mayonnaise
¼ cup finely chopped onion
1 teaspoon salt
¼ teaspoon freshly ground pepper

1. Cook the cauliflower in boiling water 2 minutes; drain well.
2. Mix all the remaining ingredients in a bowl. Add the cauliflower and toss to coat. Chill well before serving.

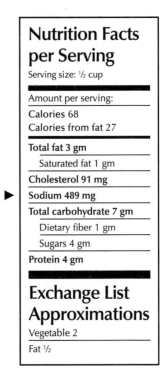

Nutrition Facts per Serving

Serving size: ½ cup

Amount per serving:

Calories 68
Calories from fat 27

Total fat 3 gm
  Saturated fat 1 gm
Cholesterol 91 mg
Sodium 489 mg
Total carbohydrate 7 gm
  Dietary fiber 1 gm
  Sugars 4 gm
Protein 4 gm

Exchange List Approximations

Vegetable 2
Fat ½

APPLE-CABBAGE SLAW

For a nice variation on this crunchy tart-sweet salad, try napa or red cabbage. Most supermarkets carry small bags of precut shredded cabbage, a convenience when you don't want half a cabbage left over. The salad, a good winter side dish, is an excellent accompaniment to roast pork and low-fat or fat-free frankfurters.

2 cups (4 servings)

¼ cup plain low-fat yogurt
2 teaspoons vinegar
½ teaspoon prepared mustard
¼ teaspoon salt
Pinch of freshly ground pepper
2 cups (8 ounces) shredded cabbage
1 large unpeeled apple, cored and
        thinly sliced

1. In a small bowl, thoroughly mix the yogurt, vinegar, mustard, salt, and pepper.
2. In a large bowl, lightly mix the cabbage and apples.
3. Pour the yogurt mixture over the cabbage mixture; toss lightly. Serve immediately.

Nutrition Facts per Serving
Serving size: ½ cup
Amount per serving:
Calories 56
Calories from fat 6
Total fat 1 gm
Saturated fat 0 gm
Cholesterol 1 mg
Sodium 174 mg
Total carbohydrate 12 gm
Dietary fiber 3 gm
Sugars 10 gm
Protein 2 gm

Exchange List Approximations

Vegetable 1

Fruit ½

FRESH TOMATO, MOZZARELLA, AND BASIL SALAD

The colors of the Italian flag—red, white, and green—are deliciously combined in this variation on a classic Italian appetizer. Ripe, juicy tomatoes and fresh, aromatic basil are the key elements in the success of this dish. Although both are at their peak in summer, when they are to be found on every local farm stand, the taste of summer can still be achieved in winter if fresh basil and ripe Holland tomatoes are available, which they are year-round in many supermarkets. Serve the salad on a bed of romaine or arugula.

4 cups (4 servings)

2 tablespoons pine nuts
2 large ripe, red tomatoes, cut into
    thin wedges
4 ounces part-skim mozzarella cheese,
    sliced and cut into ½-inch-wide
    strips
½ cup shredded fresh basil
1 small red onion, thinly sliced
¼ cup Basic Vinaigrette (page 175)
    or prepared light or fat-free
    Italian dressing

1. Place the pine nuts in a dry skillet and toast over medium heat for 4 or 5 minutes until lightly browned, shaking the pan occasionally to prevent the nuts from burning. Reserve.
2. Combine all the remaining ingredients in a large bowl. Chill several hours. Top with the pine nuts before serving.

Nutrition Facts per Serving

Serving size: 1 cup

Amount per serving:

Calories 210
Calories from fat 148

Total fat 16 gm
    Saturated fat 4 gm

Cholesterol 16 mg

Sodium 246 mg

Total carbohydrate 9 gm
    Dietary fiber 2 gm
    Sugars 5 gm

Protein 9 gm

Exchange List Approximations

Vegetable 2

Meat, medium-fat 1

Fat, monounsaturated 2

BEST-EVER COLESLAW

A peppery dressing that includes horseradish, dry mustard, cayenne pepper, and celery seed (a key ingredient) is mixed with finely chopped cabbage in the perfect side dish to serve with grilled low-fat franks, lean (90 percent) hamburgers, or skinless chicken. And it's a must for the all-American barbecue table. The flavor of this coleslaw improves on standing. After 8 hours or overnight, adjust the seasoning, if necessary, and stir well. The salad, tightly covered and refrigerated, will keep for up to 6 days.

5 cups (10 servings)

1 small or ½ large head cabbage
    (about 2 pounds)
½ cup fat-free mayonnaise
½ cup light sour cream
2 tablespoons sugar
2 green onions with green tops,
    chopped
2 tablespoons prepared horseradish
1 tablespoon fresh lemon juice
½ teaspoon salt
½ teaspoon dry mustard
⅛ teaspoon cayenne pepper
1 clove garlic, minced
½ teaspoon celery seed

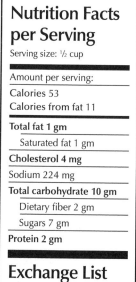

Nutrition Facts per Serving

Serving size: ½ cup

Amount per serving:

Calories 53
Calories from fat 11

Total fat 1 gm
  Saturated fat 1 gm
Cholesterol 4 mg
Sodium 224 mg
Total carbohydrate 10 gm
  Dietary fiber 2 gm
  Sugars 7 gm
Protein 2 gm

Exchange List Approximation

Vegetable 2

1.   Remove the outer leaves and core of the cabbage; chop the cabbage into large chunks. Place several chunks in a food processor fitted with the steel blade. (Do not overfill the processor.) Chop fine, using on/off turns; transfer to a large bowl. Repeat with the remaining cabbage; do not wash the bowl of the food processor.
2.   Add the remaining ingredients to the food processor; process until well combined. Pour over the cabbage; cover and refrigerate at least 8 hours or overnight.

A-TASTE-OF-CALIFORNIA SLAW

This colorful, spicy slaw is a good source of vitamins A and C. Use it with grilled or broiled meats and poultry, or serve with low-fat franks and beans.

4 cups (8 servings)

SLAW

2 cups (8 ounces) shredded cabbage
2 green onions with green tops, sliced
1/2 cup sliced celery
1/2 cup thinly sliced carrot
2 ounces provolone cheese, cut into
    thin strips
1 clove garlic, minced
1 small jalapeño pepper, seeded and
    minced
1/2 red bell pepper, cored, seeded, and
    cut into thin strips
1/8 teaspoon celery seed

DRESSING

One 8-ounce carton plain low-fat yogurt
1 teaspoon Dijon mustard
1 teaspoon fresh lemon juice
1/4 teaspoon salt
1/8 teaspoon ground white pepper

Nutrition Facts per Serving
Serving size: 1/2 cup
Amount per serving:
Calories 60
Calories from fat 22
Total fat 2 gm
Saturated fat 1 gm
Cholesterol 7 mg
Sodium 177 mg
Total carbohydrate 6 gm
Dietary fiber 1 gm
Sugars 4 gm
Protein 4 gm

Exchange List Approximations
Vegetable 1
Fat, saturated 1/2

1. Combine the slaw ingredients in a large bowl.
2. In another bowl, mix all the ingredients for the dressing; pour over the vegetables and toss. Chill several hours before serving for the flavors to blend.

CORN RELISH SALAD

Make this salad often in summer, when fresh sweet corn is in season. Cilantro and hot sauce add a Mexican touch to an easy, portable dish.

2½ cups (5 servings)

One 10-ounce package frozen whole-
      kernel corn, thawed, or 2 cups
      fresh corn kernels
1 cup diced red or orange bell pepper
3 green onions with green tops, sliced
⅓ cup chopped fresh cilantro
2 tablespoons fresh lime or lemon juice
2 tablespoons olive oil
¼ to ½ teaspoon hot pepper sauce,
      as desired
¼ teaspoon salt
5 large red leaf lettuce leaves

1. Combine the corn, bell pepper, onions, and cilantro in a medium bowl.
2. In another bowl, whisk together the lime juice, oil, pepper sauce, and salt; pour over the corn mixture. Toss well, cover, and chill at least 1 hour for flavors to blend.
3. Serve on lettuce leaves.

Nutrition Facts per Serving

Serving size: ½ cup

Amount per serving:

Calories 114
Calories from fat 50

Total fat 6 gm
  Saturated fat 1 gm

Cholesterol 0 mg

Sodium 127 mg

Total carbohydrate 17 gm
  Dietary fiber 3 gm
  Sugars 2 gm

Protein 3 gm

Exchange List Approximations

Starch 1

Fat, monounsaturated 1

GREEK SALAD

Greek salad, a combination of fresh raw vegetables dressed with a lemony vinaigrette and topped with olives, feta cheese, and chick-peas, can be served as a hearty first course or, with the addition of a few more ounces of feta, used as a refreshing main course, especially in summer when all the ingredients are at their peak. A fruity extra virgin olive oil will add its own special character to the salad.

8½ cups (6 servings)

SALAD

1 medium head lettuce, washed and
    torn into bite-size pieces
2 medium tomatoes, cut in eighths
½ medium cucumber, peeled and
    thinly sliced
3 green onions with green tops, sliced
½ cup sliced celery
½ cup diced green bell pepper
3 radishes, sliced
1 medium carrot, shredded
1 tablespoon chopped fresh parsley

DRESSING

3 tablespoons olive oil
1 tablespoon fresh lemon juice
½ teaspoon salt
⅛ teaspoon freshly ground pepper

TOPPINGS

½ cup (2 ounces) crumbled feta cheese
16 Greek olives
2 tablespoons canned chick-peas,
    rinsed and drained
8 anchovies, drained (optional)

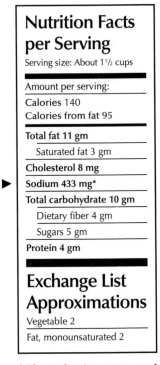

Nutrition Facts per Serving

Serving size: About 1½ cups

Amount per serving:

Calories 140
Calories from fat 95

Total fat 11 gm
    Saturated fat 3 gm
Cholesterol 8 mg
Sodium 433 mg*
Total carbohydrate 10 gm
    Dietary fiber 4 gm
    Sugars 5 gm
Protein 4 gm

Exchange List Approximations

Vegetable 2
Fat, monounsaturated 2

** If anchovies are used, sodium is **629 mg** per serving.*

1.   Combine all the salad ingredients in a large salad bowl. Toss to mix.

2.   Mix the dressing ingredients in a small bowl. Drizzle over the salad and toss again.

3.   Garnish the top of the salad with crumbled cheese, olives, and chick-peas. Add anchovies if desired.

GREEN BEAN SALAD

This salad makes a nice appetizer or buffet dish, or serve it with a main course such as chicken or fish. The green beans can be cooked in advance and chilled, but do not add the dressing until just before serving or the beans will discolor. For a slightly different texture, allow the sliced mushrooms to marinate in the vinaigrette for an hour before combining with the beans and onions. The mushrooms will lose some of their crispness but will become permeated with the flavor of the dressing.

3¾ cups (4 servings)

12 ounces fresh small green beans,
    ends trimmed
8 fresh mushrooms, sliced
½ cup chopped red onion
3 tablespoons canola or corn oil
1 tablespoon balsamic or red
    wine vinegar
1 clove garlic, minced
½ teaspoon salt
¼ teaspoon freshly ground pepper

1. Cook the green beans in a large pot of boiling water for 5 minutes; drain. Plunge the beans into a bowl of ice water to stop the cooking and retain their bright green color. Drain and place in a large bowl.

2. Add the mushrooms and onions to the beans; toss to mix.

3. For the dressing, whisk the oil into the vinegar in a small bowl; add the remaining ingredients and pour over the green beans. Toss lightly. Serve immediately.

Nutrition Facts per Serving
Serving size: About 1 cup
Amount per serving:
Calories 136
Calories from fat 99
Total fat 11 gm
Saturated fat 1 gm
Cholesterol 0 mg
Sodium 295 mg
Total carbohydrate 9 gm
Dietary fiber 3 gm
Sugars 3 gm
Protein 2 gm

Exchange List Approximations

Vegetable 2

Fat, monounsaturated 2

MARINATED CUCUMBERS

This cucumber salad and its innumerable variations have found their way into cuisines as diverse as those from the Mediterranean countries, the Middle East, and Scandinavia. This version, with its delicate flavoring, is a happy choice to serve with fish, especially fresh or smoked salmon or Salmon Mousse (page 82). Cucumbers give off a lot of water, so be sure to drain them well before serving. Fresh dill can be substituted for the parsley and works especially well if the salad will be served with fish.

2 cups (4 servings)

¼ cup vinegar
2 teaspoons sugar
½ teaspoon salt
Pinch of paprika
Pinch of freshly ground pepper
1 medium cucumber, peeled and sliced
1 medium onion, sliced and separated
        into rings
1 teaspoon chopped fresh parsley

1.   Combine the vinegar, 2 tablespoons water, sugar, salt, paprika, and pepper in a medium bowl. Add the cucumber and onion. Toss to mix.

2.   Cover and chill for at least 2 hours for the flavors to blend, stirring occasionally. Drain the liquid and sprinkle the salad with chopped parsley at serving time.

Nutrition Facts per Serving
Serving size: ½ cup
Amount per serving:
Calories 21
Calories from fat 1
Total fat 0 gm
Saturated fat 0 gm
Cholesterol 0 mg
Sodium 72 mg
Total carbohydrate 5 gm
Dietary fiber 1 gm
Sugars 4 gm
Protein 1 gm

Exchange List Approximation
Vegetable 1

JICAMA SALAD

Crisp, sweet jicama, sliced cucumbers, and orange sections, all tossed with a mildly spicy vinaigrette, make a salad that is a refreshing first course or a convenient prepare-ahead dish for a buffet.

2 cups (4 servings)

One 8-ounce jicama, peeled and cut into
     1/2-inch sticks
1 small cucumber, thinly sliced
1 medium orange, peeled and sectioned
1/4 cup white wine vinegar
2 tablespoons canola or corn oil
1 teaspoon fresh lemon juice
1/4 teaspoon chili powder
1/4 teaspoon salt

1. Combine the jicama, cucumber, and orange segments in a serving bowl.
2. Whisk together the vinegar, oil, lemon juice, chili powder, and salt. Pour over the jicama mixture; toss well. Chill.

Nutrition Facts per Serving

Serving size: 1/2 cup

Amount per serving:

Calories 104
Calories from fat 65

Total fat 7 gm
    Saturated fat 1 gm
Cholesterol 0 mg
Sodium 150 mg
Total carbohydrate 10 gm
    Dietary fiber 4 gm
    Sugars 6 gm
Protein 1 gm

Exchange List Approximations

Fruit 1/2

Vegetable 1

Fat, monounsaturated 1 1/2

FRESH MUSHROOM SALAD MIMOSA

Sliced white mushrooms have a firm texture and cool, woodsy flavor in delicious contrast to tender, leafy lettuce. Serve this light salad, which can be prepared in minutes, as an easy first or salad course.

2 cups (4 servings)

8 ounces (about 2½ cups) sliced fresh
    mushrooms
⅓ cup fat-free Thousand Island, ranch, or
    Italian dressing
4 large Boston or red leaf lettuce leaves
1 hard-cooked egg white, finely chopped
2 tablespoons chopped fresh chives
    or parsley
⅛ teaspoon freshly ground pepper

1. Put the mushrooms in a medium bowl; toss with the dressing and mix well.

2. Line 4 serving plates with lettuce; divide the mushroom mixture among the plates. Sprinkle each salad with egg white, chives, and pepper.

Nutrition Facts per Serving

Serving size: ½ cup

Amount per serving:

Calories 50
Calories from fat 2

Total fat 0 gm
  Saturated fat 0 gm

Cholesterol 0 mg

Sodium 217 mg

Total carbohydrate 10 gm
  Dietary fiber 1 gm
  Sugars 5 gm

Protein 2 gm

Exchange List Approximation

Starch ½

CALIFORNIA PEAR SALAD

Bartlett pears are a sure sign that fall has arrived. Here they are combined with crunchy celery and peanuts, then mixed with a spicy, aromatic yogurt-based dressing. Serve in lettuce cups as a first course or, better still, as an accompaniment to simply roasted poultry, pork tenderloin, or ham.

2 cups (4 servings)

One 8-ounce carton plain low-fat yogurt
$1/4$ cup light mayonnaise
$1^1/2$ teaspoons brown sugar
1 teaspoon ground ginger
1 clove garlic, minced
$1/2$ teaspoon Dijon mustard
$1/4$ teaspoon salt
$1/8$ teaspoon white pepper
2 ripe, firm, unpeeled Bartlett pears,
     cored and diced
2 teaspoons fresh lemon juice
1 green onion with green top, sliced
$1/2$ cup thinly sliced celery
$1/4$ cup unsalted coarsely chopped
     dry-roasted peanuts

1. In a medium bowl, combine the yogurt, mayonnaise, brown sugar, ginger, garlic, mustard, salt, and pepper.

2. In a large bowl, gently combine the pears with the lemon juice; add the onion, celery, and peanuts; fold in the yogurt mixture. Cover tightly and chill. Serve within 2 hours; the pears will soften and darken if stored too long.

Nutrition Facts per Serving

Serving size: $1/2$ cup

Amount per serving:

Calories 213
Calories from fat 94

Total fat 10 gm
   Saturated fat 2 gm

Cholesterol 11 mg

Sodium 321 mg

Total carbohydrate 26 gm
   Dietary fiber 3 gm
   Sugars 22 gm

Protein 6 gm

Exchange List Approximations

Starch 1

Fruit $1/2$

Fat 2

HOT GERMAN-STYLE POTATO SALAD

This is an old-fashioned recipe with a lot of down-home flavor—a perfect starch to serve with lean meat loaf, burgers, pork tenderloin, or skinless chicken breasts.

5¹/₃ cups (8 servings)

5 medium potatoes (about 1¹/₂ pounds
      total)
5 slices bacon
¹/₄ cup vinegar
1 large egg, slightly beaten
2 teaspoons sugar
¹/₂ teaspoon salt
¹/₄ teaspoon freshly ground pepper
¹/₂ cup chopped onion

Nutrition Facts per Serving
Serving size: About ²/₃ cup
Amount per serving:
Calories 112
Calories from fat 37
Total fat 4 gm
Saturated fat 1 gm
Cholesterol 31 mg
Sodium 168 mg
Total carbohydrate 16 gm
Dietary fiber 1 gm
Sugars 3 gm
Protein 3 gm

Exchange List Approximations

Starch 1

Fat ¹/₂

1. Peel and halve the potatoes and cook in boiling water until tender. Drain and slice. Set aside.

2. Cook the bacon until crisp. Drain, reserving 1 tablespoon of bacon fat. Crumble the bacon and set aside.

3. In a large nonstick skillet, combine the 1 tablespoon bacon fat, the vinegar, ¹/₄ cup water, the egg, sugar, salt, and pepper. Place over moderately low heat and stir constantly until the dressing is thickened; do not allow the egg to coagulate.

4. Add the reserved potatoes and crumbled bacon; stir in the onion. Mix and heat through. Serve hot.

NEW POTATO AND GREEN BEAN SALAD

This is the way the French make potato salad—by tossing the vinaigrette with the potatoes while they are still warm, the better to absorb the dressing. New varieties of potatoes are being developed and grown on farms across America, and they seem to be arriving in the market daily. Try Yukon Gold or other small, flavorful potatoes for this recipe, which is a refreshing change from mayonnaise-based potato salads. Served chilled or at room temperature, the salad is a good party dish, or take it to a potluck dinner.

6 cups (8 servings)

1 pound new, small, red or Yukon Gold
      potatoes, peeled
8 ounces fresh green or wax beans, ends
      trimmed, cut into 1-inch pieces
      (about 2 cups)
¼ cup olive oil
2 tablespoons Dijon mustard or grainy
      mustard
2 tablespoons cider vinegar
2 tablespoons chopped fresh chives,
      or chopped green onion tops
2 tablespoons crumbled Roquefort
      or blue cheese (optional)

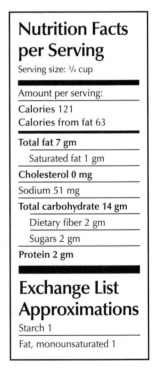

Nutrition Facts per Serving

Serving size: ¾ cup

Amount per serving:
Calories 121
Calories from fat 63
Total fat 7 gm
Saturated fat 1 gm
Cholesterol 0 mg
Sodium 51 mg
Total carbohydrate 14 gm
Dietary fiber 2 gm
Sugars 2 gm
Protein 2 gm

Exchange List Approximations

Starch 1

Fat, monounsaturated 1

1.   Cook the potatoes in a large pot of boiling water for 6 minutes. Add the beans; continue to boil until the potatoes are tender and the beans are crisp-tender, about 4 to 6 minutes longer. Drain. Cut the potatoes into bite-size pieces; transfer to a large bowl. Add the beans.

2.   In a small bowl, whisk together the oil, mustard, and vinegar; pour over the warm potatoes and beans and toss. Cover and chill at least 4 hours. Just before serving, stir in the chives. Add the cheese if desired.

FRESH SPINACH SALAD

Everyone likes spinach salad, a delectable way to get some vitamin A. This is the simplest version of the classic salad, but other ingredients—such as anchovies, black olives, orange segments, or endive spears—can be added to taste. Just be sure to add the appropriate exchange values or carbohydrate counts.

6 cups (4 servings)

5 cups (5 ounces) packed torn spinach leaves (about ½ of a 10-ounce bag), washed and thick stems removed
1½ cups (3 ounces) thinly sliced mushrooms
⅓ cup thinly sliced red onion rings
⅓ cup prepared fat-free or light red French or honey Dijon salad dressing
⅛ teaspoon freshly ground pepper
¼ cup croutons (optional)

1.   In a large bowl, combine the spinach, mushrooms, and onion; toss to mix.
2.   Drizzle the dressing over the salad; toss to coat the greens. Sprinkle the salad with freshly ground pepper and top with croutons if desired.

Nutrition Facts per Serving
Serving size: 1½ cups
Amount per serving:
Calories 50
Calories from fat 2
Total fat 0 gm
Saturated fat 0 gm
Cholesterol 0 mg
Sodium 208 mg
Total carbohydrate 10 gm
Dietary fiber 1 gm
Sugars 7 gm
Protein 2 gm

Exchange List Approximations
Starch ½
Vegetable 1

ROASTED PEPPER AND GOAT CHEESE SALAD

A farm stand salad, just right for late summer when mounds of red and yellow peppers are to be seen at every farmers' market and roadside vegetable stand, and the scent of fresh basil perfumes the air. For this simple but sophisticated dish, prepare the vinaigrette with a fruity olive oil and use fresh-tasting domestic goat cheese, a French Boucheron, or a mild feta. The peppers and vinaigrette can each be prepared and stored separately, covered and in the refrigerator, for up to 3 days in advance, then brought to room temperature before final assembly. The salad can be served as a beautiful first course or as an accompaniment to grilled meats and poultry.

2 cups (4 servings)

3 large red, yellow, or orange bell
    peppers, or one of each
    (1½ pounds total)
¼ cup packed thin strips of fresh basil
    leaves
2 tablespoons Balsamic Vinaigrette
    (page 176)
2 tablespoons finely crumbled goat
    cheese
½ teaspoon coarsely ground pepper
4 fresh basil sprigs

Nutrition Facts per Serving

Serving size: ½ cup

Amount per serving:

Calories 74
Calories from fat 45

Total fat 5 gm
   Saturated fat 2 gm

Cholesterol 6 mg

Sodium 82 mg*

Total carbohydrate 6 gm
   Dietary fiber 1 gm
   Sugars 3 gm

Protein 2 gm

Exchange List Approximations

Vegetable 1

Fat, monounsaturated 1

* If optional salt from vinaigrette recipe is used, sodium is 117 mg per serving.

1.   Cut the peppers lengthwise into 4 quarters; discard the cores, seeds, and membranes. Place the pepper quarters skin side up on a foil-lined cookie sheet.

2.   Broil 2 to 3 inches from the heat source until the skin is charred and blackened, about 10 minutes.

3.   Place the peppers in a paper bag; close and let stand about 10 minutes. Peel and discard the skin; cut the peppers into 1-inch-wide strips and place them in a shallow serving dish.

4.   Sprinkle the peppers with basil; drizzle with vinaigrette. Top with goat cheese and freshly ground pepper. Serve at room temperature, garnished with fresh basil sprigs.

SPROUT SALAD

Stuffed into pita pockets, sprinkled over salads, or quickly stir-fried, al-falfa and bean sprouts are now staple ingredients in the American kitchen. Stores selling fresh organic produce sometimes have more un-usual sprouts, such as those from radish or sunflower seeds. Radish sprouts are sharp and peppery, while those from sunflower seeds are cooler and crisper in flavor. Either or both would work very well in this salad, which is a good starter for a summer meal.

About 6 cups (6 servings)

3 tablespoons sunflower seeds
2 cups alfalfa sprouts or 1½ cups bean
      sprouts
½ cup sliced radishes
¾ cup diced cucumber (¼-inch dice)
2 green onions with green tops, sliced
4 cups bite-size torn salad greens
3 tablespoons olive oil
2 tablespoons wine vinegar
3 basil leaves, finely sliced,
      or ½ teaspoon dried basil
1 clove garlic, minced
½ teaspoon salt
2 to 3 pinches freshly ground pepper
1 large hard-cooked egg, sliced

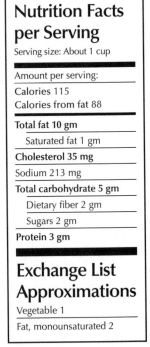

Nutrition Facts per Serving

Serving size: About 1 cup

Amount per serving:

Calories 115
Calories from fat 88

Total fat 10 gm
   Saturated fat 1 gm
Cholesterol 35 mg
Sodium 213 mg
Total carbohydrate 5 gm
   Dietary fiber 2 gm
   Sugars 2 gm
Protein 3 gm

Exchange List Approximations

Vegetable 1

Fat, monounsaturated 2

1.   Place the sunflower seeds in a dry skillet. Toast by stirring over medium heat for about 3 minutes. Allow to cool.

2.   Combine the toasted sunflower seeds, sprouts, radishes, cucumber, and onions in a large salad bowl. Add the torn salad greens and toss; cover and chill.

3.   Prepare the dressing by mixing the oil, vinegar, basil, garlic, salt, and pepper. Set aside.

4.   When ready to serve, pour the dressing over the salad and toss. Gar-nish with slices of hard-cooked egg.

FRESH TOMATO ASPIC

This Southern recipe from the 1950s is well worth saving from the archives. The texture and bright taste of chopped raw tomatoes and celery leaves heightened by a touch of winy vinegar make all the difference. Garden-fresh ripe tomatoes are the ticket for a very low-calorie appetizer that's high in vitamin A and potassium. For a more contemporary take on the recipe, substitute chopped fresh basil leaves, or use flat parsley.

6 slices (6 servings)

2 cups peeled, seeded, finely chopped
      fresh tomatoes (about 1 pound)
1 envelope unflavored gelatin
2 teaspoons balsamic or red wine
      vinegar
1/4 cup very finely chopped celery leaves
1/2 teaspoon salt
1/4 teaspoon freshly ground pepper
6 lettuce leaves
2 tablespoons light or low-fat
      mayonnaise

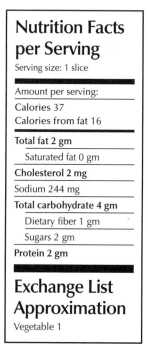

Nutrition Facts per Serving

Serving size: 1 slice

Amount per serving:

Calories 37
Calories from fat 16

Total fat 2 gm
  Saturated fat 0 gm
Cholesterol 2 mg
Sodium 244 mg
Total carbohydrate 4 gm
  Dietary fiber 1 gm
  Sugars 2 gm
Protein 2 gm

Exchange List Approximation

Vegetable 1

1. Place 1 cup of the chopped tomatoes in a small saucepan; sprinkle with the gelatin. Bring just to a boil over medium heat, stirring constantly, until the gelatin is dissolved.

2. Remove from the heat; stir in the remaining tomatoes, the vinegar, celery leaves, salt, and pepper; mix well.

3. Prepare a 7 x 3-inch loaf pan with nonstick pan spray. Pour the mixture into the pan. Cover and chill overnight or until firm.

4. Unmold; slice into 6 equal portions and place on lettuce leaves. Top each serving with 1 teaspoon light mayonnaise.

MARINATED CRISP VEGETABLE SALAD

This colorful salad is very similar to the crunchy Italian *giardiniera*. Use it as the basis for an antipasto, or serve it as part of a buffet. For variety, add peperoncini, red onion rings, and a few black or green Sicilian olives (just figure in the appropriate exchanges or carbohydrate counts). Although blanching the broccoli will prevent it from turning olive green immediately, don't marinate the salad more than a few hours.

About 3 cups (6 servings)

1 cup diagonally sliced carrots
1 cup broccoli florets
1 cup bite-size pieces cauliflower
1 red bell pepper, cut into 1-inch squares
⅓ cup tarragon vinegar or white wine
    vinegar
¼ cup extra virgin olive oil
1 tablespoon grainy or Dijon mustard
½ teaspoon freshly ground pepper

1. Bring a large pot of salted water to a boil. Blanch the vegetables by dropping the carrots, broccoli, and cauliflower into the water. Return to a boil; cook 30 to 60 seconds. The vegetables should remain very crisp. Drain and rinse under very cold running water or in a bowl of ice water. Drain well and transfer to a large bowl. Add the red pepper.
2. In a small bowl, whisk together the vinegar, oil, mustard, and pepper. Toss the dressing with the vegetables. Cover and chill until serving time.

Nutrition Facts per Serving

Serving size: About ½ cup

Amount per serving:

Calories 85
Calories from fat 63

Total fat 7 gm
    Saturated fat 1 gm
Cholesterol 0 mg
Sodium 137 mg
Total carbohydrate 6 gm
    Dietary fiber 2 gm
    Sugars 3 gm
Protein 1 gm

Exchange List Approximations

Vegetable 1

Fat, monounsaturated 1½

WALDORF SALAD

Waldorf salad is a favorite starter for fall and winter meals, often served on a bed of lettuce as the opener for Thanksgiving dinner. Although apples and walnuts are a match made in heaven, the walnuts can be omitted and one fat exchange deducted per serving.

3 cups (4 servings)

3 tablespoons light mayonnaise
1 tablespoon pineapple juice
2 medium (about 12 ounces total)
        red apples
2 teaspoons fresh lemon juice
½ cup thinly sliced celery
¼ cup chopped walnuts

1.   Mix the mayonnaise and pineapple juice in a small bowl. Set aside.
2.   Core and dice the unpeeled apples; drizzle lemon juice over the apples in a large bowl. Stir in the celery and nuts.
3.   Fold in the dressing to coat the apples. Cover tightly and chill. Use within a few hours, or the apples will darken and soften.

Nutrition Facts per Serving

Serving size: ¾ cup

Amount per serving:

Calories 136
Calories from fat 75

Total fat 8 gm
    Saturated fat 1 gm
Cholesterol 5 mg
Sodium 97 mg
Total carbohydrate 15 gm
    Dietary fiber 3 gm
    Sugars 11 gm
Protein 1 gm

Exchange List Approximations

Fruit 1

Fat, polyunsaturated 1½

AVOCADO AND GRAPEFRUIT SALAD WITH SHERRY VINAIGRETTE

This is a refreshing and beautiful salad, an ideal appetizer for a sophisticated dinner party. And, of course, it's delicious. Avocados are high in fat, but mostly monounsaturated fat. They're also a good source of folic acid and potassium.

4 servings

One 1¼-pound ruby red grapefruit, or
    1 cup grapefruit segments
2 medium-sized ripe avocados (about
    1¼ pounds total)
1 bunch watercress (about 6 ounces),
    washed and thick stems trimmed
1 tablespoon almond, walnut, or olive oil
1½ teaspoons sherry vinegar or apple
    cider vinegar
⅛ teaspoon seasoned salt
2 to 3 drops hot pepper sauce

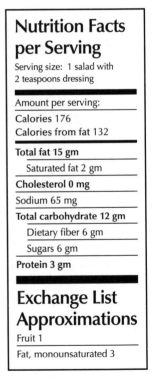

Nutrition Facts per Serving

Serving size: 1 salad with 2 teaspoons dressing

Amount per serving:

Calories 176
Calories from fat 132

Total fat 15 gm
    Saturated fat 2 gm
Cholesterol 0 mg
Sodium 65 mg
Total carbohydrate 12 gm
    Dietary fiber 6 gm
    Sugars 6 gm
Protein 3 gm

Exchange List Approximations

Fruit 1

Fat, monounsaturated 3

1. Cut the grapefruit in half; seed them and carefully remove the segments. Reserve the shells.

2. Cut each avocado in half; peel and pit.

3. Divide the trimmed watercress among 4 chilled salad plates. Put an avocado half on top of each watercress nest. Divide the grapefruit segments to fill the cavities and top the avocado halves.

4. To make the dressing, squeeze 1 tablespoon of juice from the grapefruit shells into a small bowl. Add the oil, vinegar, seasoned salt, and hot pepper sauce. Mix well with a fork.

5. Drizzle 2 teaspoons of the dressing over each salad.

PASTA SALAD

Although it's tempting to use leftover pasta in salads, it's a better idea to prepare it specially and to undercook it by several minutes so that it won't become soggy as it absorbs the dressing. To ensure an *al dente* texture, drain the pasta as soon as it is cooked, and dip the strainer or colander in cool water to stop the cooking completely, drain again, and then mix with the dressing. This is great portable food, a wonderful picnic dish, and an excellent accompaniment to grilled low-fat franks or lean (90 to 95 percent lean) hamburgers.

6 cups (6 servings)

3 cups cooked tricolor spiral pasta
       (1½ cups dry), or 3 cups other
       cooked pasta
1 large ripe tomato, cored, seeded, and
       chopped
1 medium green bell pepper, cored,
       seeded, and chopped
1 cup (4 ounces) shredded reduced-fat
       Cheddar cheese
½ cup black olives, drained and sliced
½ cup prepared fat-free Italian or
       Parmesan-pepper dressing

1.   Combine all the ingredients; toss to mix.
2.   Chill to blend the flavors. (This salad is even better the second day.)

Nutrition Facts per Serving	
Serving size: 1 cup	
Amount per serving:	
Calories 165	
Calories from fat 35	
Total fat 4 gm	
Saturated fat 1 gm	
Cholesterol 10 mg	
Sodium 355 mg	
Total carbohydrate 22 gm	
Dietary fiber 2 gm	
Sugars 5 gm	
Protein 9 gm	

Exchange List Approximations

Starch 1½	
Vegetable 1	
Fat ½	

COUSCOUS SPINACH SALAD

This is a Middle Eastern or North African version of spinach salad, with each ingredient adding its own unique texture and flavor. Couscous is a kind of Middle Eastern pasta that cooks up into small, fluffy individual grains. It cooks (or rather, soaks) in minutes, absorbs the flavor of the liquid and other ingredients it soaks with, and is nutritious. Although couscous was once available only in specialty food stores, now it can be purchased in any supermarket.

8 cups (8 servings)

1 cup Homemade Chicken Broth
    (page 101) or canned reduced-
    sodium chicken broth
¾ cup uncooked couscous
½ cup light Italian salad dressing
2 cups well-washed, shredded, tightly
    packed fresh spinach
12 cherry tomatoes, halved
One 8-ounce can water chestnuts,
    drained and sliced
1 cup well-washed, tightly packed whole
    fresh spinach leaves, for serving

1. In a saucepan, bring the chicken broth to a boil. Stir in the couscous and remove from the heat. Cover and let stand for 5 minutes.
2. Add the salad dressing. Cover and chill.
3. To serve, toss the couscous mixture with the shredded spinach, tomatoes, and water chestnuts. Serve on the whole spinach leaves.

Nutrition Facts per Serving

Serving size: 1 cup

Amount per serving:

Calories 96
Calories from fat 10

Total fat 1 gm
    Saturated fat 0 gm

Cholesterol 0 mg

Sodium 261 mg

Total carbohydrate 19 gm
    Dietary fiber 2 gm
    Sugars 3 gm

Protein 4 gm

Exchange List Approximations

Starch 1

Vegetable 1

QUINOA-VEGETABLE SALAD

Quinoa, a grain of South American origin, is fast and easy to prepare and, like couscous, tends to absorb and reflect the flavors of the foods it cooks with. This salad is similar to Tabbouleh (page 162) but has a more interesting textural contrast of herbs, grain, and crunchy vegetables. It can be served as a combination salad and starch for summer meals, or as part of a buffet.

8 cups (8 servings)

1 cup uncooked quinoa
2 cups Homemade Chicken Broth
     (page 101) or canned reduced-
     sodium chicken broth
2 ripe tomatoes, cored, seeded, and
     chopped
1 large cucumber, peeled and diced
1 cup chopped celery
1 cup packed chopped fresh parsley
1 cup packed chopped fresh mint leaves
1 medium carrot, chopped
4 green onions with green tops,
     chopped
1 clove garlic, minced
$\frac{1}{2}$ cup fresh lemon juice
1 tablespoon plus 1 teaspoon extra
     virgin olive oil
$\frac{1}{2}$ teaspoon salt

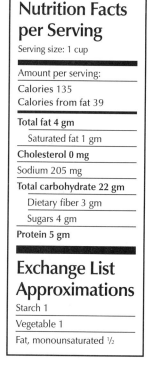

Nutrition Facts per Serving

Serving size: 1 cup

Amount per serving:

Calories 135
Calories from fat 39

Total fat 4 gm
   Saturated fat 1 gm

Cholesterol 0 mg

Sodium 205 mg

Total carbohydrate 22 gm
   Dietary fiber 3 gm
   Sugars 4 gm

Protein 5 gm

Exchange List Approximations

Starch 1

Vegetable 1

Fat, monounsaturated $\frac{1}{2}$

1. Rinse the quinoa in a medium strainer; drain. Place in a 2-quart saucepan with the chicken stock and bring to a boil. Reduce the heat, cover, and simmer for 10 to 15 minutes, or until all the water is absorbed.

2. Transfer the quinoa to a large bowl. Add the tomatoes, cucumber, celery, parsley, mint, carrots, green onions, and garlic.

3. Sprinkle the lemon juice, olive oil, and salt over the salad. Mix to combine the flavors. Chill 1 hour before serving.

BARLEY SALAD

Barley, a fat, chewy, rather bland grain, has a long history as human food. It was brought to the Americas by the Colonists, who fermented it and used it for beer as well as a starch. Like many other mild-tasting grains, barley tends to absorb flavors from other ingredients. In this salad, it is part of a delicious melange of vegetables and herbs; the salad can be used as an appetizer or to accompany grilled meats.

4 cups (6 servings)

½ cup quick-cooking pearl barley
¼ teaspoon salt
1 cup (4 ounces) sliced fresh
    mushrooms
1 medium carrot, thinly sliced
1 medium zucchini or yellow squash,
    thinly sliced
2 green onions with green tops, thinly
    sliced
3 tablespoons chopped fresh parsley
3 fresh basil leaves, chopped,
    or 1 teaspoon dried basil
3 tablespoons fresh lemon juice
2 tablespoons canola or corn oil
1 clove garlic, minced
¼ teaspoon salt
⅛ teaspoon freshly ground pepper

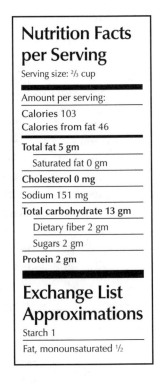

**Nutrition Facts
per Serving**

Serving size: ⅔ cup

Amount per serving:

Calories 103
Calories from fat 46

Total fat 5 gm
  Saturated fat 0 gm

Cholesterol 0 mg

Sodium 151 mg

Total carbohydrate 13 gm
  Dietary fiber 2 gm
  Sugars 2 gm

Protein 2 gm

**Exchange List
Approximations**

Starch 1

Fat, monounsaturated ½

1.   Bring 1½ cups water to a boil in a medium saucepan. Add the barley and salt; stir. Cover, lower the heat, and simmer until tender, about 10 minutes. Drain and chill in a large bowl.

2.   Add the vegetables to the chilled barley; stir to mix.

3.   In a small bowl, whisk together the lemon juice, oil, and garlic. Add to the salad. Toss lightly to coat all the ingredients. Season the salad with salt and pepper and mix well.

4.   Chill at least 3 hours or overnight. This salad will keep well in the refrigerator for several days.

BAY AREA RICE SALAD

Nestled in lettuce leaves or served over a bed of mixed greens, this salad makes an elegant first course. It combines the distinctive flavor of smoked shellfish with the equally clear textures and colors of the grains and vegetables. Smoked mussels or bay scallops, packed in plastic containers, are available in fish stores or in gourmet specialty food shops. Canned smoked mussels, packed in oil, can be bought in most supermarkets (remember to drain off the oil before using the mussels in this recipe). If you prefer, poached mussels or bay scallops can be substituted.

6 cups (8 servings)

2 cups chilled cooked white rice
1 cup chilled cooked wild rice
6 ounces smoked mussels or smoked
      bay scallops
½ cup diced red bell pepper
½ cup diced yellow or green bell
      pepper
1 cup diced peeled cucumber
3 tablespoons light mayonnaise
3 tablespoons light sour cream
1 tablespoon chopped fresh dill,
      or 1 teaspoon dried dill weed
1 tablespoon fresh lemon juice
¼ teaspoon freshly ground pepper

1.   Combine the rices, mussels, peppers, and cucumber in a large bowl.
2.   In a small bowl, combine the remaining ingredients; mix well. Toss with the rice mixture. Serve immediately or chill. Serve at room temperature.

Nutrition Facts per Serving
Serving size: ¾ cup
Amount per serving:
Calories 159
Calories from fat 42
Total fat 5 gm
Saturated fat 1 gm
Cholesterol 27 mg
Sodium 114 mg
Total carbohydrate 22 gm
Dietary fiber 1 gm
Sugars 2 gm
Protein 7 gm

Exchange List Approximations

Starch 1
Vegetable 1
Fat 1

TABBOULEH (CRACKED WHEAT SALAD)

Tabbouleh has as many variations as it does spellings, but the basic ingredients—soaked bulgur, lots of finely chopped herbs, and diced tomato—appear in every version. Depending on what's fresh in the market and what you have on your pantry shelves, you can use extra virgin olive oil (as they would in the Middle East) instead of canola or corn oil, add peeled, chopped cucumber, substitute chopped fresh mint for some of the parsley (do not use dried mint, as it tends to overwhelm the balance of flavors), or add chopped garlic. Tabbouleh will keep for 2 days in the refrigerator; after that the flavor and texture of the tomatoes begins to wilt. In Mediterranean countries, tabbouleh is served with small helpings of other appetizers: canned *mezze* such as stuffed grape leaves, Hummus (page 96), cucumber and yogurt salad, and pita bread. It is also delicious served with grilled lamb.

3 cups (6 servings)

¹/₂ cup finely cut bulgur
1 cup finely chopped fresh parsley
¹/₂ cup chopped onion
1 fresh tomato, cored, seeded, and
  chopped
3 tablespoons fresh lemon juice
3 tablespoons canola or corn oil
¹/₂ teaspoon salt
¹/₄ teaspoon freshly ground pepper

1. Soak the bulgur in 1 cup water for ¹/₂ hour. Drain well.
2. Place the bulgur in a large bowl and add the vegetables; mix well.
3. Combine the lemon juice, oil, salt, and pepper. Add to the salad; toss lightly to coat the ingredients. Refrigerate for at least 8 hours before serving.

Nutrition Facts per Serving
Serving size: ¹/₂ cup
Amount per serving:
Calories 122
Calories from fat 66
Total fat 7 gm
Saturated fat 1 gm
Cholesterol 0 mg
Sodium 206 mg
Total carbohydrate 13 gm
Dietary fiber 3 gm
Sugars 2 gm
Protein 2 gm

Exchange List Approximations

Starch 1

Fat, monounsaturated 1

GREEK CHICK-PEA SALAD

A good source of protein, fiber, and iron, chick-peas are a staple food throughout most of the Western world. Here, these crunchy, nutty legumes appear in a version of Greek salad, a pretty combination of red and green vegetables and white feta cheese. You might want to add some black Greek or Moroccan olives (add the correct exchange) and serve as a first course over lettuce. This salad will keep nicely in the refrigerator for up to two days.

3 cups (6 servings)

One 15-ounce can chick-peas (garbanzo
    beans), rinsed and drained
1 small tomato, seeded and chopped
½ cup diced peeled cucumber
2 green onions with green tops, sliced
¼ cup coarsely chopped Italian parsley
2 tablespoons red wine vinegar
2 tablespoons extra virgin olive oil
¼ cup (1 ounce) crumbled feta cheese
¼ teaspoon freshly ground pepper

1.   Combine the chick-peas, tomato, cucumber, onions, and parsley in a medium bowl.
2.   In a small bowl, whisk together the vinegar and oil; pour over the bean mixture and toss well to mix. Just before serving, sprinkle the salad with cheese and pepper.

Nutrition Facts per Serving

Serving size: ½ cup

Amount per serving:

Calories 132
Calories from fat 60

Total fat 7 gm
   Saturated fat 1 gm

Cholesterol 4 mg

Sodium 120 mg

Total carbohydrate 14 gm
   Dietary fiber 3 gm
   Sugars 3 gm

Protein 5 gm

Exchange List Approximations

Starch 1

Fat, monounsaturated 1

THREE-BEAN SALAD

In the world of portable food, is there a potluck dinner or a quickly organized picnic that's complete without a three-bean salad anointed with its characteristic slightly sweetened vinaigrette? Cooked or canned soy beans, navy beans, black-eyed peas, or limas may be substituted for the chick-peas. For a Mexican salad, omit the oregano and add 1 tablespoon of picante sauce.

3 cups (6 servings)

1 cup cut green beans, drained
     (about ½ of a 16-ounce can)
¾ cup red kidney or pinto beans,
     drained (about ½ of a
     15-ounce can)
¾ cup chick-peas (garbanzo beans),
     drained (about ½ of a
     15-ounce can)
¼ cup finely chopped onion
¼ cup chopped green bell pepper
3 tablespoons vinegar
1 tablespoon canola or corn oil
2 teaspoons sugar
1 clove garlic, minced
½ teaspoon dried oregano

1. Combine the drained beans, onion, and green pepper in a large bowl.
2. In a small bowl, whisk together ¼ cup water, the vinegar, oil, sugar, garlic, and oregano. Pour over the beans. Toss to mix.
3. Cover and chill at least 2 hours before serving.

Nutrition Facts per Serving
Serving size: ½ cup
Amount per serving:
Calories 98
Calories from fat 27
Total fat 3 gm
Saturated fat 0 gm
Cholesterol 0 mg
Sodium 124 mg
Total carbohydrate 15 gm
Dietary fiber 3 gm
Sugars 4 gm
Protein 4 gm

Exchange List Approximations

Starch 1

Fat, monounsaturated ½

HERRING SUPREME

This versatile salad, a marriage of tart and sweet flavors and tender and crunchy textures, can be arranged in a pretty glass bowl and served in a variety of ways: You can make it as an appetizer or cocktail party tidbit accompanied by crackers or cocktail rye bread, or as part of a Sunday brunch buffet served with toasted bagels or pumpernickel bread, or you can double the portions and use the salad as an entrée. If you double the recipe, be sure to double the exchange values or carbohydrate counts, too.

4 cups (8 servings)

One 12-ounce jar herring in wine sauce, rinsed, drained, and cut into bite-size pieces
$\frac{1}{2}$ cup light sour cream
$\frac{1}{4}$ cup fat-free mayonnaise
2 medium carrots, peeled and shredded
1 medium green bell pepper, cored, seeded, and diced
1 medium apple, peeled, cored, and diced
$\frac{3}{4}$ cup chopped onion
1 tablespoon fresh lemon juice
2 teaspoons sugar
1 teaspoon celery seed

1. Combine all the ingredients in a large bowl.
2. If time permits, chill several hours before serving.

Nutrition Facts per Serving
Serving size: ½ cup
Amount per serving:
Calories 111
Calories from fat 35
Total fat 4 gm
Saturated fat 1 gm
Cholesterol 21 mg
Sodium 244 mg
Total carbohydrate 15 gm
Dietary fiber 2 gm
Sugars 11 gm
Protein 4 gm

Exchange List Approximations

Starch 1

Fat, monounsaturated ½

TUNA NOODLE SALAD

Here's an upscale dinner-party version of that old favorite tuna noodle casserole. The flavor and texture will be vastly enhanced if you use pasta that is just *al dente* and grilled fresh tuna—perhaps a preplanned leftover from the night before. An easily portable dish, it can serve 6 as a light luncheon entrée or 4 as a main course, or you can use it as one of several salads for the buffet table.

6 cups (6 servings)

SALAD

1 cup broccoli florets
3 cups cooked pasta (5 ounces dry
        pasta), wagon wheels or any
        small pasta shape
1/2 pound fresh tuna, broiled, cooled, and
        cubed, or one 6½-ounce can
        water-packed tuna
1 medium zucchini, peeled and diced
1/2 cup diced red or green bell pepper
1/2 cup thinly sliced carrot
1/3 cup chopped red onion
1/4 cup drained, sliced sweet gherkin
        pickles

DRESSING

1/3 cup light mayonnaise
1/4 cup light sour cream
1½ teaspoons dried tarragon
3/4 teaspoon salt
1 tablespoon snipped fresh chervil, or
        ½ teaspoon dried chervil
        (optional)
1/4 teaspoon freshly ground pepper

Nutrition Facts per Serving
Serving size: 1 cup
Amount per serving:
Calories 213
Calories from fat 65
Total fat 7 gm
Saturated fat 2 gm
Cholesterol 23 mg
Sodium 549 mg
Total carbohydrate 23 gm
Dietary fiber 2 gm
Sugars 6 gm
Protein 13 gm

Exchange List Approximations
Starch 1
Vegetable 2
Meat, lean 1
Fat ½

1.   Blanch the broccoli florets in a pot of boiling water for 2 minutes, then plunge the drained broccoli into a bowl of ice water. (This shocks the broccoli so that it is crisp-tender but retains its bright green color.)
2.   Combine the drained broccoli and all the other salad ingredients in a large bowl. Toss to mix.
3.   In a small bowl, combine the dressing ingredients; add to the salad and toss. Serve the salad at room temperature.

TUNA NIÇOISE

This is an American version of the classic salad of Provence. Be sure to use a fruity extra virgin olive oil for the vinaigrette, and sprinkle the finished salad with small, oil-cured olives (no need to pit them) for an even prettier look. (Eight olives equal 1 fat exchange.)

4½ cups (6 servings)

One 6½-ounce can water-packed tuna,
    drained and flaked
1 medium potato (5 ounces), cooked,
    peeled, and cut into wedges
1 cup sliced mushrooms
One 9-ounce package thawed frozen
    whole green beans, or 12 ounces
    fresh green beans, blanched
    (see Note)
⅓ cup Basic Vinaigrette (page 175), or
    prepared light Italian dressing
6 leaves leaf lettuce
1 large hard-cooked egg, peeled and sliced
2 teaspoons drained capers

Nutrition Facts per Serving
Serving size: ¾ cup
Amount per serving:
Calories 148
Calories from fat 82
Total fat 9 gm
Saturated fat 1 gm
Cholesterol 44 mg
Sodium 195 mg
Total carbohydrate 8 gm
Dietary fiber 2 gm
Sugars 2 gm
Protein 9 gm

Exchange List Approximations

Starch ½
Meat, lean 1
Fat, monounsaturated 1

1. Combine the tuna, potato, mushrooms, and green beans in a large bowl.

2. Gently toss the dressing with the tuna mixture. Chill.

3. Line a pretty glass bowl with lettuce leaves; add the tuna mixture and garnish the top with egg slices and capers.

Note: To blanch beans, snap off the stem end and put the trimmed beans in a large pot of boiling water for 1 minute. Drain and plunge them into a bowl of ice water. This shocks the beans so that they are crisp-tender but retain their bright green color.

TUSCAN TUNA AND WHITE BEAN SALAD

There's no better reason to keep your pantry stocked with canned water-packed tuna and cannellini or navy beans than this satisfying, fiber-rich Italian salad, which can be prepared in less than 10 minutes. Although commercially prepared dressing is perfectly acceptable, vinaigrette made with a fruity olive oil and a good red wine vinegar will taste even better. Sprinkle the top of the salad with chopped flat parsley for a fresh, bright green color contrast.

3 cups (6 servings)

One 6½-ounce can water-packed tuna,
    drained and flaked
One 19-ounce can cannellini, or any
    cooked white beans, rinsed and
    drained (about 2 cups)
⅓ cup thinly sliced red onion rings
2 tablespoons chopped green bell pepper
¼ teaspoon freshly ground pepper
⅓ cup prepared light Italian dressing,
    or Basic Vinaigrette (page 175)

1.   Combine the tuna, beans, onion, green pepper, and ground pepper.
2.   Mix in the dressing and toss to combine. Chill before serving.

Nutrition Facts per Serving	
Serving size: ½ cup	
Amount per serving:	
Calories 129	
Calories from fat 9	
Total fat 1 gm	
Saturated fat 0 gm	
Cholesterol 8 mg	
Sodium 395 mg	
Total carbohydrate 18 gm	
Dietary fiber 3 gm	
Sugars 2 gm	
Protein 12 gm	

Exchange List Approximations

Starch 1	
Meat, very lean 1	

PACIFIC NORTHWEST SALMON SALAD

This is a beautiful salad—green, pink, white, and red—and it takes only minutes to prepare if you have leftover cooked rice on hand. Serve the salad as a main course on a bed of mixed wild greens with a basket of warm country bread.

4 cups (4 servings)

2 cups cooked white rice
8 ounces cooked salmon or canned*
    salmon, flaked
4 green onions with green tops, sliced
½ cup diced red bell pepper
¾ cup thawed frozen peas

DRESSING

½ cup plain low-fat yogurt
2 tablespoons fat-free mayonnaise
1 tablespoon chopped fresh dill, or
    1 teaspoon dried dillweed
4 to 6 dashes hot pepper sauce
1 teaspoon fresh lemon juice
¼ teaspoon salt
⅛ teaspoon freshly ground pepper

1.   In a large bowl, combine the rice, salmon, onions, red pepper, and peas.
2.   In another bowl, mix all the ingredients for the dressing. Add the dressing to the salmon mixture; toss to blend. Chill before serving.

Nutrition Facts per Serving

Serving size: 1 cup

Amount per serving:

Calories 284
Calories from fat 63

Total fat 7 gm
   Saturated fat 1 gm
Cholesterol 52 mg
Sodium 292 mg*
Total carbohydrate 32 gm
   Dietary fiber 3 gm
   Sugars 5 gm
Protein 21 gm

Exchange List Approximations

Starch 2
Meat, lean 2

* *If canned salmon is used, sodium is **532 mg** per serving.*

CURRIED CHICKEN SALAD

Leftover cooked chicken or turkey, crisp apple, and crunchy shredded carrot appear to good advantage in this tangy salad, which is moistened with a creamy, mildly spiced curried dressing. Serve the salad over greens as a first course, or use it to fill whole wheat pita pockets for a delicious sandwich.

2 cups (4 servings)

3 tablespoons chopped prepared mango
      chutney
2 tablespoons plain low-fat yogurt
2 tablespoons light sour cream
1 teaspoon curry powder
2 cups (8 ounces) diced cooked chicken
1 peeled tart medium apple, cored
      and diced
½ cup shredded carrot

1. Combine the chutney, yogurt, sour cream, and curry powder in a medium bowl.
2. Add the chicken, apple, and carrot; mix well.
3. Cover and chill at least 1 hour before serving for the flavors to blend.

Nutrition Facts per Serving

Serving size: ½ cup

Amount per serving:

Calories 180
Calories from fat 46

Total fat 5 gm
    Saturated fat 2 gm
Cholesterol 53 mg
Sodium 87 mg
Total carbohydrate 16 gm
    Dietary fiber 2 gm
    Sugars 15 gm
Protein 17 gm

Exchange List Approximations

Starch 1
Meat, very lean 2
Fat ½

WARM CHICKEN SALAD

Leftover cooked chicken is transformed into a tasty luncheon or light supper dish that's a variation on an old favorite, tuna surprise. Accompany this salad with a tossed salad and some good whole-grain bread, and follow with a fruit dessert.

4½ cups (6 servings)

2 cups diced cooked chicken (8 ounces)
2 cups chopped celery
⅓ cup light mayonnaise
¼ cup slivered almonds
2 tablespoons fresh lemon juice
¼ cup chopped green bell pepper
¼ cup finely chopped onion
2 tablespoons chopped pimiento
½ teaspoon salt
¼ teaspoon freshly ground pepper
¼ cup (about 1 ounce) grated or
     shredded Swiss cheese
2 cups (2 ounces) fat-free or reduced-fat
     potato chips, coarsely crushed

1. Preheat the oven to 350°F. Spray a 2-quart casserole with nonstick pan spray.
2. Mix all the ingredients except the cheese and potato chips in a large bowl. Turn into the casserole. Top with the cheese and crushed potato chips.
3. Bake about 25 minutes, until the cheese is melted and the salad is hot.

Nutrition Facts per Serving

Serving size: ¾ cup

Amount per serving:

Calories 212
Calories from fat 96

Total fat 11 gm
  Saturated fat 2 gm
Cholesterol 43 mg
Sodium 439 mg
Total carbohydrate 13 gm
  Dietary fiber 2 gm
  Sugars 2 gm
Protein 15 gm

Exchange List Approximations

Starch ½
Vegetable 1
Meat, medium-fat 2

BLUE CHEESE DRESSING

Use this calcium-rich dressing over mixed greens or spinach leaves, or as a creamy contrast to chunked chicken and apple salad. A moderately priced blue cheese will provide excellent flavor.

1¼ cups (10 servings)

¾ cup low-fat cottage cheese
⅓ cup low-fat (1 percent fat) buttermilk,
    or water
2 tablespoons fresh lemon juice
1 tablespoon chopped onion
2 ounces blue cheese, crumbled
¼ teaspoon salt
⅛ teaspoon freshly ground pepper

1. Put the cottage cheese, buttermilk or water, lemon juice, and onion in a blender or food processor. Blend until smooth and creamy.

2. Add the blue cheese, salt, and pepper; blend a few seconds to combine the ingredients but leave some cheese chunks. Cover and chill. The dressing will keep about 5 days. Shake or stir before serving.

Nutrition Facts per Serving

Serving size: 2 tablespoons

Amount per serving:

Calories 36
Calories from fat 17

Total fat 2 gm
  Saturated fat 1 gm
Cholesterol 5 mg
Sodium 215 mg
Total carbohydrate 1 gm
  Dietary fiber 0 gm
  Sugars 1 gm
Protein 4 gm

Exchange List Approximation

Fat, saturated ½

YOGURT-DILL DRESSING

A mild, low-calorie complement to mixed greens.

1 cup (8 servings)

One 8-ounce carton plain low-fat yogurt
1 tablespoon very finely chopped onion
2 teaspoons fresh lemon juice
1 tablespoon chopped fresh dill, or
            ½ teaspoon dried dill weed
½ teaspoon dry mustard
1 small clove garlic, finely minced
½ teaspoon seasoned salt
Dash of freshly ground pepper

1.   Mix all the ingredients thoroughly.
2.   Chill at least 2 hours to allow the flavors
to blend.

Nutrition Facts per Serving

Serving size: 2 tablespoons

Amount per serving:

Calories 19
Calories from fat 4

Total fat 0 gm
    Saturated fat 0 gm
Cholesterol 2 mg
Sodium 116 mg
Total carbohydrate 2 gm
    Dietary fiber 0 gm
    Sugars 2 gm
Protein 2 gm

Exchange List Approximation

Free food

BASIC VINAIGRETTE

If possible, buy several kinds of wine vinegar in the smallest amounts available so that you can taste and experiment with them to see which kinds suit your palate and pocketbook best. The same is even truer for olive oil, which, unlike vinegar, does not keep forever.

This vinaigrette lends itself to an infinite number of variations, depending on how you plan to use it and what flavorings you want to add or subtract: chopped fresh herbs of the widest possible variety, dried herbs, flavored vinegars or oils, prepared mustard in numerous flavorings, and hot sauce, among others. An alternative and very easy way to prepare the dressing, especially successful for vinaigrette made with prepared mustard, is to place all the ingredients in a small, clean glass jar with a tight-fitting lid, cover the jar, and shake vigorously until the dressing is creamy and emulsified. Store the vinaigrette in the refrigerator.

¾ cup (6 servings)

¼ cup red wine vinegar
1 small clove garlic, minced
½ teaspoon dry mustard
½ teaspoon salt
¼ teaspoon freshly ground pepper
½ cup olive oil (preferably extra
     virgin oil)

1.   Combine all the ingredients except the oil in a medium bowl or food processor.
2.   With the processor on or while whisking, slowly add the oil, mixing until thickened. This dressing will keep 1 to 2 weeks in the refrigerator. Shake or whisk before using to recombine the oil and vinegar.

Nutrition Facts per Serving
Serving size: 2 tablespoons
Amount per serving:
Calories 162
Calories from fat 162
Total fat 18 gm
Saturated fat 2 gm
Cholesterol 0 mg
Sodium 199 mg
Total carbohydrate 1 gm
Dietary fiber 0 gm
Sugars 1 gm
Protein 0 gm

Exchange List Approximation

Fat, monounsaturated 3½

BALSAMIC VINAIGRETTE

Balsamic vinegar has been produced for at least a thousand years in Modena, Italy. It is made from the unfermented juice, or must, of Trebbiano grapes, to which a very small amount of mature vinegar is added. This combination is aged in a succession of casks made of different woods, a process which, especially for the more rarefied and expensive balsamic vinegars, can take up to 100 years! But for most balsamics found in supermarkets or even in fancy food markets, the procedure has been speeded up somewhat, resulting in a much more affordable but still quite delicious vinegar with a flavor that is rich and intense, with a touch of sweetness and a color that ranges from dark brown to almost black.

White balsamic vinegar, made from aged white vinegar and the must of white grapes, is a recent addition to the vinegar shelf. It is a pale amber color with a light, faintly sweet flavor that works well combined with other vinegars, and you might want to substitute a tablespoon of it for the dark balsamic vinegar in this recipe. Balsamic vinaigrette is especially good on salads made from mixed greens, and on grilled chicken or fresh tuna.

1 cup (8 servings)

¹/₃ cup balsamic vinegar
1 large clove garlic, finely minced
¹/₂ teaspoon salt (optional)*
¹/₄ teaspoon freshly ground pepper
¹/₂ cup extra virgin olive oil

1.   Combine the vinegar, 2 tablespoons water, the garlic, salt (if desired), and pepper.
2.   Whisk in the oil. The dressing will keep, refrigerated, for 2 weeks. Shake or whisk before using to recombine the oil and vinegar.

Nutrition Facts per Serving

Serving size: 2 tablespoons

Amount per serving:

Calories 121
Calories from fat 122

Total fat 14 gm
  Saturated fat 2 gm

Cholesterol 0 mg

Sodium 0 mg*

Total carbohydrate 1 gm
  Dietary fiber 0 gm
  Sugars 1 gm

Protein 0 gm

Exchange List Approximation

Fat, monounsaturated 2¹/₂

* *If optional salt is added, sodium is 146 mg per serving.*

GARLIC-BUTTERMILK DRESSING

This pleasantly tart dressing is most suitable for green salads and keeps well in the refrigerator for up to a week. To make an herbed dressing, add 1 tablespoon of chopped fresh tarragon, dill, thyme, rosemary, oregano, basil, or parsley. These additions do not affect nutrient content or exchange values.

¾ cup (6 servings)

½ cup low-fat (1 percent fat) buttermilk
¼ cup olive oil
1 large clove garlic, minced
¼ teaspoon freshly ground pepper
¼ teaspoon salt

1. Whisk together all the ingredients, or combine them in a food processor or blender.
2. Cover and refrigerate for at least 2 hours for the flavors to blend.

Nutrition Facts per Serving

Serving size: 2 tablespoons

Amount per serving:

Calories 89
Calories from fat 83

Total fat 9 gm
  Saturated fat 1 gm
Cholesterol 1 mg
Sodium 118 mg
Total carbohydrate 1 gm
  Dietary fiber 0 gm
  Sugars 1 gm
Protein 1 gm

Exchange List Approximation

Fat, monounsaturated 2

THOUSAND ISLAND DRESSING

This mayonnaise-based dressing, similar to the Louis dressing on page 32, works well with crabmeat or shrimp but tends to overwhelm the more delicate flavor and texture of greens.

³/₄ cup (6 servings)

½ cup light or low-fat mayonnaise
¼ cup chili sauce
1 tablespoon sweet pickle relish
¼ teaspoon hot pepper sauce

1.   Combine all the ingredients.
2.   Chill until ready to serve. The dressing will keep up to 5 days in the refrigerator.

Nutrition Facts per Serving

Serving size: 2 tablespoons

Amount per serving:

Calories 81
Calories from fat 55

Total fat 6 gm
  Saturated fat 1 gm
Cholesterol 8 mg
Sodium 305 mg
Total carbohydrate 4 gm
  Dietary fiber 0 gm
  Sugars 3 gm
Protein 0 gm

Exchange List Approximations

Starch ½
Fat, polyunsaturated 1

6

MEAT

Americans have always been meat lovers, but in today's health-conscious climate, many people have given up eating meat in an effort to improve health and reduce fat and cholesterol.

While meat *is* a source of fat (particularly saturated fat) and cholesterol, the good news is that you don't need to eliminate it in order to eat healthfully. It's simply a matter of moderation. Meat contributes important nutrients, such as protein, B vitamins, iron, and zinc, that are often difficult to get from other foods. The trick is to balance the positive nutritional benefits of meat while limiting its negative nutritional attributes.

This is actually quite easy to do. The Exchange Lists for Meal Planning divide meat and meat substitutes into four categories: Very Lean Meat and Substitutes, Lean Meat and Substitutes, Medium-Fat Meat and Substitutes, and High-Fat Meat and Substitutes (see Appendix, page 496). Select lean or extra-lean cuts of beef, pork, or lamb whenever possible. Veal and game meats are naturally very lean. Know the terms that indicate a cut of meat is lean. Specific examples of lean cuts for the different types of meat are detailed below. Nutrition information on fresh meat can also be found on Nutrifacts posters located at the meat counters in many supermarkets.

Another important way to decrease fat is to trim any visible fat from the meat before cooking. Even lean meats will have some fat on them. By trimming fat, you can reduce total fat and saturated fat content by an average of over 50 percent and remove some but not all the cholesterol, because cholesterol is in both the lean tissue and fat in meat. Marbling, the white streaks of fat that run throughout meat, can't be trimmed away, but leaner cuts of meat have less marbling to begin with, so they are the best choices if you're trying to eat less fat and saturated fat.

Using low-fat cooking methods to maximize flavor and keep added fat to a minimum is another key step in eating lean. In general, for very lean cuts of meat such as beef eye of round or top round steak, low-fat moist-heat methods like stewing, braising, and poaching are preferred to help keep meat tender. However, some lean cuts of meat, including sirloin or flank steak, or more expensive cuts like filet mignon or tenderloin, get tough if moist-heat methods are used. Dry-heat cooking methods—such as roasting, broiling, grilling, stir-frying, or pan broiling—are best for these cuts. If dry-heat methods are used, a marinade will often help tenderize the meat. Roasting and grilling are great cooking methods because they drain fat away from the meat as it cooks. Remember to place the meat on a rack when roasting so the excess fat can drip off as the meat cooks. If you brown ground meat to use in tacos or spaghetti sauce, use a nonstick spray and a nonstick pan, and drain the meat on paper towels after browning before adding it to sauces or seasoning it.

Managing portion size is probably the most important thing you can do to decrease fat intake from meat. Health experts recommend no more than 5 to 7 ounces per day of foods from the meat, fish, poultry, dried beans, eggs, and nuts group. Yet many people often consume double this amount. A serving size is typically considered to be 3 or 4 ounces, which is about the same size as a deck of cards. In some of the recipes we've included, meat is used more as an ingredient than as the main item in the dish, such as stews. As a general rule of thumb, 4 ounces of raw meat is equal to about 3 ounces of cooked. Weigh your meat portion after cooking and removing bones and fat.

BEEF

There are many lean cuts of beef that compare favorably with the fat, calorie, and cholesterol content of skinless chicken. It's just a matter of knowing which ones to choose, such as eye of round or top round steak.

Beef is graded as select, choice, or prime. The select grade has the least amount of fat. Choice grades contain a moderate amount of fat, and prime cuts of meat have the highest amount of fat and the most marbling. Marbled fat helps keep meat juicy and flavorful, but even lean cuts that have less fat can stay juicy, tender, and flavorful if you use proper cooking and preparation methods.

In addition to choosing the select grade of beef most often, it's also important to choose lean cuts. The word *loin* or *round* in the name signals a leaner cut. Examples include eye of *round,* top *round* steak, top *round* roast, and *sirloin* steak.

When shopping for ground beef, look for packages that have a greater percentage of lean than fat. Different stores may use different terms to signal lean or very lean ground beef, but in general, ground round is the leanest, followed by ground sirloin, ground chuck, and regular ground beef.

Try New Mexico Green Chili with Beef, Steak Fajitas, or Russian Beef and Cabbage Stew when you have a hankering for the taste of beef.

VEAL

Veal has little fat and no visible marbling, so most cuts are considered lean. To enhance its delicate flavor and keep it from drying out, veal should be cooked slowly, generally using moist-heat cooking methods. A leg or loin of veal can be oven-roasted, but because it doesn't have a lot of fat, it must be basted frequently with a liquid like stock or a small amount of fat when cooking or it becomes tough and dry. Veal uses the same grading system as beef, except that the term *good* is used instead of *select* for the grade with the least amount of fat.

Veal Scallops with Lemon, Roast Brisket of Veal with Onion Gravy, and Veal Roast are three recipes included in this chapter.

PORK

The average fat and cholesterol content of trimmed lean pork is almost one-third lower today than it was twenty years ago. As a general rule, cuts that have the word *loin* or *leg* in their name (such as pork tenderloin, top *loin* roast, or *loin* rib chop) are lean.

Be careful not to overcook pork, or it becomes tough and dry. The worry over trichinosis, an illness caused by a type of foodborne parasite, is no longer a concern, thanks to modern methods of raising pigs that have virtually eliminated it, so pork need only be cooked to the medium-done stage, or 160°F.

Scandinavian Pork with Prunes, Pacific Rim Omelet Rolls, Pork

Chops Paprikash, and Herb-Roasted Pork Tenderloin showcase pork's wonderful taste and prove lean can be delicious!

LAMB

Many cuts of lamb are considered lean. As in pork, the terms *loin* and *leg* indicate that it is a lean cut. Examples include *leg* of lamb and *loin* chop.

The simpler the preparation, the better lamb tastes. The choicest, most tender lamb on the market is called spring lamb, which used to be available only from March through September. Now spring lamb is available just about year-round, since it is imported from Australia and New Zealand during our winter months.

Try Curried Lamb on Rice, Minted Lamb Kebabs, or Roast Spring Lamb for a real taste treat.

GAME MEATS

Game meats such as venison and buffalo are quite lean and can be enjoyed in many of your favorite recipes. Because these meats are so low in fat, moist-heat cooking methods are preferred to help keep them tender. If dry heat is used, game meats are often barded, or covered, with a small amount of fat (such as bacon) to prevent them from getting too dry.

Grilled Venison Steaks, Hearty Yukon Stew, and Venison with Pan-Roasted Vegetables are wonderful recipes that highlight the great taste of game meats.

PREPARATION AND COOKING

Leaner cuts of meat are often less tender than fattier cuts that have a lot of marbling. To help tenderize leaner meats and add flavor, try a marinade that has little or no fat in it. Orange, lemon, or lime juice; defatted broth; tomato juice; wine; and vinegars are all fat-free, acidic ingredients that help to tenderize meat. One word of caution: acid ingredients can react with metal containers and leach metal into the food, so marinate in a glass or nonmetallic dish—or even in a large plastic bag with a zip seal, to help make cleanup a snap. Scoring the meat before placing it in a marinade also helps the marinade penetrate the meat more quickly.

Seasoning meats with herbs and spices (other than salt) is another great way to boost flavor and cut back on fat and salt at the same time. Experiment with different seasonings and dry rubs on roasts and steaks. You'll find a number of great recipes that use rubs in this chapter.

FOOD SAFETY

Food safety is a particular concern with meats. Follow these tips to help prevent foodborne illness and keep mealtime safe for you and your family.

Thaw meat in the refrigerator, never on the counter. Bacteria thrive at room temperature, so place the meat on a plate or in a plastic bag (to collect any juices and moisture) on the lowest shelf in the refrigerator. Or place the meat in a microwave-safe container and defrost on the low or defrost setting in your microwave oven, then use it right away. Be careful not to splatter any raw juices on counters and utensils.

Use separate cutting boards, plates, trays, and utensils for cooked and uncooked meat. For example, don't carry the cooked meat to the table in the same dish you used to carry the raw meat to the grill. And don't use the same knife or cutting board to slice raw meat and then chop vegetables unless you clean it thoroughly in between. Wash hands thoroughly before and after every step in preparing foods, especially when moving from raw to cooked foods.

Don't use marinades that have been in contact with raw meat as a sauce for cooked meat unless you boil them first for at least 1 full minute. Or even better, make a double batch of the marinade and use half for marinating the meat, reserving the other half as a sauce at serving. If you decide to use a marinade as a sauce, remember to count in the appropriate exchange.

Cook meat, especially ground meat, thoroughly. Use a meat or instant-read thermometer to check internal temperatures. *E. coli,* a bacteria that can cause life-threatening health problems, can be found in ground meat and other foods. To combat *E. coli,* cook and reheat ground meats to at least 160°F and wash anything that comes into contact with raw ground beef, including cutting surfaces, utensils, plates, and your hands. Ground beef, pork, and ham should be cooked to at least 160°F. Steaks and roasts should be cooked to a minimum of 145°F.

NEW MEXICO GREEN CHILI WITH BEEF

Nothing satisfies the appetite like a piping hot bowl of chili, and this Southwestern rendition is no exception. Robust with zucchini, tomatoes, and chunks of beef, and spiced up with green chiles, it's a sure-fire crowd-pleaser.

About 6 cups (6 servings)

1 pound lean beef, cubed
1 cup chopped onion
2 cloves garlic, minced
One 7-ounce can green chiles
4 medium zucchini, quartered and sliced
One 14- to 15-ounce can diced tomatoes,
    with juice
½ cup (2 ounces) reduced-fat shredded
    Monterey Jack/Colby cheese
    blend

1. Prepare a large skillet with nonstick pan spray.
2. Sauté the beef until lightly browned; add the onion and garlic. Cook 5 minutes. Add chiles and the liquid from the can, and the zucchini; cook 5 minutes. Add the tomatoes with liquid; heat to a simmer. The mixture should be soupy. Add up to ½ cup water if needed.
3. Serve in soup bowls, with 1½ tablespoons of shredded cheese on top of each serving.

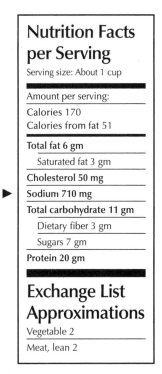

Nutrition Facts per Serving

Serving size: About 1 cup

Amount per serving:

Calories 170
Calories from fat 51

Total fat 6 gm
  Saturated fat 3 gm
Cholesterol 50 mg
Sodium 710 mg
Total carbohydrate 11 gm
  Dietary fiber 3 gm
  Sugars 7 gm
Protein 20 gm

Exchange List Approximations

Vegetable 2
Meat, lean 2

SWISS STEAK

Swiss steak, sometimes called smothered steak, uses braising—a long, slow cooking process—to help develop the flavor and tenderize the meat. Be sure to use a tight-fitting lid on your skillet to prevent the liquid from evaporating, and add water as needed as the dish simmers.

6 servings

¼ cup all-purpose flour
1 teaspoon salt
¼ teaspoon pepper
A 1½-pound beef round steak, about
        ¾ inch thick
1 tablespoon canola or corn oil
1 large onion, sliced
One 14- to 15-ounce can crushed or
        diced tomatoes, with liquid
1 cup unsalted homemade or canned
        reduced-sodium beef broth
2 cups sliced carrots

Nutrition Facts per Serving
Serving size: ⅙ of recipe
Amount per serving:
Calories 243
Calories from fat 71
Total fat 8 gm
Saturated fat 2 gm
Cholesterol 64 mg
Sodium 748 mg
Total carbohydrate 18 gm
Dietary fiber 4 gm
Sugars 8 gm
Protein 24 gm

Exchange List Approximations

Starch 1

Meat, lean 3

1.   Combine the flour, salt, and pepper in a pie pan. Dredge the steak in the seasoned flour.

2.   With a wooden or metal meat mallet, pound the steak between sheets of wax paper until it is ½ inch thick. Cut the steak into 6 pieces. Dredge the pieces in any remaining flour.

3.   Heat the oil in a large nonstick skillet. Brown the steak well on both sides. Remove from the pan and set aside.

4.   In the same skillet, sauté the onion until tender, about 5 minutes. Add the tomatoes with their liquid, and the broth. Stir to blend.

5.   Add the steak; cover and simmer 1½ hours, adding enough water to braise the meat and keep it moist.

6.   Add the carrots, cover, and simmer 30 minutes longer, or until the meat is fork-tender.

STEAK AU POIVRE

Also known as pepper steak, this recipe is the perfect solution for spur-of-the-moment company. It's simple to make, yet looks extravagant. The individual steaks are covered with cracked peppercorns before being lightly sautéed, giving them a slightly hot yet tantalizingly sweet flavor.

4 servings

Four 4-ounce tenderloin (filet mignon) steaks (1 pound total), well trimmed
2 teaspoons olive oil
1½ teaspoons cracked black peppercorns, or enough to cover both sides of the meat
½ cup dry red wine
½ cup unsalted homemade or canned reduced-sodium beef broth

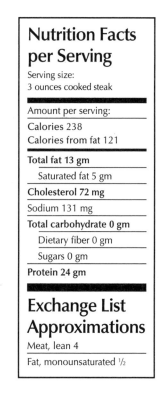

Nutrition Facts per Serving

Serving size:
3 ounces cooked steak

Amount per serving:

Calories 238
Calories from fat 121

Total fat 13 gm
   Saturated fat 5 gm
Cholesterol 72 mg
Sodium 131 mg
Total carbohydrate 0 gm
   Dietary fiber 0 gm
   Sugars 0 gm
Protein 24 gm

Exchange List Approximations

Meat, lean 4
Fat, monounsaturated ½

1. Heat a large nonstick skillet over medium-high heat until hot, about 3 minutes.
2. Brush the steaks lightly on both sides with oil. Press the peppercorns evenly onto both sides of the steaks.
3. Put the steaks in the hot skillet and sear quickly until the meat is medium-rare, about 3 minutes per side for 1-inch steaks, about 2 minutes per side for ¾-inch steaks.
4. Remove the steaks to a warm platter or 4 plates. Add the wine and broth to the skillet; simmer until the liquid is slightly reduced, about 2 minutes. Pour the sauce over the steaks; serve immediately.

BAKED STUFFED CABBAGE

Here's a traditional Hungarian dish that's sure to become a favorite in your house, if it isn't already. Cabbage leaves are folded around seasoned meat and onions and baked in a rich tomato sauce to create a dish with lots of flavor yet less fat than the traditional version.

8 rolls (4 servings)

8 large green cabbage leaves
1 pound (90 percent lean) ground beef
¼ cup chopped onion
2 tablespoons chopped fresh parsley
¾ teaspoon salt
1 teaspoon chopped fresh thyme, or
        ½ teaspoon dried thyme
1 small clove garlic, minced
Pinch of cayenne pepper
One 8-ounce can tomato sauce

Nutrition Facts per Serving

Serving size: 2 rolls

Amount per serving:

Calories 254
Calories from fat 125

Total fat 14 gm
    Saturated fat 5 gm
Cholesterol 71 mg
Sodium 876 mg
Total carbohydrate 8 gm
    Dietary fiber 2 gm
    Sugars 5 gm
Protein 25 gm

Exchange List Approximations

Vegetable 1

Meat, medium-fat 3

1.   Preheat the oven to 375°F. Prepare a flat baking dish or casserole with nonstick pan spray.
2.   Blanch the cabbage leaves by immersing them in a pot of boiling water for 1 minute. Drain and pat the leaves dry.
3.   Combine the beef, onion, parsley, salt, thyme, garlic, and pepper. Mix well. Divide the meat mixture into 8 equal portions on the cabbage leaves. Roll or fold the leaves around the filling. Secure each cabbage roll with wooden toothpicks.
4.   Place the rolls seam side down in the baking dish. Pour the tomato sauce over the rolls.
5.   Bake, covered, 50 to 60 minutes.

BEEF RAGOUT

Ragout is a French word used to describe a thick, rich, well-seasoned stew. You'll find this version particularly tasty, filled with tender cuts of lean beef, onions, mushrooms, green pepper, and a variety of unexpected spices, including orange zest and cinnamon, that add a subtly sweet flavor. Serve over noodles (½ cup of cooked noodles equals 1 starch exchange) or by itself in a deep bowl.

About 6 cups (8 servings)

1 tablespoon margarine
2 pounds round steak or other lean beef,
    cut in ¾-inch cubes
2 cups chopped onion
5 cloves garlic, minced
2 tablespoons chopped fresh parsley,
    or 2 teaspoons dried parsley
1 tablespoon grated orange zest
1 tablespoon chopped fresh rosemary,
    or 1 teaspoon dried rosemary
2 bay leaves
1 teaspoon cinnamon
½ teaspoon salt
2 cups sliced fresh mushrooms
1 cup sliced green bell pepper

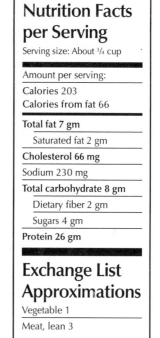

Nutrition Facts per Serving

Serving size: About ¾ cup

Amount per serving:

Calories 203
Calories from fat 66

Total fat 7 gm
  Saturated fat 2 gm
Cholesterol 66 mg
Sodium 230 mg
Total carbohydrate 8 gm
  Dietary fiber 2 gm
  Sugars 4 gm
Protein 26 gm

Exchange List Approximations

Vegetable 1

Meat, lean 3

1. Heat the margarine in a large nonstick skillet. Brown the beef cubes on all sides over high heat; transfer to a large pot or Dutch oven.

2. Lower the heat under the skillet and add the onion and garlic; stir and cook about 5 minutes. Transfer to the large pot.

3. Add ½ cup water, the parsley, orange zest, rosemary, bay leaves, cinnamon, and salt to the large pot.

4. Cover and simmer 1½ hours, or until the meat is tender. Add water if the mixture becomes dry. Remove the bay leaves.

5. Add the mushrooms and green pepper, stir, cover, and cook about 5 minutes more.

MEXICAN BAKE

Olé! Young and old alike love this casserole filled with meat, beans, and cheese. If you like, you can substitute baked or fat-free corn tortilla chips for the flour tortillas called for in the recipe. Just be sure to check labels and use an amount equal to 4 starch exchanges (or the equivalent of 60 grams of carbohydrate).

About 6 cups (6 servings)

½ pound (90 percent lean) lean ground
    beef
½ cup chopped onion
1 clove garlic, minced
1 teaspoon chili powder, hot or mild
½ teaspoon cumin
⅛ teaspoon crushed red pepper flakes
One 8-ounce can unsalted tomato sauce
One 15-ounce can ranch-style pinto
    beans in tomato and chili sauce
1 cup low-fat cottage cheese
One 8-ounce container low-fat plain
    yogurt or fat-free sour cream
¼ cup canned chopped green chiles
4 flour tortillas 7 to 8 inches in diameter
1½ cups (about 6 ounces) shredded
    reduced-fat Mexican-style
    blended cheese

Nutrition Facts per Serving
Serving size: About 1 cup
Amount per serving:
Calories 352
Calories from fat 115
Total fat 13 gm
Saturated fat 6 gm
Cholesterol 53 mg
Sodium 1026 mg
Total carbohydrate 33 gm
Dietary fiber 4 gm
Sugars 9 gm
Protein 30 gm

Exchange List Approximations

Starch	2
Meat, lean	3
Fat	½

1.   Preheat the oven to 400°F. Prepare a 2-quart casserole with nonstick pan spray.

2.   Sauté the ground beef and onions in a large skillet until crumbly. Drain off any excess fat.

3.   Add the garlic, chili powder, cumin, and pepper flakes and mix thoroughly with the meat. Add the tomato sauce and beans. Mix well.

4.   In a separate bowl, mix the cottage cheese, yogurt, and chiles.

5.   Bake the tortillas on a cookie sheet until crisp and beginning to brown, about 5 minutes. Break the tortillas into large pieces. Reduce the oven temperature to 350°F.

6.   Put half the tortillas in the bottom of the prepared casserole. Spoon half the meat mixture evenly over the tortillas. Add half the yogurt mixture and sprinkle with half the cheese. Repeat the layers, ending with the cheese on top.

7.   Bake, covered, in a 350°F oven for 30 to 35 minutes.

STEAK FAJITAS

These spectacular Southwest "sandwiches" are brimming with juicy slices of marinated flank steak and colorful red and green peppers. It's attractive to serve the steak and vegetables hot on a platter, with a basket of warm tortillas nearby. Arrange the lettuce, tomatoes, salsa, and sour cream toppings in bowls so guests can build their own fajita creations. Or you may prefer to assemble the fajitas as described in Step 6. Remember to add in the appropriate exchange values for any toppings you use. Spicy Black Beans (page 410) makes a nice accompaniment.

8 fajitas (4 servings)

1 flank steak (1 pound), well trimmed
¼ cup fresh lime juice
1 teaspoon salt
1 clove garlic, minced
¼ teaspoon freshly ground pepper
⅛ teaspoon cayenne pepper
1 medium red onion, thinly sliced
1 large red bell pepper, cored, seeded,
    and cut into thin strips
1 large green bell pepper, cored, seeded,
    and cut into thin strips
1 teaspoon canola or corn oil
8 flour tortillas 8 inches in diameter,
    warmed
½ cup chopped tomato
½ cup shredded lettuce
½ cup salsa
¼ cup fat-free sour cream

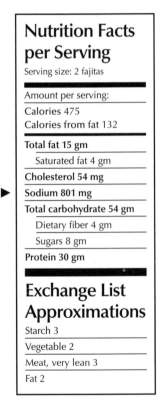

Nutrition Facts per Serving

Serving size: 2 fajitas

Amount per serving:

Calories 475
Calories from fat 132

Total fat 15 gm
   Saturated fat 4 gm
Cholesterol 54 mg
Sodium 801 mg
Total carbohydrate 54 gm
   Dietary fiber 4 gm
   Sugars 8 gm
Protein 30 gm

Exchange List Approximations

Starch 3

Vegetable 2

Meat, very lean 3

Fat 2

1.   Score the steak by making long, shallow cuts 1 inch apart in both sides.

2.   Make the marinade by mixing the lime juice, salt, garlic, black pepper, and cayenne a in large shallow dish. Add the steak; turn to coat. Refrigerate, covered, at least 3 hours or overnight, turning once.

3.   Preheat the broiler or prepare a grill.

4.   Remove the steak from the marinade. Broil or grill 6 inches from the heat for about 4 to 5 minutes on each side for medium-rare, or longer if you prefer. Slice the steak across the grain into thin strips.

5.   While the steak is cooking, sauté the onion and peppers in the oil in a medium skillet until soft, about 5 minutes. Mix the steak into the vegetables.

6.   Divide the steak, onions, and peppers to top the tortillas. Divide the diced tomato, lettuce, salsa, and sour cream to top the meat mixture on each tortilla.

STIR-FRIED BEEF AND BROCCOLI

For a quick after-work meal that takes just minutes, a stir-fry definitely fits the bill. To save even more time, chop and slice all the ingredients the night before, so you're ready to go as soon as you walk in the door. Chilling the meat (or even better, freezing it slightly) makes it much easier to cut into thin slices or strips. Round and flank steaks are lean cuts of beef and can become tough if overcooked, so stir-fry them quickly. Serve over rice (½ cup equals 1 starch exchange).

About 5 cups (4 servings)

1 round or flank steak (about 1 pound),
    chilled
2 teaspoons cornstarch
2 tablespoons light soy sauce
3 cups small broccoli florets (cut large
    florets in pieces)
2 tablespoons canola or corn oil
1 large onion, cut in thin wedges
1 tablespoon minced gingerroot
1 tablespoon sherry (optional)

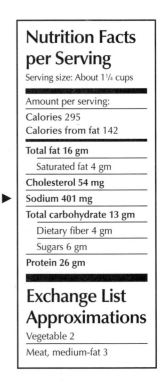

Nutrition Facts per Serving

Serving size: About 1¼ cups

Amount per serving:

Calories 295
Calories from fat 142

Total fat 16 gm
  Saturated fat 4 gm
Cholesterol 54 mg
Sodium 401 mg
Total carbohydrate 13 gm
  Dietary fiber 4 gm
  Sugars 6 gm
Protein 26 gm

Exchange List Approximations

Vegetable 2

Meat, medium-fat 3

1. Slice the meat across the grain in 1 x ¼-inch strips.
2. Sprinkle the beef with cornstarch and soy sauce. Toss to mix, and set aside.
3. Bring a pot of water to a boil and add the broccoli; return the water to a boil and cook 2 minutes. Drain immediately. Set aside.
4. Heat the oil in a wok or large nonstick skillet until very hot. Add the onion and gingerroot and stir-fry about 30 seconds.
5. Add the steak and stir-fry about 2 minutes to brown the edges of the meat. Add the broccoli, sherry, and 2 tablespoons water. Stir constantly until steaming hot, about 1 minute.

TEXAS BEEF BRISKET

Brisket is actually quite lean, and this slow-cooked, down-home recipe boasts just 10 grams of fat per serving. It's wonderful on the day it's made but gets even better on succeeding days, served hot with its spicy gravy or cold as a sandwich filling.

1 brisket (about 8 servings)

SAUCE

1½ cups finely chopped onions
2 cloves garlic, minced
2 tablespoons prepared mustard
2 packed tablespoons brown sugar
1 tablespoon Worcestershire sauce
1 teaspoon chili powder
¼ cup light soy sauce
¼ cup dry red wine
1 tablespoon molasses

One 3-pound center-cut beef brisket,
      well trimmed

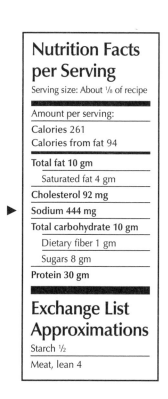

Nutrition Facts per Serving

Serving size: About ⅛ of recipe

Amount per serving:

Calories 261
Calories from fat 94

Total fat 10 gm
  Saturated fat 4 gm
Cholesterol 92 mg
Sodium 444 mg
Total carbohydrate 10 gm
  Dietary fiber 1 gm
  Sugars 8 gm
Protein 30 gm

Exchange List Approximations

Starch ½
Meat, lean 4

1.   Preheat the oven to 325°F. Place a 24-inch length of 18-inch-wide heavy-duty aluminum foil in a 13 x 9-inch baking pan.
2.   Combine all the sauce ingredients in a medium bowl.
3.   Place the brisket in the center of the foil. Pour the sauce over the meat. Bring the ends of the foil together; fold over and continue folding down to the top of meat. Fold the sides up to make a neatly sealed package.
4.   Bake 3 to 3½ hours, or until the meat is tender.
5.   Remove from the oven. Trim the excess fat and thinly slice the meat across the grain.
6.   Skim the excess fat from the sauce with a spoon or fat-separator. Serve the defatted gravy over the meat.

NEW ENGLAND BOILED BEEF

In this New England classic, corned beef, root vegetables, and cabbage are slowly simmered together to create a hearty one-pot meal. Serve with a dollop of special horseradish-mustard sauce for a real treat.

12 servings

One 4-pound corned beef brisket, well
    rinsed
1 teaspoon whole peppercorns
2 bay leaves
12 white boiling onions, peeled
4 medium turnips, peeled and quartered
12 red boiling potatoes
6 small carrots (6 to 8 ounces), peeled
    and cut into 1-inch pieces
1 pound green cabbage, cleaned,
    trimmed, cored, and cut into
    wedges

MUSTARD SAUCE

½ cup prepared mustard
¼ cup fat-free sour cream
2 tablespoons prepared horseradish

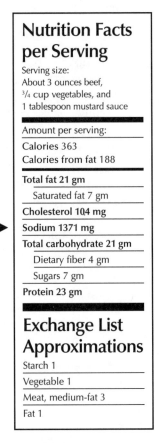

Nutrition Facts per Serving

Serving size:
About 3 ounces beef,
¾ cup vegetables, and
1 tablespoon mustard sauce

Amount per serving:

Calories 363
Calories from fat 188

Total fat 21 gm
  Saturated fat 7 gm

Cholesterol 104 mg

Sodium 1371 mg

Total carbohydrate 21 gm
  Dietary fiber 4 gm
  Sugars 7 gm

Protein 23 gm

Exchange List Approximations

Starch 1

Vegetable 1

Meat, medium-fat 3

Fat 1

1. Place the corned beef in a 6½-quart Dutch oven; cover with cold water. Add the peppercorns and bay leaves. Bring to a boil; reduce the heat and simmer for 2½ to 3 hours, or until almost tender, turning the beef several times and skimming the foam from the top as necessary.
2. Add the onions and turnips; cook for 30 minutes. Add the potatoes, carrots, and cabbage. Cook 20 minutes longer, until the meat and vegetables are tender. Discard the bay leaves; drain the liquid and keep the meat and vegetables warm.
3. Trim the fat from the beef; thinly slice the beef across the grain.
4. Combine the mustard sauce ingredients in a small bowl.
5. Serve the beef and vegetables hot with mustard sauce on the side.

GRILLED MARINATED SIRLOIN STEAK

Sirloin is one of the leaner cuts of beef and is delicious prepared with this pungently sweet balsamic vinegar marinade. Consider making a large steak (2 to 2½ pounds) and enjoy the leftovers in sandwiches and salads—just double the amount of marinade ingredients. For a side dish, consider the Asian Noodle Salad (page 372) or Golden Currant Pilaf with Cinnamon (page 395).

1 steak (4 servings)

1 pound boneless beef top sirloin steak,
    cut 1 inch thick and well
    trimmed

MARINADE

1 tablespoon balsamic vinegar
1 tablespoon tomato paste
2 cloves garlic, minced
1 tablespoon fresh thyme, or 1 teaspoon
    dried thyme
1 tablespoon fresh marjoram,
    or 1 teaspoon dried marjoram
½ teaspoon cracked black peppercorns

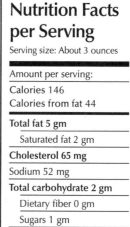

Nutrition Facts per Serving

Serving size: About 3 ounces

Amount per serving:

Calories 146
Calories from fat 44

Total fat 5 gm
  Saturated fat 2 gm
Cholesterol 65 mg
Sodium 52 mg
Total carbohydrate 2 gm
  Dietary fiber 0 gm
  Sugars 1 gm
Protein 22 gm

Exchange List Approximation

Meat, lean 3

1.   Place the steak in a shallow glass dish or pie pan.
2.   Combine the marinade ingredients; spread evenly over both sides of the steak. Let stand at room temperature 30 minutes, or cover and refrigerate up to 8 hours.
3.   Prepare a charcoal grill or preheat the broiler. Grill or broil the steak 4 to 5 inches from the heat source 4 minutes per side for medium-rare, or to desired doneness. Discard the marinade.
4.   Slice the steak into thin strips; serve immediately.

BEEF SATAY WITH PEANUT DIPPING SAUCE

Beef satay is an Indonesian favorite, usually served as an appetizer or main course accompanied by a spicy peanut sauce. Freezing the sirloin steak slightly (for about one hour) will help make slicing it into thin strips easier. Also, be careful not to overcook the meat or it may become tough and dry. Three minutes per side is plenty.

8 skewers (4 servings)

One 1-pound boneless beef sirloin steak,
　　cut 1 inch thick and well
　　trimmed

MARINADE

3 tablespoons rice wine vinegar or
　　dry sherry
2 tablespoons light soy sauce
1 tablespoon fresh lime juice
1 tablespoon grated onion
1 tablespoon peanut oil
1 teaspoon oriental dark-roasted
　　sesame oil
1 teaspoon sugar
2 large cloves garlic, minced
1/2 teaspoon crushed red pepper flakes

4 large green onions with green tops,
　　cut into 1-inch lengths
1/3 cup fat-free evaporated milk
2 tablespoons peanut butter
1/8 teaspoon crushed red pepper flakes
　　(optional)

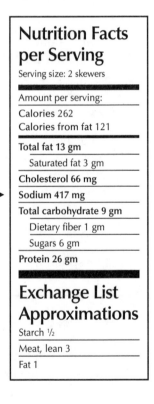

**Nutrition Facts
per Serving**

Serving size: 2 skewers

Amount per serving:

Calories 262
Calories from fat 121

Total fat 13 gm
　Saturated fat 3 gm

Cholesterol 66 mg

Sodium 417 mg

Total carbohydrate 9 gm
　Dietary fiber 1 gm
　Sugars 6 gm

Protein 26 gm

**Exchange List
Approximations**

Starch 1/2

Meat, lean 3

Fat 1

1. Cut the meat into ⅛- to ¼-inch-thick strips. (They should look like ribbons of beef.) Place in a glass dish or plastic bag.

2. Combine all the marinade ingredients in a medium bowl; pour over the meat. Cover the dish or close the bag securely and refrigerate 1 to 2 hours. If using bamboo skewers, soak them in cold water to cover while marinating the meat.

3. Prepare a charcoal grill or preheat the broiler.

4. Drain the marinade into a small saucepan. Thread the meat accordion-style onto 8 skewers, alternating the meat strips with lengths of green onions.

5. Grill over medium coals or broil 4 to 5 inches from the heat source about 3 minutes per side, or just until the meat is no longer pink, turning once.

6. While the meat is grilling, add the milk, peanut butter, and additional pepper flakes (if desired) to the reserved marinade. Simmer over low heat until thickened, stirring frequently; do not boil. Serve the peanut sauce in a small bowl for dipping the beef.

MARINATED SKIRT STEAK WITH VEGETABLE CHUTNEY

Skirt steak is from the beef flank and is a very flavorful yet somewhat tough cut of meat. The unique beer and jalepeño pepper marinade not only helps tenderize the steak, it adds a spunky flavor too. Topped with a spoonful of piquant vegetable chutney, this is a dish that's guaranteed to please.

1 steak (4 servings)

MARINATED STEAKS

One 1-pound skirt or flank steak,
    well trimmed
One 12-ounce can or bottle beer
1 cup diced onion
2 tablespoons chopped pickled jalapeño
    pepper, or 1 large fresh jalapeño
    pepper, cored, seeded, and
    chopped
2 cloves garlic, minced
1/8 teaspoon freshly ground pepper
1/4 teaspoon salt

VEGETABLE CHUTNEY

2 teaspoons olive oil
1/2 cup chopped onion
1/2 cup diced red bell pepper
1/2 cup diced yellow bell pepper
2 tablespoons orange or lime marmalade
1 teaspoon minced crystallized ginger

Nutrition Facts per Serving

Serving size:
About 3 ounces steak and
2 tablespoons chutney

Amount per serving:

Calories 254
Calories from fat 96

Total fat 11 gm
    Saturated fat 4 gm
Cholesterol 54 mg
Sodium 235 mg
Total carbohydrate 16 gm
    Dietary fiber 2 gm
    Sugars 11 gm
Protein 23 gm

Exchange List Approximations

Starch 1

Meat, lean 3

1. Place the steak in a shallow glass dish or zip-top freezer bag. Add the beer, onion, jalapeño pepper, and garlic. Turn the steak in the liquid. Cover the dish or close the bag securely and refrigerate at least 6 hours or up to 24 hours, turning several times.

2. Prepare a charcoal grill or preheat the broiler.

3. Drain the liquid from the meat, reserving the onion mixture and the meat separately. Sprinkle the steak with salt and pepper.

4. To make the chutney, heat the oil in a small saucepan. Sauté the drained onions from the marinade in oil for 3 minutes. Add the remaining chutney ingredients; cover and simmer 10 minutes. Uncover and continue to simmer until thickened, about 5 minutes longer. Cool to room temperature.

5. Grill or broil the steak 5 to 6 inches from the heat source about 4 to 5 minutes on each side for medium-rare, or to desired degree of doneness.

6. Thinly slice the steak and serve with chutney.

NEW MEXICO–STYLE FLANK STEAK

Tequila and lime juice add a simple Southwest flavor to create a steak that's utterly irresistible. Use leftovers to top salads or as a filling for pita sandwiches stuffed with fresh vegetables. Red Beans and Brown Rice (page 406) makes a nice side dish.

1 steak (4 servings)

MARINADE

¼ cup tequila
2 tablespoons fresh lime juice
2 cloves garlic, minced
½ teaspoon hot pepper sauce

1 pound flank steak
⅛ teaspoon freshly ground pepper

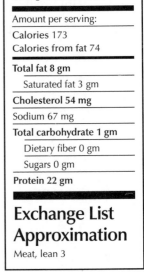

Nutrition Facts per Serving

Serving size: About 3 ounces

Amount per serving:

Calories 173
Calories from fat 74

Total fat 8 gm
    Saturated fat 3 gm
Cholesterol 54 mg
Sodium 67 mg
Total carbohydrate 1 gm
    Dietary fiber 0 gm
    Sugars 0 gm
Protein 22 gm

Exchange List Approximation

Meat, lean 3

1.   Combine the tequila, lime juice, garlic, and hot pepper sauce in a shallow glass dish or zip-top freezer bag.
2.   Add the steak; turn to coat. Cover the dish or seal the bag. Marinate in the refrigerator at least 4 hours or overnight.
3.   Prepare a charcoal grill or preheat the broiler.
4.   Drain and discard the marinade. Grill or broil the steak 4 to 5 inches from the heat source 4 minutes per side for medium-rare, or to desired doneness. Carve the steak into thin slices across the grain. Season with pepper before serving.

RUSSIAN BEEF AND CABBAGE STEW

This hearty stew—rich with cabbage, carrots, green pepper, and tomatoes—is a true meal in itself. It gets even more flavorful by the second day, so prepare enough for leftovers. To make skimming the fat from the finished stew easier, chill it for several hours or overnight. Then, just lift off the layer of fat that has risen to the top. Round out your meal with thick slices of dark pumpernickel or rye bread (add 1 starch exchange per slice).

About 3 quarts (10 servings)

One 2-pound boneless chuck roast,
    trimmed and cut into 1-inch
    cubes
1 teaspoon salt
¼ teaspoon freshly ground pepper
2 cups chopped onion
1 small head cabbage (about
    1½ pounds), shredded
One 28-ounce can tomato purée
One 28-ounce can diced tomatoes
1½ cups sliced carrots
1 cup diced green bell pepper
¼ cup packed brown sugar
1 cup plain low-fat yogurt

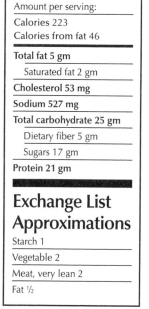

Nutrition Facts per Serving

Serving size: About 1¼ cups

Amount per serving:

Calories 223
Calories from fat 46

Total fat 5 gm
    Saturated fat 2 gm
Cholesterol 53 mg
Sodium 527 mg
Total carbohydrate 25 gm
    Dietary fiber 5 gm
    Sugars 17 gm
Protein 21 gm

Exchange List Approximations

Starch 1
Vegetable 2
Meat, very lean 2
Fat ½

1. Season the meat with salt and pepper; place in a large pot or Dutch oven. Add the onions and enough water to cover the meat (about 2 quarts). Bring to a boil, reduce the heat, cover, and simmer 1 hour.

2. Add all the remaining vegetables and the brown sugar. Cover and simmer 2 hours longer.

3. Skim the fat from the top of the stew with a spoon. Serve the stew in bowls, each topped with 1 rounded tablespoon of yogurt.

SCANDINAVIAN PORK WITH PRUNES

This scrumptious pork roast will have your family demanding seconds. Rubbed with ginger and black pepper, glazed with a slightly sweet sauce, and studded with prunes, the pork roast is as impressive in presentation as it is in flavor.

1 pork roast (4 servings)

4 prunes, pitted and halved
$\frac{1}{2}$ cup homemade or canned beef broth
1 teaspoon grated gingerroot
$\frac{1}{4}$ teaspoon black pepper
One 1$\frac{1}{4}$-pound boneless rolled pork roast

GLAZE

$\frac{1}{4}$ cup dry sherry
1 tablespoon ketchup
1 teaspoon light soy sauce
2 teaspoons honey

1. Preheat the oven to 375°F. Prepare a small roasting pan with nonstick pan spray.
2. Heat the broth to boiling in a small saucepan; add the prunes and set aside for 30 minutes.
3. Press the ginger and pepper onto the surface of the roast. Make 4 slits about 1$\frac{1}{2}$ inches deep in the roast. Remove prunes from the broth and place half a prune in each slit, reserving the broth and the remaining prunes. Place the roast in the roasting pan.
4. In a small bowl, combine all the ingredients for the glaze. Spread over the roast.
5. Bake for 50 minutes, basting occasionally, until a meat thermometer reads 160°F. Allow the roast to stand, covered with foil, for 10 minutes before slicing.
6. Remove the fat from the drippings; add the defatted drippings to the broth and prunes in a saucepan. Boil over high heat until reduced to $\frac{1}{2}$ cup. Serve with the roast.

Nutrition Facts per Serving

Serving size:
About 4 ounces pork and
2 tablespoons gravy

Amount per serving:

Calories 263
Calories from fat 90

Total fat 10 gm
    Saturated fat 4 gm
Cholesterol 85 mg
Sodium 268 mg
Total carbohydrate 10 gm
    Dietary fiber 1 gm
    Sugars 7 gm
Protein 31 gm

Exchange List Approximations

Fruit $\frac{1}{2}$

Meat 4

PORK IN APPLE-BRANDY GLAZE

These individual pork tenderloin medallions, with just 4 grams of fat per serving, are glazed with a rich apple-brandy sauce that beautifully enhances the mild flavor of the pork.

4 servings

One 1-pound pork tenderloin
2 tablespoons apple jelly
$1/4$ teaspoon salt
$1/8$ teaspoon ground white pepper
2 tablespoons brandy or Cognac
1 tablespoon chopped fresh parsley

1. Make medallions by cutting the pork tenderloin across the grain into 4 pieces (about 4 ounces each). Pound the pieces between sheets of wax paper to a thickness of $1/2$ inch. If the tenderloin is in 2 smaller pieces, cut into 8 pieces (2 ounces each).
2. Brush each medallion with apple jelly and sprinkle with salt and pepper.
3. Prepare a large nonstick skillet with nonstick pan spray, and heat over medium heat. Add the pork and cook 5 minutes per side, or until the meat is cooked through. Remove to a warm serving platter.
4. Add the brandy to the skillet; deglaze by stirring the browned bits from the bottom of the skillet into the brandy. Cook and stir 2 minutes. Drizzle the sauce over the pork; sprinkle with parsley.

Nutrition Facts per Serving

Serving size: 1 medallion (about 3½ ounces pork) or 2 smaller medallions (about 4 ounces pork)

Amount per serving:	
Calories 181	
Calories from fat 40	
Total fat 4 gm	
Saturated fat 1 gm	
Cholesterol 71 mg	
Sodium 200 mg	
Total carbohydrate 7 gm	
Dietary fiber 0 gm	
Sugars 6 gm	
Protein 25 gm	

Exchange List Approximations

Other carbohydrate ½
Meat, very lean 4

PORK CHOPS PAPRIKASH

This recipe uses two different intensities of paprika—sweet and hot—to give the pork chops not only a beautiful color but a pungent flavor as well. Paprika is made from ground aromatic sweet red pepper pods, and the Hungarian variety is considered superior to others. For this recipe, splurge on the more expensive Hungarian brand. It's worth the taste.

4 chops (4 servings)

1 large onion, thinly sliced
1 clove garlic, minced
1 teaspoon olive oil
Four center-cut pork chops (1¼ pounds
        total), cut ½ inch thick and well
        trimmed
2 teaspoons paprika, preferably sweet
        Hungarian
¼ teaspoon hot Hungarian paprika or
        cayenne pepper (optional)
⅓ cup sauerkraut, rinsed, drained, and
        patted dry

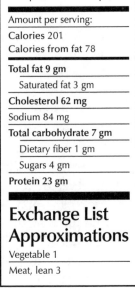

Nutrition Facts per Serving

Serving size:
1 chop with about ¼ cup sauce

Amount per serving:

Calories 201
Calories from fat 78

Total fat 9 gm
    Saturated fat 3 gm
Cholesterol 62 mg
Sodium 84 mg
Total carbohydrate 7 gm
    Dietary fiber 1 gm
    Sugars 4 gm
Protein 23 gm

Exchange List Approximations

Vegetable 1
Meat, lean 3

1.   Sauté the onion and garlic in the oil in a large nonstick skillet until very tender, about 6 to 8 minutes. Remove and set aside.

2.   Sprinkle the pork chops with the sweet and hot paprikas. Brown in the same skillet over medium heat, 3 minutes per side.

3.   Combine the onion mixture and the sauerkraut; spoon over the chops. Sprinkle with additional paprika, if desired.

4.   Cover and cook until the pork chops are no longer pink, about 6 to 8 minutes longer. Serve hot.

PACIFIC RIM OMELET ROLLS

Omelets are used in this recipe as a type of wrap, in place of a tortilla or crêpe. These are delightful as an entrée at brunch or for a light lunch. The pan-Asian–influenced pork and spinach filling is both creative and delicious.

4 rolls (4 servings)

³/₄ pound lean ground pork
3 large cloves garlic, minced
1 teaspoon crushed red pepper flakes
2 cups packed sliced fresh spinach
      leaves
1 tablespoon cornstarch
1 tablespoon light soy sauce
2 large eggs, or ¹/₂ cup egg substitute

Nutrition Facts per Serving

Serving size: 1 omelet roll

Amount per serving:

Calories 159
Calories from fat 51

Total fat 6 gm
   Saturated fat 2 gm
Cholesterol 156 mg
Sodium 241 mg
Total carbohydrate 4 gm
   Dietary fiber 1 gm
   Sugars 1 gm
Protein 22 gm

Exchange List Approximations

Vegetable 1
Meat, very lean 3
Fat ¹/₂

1. Brown the pork, garlic, and pepper flakes in a large nonstick skillet; pour off the drippings. Add the spinach and cook just until wilted, 1 to 2 minutes.

2. In a small bowl, combine ¹/₂ cup water, the cornstarch, and 2 teaspoons of the soy sauce; mix well. Pour into the skillet, stirring until the mixture thickens. Set aside.

3. In a small bowl, beat the eggs with the remaining 1 teaspoon of soy sauce.

4. Heat an 8- or 9-inch nonstick skillet or crêpe pan over medium-high heat and prepare with nonstick pan spray. Pour in ¹/₄ of the egg mixture, tilting the skillet so the eggs cover the bottom of the pan in a thin layer. Cook about 1 minute, just until the egg looks dry and the bottom is golden brown. Slide out onto a plate; spoon ¹/₄ of the pork mixture down the center of the uncooked side of the omelet; roll up and keep warm.

5. Repeat the process 3 times with the remaining egg mixture and filling to make 4 omelet rolls.

PORK WITH GREEN CHILE SAUCE

(Puerco con Salsa de Chile Verde)

Pork shoulder is a lean but not very tender cut. The slow cooking of the pork, which is accented with an abundance of spices and seasonings, helps make the meat tender and tasty. Serve with hot cooked rice or use as a filling for warmed flour tortillas. Add 1 starch exchange for ½ cup of rice or one 7-inch tortilla.

About 7 cups (7 servings)

3 pounds lean boneless pork shoulder or
      butt, well trimmed and cut into
      1-inch cubes
1 tablespoon canola or corn oil
1 cup chopped onion
2 cloves garlic, minced
Three 4-ounce cans green chiles, or one
      10-ounce can jalapeño peppers,
      or 6 to 7 large fresh Anaheim
      or California peppers, seeded
      and chopped
3 medium tomatoes, seeded and
      chopped
½ cup packed chopped cilantro, or
      2 tablespoons ground coriander
1 tablespoon wine vinegar
1 teaspoon salt
1 tablespoon chopped fresh oregano,
      or 1 teaspoon dried oregano
½ teaspoon dried cumin

Nutrition Facts per Serving

Serving size: About 1 cup

Amount per serving:

Calories 257
Calories from fat 86

Total fat 10 gm
  Saturated fat 3 gm

Cholesterol 92 mg

Sodium 624 mg

Total carbohydrate 8 gm
  Dietary fiber 2 gm
  Sugars 5 gm

Protein 33 gm

Exchange List Approximations

Vegetable 2

Meat, lean 4

1.   Brown the pork in the oil in small batches in a large nonstick skillet or Dutch oven. Remove and set aside.

2.   Sauté the onion and garlic in the pan about 5 minutes, until lightly browned. Add the pork and all the remaining ingredients, plus $\frac{1}{4}$ cup water.

3.   Cover and simmer on top of the stove, or bake in a 325°F oven, for $1\frac{1}{2}$ to 2 hours, or until the pork is tender. Skim any fat from the surface before serving.

MOO SHU PORK

Moo shu pork is a Chinese restaurant favorite that's easy to make at home. Hoisin sauce is the only moderately unusual ingredient, and it is available in most supermarkets in the ethnic food section. Although this is traditionally served with paper-thin pancakes as wrappers, we use store-bought flour tortillas to cut preparation time.

8 rolls (8 servings as an appetizer; 4 servings as an entrée)

MARINADE

2 tablespoons light soy sauce
1 tablespoon Oriental dark-roasted
      sesame oil
2 cloves garlic, minced
2 teaspoons sugar

1 pound pork loin or tenderloin, sliced
      into ⅛-inch x ½-inch strips
1 tablespoon cornstarch
3 cups packaged shredded coleslaw
      mix (cabbage or cabbage with
      carrots)
6 green onions with green tops, thinly
      sliced
Eight 8-inch-diameter flour tortillas,
      warmed
⅓ cup hoisin sauce

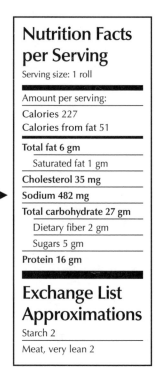

**Nutrition Facts
per Serving**

Serving size: 1 roll

Amount per serving:

Calories 227
Calories from fat 51

Total fat 6 gm
   Saturated fat 1 gm
Cholesterol 35 mg
Sodium 482 mg
Total carbohydrate 27 gm
   Dietary fiber 2 gm
   Sugars 5 gm
Protein 16 gm

**Exchange List
Approximations**

Starch 2

Meat, very lean 2

1. In a medium bowl, combine 2 tablespoons water with the marinade ingredients; add the pork, tossing to coat. Cover and marinate in the refrigerator 20 minutes.

2. Remove the pork from the marinade; discard the marinade. Heat a large nonstick skillet prepared with nonstick pan spray over medium-high heat until hot. Add the pork (half at a time) and stir-fry only 1 to 2 minutes, or until the outside surface is no longer pink. Repeat with the remaining pork.

3. In a small bowl, mix the cornstarch with $1/4$ cup water; stir to dissolve. Add the coleslaw mix, cornstarch mixture, and green onions to the pork. Cook and stir until the mixture has thickened.

4. To assemble, spread 1 side of each tortilla with 2 teaspoons hoisin sauce. Spoon about $1/2$ cup of the pork mixture in the center of each tortilla. Fold the bottom edge up over the filling. Fold the right and left sides to the center, overlapping the edges. (This makes a folded packet with one closed end.)

HERB-ROASTED PORK TENDERLOIN

A dry rub of herbs lends a fragrant undertone to the tenderloin in this recipe, adding a ton of flavor without any fat. Remember, fresh herbs yield more and better flavor than dried varieties. Look for fresh herbs year-round in the produce department of your local supermarket.

1 tenderloin (4 servings)

1 whole pork tenderloin (1 pound)
1 tablespoon grainy Dijon mustard
1 tablespoon chopped fresh rosemary,
    or 1 teaspoon dried rosemary
1 tablespoon chopped fresh oregano,
    or 1 teaspoon dried oregano
1 tablespoon chopped fresh sage, or
    1 teaspoon dried sage
1 tablespoon chopped fresh thyme,
    or 1 teaspoon dried thyme
1/2 teaspoon freshly ground pepper

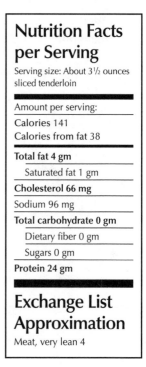

Nutrition Facts per Serving

Serving size: About 3 1/2 ounces sliced tenderloin

Amount per serving:

Calories 141
Calories from fat 38

Total fat 4 gm
  Saturated fat 1 gm
Cholesterol 66 mg
Sodium 96 mg
Total carbohydrate 0 gm
  Dietary fiber 0 gm
  Sugars 0 gm
Protein 24 gm

Exchange List Approximation

Meat, very lean 4

1. Preheat the oven to 450°F. Prepare a shallow roasting pan and rack with nonstick pan spray.

2. Brush the tenderloin with the mustard. Combine the herbs; pat them evenly onto the tenderloin and sprinkle with pepper.

3. Place the pork on the rack in the roasting pan, set it in the oven, and immediately reduce the oven temperature to 350°F. Roast until a meat thermometer inserted in the thickest part of the tenderloin registers 145°F, about 25 minutes (depending on the size of the tenderloin). Remove the pork from the oven and let rest 5 minutes. Carve in 1/2-inch slices and serve with the pan juices.

CURRIED LAMB ON RICE

This curried lamb dish, made flavorful with a combination of ginger, curry, and carrot, is wonderful garnished with thin slices of fresh apple. The apple lends crispness and a nice color contrast to the dish. One medium apple is enough for 4 servings, so add ¼ fruit exchange per serving.

About 3 cups (4 servings)

1 pound lean lamb, well trimmed
        and cubed
½ cup chopped onion
1 clove garlic, minced
1 tablespoon margarine
1 cup homemade or canned beef broth
2 teaspoons curry powder
¾ teaspoon salt
¼ teaspoon ground ginger
1 medium tomato, peeled, seeded,
        and chopped
1½ tablespoons all-purpose flour
½ cup grated carrot
2 cups cooked rice

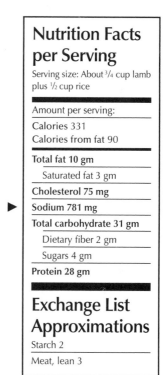

Nutrition Facts per Serving

Serving size: About ¾ cup lamb plus ½ cup rice

Amount per serving:
Calories 331
Calories from fat 90
Total fat 10 gm
Saturated fat 3 gm
Cholesterol 75 mg
Sodium 781 mg
Total carbohydrate 31 gm
Dietary fiber 2 gm
Sugars 4 gm
Protein 28 gm

Exchange List Approximations

Starch 2
Meat, lean 3

1. Heat a large nonstick skillet. Brown the lamb, onion, and garlic in the margarine about 5 minutes. Add the broth, curry powder, salt, ginger, tomato, and flour. Stir to mix well.
2. Cover and simmer 30 to 40 minutes, or until the lamb is tender. Stir occasionally and add a little water if the liquid evaporates.
3. Toss the grated carrot with the rice in a small nonstick saucepan. Heat through.
4. Divide the rice among 4 serving plates; divide the lamb over the rice.

STUFFED PEPPERS WITH GROUND LAMB

Stuffed peppers take on a whole new taste when filled with spiced ground lamb. When selecting peppers for this recipe, choose those with flat bottoms and place them carefully in a baking dish or large cupcake tins so they don't tip over while they're cooking.

4 stuffed peppers (4 servings)

4 medium green bell peppers
$\frac{1}{2}$ pound lean ground lamb
$\frac{1}{4}$ cup chopped onion
1 cup cooked brown or white rice
One 8-ounce can tomato sauce
1 clove garlic, minced
$\frac{1}{2}$ teaspoon salt
$\frac{1}{4}$ teaspoon dried oregano
$\frac{1}{8}$ teaspoon freshly ground pepper

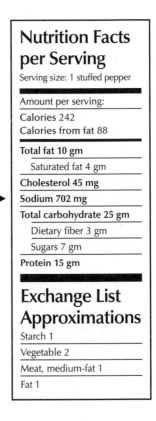

1. Preheat the oven to 350°F. Prepare an 8-inch square or round baking dish with non-stick pan spray.
2. Cut a thin slice from the stem end of each pepper. Remove all the seeds and membranes. Partially cook the peppers in a large pot of boiling water for 5 minutes. Drain and set aside.
3. In a large nonstick skillet, sauté the ground lamb and the onion over medium-high heat about 5 minutes, until the lamb is browned and the onion is tender; drain off the fat. Stir in the rice, $\frac{1}{2}$ cup of the tomato sauce, the garlic, salt, oregano, and pepper.
4. Divide the mixture evenly to fill the peppers. Stand the peppers upright in the prepared baking dish and top them with the remaining tomato sauce.
5. Cover the peppers with foil and bake for 40 minutes; uncover and bake for an additional 10 to 15 minutes.

Nutrition Facts per Serving

Serving size: 1 stuffed pepper

Amount per serving:

Calories 242
Calories from fat 88

Total fat 10 gm
  Saturated fat 4 gm
Cholesterol 45 mg
Sodium 702 mg
Total carbohydrate 25 gm
  Dietary fiber 3 gm
  Sugars 7 gm
Protein 15 gm

Exchange List Approximations

Starch 1
Vegetable 2
Meat, medium-fat 1
Fat 1

MINTED LAMB KEBABS

Kebabs are wonderful. If you like, you can alternate vegetables—such as onion wedges, whole mushrooms, green or red bell pepper chunks, and cherry tomatoes—with the skewered lamb chunks to make a shish kebab variation. Then you'll have enough for 8 kebabs instead of 4 (serve 2 skewers per portion and add 1 Vegetable Exchange).

4 servings

1 pound boneless lean leg of lamb, cut
      into 1-inch cubes
¾ cup plain low-fat yogurt
2 cloves garlic, minced
2 tablespoons chopped fresh mint
      leaves, or 1 teaspoon dried mint
½ teaspoon seasoned salt
¼ teaspoon crushed saffron (optional)
⅛ teaspoon freshly ground pepper

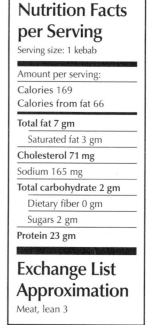

Nutrition Facts per Serving

Serving size: 1 kebab

Amount per serving:

Calories 169
Calories from fat 66

Total fat 7 gm
    Saturated fat 3 gm
Cholesterol 71 mg
Sodium 165 mg
Total carbohydrate 2 gm
    Dietary fiber 0 gm
    Sugars 2 gm
Protein 23 gm

Exchange List Approximation

Meat, lean 3

1. Place the lamb cubes in a shallow glass dish or plastic bag. Combine the remaining ingredients in a medium bowl; mix well. Pour over the lamb. Cover and refrigerate at least 2 hours or overnight.

2. Preheat the broiler or grill.

3. Thread the lamb onto 4 skewers, reserving the marinade. Broil or grill 6 to 8 inches from the heat source, turning and basting with the marinade several times, until the lamb is browned on all sides, about 9 to 12 minutes. Do not overcook; the lamb cubes should be pink in the middle to retain flavor and tenderness. Discard the remaining marinade; do not serve it with the cooked kebabs.

LAMB OVER MINTED COUSCOUS

Warm spices, tomato sauce, and raisins add a complex flavor to simmering lamb, resulting in a dish that's both pungent and sweet. Couscous, flavored with fresh mint in this recipe, can be found in most major supermarkets and is a nice change of pace from rice.

4 servings

1 pound lean ground lamb
1½ cups chopped onion
2 cloves garlic, minced
1½ teaspoons cinnamon
One 14- to 15-ounce can tomato sauce
⅓ cup raisins or dried currants
1 cup Homemade Chicken Broth
      (page 101), or canned reduced-
      sodium chicken broth
⅔ cup uncooked couscous
3 tablespoons chopped fresh mint leaves,
      or 1½ teaspoons dried mint
2 tablespoons slivered almonds

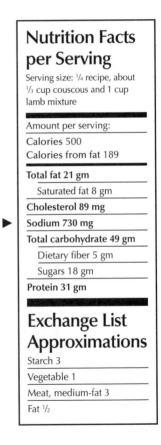

Nutrition Facts per Serving

Serving size: ¼ recipe, about ⅓ cup couscous and 1 cup lamb mixture

Amount per serving:

Calories 500
Calories from fat 189

Total fat 21 gm
   Saturated fat 8 gm
Cholesterol 89 mg
Sodium 730 mg
Total carbohydrate 49 gm
   Dietary fiber 5 gm
   Sugars 18 gm
Protein 31 gm

Exchange List Approximations

Starch 3

Vegetable 1

Meat, medium-fat 3

Fat ½

1.   Sauté the lamb, onion, and garlic in a non-stick skillet over medium-high heat until the meat is no longer pink. Drain well. Sprinkle with cinnamon.

2.   Stir in the tomato sauce and raisins; simmer, uncovered, 15 minutes, stirring occasionally.

3.   While the lamb is simmering, bring the broth to a boil in a small saucepan. Stir in the couscous and mint; cover and let stand 5 minutes. Fluff with a fork.

4.   Toast the almonds in a small skillet over medium heat about 3 minutes, or until lightly browned and fragrant.

5.   Divide the couscous among 4 warm plates; divide the lamb over the couscous and sprinkle with almonds.

ROAST SPRING LAMB

The leg is a very lean cut of lamb. You can ask the butcher to butterfly the leg for you or you can easily do it yourself. Simply split the meat down the middle, cutting almost—but not completely—through. Open the two halves and lay them flat to resemble a butterfly shape. Lamb is best cooked to 145°F, or rare to medium-rare. Once you remove it from the oven, it continues to cook internally for about 10 minutes, so take care not to overcook it.

1 half leg of lamb (about 10 servings)

One 2½- to 3-pound sirloin half leg of
    lamb, well trimmed, boned, and
    butterflied
3 cloves garlic, cut into slivers
2 tablespoons chopped fresh rosemary,
    or 2 teaspoons dried rosemary
1 teaspoon salt
1 teaspoon cracked black peppercorns
Sprigs of fresh rosemary or mint, for
    garnish

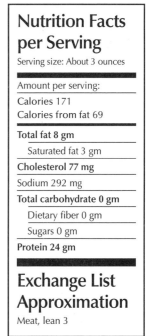

Nutrition Facts per Serving

Serving size: About 3 ounces

Amount per serving:

Calories 171
Calories from fat 69

Total fat 8 gm
    Saturated fat 3 gm
Cholesterol 77 mg
Sodium 292 mg
Total carbohydrate 0 gm
    Dietary fiber 0 gm
    Sugars 0 gm
Protein 24 gm

Exchange List Approximation

Meat, lean 3

1. Preheat the oven to 325°F.
2. Cut small, deep slits in the lamb with the point of a sharp knife; insert 1 garlic silver in each slit. Rub the surface of the lamb with rosemary, salt, and pepper. Place on a rack in a shallow roasting pan. Roast until a meat thermometer inserted in the thickest part of the meat registers 145°F (about 1 hour, depending on the thickness of the lamb). Let stand, tented with foil, 10 minutes before carving, to set juices.
3. Thinly slice the lamb across the grain. Pour any accumulated juices from the carving board over the lamb slices. Serve immediately, garnished with herb sprigs.

MOUSSAKA WITH LAMB

Moussaka is a classic Greek casserole that's traditionally prepared by layering slices of eggplant with ground meat. Through the years, there have been many variations on the dish; our recipe uses potatoes in place of the eggplant. Moussaka is often covered with a rich béchamel sauce, but we've lightened the topping by using a mixture of yogurt, eggs, and Parmesan cheese.

About 6 cups (4 servings)

1 pound lean ground lamb
1/2 cup chopped onion
2 cloves garlic, minced
1 cup tomato purée
1/2 cup dry red wine
1 tablespoon chopped fresh parsley,
        or 1/2 teaspoon dried parsley
1 tablespoon chopped fresh mint leaves,
        or 1 teaspoon dried mint
2 teaspoons chopped fresh oregano,
        or 1/2 teaspoon dried oregano
3/4 teaspoon salt
1/4 teaspoon freshly ground pepper
Pinch of cinnamon
3 medium potatoes (1 pound total),
        boiled, peeled, and thinly sliced
1/4 cup grated Parmesan cheese
2 cups plain low-fat yogurt
2 large egg yolks, or 1/4 cup egg
        substitute
2 tablespoons all-purpose flour

Nutrition Facts per Serving

Serving size: About 1 1/2 cups

Amount per serving:

Calories 524
Calories from fat 219

Total fat 24 gm
   Saturated fat 10 gm
Cholesterol 209 mg
Sodium 801 mg
Total carbohydrate 39 gm
   Dietary fiber 4 gm
   Sugars 16 gm
Protein 36 gm

Exchange List Approximations

Starch 2 1/2
Vegetable 1
Meat, medium-fat 4

1.   Preheat the oven to 350°F. Prepare a 2-quart baking dish with non-stick pan spray.

2.   Sauté the ground lamb, onion, and garlic in a large nonstick skillet until the meat is no longer pink; drain well. Stir in the tomato purée, wine, parsley, mint, oregano, salt, pepper, and cinnamon. Simmer for 5 minutes.

3.   Arrange half of the potato slices in the prepared dish. Top with half the meat mixture and sprinkle with half the cheese. Repeat the potato and meat layers.

4.   Combine the yogurt, egg yolks, and flour in a small bowl; spread over the top of the casserole. Top with the remaining cheese. Bake for 30 minutes, or until golden brown.

VEAL ROAST

Sometimes, simpler is better. That's certainly the case with veal, which has such a wonderfully delicate flavor that you want to enhance, not overwhelm. A dry rub of rosemary, thyme, and garlic is all that's needed.

1 roast (4 servings)

One 1½-pound veal breast or leg, boned
    and rolled
2 teaspoons chopped fresh rosemary,
    or ½ teaspoon dried rosemary
2 teaspoons chopped fresh thyme,
    or ½ teaspoon dried thyme
1 clove garlic, minced
½ teaspoon salt
¼ teaspoon freshly ground pepper
1 cup coarsely chopped carrot
1 cup coarsely chopped onion
4 small red potatoes, peeled and halved
¼ cup dry white wine

Nutrition Facts per Serving
Serving size: About 4 ounces meat plus ½ cup vegetables
Amount per serving:
Calories 260
Calories from fat 38
Total fat 4 gm
Saturated fat 1 gm
Cholesterol 116 mg
Sodium 397 mg
Total carbohydrate 21 gm
Dietary fiber 3 gm
Sugars 5 gm
Protein 34 gm

Exchange List Approximations
Starch 1
Vegetable 1
Meat, very lean 4

1. Preheat the oven to 325°F. Prepare a roasting pan with nonstick pan spray.

2. Place the veal in the pan and press the herbs, garlic, and salt and pepper on all sides of the roast. Surround the roast with the vegetables; add ¾ cup water and the wine. Cover tightly with foil. Roast for about 2 hours, or until the veal is tender. If necessary, add additional water to the pan to keep the roast moist and prevent burning.

3. Remove the roast to a heated platter. Skim the fat from the pan juices with a spoon, or use a gravy separator and set aside.

4. Allow the meat to rest 10 minutes before carving. Slice the roast and divide the meat and vegetables to serve 4. Top the veal with natural juices.

VEAL STEW

We've lightened up this traditionally creamy French stew by using "skinny" ingredients, like fat-free evaporated milk and cornstarch, to create a slurry that thickens the white sauce without a lot of fat.

About 5 cups (4 servings)

1 pound veal shoulder or stew meat,
      cut into 1-inch cubes
¾ cup chopped onion
1 large leek, white part only, sliced
¼ cup sliced carrot
½ cup (2 ounces) sliced mushrooms
2 cloves garlic, minced
1 teaspoon chopped fresh rosemary,
      or ¼ teaspoon dried rosemary
½ teaspoon salt
¼ teaspoon freshly ground pepper
1 cup Homemade Chicken Broth
      (page 101), or canned reduced-
      sodium chicken broth
½ cup dry white wine
1 tablespoon cornstarch
¼ cup fat-free evaporated milk
1 tablespoon Dijon mustard
1 cup frozen petite peas

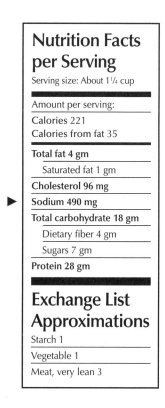

Nutrition Facts per Serving

Serving size: About 1¼ cup

Amount per serving:

Calories 221
Calories from fat 35

Total fat 4 gm
   Saturated fat 1 gm
Cholesterol 96 mg
Sodium 490 mg
Total carbohydrate 18 gm
   Dietary fiber 4 gm
   Sugars 7 gm
Protein 28 gm

Exchange List Approximations

Starch 1
Vegetable 1
Meat, very lean 3

1. Preheat the oven to 325°F. Prepare a Dutch oven with nonstick pan spray.

2. In the Dutch oven, brown the veal cubes on all sides. Stir in the onion, leek, carrot, mushrooms, garlic, rosemary, salt, and pepper. Cook for 5 minutes; remove from the heat.

3. Stir in the chicken broth and wine. Cover and bake for 1 to 1½ hours, or until the veal is tender. With a slotted spoon, remove the veal and vegetables, leaving the liquid in the pot.

4. In a small bowl, dissolve the cornstarch in 2 tablespoons water. Add the cornstarch mixture, fat-free evaporated milk, and mustard to the pot. Whisk over medium heat until the sauce is thickened. Do not boil. Add the peas; simmer 5 minutes.

5. Return the veal and vegetables to the pot and heat through.

VEAL SCALLOPS WITH LEMON

This simple yet elegant dish takes just minutes to make. Dry white wine, lemon juice, and capers combine to create a light lemony sauce that enhances the subtle flavor of veal.

4 servings

1 pound veal scallops, pounded to
        1/8-inch thickness
1/8 teaspoon ground white pepper
1 tablespoon margarine
1 clove garlic, minced
1/4 cup dry white wine
2 tablespoons fresh lemon juice
1 tablespoon drained capers
1 tablespoon chopped fresh parsley,
        preferably Italian or flat-leaf
        parsley
1/2 lemon, thinly sliced

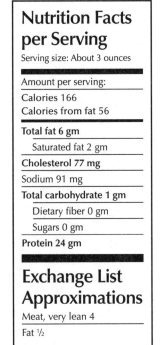

Nutrition Facts per Serving

Serving size: About 3 ounces

Amount per serving:

Calories 166
Calories from fat 56

Total fat 6 gm
    Saturated fat 2 gm
Cholesterol 77 mg
Sodium 91 mg
Total carbohydrate 1 gm
    Dietary fiber 0 gm
    Sugars 0 gm
Protein 24 gm

Exchange List Approximations

Meat, very lean 4
Fat 1/2

1.   Season the veal with pepper. Heat the margarine in a large nonstick skillet over medium-high heat.
2.   Sauté the veal (in batches if necessary) until lightly browned, about 2 minutes per side. Remove to a warm serving platter; cover with foil.
3.   Add the garlic to the skillet; sauté 1 minute. Add the wine, lemon juice, and capers; simmer 1 minute. Pour the sauce over the veal scallops; sprinkle with parsley and garnish with lemon slices.

ROAST BRISKET OF VEAL WITH ONION GRAVY

This brisket—lively with a gravy made with onions, chili sauce, and beer—is even better served the next day. Brisket doesn't take a lot of time to prepare, but it does take a long, slow time to cook, yielding a meat that's very tender and flavorful. The yield will vary depending on the size of the brisket.

One pound of cooked meat will yield about 5 servings.

2 medium onions, sliced and separated
      into rings
One 3- to 3½-pound veal brisket,
      well trimmed
½ teaspoon freshly ground pepper
1 cup chili sauce
One 12-ounce bottle or can beer

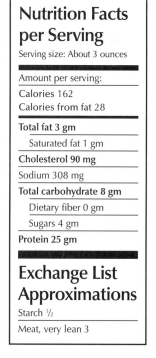

Nutrition Facts per Serving

Serving size: About 3 ounces

Amount per serving:

Calories 162
Calories from fat 28

Total fat 3 gm
   Saturated fat 1 gm
Cholesterol 90 mg
Sodium 308 mg
Total carbohydrate 8 gm
   Dietary fiber 0 gm
   Sugars 4 gm
Protein 25 gm

Exchange List Approximations

Starch ½

Meat, very lean 3

1. Heat the oven to 325°F. Prepare a roasting pan with nonstick pan spray.
2. Scatter half the onion rings over the bottom of the pan. Place the brisket over the onions; sprinkle with pepper. Spread the remaining onions over the brisket. Stir the chili sauce and beer together and pour over the meat.
3. Cover and roast until the veal is fork-tender, about 2½ to 3 hours, basting with the pan juices several times.
4. Remove the brisket to a carving board. Skim the fat from the surface of the pan juices with a spoon. Transfer the defatted juices and onions to a saucepan and cook over high heat until slightly thickened and reduced to 2½ cups.
5. Thinly slice brisket across the grain; pour ¼ cup of onion gravy over each serving.

GRILLED VENISON STEAKS

Venison is very lean, and the little bit of bacon called for in this recipe adds both flavor and fat, which helps keep the meat from getting too dry. If time permits, marinate the venison steaks in ½ cup dry red wine for 2 hours before cooking to add more flavor; just drain the wine before seasoning and cooking.

4 steaks (4 servings)

Four 4-ounce venison steaks (1 pound
        total), trimmed
2 cloves garlic, minced
2 tablespoons finely chopped onion
¼ teaspoon salt
¼ teaspoon freshly ground pepper
4 strips bacon

1. Soak 4 bamboo skewers for 10 to 15 minutes in water. Preheat the broiler or prepare a charcoal grill.
2. Rub the garlic and onion into both sides of steaks; sprinkle with salt and pepper.
3. Place 1 strip of bacon on each steak. Roll up with the bacon on the outside and secure each roll with a bamboo skewer.
4. Grill for 3 to 5 minutes per side over a moderately hot fire or with broiler (do not overcook). Remove the skewers before serving.

Nutrition Facts per Serving
Serving size: 1 steak
Amount per serving:
Calories 218
Calories from fat 99
Total fat 11 gm
Saturated fat 4 gm
Cholesterol 105 mg
Sodium 308 mg
Total carbohydrate 1 gm
Dietary fiber 0 gm
Sugars 1 gm
Protein 27 gm

Exchange List Approximation

Meat, lean 4

VENISON WITH PAN-ROASTED VEGETABLES

Venison is such a lean meat that it needs a barding of fat (such as bacon) to help baste the venison and prevent it from drying out during roasting. Simply seasoned with slivers of garlic and a sprinkling of rosemary, this roast is ideal for Sunday dinner.

1 roast (8 servings)

1 clove garlic, split
1 teaspoon chopped fresh rosemary, or
      ½ teaspoon dried rosemary
One 2-pound venison roast, trimmed
5 strips bacon
2 large baking potatoes (1¼ pounds
      total), unpeeled, cut into
      8 wedges
2 medium carrots, cut into 1-inch pieces
1 medium onion, cut into eighths
½ cup dry red wine

Nutrition Facts per Serving

Serving size: ⅛ of recipe

Amount per serving:

Calories 271
Calories from fat 80

Total fat 9 gm
   Saturated fat 3 gm
Cholesterol 101 mg
Sodium 161 mg
Total carbohydrate 19 gm
   Dietary fiber 2 gm
   Sugars 3 gm
Protein 28 gm

Exchange List Approximations

Starch 1
Vegetable 1
Meat, lean 3

1. Preheat the oven to 350°F. Prepare a shallow roasting pan with nonstick pan spray.

2. Rub the garlic halves and rosemary over the roast. Sliver the garlic; make a few small slits in the roast and insert the slivered garlic into the slits.

3. Place the roast in the roasting pan. Cover with bacon strips and tie with string or secure the bacon with wooden toothpicks. Add the potatoes, carrots, and onion to the pan. Pour the wine and ½ cup water into the pan.

4. Insert a meat thermometer into the roast and cook until the thermometer reaches 165°F, about 1½ hours. Baste often; if the pan bottom becomes dry, add more water during cooking.

5. Allow the roast to stand, covered, about 10 minutes before carving, to set the juices. Remove the string or toothpicks and discard the bacon. Carve the roast in thin slices and serve with the vegetables and natural pan juices.

HEARTY YUKON STEW

You can use shoulder cuts of venison, veal, or buffalo in this robust stew, cooked slowly to render chunks of meat that are fork-tender. Serve the stew over a heaping pile of egg noodles or with a slice of crusty French bread. Add 1 starch exchange for ½ cup of noodles or 1 slice of bread.

About 6 cups (6 servings)

3 tablespoons all-purpose flour
½ teaspoon salt
½ teaspoon freshly ground pepper
1½ pounds boneless venison, buffalo,
    or veal shoulder, cut into 1½-inch
    pieces
1 tablespoon olive oil
2 cloves garlic, minced
2 cups dry red wine
2 tablespoons tomato paste
2 cups sliced carrots
1 bay leaf
12 small whole white onions (¾ pound
    total), peeled
8 ounces mushrooms, stems trimmed
1 tablespoon chopped fresh thyme, or
    1 teaspoon dried thyme

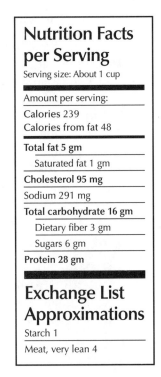

Nutrition Facts per Serving

Serving size: About 1 cup

Amount per serving:

Calories 239
Calories from fat 48

Total fat 5 gm
  Saturated fat 1 gm
Cholesterol 95 mg
Sodium 291 mg
Total carbohydrate 16 gm
  Dietary fiber 3 gm
  Sugars 6 gm
Protein 28 gm

Exchange List Approximations

Starch 1

Meat, very lean 4

1. Combine the flour with the salt and pepper in a pie plate. Dredge the venison in the seasoned flour.

2. Heat the oil and garlic in a large nonstick skillet over medium-high heat. Brown the meat in the oil, in batches if necessary.

3. Add the wine, 1 cup water, and the tomato paste; bring to a boil. Add the carrots and bay leaf. Reduce the heat; cover and simmer 30 minutes, stirring occasionally.

4. Add the onions, mushrooms, and thyme; cover and simmer 30 minutes longer, or until the venison and onions are fork-tender. Uncover and simmer until the sauce reaches the desired consistency.

7

POULTRY

It seems that there are more than 1001 ways to prepare poultry, a category that includes chicken, turkey, duck, game hens, and capons. Reasonably priced, versatile, and easy to fix, poultry—especially chicken—has become a mainstay in our fast-paced, health-conscious society. With good reason, too: besides protein, poultry supplies iron, important B vitamins, zinc, and magnesium. And it's lean—poultry without skin has less fat than most other meats.

Most of poultry's fat is found just under its skin. Leave the skin on poultry when roasting, to keep the meat from drying out, but remove it before eating to save fat and calories. (Removing the skin before eating can cut the total saturated fat intake by a whopping one-half.) Individual parts, like breasts or thighs, can be cooked skinless. To save money, consider buying a whole bird and skinning it yourself; if you're tight on time, purchase skinless parts.

Light meat has less fat than dark meat, and cooks more quickly. Three and a half ounces of roasted, skinless dark meat has about 10 grams of fat and 3 grams of saturated fat compared with 3 grams and 1 gram in the same amount of light meat. The cholesterol content for both light and dark meat is similar.

Poultry is delicious prepared in any number of ways. Roasting poultry on a rack so the fat drips off, grilling, baking, braising, broiling, stewing, and oven-frying are some of the low-fat cooking methods we use in our recipes. Poultry is great for entertaining or for the family;

we've updated some classic recipes in this chapter and added new ones to spice up your meals. Try Tandoori Chicken, Stuffed Turkey Tenderloin, Hunan Chicken, Grilled Duck Breast, or Lemon Barbecued Chicken tonight!

FOOD SAFETY

One word of caution: Salmonella is a type of bacteria commonly found in raw or undercooked poultry and eggs; it can cause foodborne illness. Proper cooking destroys salmonella, so be sure to cook poultry thoroughly to at least 160°F, until it is no longer pink inside and the juices run clear. A few other food safety tips:

Rinse poultry in cold water before cooking and pat dry with paper towels before preparing. Check for any off odors, too.

Use separate cutting boards, plates, and trays for cooked and uncooked poultry, and avoid cross-contamination with utensils. Unless it's washed thoroughly in between, don't use the same knife to slice raw poultry and chop vegetables.

Wash hands before and after each step in preparing foods.

Keep packages of raw poultry in separate plastic bags in a bowl or pan on the lowest refrigerator shelf. This helps keep the juices from dripping onto other foods.

Marinate poultry in covered nonmetallic containers in the refrigerator. Many marinades contain acidic ingredients, like wine, citrus juice, or vinegar; these react with metals that can then leach into the food.

LEMON BARBECUED CHICKEN

The lemony tang of this chicken recipe comes compliments of the marinade. Marinades are wonderful at adding flavor with very little fat, since the marinade mix is drained off before cooking. This dish is equally good hot off the grill or at room temperature tossed in a green salad the next day. If grilling isn't an option, you can broil the chicken 4 to 5 inches from the heat, turning every 8 to 10 minutes until it is cooked through.

6 servings

2 teaspoons Worcestershire sauce
1 teaspoon grated lemon zest
1 teaspoon salt
½ teaspoon dry mustard
½ teaspoon dried oregano
½ cup fresh lemon juice
½ cup olive, canola, or corn oil
1 green onion with green top, chopped
6 chicken breast halves, or 6 legs and
      6 thighs (2½ to 3 pounds)

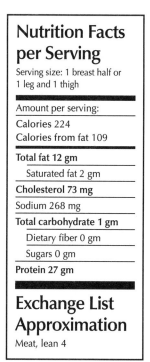

Nutrition Facts
per Serving
Serving size: 1 breast half or
1 leg and 1 thigh

Amount per serving:
Calories 224
Calories from fat 109

Total fat 12 gm
  Saturated fat 2 gm
Cholesterol 73 mg
Sodium 268 mg
Total carbohydrate 1 gm
  Dietary fiber 0 gm
  Sugars 0 gm
Protein 27 gm

Exchange List
Approximation
Meat, lean 4

1.   Mix the Worcestershire sauce, lemon zest, salt, dry mustard, and oregano in a small bowl. Gradually stir in the lemon juice, followed by the oil and chopped green onions.
2.   Brush the mixture over the chicken pieces. Cover and marinate in the refrigerator for at least 2 hours.
3.   Prepare a charcoal grill.
4.   Remove the chicken from the marinade and place skin side down on the grill. Set 3 to 6 inches from charcoal that has reached the light gray ash stage. Cook 30 minutes for breast halves and 40 minutes for thighs, turning every 10 to 15 minutes.

CHICKEN PAPRIKA

Serve this traditional Hungarian dish, made rich with a low-fat sour cream sauce, over steaming egg noodles or yolk-free noodles. Paprika, an essential spice in Hungarian cooking, adds important flavor and a rosy color to the chicken, so don't skimp on quality. Buy Hungarian paprika, which is sweeter (and more expensive) than regular paprika, to make the most of this dish.

4 servings

4 boneless, skinless chicken breast
    halves (about 1 pound)
1 clove garlic, minced
1 tablespoon margarine
2 cups chopped onions
1½ cups (about 4 ounces) sliced fresh
    mushrooms
2 tablespoons fresh lemon juice
2 teaspoons paprika, Hungarian
    preferred
½ teaspoon salt
¼ teaspoon freshly ground pepper
1 tablespoon flour
⅔ cup fat-free milk
½ cup nonfat sour cream

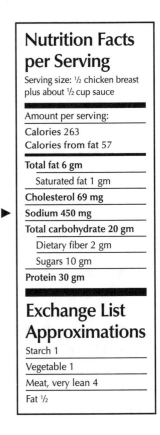

**Nutrition Facts
per Serving**

Serving size: ½ chicken breast plus about ½ cup sauce

Amount per serving:

Calories 263
Calories from fat 57

Total fat 6 gm
  Saturated fat 1 gm
Cholesterol 69 mg
Sodium 450 mg
Total carbohydrate 20 gm
  Dietary fiber 2 gm
  Sugars 10 gm
Protein 30 gm

**Exchange List
Approximations**

Starch 1
Vegetable 1
Meat, very lean 4
Fat ½

1.   Season the chicken with the garlic and set aside.

2.   Prepare a large skillet with nonstick pan spray. Add the margarine and cook the onions and mushrooms over medium-high heat about 2 to 3 minutes. Push the onions to one side and brown the chicken breasts about 3 minutes per side. Sprinkle the chicken with lemon juice, paprika, salt, and pepper. Cover tightly and cook over low heat until the chicken is tender, about 30 minutes. Remove the chicken from the skillet and keep warm.

3.   Make the sauce by sprinkling the flour over the onions and mushrooms; stir and cook about 1 minute. Add the milk and stir and simmer until thickened.

4.   Stir in the sour cream. Taste and add more paprika if desired. Add the chicken and heat through. Do not boil.

ROAST CHICKEN OR CAPON

Roasted chicken is an all-time favorite, with its deliciously moist and tender meat. Filling the cavity of the bird with wedges of lemon, cloves of garlic, parsley, and rosemary imparts a wonderful flavor to the meat, as does the lemon-oil mixture that's brushed on the skin of the bird. Don't be concerned about the fat added by the lemon-oil mixture—it's used only for seasoning and to crisp the skin so the meat stays moist. If you remove the skin and don't eat the drippings, the added fat is negligible. Calculate your exchange value based on the amount of chicken you eat (1 ounce of chicken counts as 1 lean meat exchange). Any size chicken, roasting chicken, or capon can be used in this recipe, but keep in mind that if you use a larger bird you'll have more lean meat—and leftovers, too, which you can use in a variety of other recipes.

1 roasted bird (servings depend on size of bird)

1 roasting chicken or capon
     (about 5 to 7 pounds)
6 cloves garlic
1 medium lemon, cut in half
2 tablespoons olive oil
1 teaspoon salt
½ teaspoon freshly ground pepper
½ cup chopped fresh parsley
1 tablespoon chopped fresh rosemary,
     or 1 teaspoon dried rosemary

Nutrition Facts per Serving
Serving size: 3 ounces cooked poultry
Amount per serving:
Calories 179
Calories from fat 70
Total fat 8 gm
Saturated fat 2 gm
Cholesterol 78 mg
Sodium 192 mg
Total carbohydrate 0 gm
Dietary fiber 0 gm
Sugars 0 gm
Protein 25 gm

Exchange List Approximation

Meat, lean 3

1. Preheat the oven to 425°F. Wash the chicken under cold running water and pat dry with paper towels. Trim and discard the extra fat.

2. Crush 2 of the garlic cloves. In a small bowl, combine the crushed garlic, the juice of ½ lemon, the olive oil, salt, and pepper.

3. Brush the cavity of the bird with some of the lemon-oil mixture. Reserve the remainder. Cut the remaining lemon half in pieces; put the lemon pieces, the remaining 4 garlic cloves, the parsley, and rosemary in the cavity of the chicken. Tie the legs together with cotton string, or tuck them in the cavity of the bird.

4. Set the chicken, breast side up, on a rack in a roasting pan. Brush all the outside surfaces of the bird with the remaining lemon-oil mixture. Roast on the lower or middle rack of the oven, turning the bird over every 30 minutes and basting with pan juices at each turn. Cooking time depends on the size of the bird. Allow 25 minutes per pound; the chicken is done when an instant-read thermometer registers 165°F.

5. Remove the chicken from the oven; let it rest about 15 minutes to set the juices, covered lightly with foil to keep it hot.

6. Carve the chicken or cut in pieces. Remove the skin before eating.

FANNY'S CHICKEN AND RICE

Although this chicken dish takes a bit of time to prepare, it's well worth the time and effort. Sweet currants offset the flavors of peppers, onions, garlic, and tomatoes, and a dash of curry radiates beautiful color while lending a spicy, exotic flavor to the dish.

6 servings

¾ cup uncooked brown rice
6 skinless chicken breasts, or 6 skinless
     chicken thighs and drumsticks
     (about 2 pounds)
1 cup chopped onion
¾ cup chopped green bell pepper
2 cloves garlic, minced
1 tablespoon canola or corn oil
2 teaspoons curry powder
1½ teaspoons fresh thyme, or
     ½ teaspoon dried thyme
¾ teaspoon salt
One 14- to 15-ounce can diced tomatoes,
     with juice
1 tablespoon chopped fresh parsley
2 tablespoons dried currants
2 tablespoons slivered almonds

Nutrition Facts per Serving

Serving size: 1 breast half, or 1 drumstick and thigh, plus ½ cup rice and ½ cup sauce

Amount per serving:

Calories 304
Calories from fat 68

Total fat 8 gm
   Saturated fat 1 gm
Cholesterol 73 mg
Sodium 469 mg
Total carbohydrate 28 gm
   Dietary fiber 3 gm
   Sugars 7 gm
Protein 30 gm

Exchange List Approximations

Starch 1½
Vegetable 1
Meat, very lean 4
Fat, monounsaturated ½

1.   Preheat the oven to 425°F. Prepare a shallow baking pan with non-stick pan spray.

2.   Add the rice to 3 cups boiling water in a medium saucepan; cover and simmer 50 to 60 minutes.

3.   While the rice is cooking, put the chicken in the prepared pan. Bake, uncovered, 20 minutes.

4.   While the chicken is cooking, sauté the onion, pepper, and garlic in the oil in a large skillet for 5 minutes, until tender; add the curry powder, thyme, and salt and blend thoroughly. Add the tomatoes with their liquid, and the parsley; heat to a simmer.

5.   Pour the sauce over the chicken and sprinkle with the currants. Cover and bake at 350°F for 25 minutes.

6.   While the chicken is cooking, toast the almonds in a small skillet over medium heat for 3 minutes, or until lightly browned and fragrant.

7.   To serve, arrange the chicken parts next to ½ cup rice on individual plates. Divide the sauce over the rice. Sprinkle the almonds over the chicken.

PAELLA

Paella is a favorite party dish originally created by Spanish cowboys. We've developed a lighter version of this classic, using lean sausage, skinless chicken, shellfish, and just a touch of oil for sautéing. Paella's secret ingredient, saffron, is the most expensive spice in the world, but fortunately, a little goes a long way. Besides adding its trademark yellow color to the dish, saffron also lends a pungent, aromatic flavor.

6 servings

2 tablespoons olive oil
1½ to 2 pounds skinless chicken pieces
      (breasts, drumsticks, and thighs
      of 1 chicken)
½ cup thinly sliced red bell pepper
½ cup thinly sliced green bell pepper
¾ cup coarsely chopped onion
2 cloves garlic, minced
4 ounces reduced-fat Italian sausage or
      lean chorizo
1½ cups uncooked rice
One 14- to 15-ounce can diced tomatoes
      in tomato sauce
½ teaspoon salt
⅛ teaspoon ground saffron, or
      ½ teaspoon turmeric
½ cup thawed frozen peas
6 clams, scrubbed
6 mussels, scrubbed
12 medium shrimp, in the shell

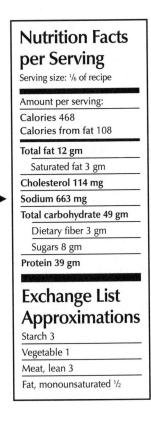

Nutrition Facts per Serving	
Serving size: ⅙ of recipe	
Amount per serving:	
Calories 468	
Calories from fat 108	
Total fat 12 gm	
Saturated fat 3 gm	
Cholesterol 114 mg	
Sodium 663 mg	
Total carbohydrate 49 gm	
Dietary fiber 3 gm	
Sugars 8 gm	
Protein 39 gm	

Exchange List Approximations

Starch	3
Vegetable	1
Meat, lean	3
Fat, monounsaturated	½

1.   Heat a paella pan or large ovenproof skillet over medium heat. Add the olive oil. Sauté the chicken over medium heat for 10 to 15 minutes, or until browned on both sides. Drain on paper towel and set aside.

2.   In the same skillet, sauté the red and green peppers, onion, and garlic for 5 minutes, stirring often; set aside.

3.   Preheat the oven to 400°F.

4.   Cook the sausage in the skillet for 5 to 10 minutes, or until browned; drain on paper towel, slice, and set aside.

5.   In the same large skillet, combine the rice, vegetable mixture, tomatoes, salt, saffron, and 3 cups water. Bring to a boil, stirring constantly; remove from the heat.

6.   Add the chicken and sausage to the skillet. Cover and bake for 30 minutes.

7.   Stir the peas into the mixture. Arrange the clams, mussels, and shrimp around the chicken. Bake, covered, 10 minutes longer, or until the mussels and clams open. (Discard any that do not open.)

CHICKEN TACOS

You can use leftover roasted chicken in this easy-to-fix dinner that's bound to become a staple in your house.

12 tacos (6 servings)

One package 6-inch-diameter taco shells
    (12 shells)
One 1¼-ounce package taco seasoning
    mix
2⅔ cups cooked chicken (1 pound),
    torn into small pieces or
    shredded
1½ cups (6 ounces) shredded reduced-
    fat Cheddar cheese
¾ cup nonfat sour cream
2 cups shredded lettuce
1 cup diced tomato
¾ cup chopped onion

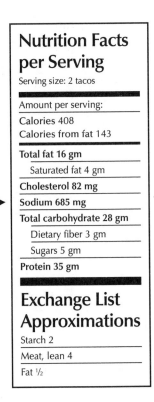

Nutrition Facts per Serving

Serving size: 2 tacos

Amount per serving:

Calories 408
Calories from fat 143

Total fat 16 gm
  Saturated fat 4 gm

Cholesterol 82 mg

Sodium 685 mg

Total carbohydrate 28 gm
  Dietary fiber 3 gm
  Sugars 5 gm

Protein 35 gm

Exchange List Approximations

Starch 2

Meat, lean 4

Fat ½

1.   Preheat the oven to 350°F. Put the taco shells on a cookie sheet.

2.   In a skillet, combine the taco seasoning and 1 cup water. Bring to a boil; add the cooked chicken and simmer 10 to 15 minutes, until most of the liquid is absorbed into the chicken.

3.   Bake the taco shells 5 to 7 minutes, until warm.

4.   Place ¼ cup of the chicken mixture in each taco shell. Top each with 2 tablespoons Cheddar cheese, 1 tablespoon sour cream, some shredded lettuce, diced tomato, and chopped onion. Serve immediately.

TANDOORI CHICKEN

The aromatic spices ginger, paprika, cumin, cardamom, and crushed red pepper flakes are mixed with yogurt and used as both a marinade and a sauce in this Indian-inspired dish.

4 servings

1 whole chicken (3 to 3½ pounds),
    cut in 8 pieces
1 teaspoon salt
½ cup plain nonfat or low-fat yogurt
¼ cup fresh lime juice (juice of 1 large
    or 2 small limes)
2 cloves garlic, chopped
2 teaspoons grated gingerroot
2 teaspoons paprika
½ teaspoon ground cumin
¼ teaspoon ground cardamom
¼ teaspoon crushed red pepper flakes

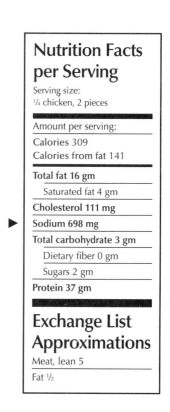

Nutrition Facts per Serving

Serving size:
¼ chicken, 2 pieces

Amount per serving:
Calories 309
Calories from fat 141

Total fat 16 gm
    Saturated fat 4 gm
Cholesterol 111 mg
Sodium 698 mg
Total carbohydrate 3 gm
    Dietary fiber 0 gm
    Sugars 2 gm
Protein 37 gm

Exchange List Approximations

Meat, lean 5

Fat ½

1. Prick the chicken skin with a fork. Make diagonal slashes through the skin about ¼ inch deep and about 1 inch apart. Place the chicken in a flat glass baking dish. Sprinkle with salt.

2. In a small bowl, combine all the remaining ingredients. Brush generously over all surfaces of the chicken and pour the remaining marinade on top. Cover and marinate for at least 8 hours or as long as 24 hours in the refrigerator.

3. Preheat the oven to 450°F. Bake the chicken in the marinade for 20 minutes; turn, baste with the sauce in the pan, and cook 20 minutes more, until the chicken is browned and thoroughly cooked.

NEW ENGLAND CHICKEN CROQUETTES

A traditional New England favorite, croquettes are crunchy on the outside, rich and creamy on the inside. Usually deep-fat fried, they are equally delicious in this recipe, which reduces the fat content by baking them instead.

8 croquettes (4 servings)

2 tablespoons margarine
2 tablespoons all-purpose flour
1 cup fat-free milk
1 teaspoon Worcestershire sauce
2 teaspoons snipped fresh chervil, or
      ½ teaspoon dried chervil
½ teaspoon salt
⅛ teaspoon white pepper
2 cups (12 ounces) finely chopped
    cooked chicken
⅔ cup bread crumbs
2 large eggs, lightly beaten in a shallow
    bowl, or ½ cup egg substitute

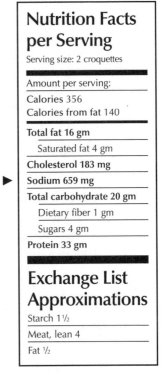

Nutrition Facts per Serving

Serving size: 2 croquettes

Amount per serving:

Calories 356
Calories from fat 140

Total fat 16 gm
   Saturated fat 4 gm
Cholesterol 183 mg
Sodium 659 mg
Total carbohydrate 20 gm
   Dietary fiber 1 gm
   Sugars 4 gm
Protein 33 gm

Exchange List Approximations

Starch 1½
Meat, lean 4
Fat ½

1.   Melt the margarine in a nonstick skillet over low heat; stir in the flour and mix to a smooth paste. Add the milk gradually, whisking until smooth; stir in the Worcestershire sauce, chervil, salt, and pepper. Add the chicken; mix well. Cover and refrigerate at least 1 hour.

2.   Preheat the oven to 375°F. Prepare a cookie sheet with nonstick pan spray.

3.   Spread the bread crumbs on a plate.

4.   When the croquette mixture is cold, form it into 8 balls, using ⅓ cup per ball. Roll each ball in bread crumbs, then in eggs, and again in bread crumbs.

5.   Place the croquettes on the prepared cookie sheet. Bake for 25 to 30 minutes, until they are a light golden brown.

CHICKEN NUGGETS WITH BBQ DIPPING SAUCE

Kids especially love these crispy nuggets, ideal for a casual supper or as a party appetizer.

24 nuggets (4 servings)

4 to 5 skinless, boneless chicken breasts
      (1 pound), cut in 1 x 1 x ½-inch
      pieces (about 24 pieces)
½ teaspoon salt
¼ teaspoon freshly ground pepper
1 large egg, beaten, or ¼ cup egg
      substitute
½ cup bread crumbs
⅓ cup prepared barbecue sauce or
      Dijon and honey mustard
      barbecue sauce

1. Preheat the oven to 350°F. Prepare a cookie sheet with nonstick pan spray.
2. Sprinkle the nuggets with salt and pepper. Dip them in egg, then in bread crumbs. Place on the cookie sheet.
3. Bake for 15 minutes; turn them and bake 5 minutes longer, to a light golden brown.
4. Serve hot with barbecue sauce for dipping.

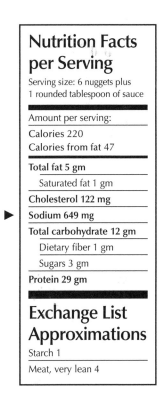

Nutrition Facts per Serving

Serving size: 6 nuggets plus 1 rounded tablespoon of sauce

Amount per serving:

Calories 220
Calories from fat 47

Total fat 5 gm
   Saturated fat 1 gm
Cholesterol 122 mg
Sodium 649 mg
Total carbohydrate 12 gm
   Dietary fiber 1 gm
   Sugars 3 gm
Protein 29 gm

Exchange List Approximations

Starch 1
Meat, very lean 4

SPINACH-STUFFED CHICKEN BREASTS

An herbed spinach and cheese mixture is stuffed under the skin of plump chicken breasts, creating a dish that's perfect for a dinner party or a special romantic dinner. The skin is needed to encase the stuffing in the chicken breasts, but you may wish to remove it before eating to help reduce calories and fat grams. Mushroom Risotto (page 396) makes a great side dish.

4 servings

$^3/_4$ cup frozen chopped spinach, thawed
    and drained
$^1/_4$ cup (2 ounces) low-fat ricotta cheese
$^1/_2$ cup (2 ounces) shredded part-skim
    mozzarella cheese
2 teaspoons chopped fresh tarragon, or
    $^1/_4$ teaspoon dried tarragon
$^1/_4$ teaspoon salt
$^1/_8$ teaspoon freshly ground pepper
4 chicken breast halves (1$^3/_4$ pounds)
2 teaspoons olive oil

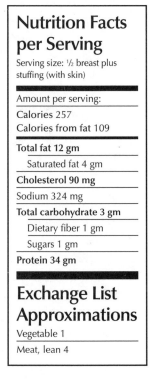

Nutrition Facts per Serving

Serving size: $^1/_2$ breast plus stuffing (with skin)

Amount per serving:

Calories 257
Calories from fat 109

Total fat 12 gm
    Saturated fat 4 gm
Cholesterol 90 mg
Sodium 324 mg
Total carbohydrate 3 gm
    Dietary fiber 1 gm
    Sugars 1 gm
Protein 34 gm

Exchange List Approximations

Vegetable 1
Meat, lean 4

1.   Preheat the oven to 350°F. Prepare a shallow baking pan with nonstick pan spray.
2.   Combine the spinach, cheeses, and seasonings in a small bowl. Lift up the skin from each chicken breast half and stuff the spinach mixture between the skin and chicken meat. (Be careful not to tear the skin.) Smooth the skin over the stuffing, tucking it underneath to form a neat package.
3.   Brush the stuffed breasts with olive oil and place them bone side down in a baking pan. Bake, uncovered, for 45 minutes, until the chicken is cooked and brown.

CALIFORNIA-STYLE CHICKEN

For garlic lovers only! This chicken dish is loaded with garlic cloves that infuse their fragrance into the chicken as it roasts. In addition to adding ample flavor, the cloves can do double duty as a delicious, fat-free spread. Simply squeeze out the baked garlic and spread on bread slices. Round out the meal with Green Beans with Sunflower Seeds (page 313) and wild rice.

4 servings

1 chicken, cut in 8 pieces
    (about 3 pounds)
2 teaspoons olive oil
¼ cup chopped fresh basil leaves,
    or 2 teaspoons dried basil
1 tablespoon chopped fresh oregano
    leaves, or 1 teaspoon dried
    oregano
½ teaspoon salt
¼ teaspoon freshly ground pepper
40 cloves garlic, separated, peeled
4 ribs celery, cut into 1-inch pieces
1 cup chopped onion
¼ cup chopped fresh parsley
¾ cup dry white wine
2 tablespoons fresh lemon juice

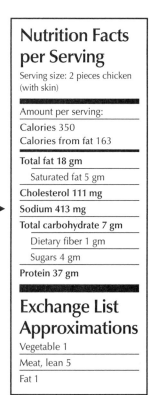

Nutrition Facts per Serving

Serving size: 2 pieces chicken (with skin)

Amount per serving:

Calories 350
Calories from fat 163

Total fat 18 gm
    Saturated fat 5 gm
Cholesterol 111 mg
Sodium 413 mg
Total carbohydrate 7 gm
    Dietary fiber 1 gm
    Sugars 4 gm
Protein 37 gm

Exchange List Approximations

Vegetable 1
Meat, lean 5
Fat 1

1. Preheat the oven to 375°F. Prepare a medium baking dish with olive oil–flavored nonstick pan spray.

2. Place the chicken in the prepared baking dish and brush with oil. Sprinkle basil, oregano, salt, and pepper over the chicken. Spread the garlic cloves, celery, onion, and parsley over and around the chicken. Pour the wine and lemon juice into the baking dish.

3. Cover with foil and bake for 40 minutes. Uncover and bake for an additional 30 minutes.

SOUTHERN CHICKEN HASH

Seasoned with paprika, mace, and a pinch of cayenne pepper, this hearty hash has its roots in the Deep South. Serve as a main dish or at brunch as an accompaniment to omelets and other egg dishes. It's a tasty way to use up leftover chicken.

4 servings

½ cup chopped onion
¼ cup chopped green bell pepper
1 tablespoon canola or corn oil
2½ cups (about 1 pound) coarsely
      chopped cooked chicken
1 cup diced, peeled, boiled red potatoes
¼ cup fat-free evaporated milk
1 teaspoon Worcestershire sauce
½ teaspoon salt
½ teaspoon paprika
⅛ teaspoon mace
Pinch of cayenne pepper

1. Prepare a large skillet with nonstick pan spray. Sauté the onion and green pepper in oil over medium heat for about 5 minutes.
2. Stir in all the remaining ingredients and press the mixture to flatten. Cover the pan and cook for 5 minutes, until the hash is heated thoroughly.
3. Uncover and cook over low heat, allowing the hash to brown. Turn the hash over (it will probably break apart). Pat it down and brown on the other side. Divide in 4 equal portions; serve hot.

Nutrition Facts per Serving

Serving size: ¼ of recipe

Amount per serving:

Calories 302
Calories from fat 108

Total fat 12 gm
   Saturated fat 3 gm
Cholesterol 101 mg
Sodium 421 mg
Total carbohydrate 12 gm
   Dietary fiber 1 gm
   Sugars 4 gm
Protein 35 gm

Exchange List Approximations

Starch 1

Meat, very lean 5

Fat 1

SAUTÉ OF CHICKEN WITH CARAMELIZED ONIONS

This dish is especially good in the late spring when sweet onions like Vidalia, Walla Walla, and Texas 1015 varieties are in season. Sautéing the onions helps caramelize their natural sugars.

4 servings

1 tablespoon olive oil
2 large sweet or Spanish onions (about
      12 ounces total), thinly sliced and
      separated into rings
2 teaspoons sugar
4 skinless, boneless chicken breast
      halves (about 1 pound)
2 tablespoons grainy Dijon mustard
3/4 teaspoon cracked black peppercorns

1. Heat the oil in a large nonstick skillet. Sauté the onions over medium-low heat until tender and golden. Add the sugar after the first 5 minutes of cooking. Caramelizing the onions will take about 15 minutes; stir occasionally. Remove the onions from the skillet with a slotted spatula; set aside.
2. Brush the chicken on both sides with mustard; sprinkle with pepper. Sauté in the same skillet over medium heat, about 5 minutes per side, or until cooked through.
3. Arrange the reserved onions over the chicken; heat through. Serve with additional cracked pepper, if desired.

Nutrition Facts per Serving	
Serving size: 1/2 chicken breast with about 1/3 cup onions	
Amount per serving:	
Calories 207	
Calories from fat 60	
Total fat 7 gm	
Saturated fat 1 gm	
Cholesterol 69 mg	
Sodium 156 mg	
Total carbohydrate 9 gm	
Dietary fiber 1 gm	
Sugars 7 gm	
Protein 26 gm	

Exchange List Approximations

Vegetable 2	
Meat, very lean 3	
Fat, monounsaturated 1	

GRILLED ORANGE-MUSTARD CHICKEN

Glazed with a fruity mustard and orange marinade, this chicken dish is a delight. Liqueurs add a lot of flavor and no fat to recipes, and the alcohol burns off during cooking. Try nutty Apple-Pecan Wild Rice (page 398) and steamed broccoli on the side.

4 servings

4 skinless chicken breast halves,
      or 4 skinless leg quarters
      (about 1³/₄ pounds)
¹/₂ cup orange juice
¹/₄ cup orange-flavored liqueur
1 tablespoon plus 1 teaspoon grainy
      Dijon mustard
2 tablespoons chopped fresh thyme
      leaves, or 1 teaspoon dried thyme
2 cloves garlic, minced
1 medium orange, peeled and cut in
      8 wedges

Nutrition Facts per Serving

Serving size: ¹/₂ chicken breast plus 2 orange wedges

Amount per serving:

Calories 175
Calories from fat 28

Total fat 3 gm
   Saturated fat 1 gm
Cholesterol 69 mg
Sodium 93 mg
Total carbohydrate 10 gm
   Dietary fiber 1 gm
   Sugars 9 gm
Protein 26 gm

Exchange List Approximations

Fruit ¹/₂

Meat, very lean 4

1.   Place the chicken in a shallow glass dish or plastic bag.

2.   To make the marinade, combine the remaining ingredients except the orange wedges in a small bowl; pour over the chicken. Cover and refrigerate at least 1 hour. Drain the chicken, reserving the marinade.

3.   Preheat a grill or the broiler.

4.   Grill over medium coals, covered with foil or with a grill cover, or broil 4 to 5 inches from the heat source 5 minutes per side, or until the chicken is cooked through, basting often with the marinade. (Discard any remaining marinade. Do not pour it over the cooked chicken.)

5.   Garnish the chicken portions with orange wedges at serving time.

BASQUE-STYLE CHICKEN

Roasted red pepper and parsley lend a dash of color to this savory chicken dish simmered with wine and aromatic vegetables.

4 servings

2 tablespoons all-purpose flour
1 tablespoon chopped fresh thyme,
    or 1 teaspoon dried thyme
1 teaspoon paprika
1/2 teaspoon freshly ground pepper
1/2 teaspoon salt
4 skinless chicken breast halves
    (1 1/4 to 1 1/2 pounds)
2 teaspoons olive oil
1 large onion, coarsely chopped
2 cloves garlic, minced
1 cup dry white wine
1 bay leaf
1 tablespoon chopped roasted red
    bell pepper or chopped, drained
    pimiento
2 tablespoons chopped fresh parsley

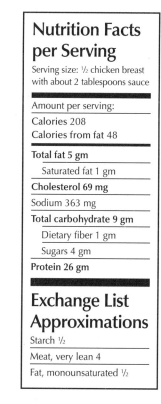

Nutrition Facts per Serving

Serving size: 1/2 chicken breast with about 2 tablespoons sauce

Amount per serving:

Calories 208
Calories from fat 48

Total fat 5 gm
  Saturated fat 1 gm
Cholesterol 69 mg
Sodium 363 mg
Total carbohydrate 9 gm
  Dietary fiber 1 gm
  Sugars 4 gm
Protein 26 gm

Exchange List Approximations

Starch 1/2
Meat, very lean 4
Fat, monounsaturated 1/2

1. Combine the flour, thyme, paprika, pepper, and salt in a large bowl or plastic bag. Dredge the chicken in the flour mixture.
2. Heat the oil in a large nonstick skillet. Brown the chicken over medium heat, about 4 minutes per side. Remove and reserve.
3. Sauté the onion and garlic in the same skillet until tender, about 5 minutes. Add the wine and bay leaf; bring to a boil, stirring constantly.
4. Return the chicken to the skillet; add the roasted pepper. Cover and simmer over low heat until the chicken is cooked through, about 20 minutes. Discard the bay leaf. Serve the hot chicken in the sauce; sprinkle with parsley.

CHICKEN VESUVIO

The traditional Italian gremolata garnish of parsley, lemon zest, and raw garlic provides a burst of fresh flavor and texture to this traditional chicken and roasted potato dish. There is so much good garlic taste in this recipe that you don't even need salt to enhance its flavor.

4 servings

1 whole chicken, cut in 8 pieces, skin
    removed (about 3 pounds)
1 tablespoon extra virgin olive oil
1 tablespoon chopped fresh rosemary,
    or 1 teaspoon dried rosemary
3 large cloves garlic, minced
¼ teaspoon freshly ground pepper
1 large baking potato (12 ounces),
    peeled and cut into 8 wedges
3 tablespoons chopped Italian parsley
½ teaspoon grated lemon zest

1. Preheat the oven to 375°F.

2. Place the chicken in an ovenproof casserole dish or small roasting pan. Brush with oil and sprinkle with the rosemary, ⅔ of the chopped garlic, and the pepper. Place the potato wedges around the chicken. Cover with foil and bake 30 minutes.

3. Uncover; baste the chicken with the pan juices and continue to bake 20 minutes longer, or until the chicken and potatoes are tender.

4. Combine the parsley, lemon zest, and remaining chopped garlic; sprinkle over the chicken.

Nutrition Facts per Serving
Serving size: ¼ chicken with 2 potato wedges
Amount per serving:
Calories 288
Calories from fat 99
Total fat 11 gm
Saturated fat 3 gm
Cholesterol 93 mg
Sodium 94 mg
Total carbohydrate 15 gm
Dietary fiber 1 gm
Sugars 2 gm
Protein 31 gm

Exchange List Approximations

Starch 1

Meat, lean 4

WEST COAST CHICKEN BREAST

Serve this chicken dish at your next dinner party—it's both elegant and scrumptious. Chicken breasts are stuffed with an herbed sun-dried tomato mixture and topped with golden bread crumbs. You can even prepare the chicken and refrigerate it up to 4 hours before baking, so there's no need to worry about last-minute preparation while guests are arriving. Just add 2 minutes to the baking time if the breasts are chilled.

4 servings

4 large skinless, boneless chicken breast
      halves (about 1 pound)
¼ cup chopped sun-dried tomatoes
      packed in oil, well drained
¼ cup packed chopped fresh basil
      leaves
1 clove garlic, minced
1 tablespoon olive oil
¼ teaspoon freshly ground pepper
¼ teaspoon paprika
1 slice whole wheat bread, crumbled to
      make soft crumbs

Nutrition Facts per Serving

Serving size:
1 stuffed chicken breast half

Amount per serving:

Calories 198
Calories from fat 68

Total fat 8 gm
  Saturated fat 1 gm
Cholesterol 69 mg
Sodium 118 mg
Total carbohydrate 5 gm
  Dietary fiber 1 gm
  Sugars 1 gm
Protein 26 gm

Exchange List Approximations

Starch ½

Meat, very lean 4

Fat, monounsaturated ½

1.   Preheat the oven to 425°F. Prepare a shallow baking dish with olive oil–flavored nonstick pan spray.

2.   Pound the chicken breasts to ¼-inch thickness. Combine the tomatoes, basil, and garlic in a small bowl. Spread the tomato mixture evenly over the chicken breasts; roll up and place seam side down in the prepared baking dish.

3.   Combine the oil, pepper, and paprika in a small bowl; brush evenly over the chicken rolls. Sprinkle with the bread crumbs. Press the crumbs onto the chicken rolls so they adhere.

4.   Bake 15 minutes, or until the chicken is tender and the crumbs are browned.

COQ AU VIN

Here's a lighter version of the classic French dish, guaranteed to perfume the house with its heady aroma. Serve with parsleyed new potatoes, a leafy green salad, and a warm baguette.

4 servings

3 tablespoons all-purpose flour
¼ teaspoon salt
¼ teaspoon freshly ground pepper
1 whole chicken, cut in quarters, skin
     removed (about 3 pounds)
1 tablespoon olive oil
8 small white boiling onions
     (each 1 inch in diameter,
     8 ounces total), peeled
1 teaspoon sugar
2 cloves garlic, minced
8 ounces whole medium mushrooms,
     stems trimmed
1 cup dry red wine
1 cup Homemade Chicken Broth
     (page 101) or canned reduced-
     sodium chicken broth
1 bay leaf
1 tablespoon chopped fresh thyme,
     or 1 teaspoon dried thyme
1 tablespoon chopped fresh parsley

Nutrition Facts per Serving
Serving size: ¼ chicken
Amount per serving:
Calories 297
Calories from fat 106
Total fat 12 gm
Saturated fat 3 gm
Cholesterol 93 mg
Sodium 264 mg
Total carbohydrate 13 gm
Dietary fiber 2 gm
Sugars 5 gm
Protein 33 gm

Exchange List Approximations

Starch ½	
Vegetable 1	
Meat, lean 4	

1. Combine the flour, salt, and pepper in a large bowl or plastic bag. Dredge the chicken pieces, using all of the flour mixture. Heat the oil in a large nonstick skillet over medium heat. Lightly brown the chicken in the oil, about 4 minutes per side.

2. Remove the chicken; reserve. Add the onions to the skillet; sprinkle with sugar. Sauté until lightly browned. Add the garlic and mushrooms; sauté about 2 minutes.

3. Add the wine, broth, bay leaf, and thyme; bring to a boil. Add the chicken; reduce the heat, cover, and simmer 40 minutes, or until the chicken is tender, turning the chicken midway through the cooking time.

4. Transfer the chicken and vegetables to 4 shallow bowls. Simmer the sauce over medium-high heat about 3 minutes, stirring and scraping to incorporate the browned bits from the bottom of the pan. Discard the bay leaf; pour the sauce over the chicken. Sprinkle with parsley.

SPICY CHICKEN THIGHS

The heat of the salsa you choose to use—hot, medium, or mild—will dictate the spiciness of this dish. Some salsas become hotter the longer they are kept in the refrigerator, so beware. For the best flavor, marinate the thighs for at least 6 hours before cooking.

4 chicken thighs (4 servings)

4 medium to large skinless chicken
    thighs (1½ pounds)
One 8-ounce container plain low-fat
    yogurt
¼ cup hot salsa or picante sauce
1 tablespoon curry powder
1 teaspoon ground cumin

1. Place the chicken in a glass dish. In a small bowl, combine the yogurt, salsa, curry powder, and cumin. Pour over the chicken, turning to coat. Cover and refrigerate at least 6 hours or up to 24 hours.

2. Heat the oven to 375°F. Transfer the chicken and sauce to an ovenproof dish prepared with nonstick pan spray. Bake, uncovered, 40 to 45 minutes, or until the chicken is tender and cooked through.

Nutrition Facts per Serving

Serving size: 1 thigh

Amount per serving:

Calories 186
Calories from fat 75

Total fat 8 gm
    Saturated fat 3 gm
Cholesterol 73 mg
Sodium 139 mg
Total carbohydrate 5 gm
    Dietary fiber 0 gm
    Sugars 4 gm
Protein 22 gm

Exchange List Approximations

Starch ½

Meat, lean 3

RAGOUT OF CHICKEN, SWEET POTATO, AND BROCCOLI

Ragouts are thick, rich, well-seasoned stews, and this chicken version is one of the best. Sweet potatoes and broccoli add not only bright, beautiful color but wonderful flavor to the stew as well.

4 servings

2 tablespoons all-purpose flour
1 teaspoon paprika, preferably
    Hungarian
¼ teaspoon freshly ground pepper
¼ teaspoon salt
4 medium to large skinless chicken
    thighs (1½ pounds)
1 tablespoon olive oil
1 large onion, thinly sliced
2 cloves garlic, minced
1⅓ cups Homemade Chicken Broth
    (page 101), or canned reduced-
    sodium chicken broth
2 medium sweet potatoes (1 pound
    total), peeled and quartered
1 bay leaf
3 cups broccoli florets (8 ounces)
1 teaspoon grated lemon zest

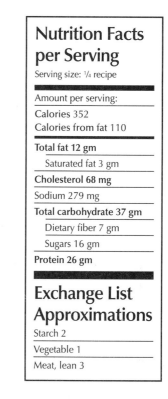

Nutrition Facts per Serving

Serving size: ¼ recipe

Amount per serving:

Calories 352
Calories from fat 110

Total fat 12 gm
    Saturated fat 3 gm

Cholesterol 68 mg

Sodium 279 mg

Total carbohydrate 37 gm
    Dietary fiber 7 gm
    Sugars 16 gm

Protein 26 gm

Exchange List Approximations

Starch 2

Vegetable 1

Meat, lean 3

1.   Combine the flour with the paprika, pepper, and salt. Dredge the chicken, using all of the flour mixture.

2.   Heat the oil in a large, deep nonstick skillet over medium heat. Sauté the chicken in the oil until lightly browned, about 4 minutes per side. Add the onion and garlic; cook 1 minute.

3.   Add the broth, potatoes, and bay leaf. Cover and simmer over low heat 30 minutes. Add the broccoli; cover and continue to simmer until the chicken and potatoes are tender and the broccoli is crisp-tender, about 5 minutes. Remove and discard the bay leaf.

4.   Remove the chicken and vegetables to a serving platter; boil the pan juices over high heat until thickened, about 5 minutes. Spoon the sauce over the chicken and vegetables; sprinkle with lemon zest.

CHICKEN IN MOLE SAUCE

Mole is a deep, dark sauce that's a Mexican specialty. Its unique flavor and reddish brown color results from blending onions, garlic, and chiles with—surprise—a small amount of cocoa powder or chocolate, which adds richness without sweetness. Try jalapeño relish in place of the salsa if you're a fan of spicy food. Its intensity varies from hot to super-hot, so use sparingly if you're a first-timer.

6 servings

1 cup uncooked white rice
1 large onion, coarsely chopped
2 cloves garlic, minced
2 teaspoons olive, canola, or corn oil
One 15-ounce can tomato sauce
⅓ cup prepared salsa, picante sauce,
    or jalapeño relish
4 teaspoons unsweetened cocoa powder
1 teaspoon ground cumin
⅛ teaspoon ground allspice
6 skinless chicken breast halves or
    skinless chicken thighs
    (about 2 pounds)
⅓ cup coarsely chopped cilantro

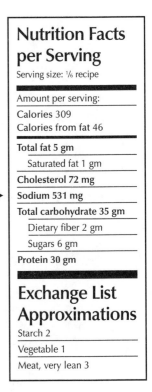

Nutrition Facts per Serving

Serving size: ⅙ recipe

Amount per serving:

Calories 309
Calories from fat 46

Total fat 5 gm
    Saturated fat 1 gm
Cholesterol 72 mg
Sodium 531 mg
Total carbohydrate 35 gm
    Dietary fiber 2 gm
    Sugars 6 gm
Protein 30 gm

Exchange List Approximations

Starch 2

Vegetable 1

Meat, very lean 3

1.   Cook the rice according to the package directions, without salt.
2.   While the rice is cooking, sauté the onion and garlic in oil in a large nonstick skillet until tender, about 5 minutes. Add the tomato sauce, salsa, cocoa, cumin, and allspice. Bring to a boil, stirring well.
3.   Add the chicken; reduce the heat. Cover and simmer until the chicken is tender, about 25 minutes.
4.   Arrange the rice on a serving platter and top with the chicken. Stir the sauce; pour over the chicken and rice. Sprinkle the top with cilantro.

GEORGIA-STYLE COUNTRY CAPTAIN CHICKEN

Legend has it that this recipe originated in Savannah, Georgia, from a sea captain selling spices. Whether or not the tale is true, the mix of currants, thyme, almonds, cayenne pepper, curry powder, and garlic certainly adds an enjoyable flavor.

4 servings

1 chicken, cut into 8 pieces, skin
        removed (about 3 pounds)
2 teaspoons curry powder
½ teaspoon salt
¼ to ½ teaspoon cayenne pepper
1 tablespoon olive oil
1 medium onion, cut into thin wedges
2 cloves garlic, minced
1 large green bell pepper, cut into 1-inch
        pieces
One 14- to 15-ounce can diced tomatoes
        with juice
¼ cup dried currants or raisins
½ teaspoon dried thyme
2 tablespoons sliced almonds

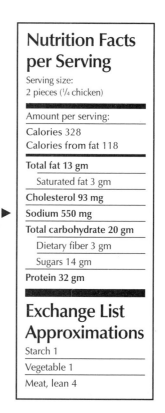

Nutrition Facts per Serving

Serving size:
2 pieces (¼ chicken)

Amount per serving:

Calories 328
Calories from fat 118

Total fat 13 gm
    Saturated fat 3 gm
Cholesterol 93 mg
Sodium 550 mg
Total carbohydrate 20 gm
    Dietary fiber 3 gm
    Sugars 14 gm
Protein 32 gm

Exchange List Approximations

Starch 1
Vegetable 1
Meat, lean 4

1. Sprinkle the chicken pieces with curry powder, salt, and cayenne.

2. Heat the oil in a large nonstick skillet. Brown the chicken in oil on all sides, about 10 minutes. Remove and set aside.

3. Sauté the onion and garlic in the same skillet for 3 minutes. Add the green pepper, tomatoes with liquid, currants, and thyme. Bring to a boil. Return the chicken to the skillet; reduce the heat. Cover and simmer until the chicken is tender, about 15 minutes, spooning the juices over the chicken occasionally. While the chicken is cooking, heat the almonds in a small skillet over medium heat for about 3 minutes, until slightly browned and fragrant.

4. Sprinkle the dish with toasted almonds at serving time.

CHICKEN CANNELLONI WITH RED AND WHITE SAUCE

We used crêpes in this recipe instead of pasta to wrap around a rich chicken and spinach filling. Topped with both tomato sauce and "skinny" white sauce, this dish is delicious and pretty to look at, too.

10 filled crêpes (5 servings)

CRÊPES

³/₄ cup all-purpose flour
¹/₈ teaspoon salt
2 large eggs

WHITE SAUCE

4 tablespoons (¹/₂ stick) margarine
¹/₄ cup all-purpose flour
1 cup Homemade Chicken Broth
     (page 101) or canned reduced-
     sodium chicken broth
¹/₃ cup fat-free milk
¹/₄ cup dry white wine
¹/₈ teaspoon white pepper
Pinch of nutmeg

FILLING

1¹/₂ cups cooked, diced chicken
     (9 ounces)
One 10-ounce package frozen chopped
     spinach, thawed and squeezed
     dry

RED SAUCE

1 cup prepared marinara pasta sauce
¹/₄ cup freshly grated Parmesan cheese

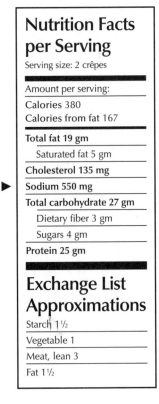

Nutrition Facts per Serving

Serving size: 2 crêpes

Amount per serving:

Calories 380
Calories from fat 167

Total fat 19 gm
    Saturated fat 5 gm

Cholesterol 135 mg

Sodium 550 mg

Total carbohydrate 27 gm
    Dietary fiber 3 gm
    Sugars 4 gm

Protein 25 gm

Exchange List Approximations

Starch 1¹/₂

Vegetable 1

Meat, lean 3

Fat 1¹/₂

1.   To make the crêpes, combine ³/₄ cup water with the flour, salt, and eggs in a food processor or blender and process until smooth.

2.   Heat a 5- or 6-inch skillet or crêpe pan until moderately hot. Prepare the pan with nonstick pan spray.

3.   Pour 1 ounce (2 tablespoons) of batter into the pan; tilt quickly to cover the pan with the thinnest possible layer.

4.   Cook until the bottom is lightly browned and the edges lift easily. Turn and cook the other side for a few minutes. Remove each crêpe to a sheet of wax paper and repeat the process until all the batter is used.

5.   For the white sauce, melt the margarine in a 1-quart saucepan over medium-high heat. Whisk in the flour and cook until blended. Gradually add the chicken broth and milk. Cook, whisking until smooth and thickened. Remove from the heat; stir in the wine, pepper, and nutmeg.

6.   To make the filling, place the chicken and spinach in a food processor or use a sharp knife; chop until well blended. Add enough white sauce (about ¹/₄ cup) to make the chicken mixture spreadable.

7.   Preheat the oven to 350°F. Prepare a 2-quart shallow baking dish with nonstick pan spray.

8.   Place 1¹/₂ tablespoons of chicken filling down the center of each crêpe; roll up. Place the crêpes seam side down in the baking dish in a single layer.

9.   Spread the remaining white sauce over the crêpes. Pour the red sauce in a strip over the white sauce. Sprinkle Parmesan cheese over all.

10.   Bake for 30 minutes, or until the cheese is brown and bubbly.

CHICKEN IN SAFFRON CREAM SAUCE

Saffron is a very expensive spice, but just a little bit provides a unique pungent flavor and an exquisite color. You can purchase saffron in powdered form or in threads. Threads are preferred, since the powdered variety loses its flavor more quickly during storage, but threads cost a bit more. This chicken is superb spooned over rice or pasta; add 1 starch exchange for 1/3 cup of rice or 1/2 cup of pasta.

6 chicken thighs and/or breast halves (6 servings)

3/4 cup chopped onion
2 cloves garlic, minced
1 tablespoon olive oil
2 tablespoons all-purpose flour
3/4 cup Homemade Chicken Broth
      (page 101) or canned reduced-
      sodium chicken broth
1/4 cup dry white wine or vermouth
1 tablespoon chopped fresh thyme
      or 1 teaspoon dried thyme
1/2 teaspoon salt
1/4 teaspoon powdered saffron or
      8 saffron threads
6 skinless chicken thighs and/or
      6 boneless, skinless breast halves
      (about 2 pounds)
1/4 cup sour half-and-half or light sour
      cream
2 tablespoons chopped fresh parsley
      or cilantro

Nutrition Facts per Serving

Serving size: 1/6 recipe (1 chicken thigh or breast half with 1/4 cup sauce)

Amount per serving:

Calories 193
Calories from fat 74

Total fat 8 gm
   Saturated fat 2 gm
Cholesterol 70 mg
Sodium 271 mg
Total carbohydrate 5 gm
   Dietary fiber 0 gm
   Sugars 2 gm
Protein 23 gm

Exchange List Approximations

Starch 1/2

Meat, lean 3

1. Sauté the onion and garlic in oil in a large nonstick skillet until tender, about 5 minutes. Sprinkle with flour; cook and stir 1 minute. Add the broth, wine, thyme, salt, and saffron; mix well. Add the chicken, spooning the sauce over the pieces. Cover and simmer over low heat until the chicken is tender, about 30 minutes, turning occasionally.

2. Transfer the chicken to a warm serving platter. Remove the skillet from the heat; stir in the sour cream until well blended. Pour over the chicken and sprinkle with parsley.

LOW-FAT OVEN-FRIED CHICKEN

Love the taste of fried chicken but hate the excess calories and fat? Here's a solution that's sure to please. Spicy yogurt sauce adds both flavor and practicality, acting as a base for the seasoned bread crumbs to keep the chicken moist during baking.

6 servings

1 cup plain low-fat yogurt
1 teaspoon paprika
1 teaspoon dried thyme
½ teaspoon salt
¼ teaspoon cayenne pepper
1 clove garlic, minced
6 skinless chicken breast halves or
      6 skinless chicken thighs
      (1¾ to 2 pounds)
1 cup seasoned bread crumbs
1 tablespoon margarine, melted

1.   Preheat the oven to 400°F.
2.   Combine the yogurt, paprika, thyme, salt, pepper, and garlic in a large bowl; mix well. Coat the chicken with the mixture. (The chicken may be covered and refrigerated overnight or baked immediately.)
3.   Prepare a shallow roasting pan or jelly roll pan with nonstick pan spray. Combine the bread crumbs and margarine in a shallow dish. Coat the chicken with the crumbs; place in the pan.
4.   Bake breasts for 25 minutes, thighs for 30 to 35 minutes, or until tender.

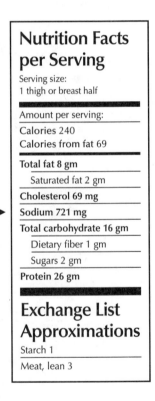

Nutrition Facts per Serving

Serving size:
1 thigh or breast half

Amount per serving:

Calories 240
Calories from fat 69

Total fat 8 gm
   Saturated fat 2 gm

Cholesterol 69 mg

Sodium 721 mg

Total carbohydrate 16 gm
   Dietary fiber 1 gm
   Sugars 2 gm

Protein 26 gm

Exchange List Approximations

Starch 1

Meat, lean 3

CHICKEN CALDO

A Spanish rendition of chicken soup that's made substantial with a mix of vegetables and beans. It's certain to give Mom's classic recipe a run for its money.

About 3 quarts (8 servings)

1 whole chicken, cut in 8 pieces, skin
     removed (about 2½ to 3 pounds)
1 cup chopped onion
3 cloves garlic, minced
½ teaspoon peppercorns
1 rib celery, sliced
1 medium turnip, peeled and cut into
     ½-inch cubes
2 medium carrots, sliced
1 medium zucchini, sliced
One 15-ounce can kidney beans or
     hominy, drained
2 cups chopped cabbage
1 teaspoon salt
½ teaspoon freshly ground pepper

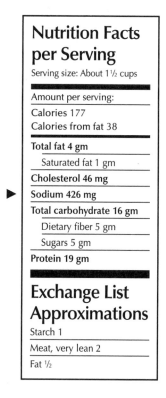

Nutrition Facts per Serving

Serving size: About 1½ cups

Amount per serving:

Calories 177
Calories from fat 38

Total fat 4 gm
   Saturated fat 1 gm
Cholesterol 46 mg
Sodium 426 mg
Total carbohydrate 16 gm
   Dietary fiber 5 gm
   Sugars 5 gm
Protein 19 gm

Exchange List Approximations

Starch 1
Meat, very lean 2
Fat ½

1.   Place the chicken, onion, garlic, and peppercorns in a large pot or Dutch oven. Cover with 2 quarts water; bring to a boil. Reduce the heat and simmer for 50 to 60 minutes, or until the chicken is very tender.
2.   Remove the chicken from the broth, cool, and remove the meat from the bones. Skim any fat from broth; return the chicken to the pot.
3.   Add the remaining ingredients; simmer for 20 to 30 minutes, or until the vegetables are tender. Serve in large soup bowls.

HUNAN CHICKEN

This recipe is terrific served over hot rice or chilled as a salad. Stir-frying is a great low-fat preparation method, but it requires constant stirring to cook the food thoroughly and evenly. A few quick tips: Have all the ingredients chopped and measured before starting to cook. Be careful not to overload the pan—otherwise, the food steams instead of frying. Cook in batches if necessary. And add the ingredients in the order in which they are listed in the recipe. Some items take longer to cook than others, so are listed first.

4 servings

1½ teaspoons canola or corn oil
1 boneless, skinless chicken breast
      (about 8 ounces), cubed
¾ cup sliced mushrooms
1 green onion with green top, sliced
      diagonally
½ medium red bell pepper, seeded,
      cored and cut into strips
1 clove garlic, minced
1 cup sliced bok choy
½ cup fresh bean sprouts or ¼ cup
      drained canned bean sprouts
½ cup snow peas, strings removed
1 tablespoon light soy sauce
¼ teaspoon crushed red pepper flakes
1½ teaspoons cornstarch
2 tablespoons cashews

Nutrition Facts per Serving
Serving size: ¼ recipe
Amount per serving:
Calories 146
Calories from fat 51
Total fat 6 gm
Saturated fat 1 gm
Cholesterol 36 mg
Sodium 201 mg
Total carbohydrate 8 gm
Dietary fiber 2 gm
Sugars 3 gm
Protein 16 gm

Exchange List Approximations	
Vegetable	2
Meat, very lean	2
Fat, monounsaturated	½

1. Heat the oil in a large nonstick skillet or wok. Stir-fry the chicken over medium-high heat until opaque, about 5 minutes. Set aside.
2. In the same skillet, cook the mushrooms, green onion, red pepper, garlic, and bok choy on medium heat, stirring constantly, for about 5 minutes. Add the bean sprouts and snow peas. Cook 2 minutes longer.
3. Stir in the chicken, soy sauce, and red pepper flakes. Cook gently for 2 minutes, or until chicken is heated thoroughly.
4. In a small bowl, mix the cornstarch into 1 tablespoon water; add to the skillet and cook until the sauce thickens. Stir in the cashews.

TURKEY LOAF

The classic American comfort food is made leaner by using ground turkey in place of hamburger. Ground turkey's mild taste easily takes on the flavors of spices and seasonings. For a pretty glaze, reserve 2 tablespoons of the catsup or chili sauce to brush over the top of the formed loaf toward the end of the baking time.

1 loaf (8 servings)

$^{1}/_{2}$ cup catsup or chili sauce
2 large eggs, or $^{1}/_{2}$ cup egg substitute
$^{1}/_{2}$ cup finely chopped onion
$^{1}/_{3}$ cup uncooked oatmeal
$^{1}/_{4}$ cup chopped fresh parsley, or
      1 tablespoon dried parsley
2 teaspoons chopped fresh oregano, or
      $^{3}/_{4}$ teaspoon dried oregano
$^{3}/_{4}$ teaspoon salt
$^{1}/_{2}$ teaspoon freshly ground pepper
2 pounds lean ground turkey

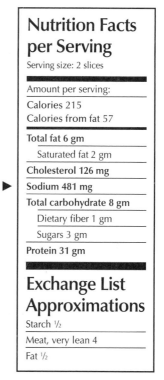

Nutrition Facts per Serving

Serving size: 2 slices

Amount per serving:

Calories 215
Calories from fat 57

Total fat 6 gm
   Saturated fat 2 gm
Cholesterol 126 mg
Sodium 481 mg
Total carbohydrate 8 gm
   Dietary fiber 1 gm
   Sugars 3 gm
Protein 31 gm

Exchange List Approximations

Starch $^{1}/_{2}$
Meat, very lean 4
Fat $^{1}/_{2}$

1.   Preheat the oven to 325°F. Prepare a 5 x 9-inch loaf pan with nonstick pan spray.
2.   Combine all the ingredients except the turkey in a large mixing bowl. Add the turkey and mix until well blended. Place the turkey mixture in the prepared pan and shape into a loaf.
3.   Bake for 1 hour, or until a meat thermometer registers 160° to 165°F.
4.   Allow the loaf to cool 5 to 10 minutes before slicing in $^{1}/_{2}$-inch slices. Extra slices are good for sandwiches.

TURKEY CUTLETS CREOLE

This recipe uses the trademarks of Creole cooking—chopped bell peppers, onions, and celery—as a flavor base. If you're in a hurry, you can substitute a 16-ounce can of chopped tomatoes with onions and peppers for the vegetables and 2 teaspoons of commercially prepared Creole or Cajun seasoning for all the spices.

4 servings

4 turkey cutlets (about 1 pound),
    or 1 pound turkey breast,
    cut in 4 slices
1 cup chopped green bell pepper
1/2 cup sliced mushrooms
1/2 cup chopped celery
1/2 cup chopped onion
2 cloves garlic, minced
1 cup stewed tomatoes with juice
1 cup Homemade Chicken Broth
    (page 101) or canned reduced-
    sodium chicken broth
1 bay leaf
2 teaspoons chopped fresh oregano,
    or 1/2 teaspoon dried oregano
2 teaspoons chopped fresh basil,
    or 1/2 teaspoon dried basil
1 teaspoon chopped fresh thyme,
    or 1/4 teaspoon dried thyme
1/2 teaspoon salt
1/4 teaspoon freshly ground pepper
1/4 teaspoon paprika
1/4 teaspoon cayenne pepper
4 to 6 drops hot pepper sauce
1 tablespoon cornstarch

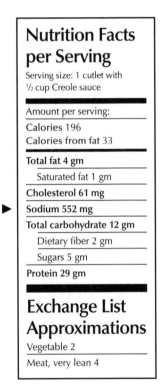

Nutrition Facts per Serving

Serving size: 1 cutlet with 1/2 cup Creole sauce

Amount per serving:

Calories 196
Calories from fat 33

Total fat 4 gm
  Saturated fat 1 gm
Cholesterol 61 mg
Sodium 552 mg
Total carbohydrate 12 gm
  Dietary fiber 2 gm
  Sugars 5 gm
Protein 29 gm

Exchange List Approximations

Vegetable 2

Meat, very lean 4

1.   Prepare a large skillet with nonstick pan spray. Heat the pan over high heat.

2.   Brown the turkey cutlets quickly on both sides. Set aside.

3.   Reduce the heat and sauté the green pepper, mushrooms, celery, onion, and garlic about 5 minutes. Add the tomatoes with juice, the chicken broth, all the herbs and seasonings, and the hot pepper sauce. Mix the cornstarch with 2 tablespoons water; add to the skillet. Bring to a boil. Simmer for about 20 minutes.

4.   Add the cutlets; spoon the sauce over them and simmer for another 4 to 6 minutes. Remove the bay leaf before serving.

TIMELY TURKEY TOSTADAS

Salsa is a terrific condiment for adding zip to recipes. Try some of the more interesting flavor combinations, like pineapple salsa or garlic salsa. Instead of using tortillas, you can substitute baked reduced-fat or fat-free corn tortilla chips if you like, using an amount equal to 1 starch exchange per serving. Serve the tostadas with Spanish Rice Picante (page 397).

4 tostadas (4 servings)

½ pound lean ground turkey
½ cup coarsely chopped onion
1 clove garlic, minced
¼ cup salsa or picante sauce
¼ cup Homemade Chicken Broth
      (page 101) or canned reduced-
      sodium chicken broth
1 teaspoon chili powder
½ teaspoon cumin seeds, or ¼ teaspoon
      ground cumin
Four 6-inch-diameter flour tortillas
2 tablespoons coarsely chopped cilantro
¼ cup (1 ounce) shredded reduced-fat
      Cheddar or reduced-fat Monterey
      Jack/Colby blend cheese
½ cup shredded lettuce
¼ cup chopped tomato
1 chopped fresh jalapeño pepper
      (optional)

Nutrition Facts per Serving	
Serving size: 1 tostada	
Amount per serving:	
Calories 177	
Calories from fat 38	
Total fat 4 gm	
Saturated fat 1 gm	
Cholesterol 31 mg	
Sodium 231 mg	
Total carbohydrate 17 gm	
Dietary fiber 2 gm	
Sugars 3 gm	
Protein 17 gm	

Exchange List Approximations

Starch	1
Meat, very lean	2
Fat	½

1.   Sauté the turkey, onion, and garlic in a large nonstick skillet over medium heat until no longer pink. Drain and return to the skillet.

2.   Add the salsa, broth, chili powder, and cumin. Simmer, uncovered, until most of the liquid has evaporated, about 10 to 12 minutes, stirring occasionally.

3.   While the turkey mixture simmers, broil the tortillas about 4 to 5 inches from the heat source until crisp and golden brown, turning occasionally.

4.   Stir the cilantro into the turkey mixture. Top each tortilla with ¼ cup turkey mixture, 1 tablespoon cheese, 2 tablespoons lettuce, and 1 tablespoon chopped tomato. Sprinkle with jalapeño pepper, if desired.

STUFFED TURKEY TENDERLOIN

Lean turkey tenderloins are stuffed with green chiles, cilantro, garlic, and other seasonings for a flavorful dish with a Southwest flair.

2 tenderloins (4 servings)

2 small turkey tenderloins (about
    ½ pound each)
¼ teaspoon salt
⅛ teaspoon freshly ground pepper
1 cup chopped onion
2 cloves garlic, minced
One 4-ounce can chopped green chiles,
    or ½ cup mild *giardiniera*
    pepper-vegetable mixture,
    drained
½ cup coarsely chopped cilantro
1 tablespoon olive oil

Nutrition Facts per Serving
Serving size: 3 or 4 slices
Amount per serving:
Calories 194
Calories from fat 57
Total fat 6 gm
Saturated fat 1 gm
Cholesterol 61 mg
Sodium 259 mg
Total carbohydrate 5 gm
Dietary fiber 1 gm
Sugars 3 gm
Protein 27 gm

Exchange List Approximations	
Vegetable	1
Meat, very lean	4
Fat, monounsaturated	½

1. Prepare a charcoal grill or preheat the broiler.
2. Cut a pocket horizontally along the side of each tenderloin, making sure not to cut all the way through. Season with salt and pepper.
3. Spray a medium skillet with nonstick pan spray. Sauté the onion and garlic until softened, about 3 minutes. Stir in the green chiles and cilantro.
4. Stuff the onion mixture into the pockets in the tenderloins; secure with small metal skewers or wooden toothpicks. Brush the tenderloins lightly with oil.
5. Grill, covered, over medium-hot coals, or broil 6 inches from the heat source, about 8 to 10 minutes per side or until the tenderloins are cooked through. Cut on the diagonal into ½-inch slices.

HEARTLAND STUFFED PEPPERS

Peppers in a rainbow of colors are the casings for this tasty stuffing made with lean ground turkey, corn kernels, and nutty brown rice. To keep the peppers from tipping over, bake them in large cupcake tins instead of a baking dish.

4 peppers (4 servings)

4 large bell peppers, red, yellow,
  green, or a combination
  (about 1½ pounds total)
¾ pound lean ground turkey
1 cup chopped onion
1 clove garlic, minced
1½ teaspoons paprika
1½ teaspoons dried sage
½ teaspoon salt
½ teaspoon hot pepper sauce
1 cup cooked brown rice
1 cup thawed frozen corn kernels
  or 1 cup drained canned corn
½ cup (2 ounces) shredded part-skim
  mozzarella cheese

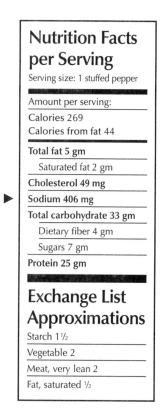

Nutrition Facts per Serving

Serving size: 1 stuffed pepper

Amount per serving:

Calories 269
Calories from fat 44

Total fat 5 gm
 Saturated fat 2 gm
Cholesterol 49 mg
Sodium 406 mg
Total carbohydrate 33 gm
 Dietary fiber 4 gm
 Sugars 7 gm
Protein 25 gm

Exchange List Approximations

Starch 1½
Vegetable 2
Meat, very lean 2
Fat, saturated ½

1. Preheat the oven to 350°F. Prepare a large skillet with nonstick pan spray.

2. Cut the tops off the peppers ½ inch from the stem end. Discard the membranes and seeds. Discard the stems; chop the tops. Parboil the pepper bottoms in boiling water 4 minutes. Drain well; stand the peppers upright in a shallow baking dish.

3. Sauté the turkey with the chopped pepper tops, onion, and garlic in the prepared skillet until the turkey is no longer pink. Add the paprika, sage, salt, and pepper sauce; cook 1 minute.

4. Stir in the rice, corn, and cheese. Pack the filling into the pepper cups. (Bake any leftover filling separately and serve it around the peppers.) Bake the peppers, uncovered, about 30 minutes, or until the stuffing is heated through and the peppers are tender.

ITALIAN TURKEY SAUSAGE WITH PEPPERS AND ONIONS

These sausages, smothered with sautéed peppers and onions, make terrific sandwiches or, along with the well-seasoned broth, a great topping for pasta. Turkey sausage is widely available in supermarkets and you can choose hot or mild varieties, depending on your tastes.

About 6 cups (4 servings)

1 pound lean fresh hot or mild Italian
      turkey sausage links (about 4 to
      5 links), each cut in 3 pieces
2 medium onions, sliced
2 medium green bell peppers, cored,
      seeded, and cut in 1-inch squares
1¾ cups Homemade Chicken Broth
      (page 101) or canned reduced-
      sodium chicken broth
2 teaspoons chopped fresh oregano, or
      ½ teaspoon dried oregano
Freshly ground pepper (optional)

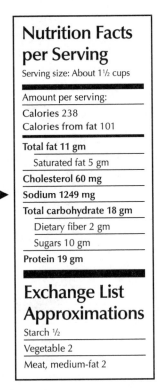

Nutrition Facts per Serving

Serving size: About 1½ cups

Amount per serving:
Calories 238
Calories from fat 101

Total fat 11 gm
Saturated fat 5 gm
Cholesterol 60 mg
Sodium 1249 mg
Total carbohydrate 18 gm
Dietary fiber 2 gm
Sugars 10 gm
Protein 19 gm

Exchange List Approximations

Starch ½
Vegetable 2
Meat, medium-fat 2

1. Brown the sausage pieces over medium heat in a large nonstick skillet. Remove from the skillet and set aside.

2. Add the onions, peppers, and ½ cup water to the skillet. Lower the heat and sauté the vegetables until lightly browned, about 8 to 10 minutes; stir to scrape any small browned bits from the sausage into the vegetables.

3. Add the broth, sausage, and oregano; cover and simmer 10 minutes. Taste and add freshly ground pepper, if desired.

TURKEY BROCCOLI CASSEROLE

You can bet this casserole will become a family favorite. Keep the ingredients on hand in your cupboard and freezer so you're always ready when you need a meal in a hurry.

1 casserole (6 servings)

2 pounds fresh broccoli, trimmed and
      cut in spears, or two 10-ounce
      packages frozen broccoli spears
2 cups coarsely diced cooked turkey
      (12 ounces)
One 10½-ounce can reduced-fat
      condensed cream of mushroom
      soup
¾ cup fat-free milk
½ cup (about 2 ounces) shredded
      reduced-fat Cheddar cheese

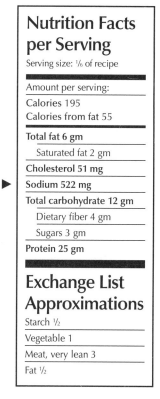

Nutrition Facts per Serving

Serving size: ⅙ of recipe

Amount per serving:

Calories 195
Calories from fat 55

Total fat 6 gm
    Saturated fat 2 gm
Cholesterol 51 mg
Sodium 522 mg
Total carbohydrate 12 gm
    Dietary fiber 4 gm
    Sugars 3 gm
Protein 25 gm

Exchange List Approximations

Starch ½
Vegetable 1
Meat, very lean 3
Fat ½

1. Preheat the oven to 375°F. Prepare a large shallow casserole dish with nonstick pan spray.
2. Cook the broccoli spears in a large pot of boiling water for 5 minutes and drain, or cook frozen broccoli according to the package directions. Arrange the broccoli in the bottom of the prepared baking dish. Spread the turkey on top.
3. In a medium bowl, combine the soup with the milk; mix until smooth and pour over the turkey. Top with shredded cheese.
4. Bake for 30 minutes. Let stand 5 minutes before dividing into 6 equal portions.

TURKEY SCALOPPINE WITH MARSALA GLAZE

Thin cuts of sautéed turkey are glazed with a marsala wine sauce that adds sweetness and a rich smoky flavor.

4 servings

3 tablespoons all-purpose flour
½ teaspoon seasoned salt
¼ teaspoon ground white pepper
1 pound boneless turkey breast, thinly
    sliced
¼ cup dry white wine
½ cup Homemade Chicken Broth
    (page 101) or canned reduced-
    sodium chicken broth
¼ cup sweet marsala wine
1 clove garlic, minced
2 teaspoons brown sugar
1 teaspoon cornstarch
½ teaspoon grated lemon zest

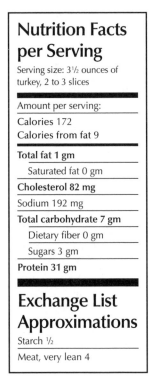

Nutrition Facts per Serving

Serving size: 3½ ounces of turkey, 2 to 3 slices

Amount per serving:

Calories 172
Calories from fat 9

Total fat 1 gm
  Saturated fat 0 gm
Cholesterol 82 mg
Sodium 192 mg
Total carbohydrate 7 gm
  Dietary fiber 0 gm
  Sugars 3 gm
Protein 31 gm

Exchange List Approximations

Starch ½

Meat, very lean 4

1. Mix the flour with the seasoned salt and pepper in a pie plate or plastic bag. Dredge the turkey slices and shake off the excess.
2. Heat a large skillet and spray well with nonstick pan spray. Cook the cutlets in a single layer over medium-high heat about 2 minutes on each side, or until light tan in color. Remove the turkey to a warm platter.
3. Add the white wine, chicken broth, marsala, garlic, and brown sugar to the skillet. Stir, scraping any bits from the bottom of the pan. Bring to a boil and reduce the sauce to about ½ cup.
4. In a small bowl, mix the cornstarch with 2 tablespoons water. Add to the sauce, bring to a boil, and stir in the lemon zest.
5. Reduce the heat. Return the turkey to the skillet. Coat with sauce to glaze, and heat thoroughly, about 5 minutes.

GAME HENS WITH CHUTNEY-MUSTARD GLAZE

Game hens are lovely dinner party entrées and this recipe couldn't be easier to fix. The slightly sweet, tangy glaze brushed on the hens adds just the right touch.

4 servings

¼ cup prepared mango chutney,
    chopped
1 tablespoon Dijon mustard
2 Cornish game hens, split and skinned
    (about 1¼ pounds each)

1. Preheat the oven to 325°F. Prepare the rack of a shallow roasting pan with nonstick pan spray.

2. Combine the chutney and mustard; brush about ½ of the mixture over all surfaces of the hens. Place the hen halves meaty side up on the prepared rack in the roasting pan.

3. Bake about 50 minutes, or until the hen halves are tender, brushing often with the remaining chutney mixture and pan drippings during the cooking time.

Nutrition Facts per Serving
Serving size: ½ hen
Amount per serving:
Calories 145
Calories from fat 28
Total fat 3 gm
Saturated fat 1 gm
Cholesterol 79 mg
Sodium 128 mg
Total carbohydrate 11 gm
Dietary fiber 0 gm
Sugars 11 gm
Protein 18 gm

Exchange List Approximations
Fruit ½
Meat, very lean 3

GRILLED DUCK BREAST

Ducks are much leaner than in years past, thanks to new breeding techniques. Scoring the duck skin decreases the fat content even further by helping to release excess fat as it cooks. Be careful not to cut into the flesh when scoring the skin, or the meat will dry out as it cooks. Serve each half duck breast topped with ¼ cup Gingered Peach Sauce (page 426) or warmed Blueberry Chutney (page 423), along with Apple-Pecan Wild Rice (page 398). Refer to the suggested recipes for exchange information. If you have leftovers, use them as a topping for salads or tossed with pasta.

4 servings

2 whole boneless duck breasts with skin
      (1½ pounds total)
¾ teaspoon salt or seasoned salt
½ teaspoon freshly ground pepper

1. Preheat the oven to 350°F.
2. Cut each breast in half. Score the skin by making diagonal cuts ¾ inches apart on the surface about halfway through the fat. Do not cut into the meat. Season on all sides with salt and pepper.
3. Heat a heavy skillet or grill over medium heat. Sear the duck breasts skin side down for 10 minutes, draining the fat every 2 to 3 minutes, until the skin is browned and most of the fat is released from the skin layer. Score again if necessary to promote fat release. Cook only skin side down.
4. Transfer the breasts to an ovenproof pan and place skin side up. Bake for about 12 minutes, or until an instant-read thermometer registers 145 to 150°F. The breast halves will be cooked to medium, with the duck meat pink and tender. Serve whole or thinly sliced and fanned.

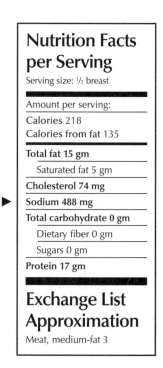

Nutrition Facts per Serving

Serving size: ½ breast

Amount per serving:

Calories 218
Calories from fat 135

Total fat 15 gm
    Saturated fat 5 gm

Cholesterol 74 mg

Sodium 488 mg

Total carbohydrate 0 gm
    Dietary fiber 0 gm
    Sugars 0 gm

Protein 17 gm

Exchange List Approximation

Meat, medium-fat 3

8

FISH AND SHELLFISH

If you're looking for a delicious source of protein that's relatively low in calories and fat (especially saturated fat) and rich in vitamins and minerals, you'll fall hook, line, and sinker for seafood.

Seafood is a general term used to describe both finfish (or fish) and shellfish. Flounder, swordfish, catfish, cod, and trout are all examples of finfish, while the shellfish category includes both crustaceans, like lobsters, shrimp, and crab, and mollusks, like clams, scallops, oysters, and mussels.

BUYING SEAFOOD

Good fresh seafood isn't readily available in all areas of the country and can be expensive if it is, so feel free to substitute frozen or canned seafood in the following recipes. Much of the seafood today is flash-frozen right on the boat to maximize flavor, and there is quite a variety of fish available. When purchasing frozen seafood, make sure it's solid, mild in odor, and free of ice crystals or freezer burn. For canned seafood, opt for those items packed in water, not oil, to save on fat and calories.

If you buy fresh seafood, make sure it's from a reputable source. Fresh fish fillets and steaks should have a mild ocean scent, not a strong "fishy" smell. The flesh should be moist and firm to the touch, springing back when pressed, with no browning on the edges.

With the exception of shrimp and preshucked clams, scallops, or oysters, all fresh shellfish should be alive when bought. Fresh clams, oysters, and mussels may have shells that are slightly open, but should close tightly when tapped. If you buy freshly shucked mollusks, make sure the liquid they are packed in is clear, not milky, in color and has a fresh, mild scent. Also, the liquid should completely cover the mollusk "meat." Shrimp are usually frozen or thawed and have had their heads removed. Shrimp should have a fresh smell and firm texture, with meat that completely fills the shell. The "vein" in shrimp is really its intestinal tract. It poses no health risk, so there's no need to remove it, unless you don't like its appearance.

PREPARING AND COOKING SEAFOOD

Be safe when preparing seafood, too. No matter the variety, all fresh fish and shellfish should be cooked within 1 day of purchase. Use separate cutting boards, plates, trays, and utensils for cooked and uncooked fish to avoid cross-contamination.

Seafood cooks much more quickly than meat or chicken. The biggest mistake people make when preparing seafood is overcooking it, resulting in a tough and tasteless product. As a general rule of thumb, cook fish steaks and fillets 10 minutes for every inch, at a temperature of 425° to 450°F. Fish is done when the flesh turns opaque and milky in color all the way through and flakes easily with a fork. Its internal temperature should reach 145°F. Scallops turn white and firm when done, shrimp turn pink, and lobster shells change to bright red. Live clams, mussels, and oysters should be cooked for about 3 to 5 minutes, until the shells open. Discard any mollusks whose shells do not open.

NUTRITION

There are two categories by which fish are classified: fatty and lean. Fatty fish are richer in flavor and darker in color—salmon, swordfish, trout, and tuna are examples. Fatty fish are also richer than lean fish in a compound called omega-3 fatty acids, which researchers think may help to prevent heart attacks and strokes. Lean fish, such as cod, red snapper, ocean perch, and orange roughy, generally have a milder flavor and less fat compared with fatty fish. However, even fatty fish varieties are still leaner than almost any other animal protein food. When it comes to cooking methods, fattier fish are usually better for grilling or roasting than lean varieties because they won't dry out as quickly. Lean fish are best suited for baking, microwaving, and poaching. Shellfish is usually best steamed or boiled, but in the case of shrimp, almost any cooking method—sautéing in a small amount of oil, broiling, or steaming—works well.

Health experts recommend eating seafood several times a week. In addition to being a great lean source of protein, seafood is low in fat (especially saturated fat), rich in B vitamins (especially B_{12}), and contains omega-3 fatty acids. Researchers believe omega-3 fatty acids help to *lower* blood cholesterol levels. Fatty fish are richest in omega-3 oils, but lean fish and shellfish also contain some.

Many types of shellfish (such as oysters, mussels, and clams) and some varieties of fish (such as mackerel, bluefish, and sardines) contain iron, and fish that are eaten with their small bones (such as canned sardines or salmon) are rich in calcium. All fish are naturally low in sodium, even those that come from the sea. There used to be some concern about the cholesterol content of seafood, but by and large, fish and most shellfish have less cholesterol per serving than other high-protein animal foods like beef or chicken. And contrary to a long-held belief, shellfish actually have less cholesterol than previously thought. Even shrimp, with 125 to 160 mg of cholesterol in a 3.5-ounce serving, is not outlandishly high, and is considered an acceptable alternative to red meat by the American Heart Association. Clams, mussels, and oysters average between 25 and 60 mg per 3.5-ounce serving, and even lobster, long "forbidden" and avoided by those watching cholesterol intake, has only 70 to 95 mg per 3.5-ounce portion.

We've included an array of tempting seafood recipes in this chapter. Try Baked Orange Roughy with Tomatoes and Herbs for a quick-to-fix meal, Lime-Grilled Fish with Fresh Salsa at a summer evening barbecue, Shrimp and Asparagus with Fettuccine in Mustard Cream Sauce for an elegant company dinner, or Mussels in Broth as a special appetizer. Whatever the occasion, if you're "fishing around" for a great meal idea, you've come to the right place.

BAKED CATFISH

An old Southern favorite, this breaded catfish is baked, not fried, to save calories and fat. Serve with Southern Corn Bread (page 56) and Best-Ever Coleslaw (page 137) for a real down-home picnic.

4 servings

4 catfish or ocean perch fillets (1 pound
    total), thawed if frozen
2 slices white bread, crumbled, or 1 cup
    fresh bread crumbs
2 tablespoons grated Romano or
    Parmesan cheese
2 teaspoons chopped fresh basil or
    oregano, or 1 teaspoon dried basil
    or oregano
1/2 teaspoon salt
1/4 teaspoon freshly ground pepper
1 large egg, beaten, or 1/4 cup egg
    substitute
1/4 cup low-fat (1 percent) buttermilk

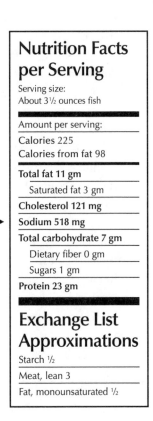

Nutrition Facts per Serving

Serving size:
About 3 1/2 ounces fish

Amount per serving:

Calories 225
Calories from fat 98

Total fat 11 gm
   Saturated fat 3 gm
Cholesterol 121 mg
Sodium 518 mg
Total carbohydrate 7 gm
   Dietary fiber 0 gm
   Sugars 1 gm
Protein 23 gm

Exchange List Approximations

Starch 1/2

Meat, lean 3

Fat, monounsaturated 1/2

1. Preheat the oven to 400°F. Prepare a baking pan with nonstick pan spray.
2. In a pie pan or shallow dish, mix the bread crumbs, cheese, basil or oregano, salt, and pepper. Set aside.
3. In another pie pan or dish, combine the egg and buttermilk.
4. Dip each fish fillet first in the milk mixture, then in the crumb mixture to coat both sides with crumbs.
5. Arrange the fillets in 1 layer in the baking pan. Bake 15 to 20 minutes, until the fish flakes easily with a fork.

TARRAGON COD WITH VEGETABLES

Cod is a mild, slightly sweet-tasting fish that's inexpensive and widely available fresh or frozen. This simplified version of "fish en papillote" uses foil instead of a parchment paper wrap and allows the fish to steam in its own juices. Prep the fish packet in advance if you like—just keep it refrigerated until ready to bake.

6 servings

6 frozen cod fillets (1 1/2 pounds total)
1/4 teaspoon salt
1/4 teaspoon freshly ground pepper
1 tablespoon fresh tarragon leaves,
      or 1 teaspoon dried tarragon
1 tablespoon fresh lemon juice
1 1/2 cups chopped mushrooms
1 1/2 cups thinly sliced carrot
3/4 cup chopped celery
2 tablespoons chopped fresh parsley
1 tablespoon margarine, cut into 6 small
      pieces

Nutrition Facts per Serving
Serving size: About 3 1/2 ounces fish plus 1/3 cup vegetables
Amount per serving:
Calories 130
Calories from fat 25
Total fat 3 gm
Saturated fat 1 gm
Cholesterol 49 mg
Sodium 205 mg
Total carbohydrate 4 gm
Dietary fiber 1 gm
Sugars 2 gm
Protein 21 gm

Exchange List Approximations

Vegetable 1

Meat, very lean 3

1.   Preheat the oven to 350°F.

2.   Place the frozen fish on a sheet of heavy-duty aluminum foil; season with salt and pepper.

3.   Sprinkle the tarragon and lemon juice on the fish. Add all the chopped vegetables and the fresh parsley. Dot with margarine; fold and crimp the foil to make a tight package.

4.   Bake for 40 minutes if the fish was frozen or 35 minutes if it was thawed when it was put in the oven. To serve, put on individual plates and slit the foil across the top so diners can easily fold it back to enjoy the entrée.

GRILLED TUNA STEAKS

The marinade in this recipe uses a minimum of oil and a maximum of aromatic spices to impart a superb flavor. If tuna is not available, use any meaty, firm-flesh fish like halibut, marlin, or swordfish. Fish is fabulous on the grill, but be careful not to overcook it or it will dry out. If desired, you can substitute 1 tablespoon of wine vinegar or apple cider vinegar for the vermouth.

4 servings

MARINADE

2 tablespoons dry vermouth
1 tablespoon olive oil
2 green onions with green tops,
        chopped
2 tablespoons chopped fresh basil,
        or 2 teaspoons dried basil
1 clove garlic, minced
2 teaspoons chopped fresh marjoram,
        or ½ teaspoon dried marjoram
¼ teaspoon crushed red pepper flakes
¼ teaspoon salt

4 tuna or halibut steaks (1 pound total),
        ¾ to 1 inch thick, thawed if
        frozen
1 lemon or lime, cut in wedges

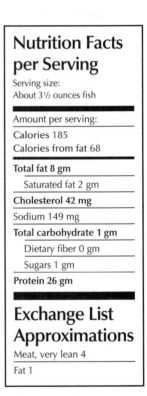

**Nutrition Facts
per Serving**

Serving size:
About 3½ ounces fish

Amount per serving:

Calories 185
Calories from fat 68

Total fat 8 gm
    Saturated fat 2 gm
Cholesterol 42 mg
Sodium 149 mg
Total carbohydrate 1 gm
    Dietary fiber 0 gm
    Sugars 1 gm
Protein 26 gm

**Exchange List
Approximations**

Meat, very lean 4
Fat 1

1.   Prepare a charcoal grill or preheat the broiler and prepare the broiler pan with non-stick pan spray.
2.   Combine the marinade ingredients and pour over the fish. Cover and refrigerate 1 to 2 hours.
3.   Grill, covered, over medium coals, or broil 6 inches from the heat source about 4 minutes per side, or until the fish is firm and opaque, basting twice with the marinade. Do not overcook, or the fish will be tough and dry.
4.   Serve with lemon wedges.

BAKED ORANGE ROUGHY WITH TOMATOES AND HERBS

The tangy tomato-and-herb sauce in this recipe enhances the mild flavor of orange roughy. Designed to be assembled and cooked in about half an hour, this dish is perfect when you're in a rush to get dinner on the table.

4 servings

½ cup chopped onion
2 cloves garlic, minced
1 teaspoon margarine
1 large tomato, seeded and chopped
½ teaspoon salt
1 teaspoon chopped fresh oregano,
     or ¼ teaspoon dried oregano
1 teaspoon chopped fresh thyme,
     or ¼ teaspoon dried thyme
⅛ teaspoon freshly ground pepper
4 orange roughy fillets (1 pound total),
     thawed if frozen
½ cup dry white wine
2 tablespoons tomato paste

Nutrition Facts per Serving
Serving size: About 3½ ounces fish plus 3 tablespoons sauce
Amount per serving:
Calories 123
Calories from fat 18
Total fat 2 gm
Saturated fat 0 gm
Cholesterol 23 mg
Sodium 384 mg
Total carbohydrate 7 gm
Dietary fiber 1 gm
Sugars 3 gm
Protein 18 gm

Exchange List Approximations

Vegetable 1	
Meat, very lean 3	

1. Preheat the oven to 350°F. Prepare an ovenproof skillet with nonstick pan spray.
2. In the skillet over medium heat, sauté the onion and garlic in the margarine until soft, about 5 minutes. Stir in the tomato and seasonings. Cover and simmer for 5 minutes.
3. Place the fish in the skillet; cover with the sauce and pour the wine over the fish. Cover and bake for 15 to 20 minutes, or until the fish flakes with a fork.
4. Remove the fish to a heated platter. Simmer the sauce in the skillet until reduced to ⅔ cup. Stir in the tomato paste, reheat, and pour over the fish.

BAKED SALMON WITH HORSERADISH MAYONNAISE

Salmon's distinctive flavor is complemented by the pungent spiciness of the horseradish mayonnaise. It's a simple way to prepare fish and makes any weeknight dinner extra special. Try a rice pilaf and Sugar Snap Peas with Basil and Lemon (page 334) as sides.

4 servings

SALMON

1 salmon fillet (1 pound total), cut into
      4 pieces
2 tablespoons finely chopped shallots
¼ cup dry white wine or vermouth

HORSERADISH MAYONNAISE

2 tablespoons light mayonnaise
2 tablespoons light sour cream
2 teaspoons fresh lemon juice
2 to 3 teaspoons freshly grated
      horseradish, or prepared
      horseradish, drained
2 teaspoons drained capers (optional)

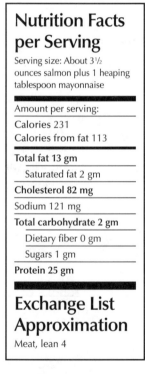

Nutrition Facts per Serving

Serving size: About 3½ ounces salmon plus 1 heaping tablespoon mayonnaise

Amount per serving:

Calories 231
Calories from fat 113

Total fat 13 gm
  Saturated fat 2 gm
Cholesterol 82 mg
Sodium 121 mg
Total carbohydrate 2 gm
  Dietary fiber 0 gm
  Sugars 1 gm
Protein 25 gm

Exchange List Approximation

Meat, lean 4

1.   Preheat the oven to 450°F. Prepare a shallow roasting pan or baking dish with nonstick pan spray.

2.   Place the salmon fillets, skin side down, in the pan. Sprinkle the shallots over the slices; pour wine evenly over all. Bake 6 to 8 minutes, or just until the fish is opaque.

3.   While the fish is cooking, combine the mayonnaise, sour cream, lemon juice, horseradish, and capers, if desired, in a small bowl; mix well.

4.   Transfer the salmon and shallots to warm serving plates with a slotted spatula. Top each serving with a heaping tablespoon of horseradish mayonnaise. Garnish with capers, if desired.

SALMON WITH GRAPEFRUIT SAUCE

Salmon definitely tastes better the more simply it's prepared. Slightly sweet yet tart grapefruit juice intensifies the flavor of the sauce and also helps keep the fish from drying out. Garnish the fish with ruby red grapefruit segments mixed with chopped fresh basil to complement the beautiful orange-pink color of the fish. One whole grapefruit equals 2 fruit exchanges or 1/2 fruit exchange per serving.

4 servings

1/2 cup minced shallots or finely
    chopped sweet onion
2 teaspoons olive oil
1 large salmon fillet (1 pound), cut into
    4 pieces
3/4 cup fresh grapefruit juice, preferably
    pink or ruby red

1.   Sauté the shallots in the oil in a nonstick skillet until tender, about 4 minutes. Add the salmon and grapefruit juice. Cover and simmer over low heat until the salmon is opaque, about 6 to 8 minutes. Transfer the salmon to warm serving plates.

2.   Increase the heat and simmer the juices about 2 minutes until reduced to 1/2 cup; pour over the salmon.

Nutrition Facts per Serving

Serving size:
About 3 1/2 ounces salmon
plus 2 tablespoons sauce

Amount per serving:

Calories 242
Calories from fat 108

Total fat 12 gm
  Saturated fat 2 gm
Cholesterol 70 mg
Sodium 56 mg
Total carbohydrate 8 gm
  Dietary fiber 1 gm
  Sugars 4 gm
Protein 25 gm

Exchange List Approximations

Fruit 1/2
Meat, lean 4

CAJUN GRILLED RED SNAPPER

The Cajun seasonings really spice up mild-mannered red snapper and add a nice, crunchy coating, too. Best of all, this recipe takes just 10 minutes from stovetop to table.

4 servings

4 red snapper, perch, or other firm, white
      fish fillets (1 pound total)
1 tablespoon olive oil
2 tablespoons Cajun seasoning blend or
      blackened fish seasoning blend
1 small lemon, cut in wedges

1.   Heat a large heavy skillet over high heat. Brush the fish with oil. Press the seasoning blend into both sides of the fish.
2.   Spray the hot skillet with nonstick pan spray. Add the fish and pan-fry over high heat about 4 minutes per side, or until the fish is firm and the surface is crusty. Serve with lemon wedges.

Nutrition Facts per Serving

Serving size:
About 3½ ounces fish

Amount per serving:

Calories 143
Calories from fat 44

Total fat 5 gm
   Saturated fat 1 gm
Cholesterol 42 mg
Sodium 950 mg
Total carbohydrate 0 gm
   Dietary fiber 0 gm
   Sugars 0 gm
Protein 23 gm

Exchange List Approximation

Meat, very lean 4

RED SNAPPER PROVENÇAL

Garlic, tomatoes, and olive oil—the trademarks of Provençal cooking—invigorate the sweet delicate flavor of red snapper in this delightful recipe.

4 servings

1 cup finely chopped onion
2 cloves garlic, minced
1 tablespoon olive oil
1 zucchini, cut in thin strips
2 medium tomatoes, seeded and diced
2 tablespoons tomato paste
2 tablespoons chopped fresh parsley
2 teaspoons chopped fresh basil,
       or ½ teaspoon dried basil
2 teaspoons chopped fresh oregano,
       or ½ teaspoon dried oregano
1 teaspoon chopped fresh thyme,
       or ⅛ teaspoon dried thyme
¼ teaspoon salt
⅛ teaspoon freshly ground pepper
1 pound red snapper fillets, thawed
       if frozen

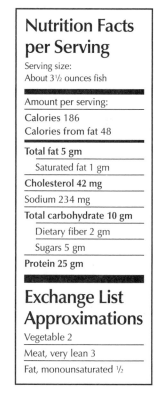

Nutrition Facts per Serving

Serving size:
About 3½ ounces fish

Amount per serving:

Calories 186
Calories from fat 48

Total fat 5 gm
  Saturated fat 1 gm
Cholesterol 42 mg
Sodium 234 mg
Total carbohydrate 10 gm
  Dietary fiber 2 gm
  Sugars 5 gm
Protein 25 gm

Exchange List Approximations

Vegetable 2
Meat, very lean 3
Fat, monounsaturated ½

1. Preheat the oven to 350°F. Prepare an 8-inch-square baking dish with nonstick pan spray.

2. Sauté the onion and garlic in oil in a non-stick skillet for 5 minutes, or until soft. Stir in the zucchini, tomatoes, tomato paste, parsley, basil, oregano, thyme, and seasonings. Simmer for 10 to 15 minutes.

3. Pour half of the sauce on the bottom of the prepared baking dish. Top with the fish fillets and the remaining sauce.

4. Cover with foil and bake for 20 to 25 minutes, or until the fish flakes with a fork.

FLOUNDER WITH PARMESAN CRUST

Simple preparations such as this Parmesan crust are ideal for flounder, and keep fat at just 2 grams per serving. Try Asparagus with Dijon Sauce (page 312) and saffron rice as sides.

6 servings

6 flounder or sole fillets (1½ pounds
      total), thawed if frozen
⅓ cup plain low-fat yogurt
2 tablespoons grated Parmesan cheese
1 tablespoon Dijon mustard
1 tablespoon fresh lemon juice
1½ teaspoons prepared horseradish,
      drained

1. Preheat the broiler and prepare the broiler pan with nonstick pan spray. Arrange the fish on the broiler pan.
2. In a small bowl, combine the yogurt, Parmesan, mustard, lemon juice, and horseradish. Spread the mixture over both sides of the fillets.
3. Broil about 8 inches from the heat, turning once, for about 6 minutes, or until the fish flakes easily with a fork.

Nutrition Facts per Serving

Serving size:
About 3½ ounces fish

Amount per serving:

Calories 122
Calories from fat 19

Total fat 2 gm
  Saturated fat 1 gm

Cholesterol 62 mg

Sodium 166 mg

Total carbohydrate 1 gm
  Dietary fiber 0 gm
  Sugars 1 gm

Protein 23 gm

Exchange List Approximation

Meat, very lean 3

STUFFED SOLE FILLETS

These elegant parcels are stuffed with a medley of aromatic vegetables and rice that nicely complement the mild flavor of sole. They are perfect for a dinner party or romantic meal. You can stuff the fillets several hours ahead of time, store them in the refrigerator, and bake when ready.

4 servings

1/2 cup finely chopped onion
1 clove garlic, minced
2 teaspoons olive oil
1/3 cup shredded carrot
1/3 cup shredded zucchini or yellow
        squash
1/2 cup cooked wild or brown rice
2 tablespoons chopped fresh flat-leaf
        (Italian) or regular parsley
1/8 teaspoon freshly ground pepper
4 sole fillets (1 1/2 pounds total), thawed
        if frozen
2 tablespoons dry white wine
2 teaspoons margarine, melted
1 teaspoon sweet Hungarian paprika
1 lemon, cut in wedges

Nutrition Facts per Serving
Serving size: 1 stuffed fillet
Amount per serving:
Calories 233
Calories from fat 56
Total fat 6 gm
Saturated fat 1 gm
Cholesterol 91 mg
Sodium 173 mg
Total carbohydrate 9 gm
Dietary fiber 1 gm
Sugars 2 gm
Protein 34 gm

Exchange List Approximations
Starch 1/2
Meat, very lean 5
Fat, monounsaturated 1/2

1. Preheat the oven to 400°F. Prepare a shallow baking dish with nonstick pan spray.

2. In a small skillet, sauté the onion and garlic in oil until tender, about 4 minutes. Add the carrot and zucchini; sauté 2 minutes. Add the rice; sauté 1 minute more. Remove from the heat; stir in the parsley and pepper.

3. Sprinkle the sole with wine. Spoon the rice mixture evenly down the center of each fillet; roll up from the short side. Place, seam side down, in the prepared baking dish. Brush with margarine and sprinkle with paprika.

4. Bake 15 to 17 minutes, or until the fish is opaque and the stuffing is hot. Serve with lemon wedges.

QUENELLES OF SOLE WITH SHRIMP SAUCE

This recipe takes some time to prepare but it is well worth the fuss. Quenelles are light, delicate dumplings made of minced fish formed into small rounds and gently poached. In this recipe, we use mild-flavored sole as the fish of choice and serve with a rich shrimp sauce. Try quenelles as appetizers or a main course.

6 servings

QUENELLES

2 tablespoons margarine
$^1/_8$ teaspoon plus 1$^1/_2$ teaspoons salt
$^1/_2$ cup all-purpose flour
2 large eggs
$^3/_4$ pound sole fillets, cut into pieces,
     thawed if frozen
$^1/_4$ teaspoon ground white pepper
$^1/_4$ teaspoon ground nutmeg
1 large egg white
$^1/_4$ cup fat-free evaporated milk, chilled

SHRIMP SAUCE

2 tablespoons margarine
2 tablespoons all-purpose flour
1 cup fat-free milk
$^1/_2$ teaspoon salt
$^1/_4$ teaspoon ground white pepper
$^1/_8$ teaspoon ground nutmeg
$^1/_4$ cup fat-free evaporated milk
1 tablespoon tomato paste
2 tablespoons dry sherry (optional)
1$^1/_2$ cups cooked fresh shrimp, chopped,
     or $^1/_2$ cup tiny canned shrimp,
     drained

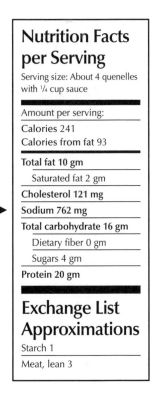

Nutrition Facts per Serving

Serving size: About 4 quenelles with $^1/_4$ cup sauce

Amount per serving:

Calories 241
Calories from fat 93

Total fat 10 gm
  Saturated fat 2 gm
Cholesterol 121 mg
Sodium 762 mg
Total carbohydrate 16 gm
  Dietary fiber 0 gm
  Sugars 4 gm
Protein 20 gm

Exchange List Approximations

Starch 1

Meat, lean 3

1.   Combine ½ cup water with the margarine and ⅛ teaspoon salt in a small saucepan; bring to a boil. Remove from the heat and stir in the flour. Beat vigorously with a wooden spoon until the mixture forms a ball. Allow to cool slightly.

2.   Beat in the eggs 1 at a time. Chill until cold.

3.   Place the fish in a food processor. Add the remaining 1½ teaspoons salt, the pepper, and nutmeg; process until smooth. Add the egg white through the feed tube while processing to blend. Add the chilled flour mixture and mix with several on/off pulses just until blended. Add the evaporated milk; process 15 seconds. Chill the fish mixture until ready to poach.

4.   Heat a medium pot of water to a slow simmer.

5.   Shape rounded teaspoonfuls of the fish mixture and drop into the simmering water. Cook for 10 to 12 minutes; drain.

6.   Make the shrimp sauce while the quenelles are poaching. Heat the margarine in a small saucepan over medium heat. Blend in the flour and cook until bubbly. Whisk in the fat-free milk, salt, pepper, and nutmeg. Cook over medium heat until thickened, whisking often.

7.   Stir in the evaporated milk, tomato paste, and sherry if desired. Simmer for 5 minutes, or until thoroughly heated. Add the shrimp. Serve hot with the quenelles.

FISH FILLETS IN RED PEPPER PURÉE

Red pepper purée adds a bright and beautiful color to these fish fillets and also helps keep them moist and flaky. When making the sauce, be sure to cover the pan tightly so the liquid does not boil away. If the sauce starts evaporating, add 1 to 2 tablespoons of water.

4 servings

1 cup coarsely chopped onion
1 clove garlic, minced
2 teaspoons olive oil
2 large red bell peppers (12 ounces
      total), cored, seeded, and coarsely
      chopped
1 teaspoon ground coriander
$\frac{1}{8}$ to $\frac{1}{4}$ teaspoon crushed red pepper
      flakes
Four 4-ounce fish fillets such as scrod,
      cod, white fish, haddock,
      or orange roughy
$\frac{1}{2}$ teaspoon salt
1 lime, cut in wedges

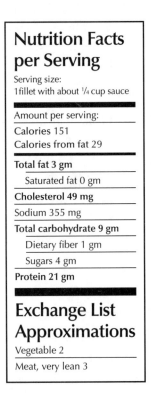

Nutrition Facts per Serving

Serving size:
1 fillet with about ¼ cup sauce

Amount per serving:

Calories 151
Calories from fat 29

Total fat 3 gm
  Saturated fat 0 gm
Cholesterol 49 mg
Sodium 355 mg
Total carbohydrate 9 gm
  Dietary fiber 1 gm
  Sugars 4 gm
Protein 21 gm

Exchange List Approximations

Vegetable 2
Meat, very lean 3

1.   In a large nonstick skillet, sauté the onion and garlic in oil until tender, about 5 minutes. Add the red peppers, coriander, and pepper flakes; sauté 1 minute. Cover and cook over low heat until the peppers are very tender, about 8 minutes.

2.   Transfer the mixture to a food processor or blender; blend until smooth, scraping down the sides twice. Stir in ¼ teaspoon of the salt.

3.   Sprinkle the fish with the remaining ¼ teaspoon salt and place in the same skillet. Spoon the purée over the fish; cover and simmer until the fish is opaque, about 8 minutes. Serve the fish topped with the pepper purée and with lime wedges.

SWORDFISH WITH RED PEPPER SAUCE

Swordfish is a very meaty, flavorful fish that's often broiled or grilled. This recipe takes a slightly unusual approach by poaching it instead. The robust red pepper sauce is simple to make and looks beautiful with the swordfish. To serve, spread a pool of sauce about 1 inch larger than the swordfish steak on each warmed plate and arrange the swordfish on top of the sauce.

4 servings

1 tablespoon fresh lemon juice
1/2 teaspoon black peppercorns
Four 4-ounce swordfish steaks, thawed if
    frozen

RED PEPPER SAUCE

One 7-ounce jar roasted red peppers,
    drained and rinsed, or 6 ounces
    roasted red peppers (page 151)
2 tablespoons fat-free evaporated milk
1/2 cup dry white wine
2 tablespoons fresh lemon juice
1 teaspoon minced shallot
2 teaspoons chopped fresh gingerroot
2 tablespoons margarine, cut in small
    pieces

Nutrition Facts per Serving
Serving size: About 3 1/2 ounces fish plus 1/4 cup sauce
Amount per serving:
Calories 212
Calories from fat 94
Total fat 10 gm
Saturated fat 2 gm
Cholesterol 44 mg
Sodium 277 mg
Total carbohydrate 3 gm
Dietary fiber 1 gm
Sugars 2 gm
Protein 23 gm

Exchange List Approximations
Vegetable 1
Meat, lean 3
Fat 1/2

1. Fill a large skillet half full of water; add the lemon juice and peppercorns; bring to a boil. Add the fish, cover, reduce the heat to a simmer, and cook for 10 minutes. Drain the fish and reserve.

2. While the fish is cooking, purée the peppers with the milk in a food processor or blender. Set aside.

3. In a small saucepan, combine the wine, lemon juice, shallot, and ginger. Cook over high heat until the sauce is reduced to 1/4 cup. Stir in the pepper purée. Add the margarine 1 small piece at a time, whisking over low heat until just melted. Serve the sauce with the fish.

SWORDFISH OR SALMON KEBABS

Any firm-fleshed fish like swordfish or salmon is ideal for kebabs, and the alternating vegetables in this recipe add gorgeous color. Serve the kebabs over a bed of brown or white rice (add 1 starch exchange for ⅓ cup rice).

4 servings

1 pound swordfish, salmon, or other
    firm-fleshed fish, cut into 1-inch
    cubes
½ cup chopped onion
3 tablespoons fresh lemon juice
1 tablespoon teriyaki sauce (optional)
⅛ teaspoon freshly ground pepper
1 small onion, cut in wedges
½ green bell pepper, seeded and cut into
    1- to 1½-inch cubes
4 cherry tomatoes
1 zucchini, cut into 1-inch pieces
4 whole mushrooms

Nutrition Facts per Serving	
Serving size: 1 skewer	
Amount per serving:	
Calories 165	
Calories from fat 42	
Total fat 5 gm	
Saturated fat 1 gm	
Cholesterol 44 mg	
Sodium 107 mg	
Total carbohydrate 7 gm	
Dietary fiber 2 gm	
Sugars 3 gm	
Protein 23 gm	

Exchange List Approximations

Vegetable	2
Meat, very lean	3

1.   Combine the fish, chopped onion, lemon juice, teriyaki sauce (if desired) and pepper in a glass bowl. Mix well, cover and marinate for 2 to 6 hours in the refrigerator.

2.   If using bamboo skewers, soak them in water for 15 minutes. Preheat the broiler and prepare the broiler pan with nonstick pan spray, or prepare a charcoal grill.

3.   On 4 skewers, alternate fish cubes and vegetables. Brush the marinade over the skewered food.

4.   Barbecue or broil about 8 minutes, turning once and basting with marinade, until the fish is opaque and flakes easily. Discard any remaining marinade.

TUNA RICE PIE

Here's an easy and tasty solution for last-minute dinners—you probably have most of the ingredients in your cupboard.

1 pie (6 servings)

1/3 cup uncooked white rice
1/4 teaspoon salt
1 teaspoon margarine
2 large eggs, or 1/2 cup egg substitute
One 6 1/2-ounce can water-packed tuna or
     salmon, drained and flaked
3/4 cup fat-free milk
1 1/2 cups fresh or thawed frozen peas
1 tablespoon chopped fresh parsley, or
     1/2 teaspoon dried parsley flakes
1/4 teaspoon freshly ground pepper
1/8 teaspoon ground nutmeg
4 slices (4 ounces) reduced-fat Swiss or
     reduced-fat Colby cheese

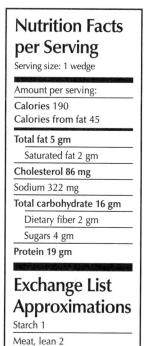

Nutrition Facts per Serving

Serving size: 1 wedge

Amount per serving:

Calories 190
Calories from fat 45

Total fat 5 gm
  Saturated fat 2 gm
Cholesterol 86 mg
Sodium 322 mg
Total carbohydrate 16 gm
  Dietary fiber 2 gm
  Sugars 4 gm
Protein 19 gm

Exchange List Approximations

Starch 1
Meat, lean 2

1. Preheat the oven to 350°F. Prepare a 9-inch pie pan with nonstick pan spray.
2. Combine the rice, 1 cup water, and the salt in a small saucepan; bring to a boil, cover, and simmer 14 minutes. Separate the rice grains with a fork.
3. Beat 1 egg in a small bowl. Stir the margarine and beaten egg (or 1/4 cup egg substitute) into the rice mixture. Press the rice against the sides and bottom of the pie pan to make a crust. Spread the tuna or salmon evenly over the rice.
4. In a saucepan, heat the milk and peas to a simmer. Add the parsley, pepper, and nutmeg. Beat the remaining egg and stir it into the milk mixture. Pour over the tuna.
5. Layer slices of cheese over the top. Bake for about 25 minutes. Cut the pie in 6 equal wedges.

WHITEFISH WITH CILANTRO PESTO

Cilantro pesto adds marvelous color and flavor to mild-flavored white-fish. Using cilantro instead of more traditional basil in the pesto sauce induces a lively, pungent fragrance. Serve with Corn Relish Salad (page 139) or Spicy Black Beans (page 410).

4 servings

4 whitefish, scrod, sole, or flounder fillets
      (1 pound total), thawed if frozen
2 tablespoons fresh lemon or lime juice
2 cloves garlic
2 cups packed fresh cilantro leaves,
      stems removed
1 tablespoon olive oil
1/2 teaspoon salt
1/2 teaspoon crushed red pepper flakes,
      or 1/8 teaspoon cayenne pepper

1. Preheat the oven to 400°F. Prepare a shallow baking dish with nonstick pan spray.
2. Sprinkle the fish with lemon juice and place in the dish.
3. Mince the garlic in a food processor or blender. Add the cilantro; process until minced. Add the oil, salt, and pepper flakes; process until well mixed. (Alternatively, mince the garlic and cilantro by hand; stir in the oil, salt, and pepper until well blended.)
4. Spread the pesto evenly over the fish. Bake 10 minutes, or until the fish is opaque and flakes easily with a fork. Serve hot.

Nutrition Facts per Serving

Serving size:
About 3 1/2 ounces fish

Amount per serving:

Calories 187
Calories from fat 90

Total fat 10 gm
  Saturated fat 1 gm
Cholesterol 68 mg
Sodium 353 mg
Total carbohydrate 1 gm
  Dietary fiber 0 gm
  Sugars 1 gm
Protein 22 gm

Exchange List Approximations

Meat, lean 3

Fat, monounsaturated 1/2

SPICY FISH STEW

A zesty mix of fish and vegetables, this stew is sure to become a family favorite. Use any firm, white-fleshed fish you prefer, such as catfish, cod, or perch. To serve, ladle the stew over cooked rice or a slice of toasted garlic bread. Add 1 starch exchange for ⅓ cup of rice or 1 starch plus 1 fat exchange for each slice of garlic bread.

About 2 quarts (8 servings)

2 cups (8 ounces) sliced mushrooms
1 cup thinly sliced celery
1 cup chopped onion
2 cloves garlic, minced
1 tablespoon olive oil
1 tablespoon chopped fresh thyme, or
        1 teaspoon dried thyme
2 teaspoons sugar
1 quart tomato juice or vegetable juice
        cocktail
1 bay leaf
½ teaspoon hot pepper sauce
½ teaspoon freshly ground pepper
1 pound firm, white fish fillets such as
        catfish, cod, or perch, cut into
        1-inch pieces, thawed if frozen
¼ cup chopped fresh parsley

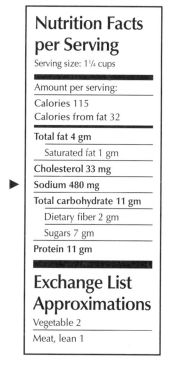

Nutrition Facts per Serving

Serving size: 1¼ cups

Amount per serving:

Calories 115
Calories from fat 32

Total fat 4 gm
    Saturated fat 1 gm
Cholesterol 33 mg
Sodium 480 mg
Total carbohydrate 11 gm
    Dietary fiber 2 gm
    Sugars 7 gm
Protein 11 gm

Exchange List Approximations

Vegetable 2
Meat, lean 1

1.   In a large saucepan, sauté the mushrooms, celery, onion, and garlic in oil over medium heat about 5 minutes. Add the thyme and sugar; sauté 1 minute. Add the tomato juice, bay leaf, pepper sauce, and pepper; bring to a boil.
2.   Reduce the heat; add the fish and simmer, uncovered, about 10 minutes.
3.   Discard the bay leaf; stir in the parsley and serve hot.

WISCONSIN-STYLE FISH BOIL

Fish boils are a Door County, Wisconsin, tradition and a delicious way to enjoy lake fish. Typically, a huge cauldron is set over an open flame outdoors to boil the fish. We've modified the recipe for home use. To save time, you can add 1 cup of clam juice to one 14-ounce can of vegetable broth to make the fish stock and begin the recipe at Step 2.

4 servings

1 cup clam juice
³/₄ cup chopped carrot
³/₄ cup chopped onion
³/₄ cup chopped celery
3 parsley sprigs or celery tops
2 teaspoons whole peppercorns
1 pound red potatoes, peeled, cut in
    halves or quarters
4 small yellow onions, peeled and
    quartered
1 pound lake trout, whitefish, walleye,
    or pike fillets, thawed if frozen
1 tablespoon chopped fresh parsley
4 lemon wedges

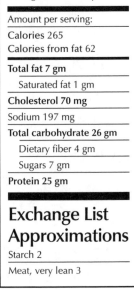

Nutrition Facts per Serving

Serving size: ¼ of recipe

Amount per serving:

Calories 265
Calories from fat 62

Total fat 7 gm
  Saturated fat 1 gm

Cholesterol 70 mg

Sodium 197 mg

Total carbohydrate 26 gm
  Dietary fiber 4 gm
  Sugars 7 gm

Protein 25 gm

Exchange List Approximations

Starch 2

Meat, very lean 3

1.   Combine 2 cups water, the clam juice, carrot, onion, celery, parsley sprigs, and peppercorns in a large saucepan or Dutch oven. Bring to a boil; reduce the heat. Cover and simmer 20 minutes. Strain the liquid and discard the vegetables.
2.   Return the broth to the pan. Add the potatoes and onions; bring to a boil. Cover and simmer 17 to 20 minutes, or until the potatoes are tender.
3.   Add the fish; simmer until it is opaque, about 6 to 7 minutes.
4.   Divide the fish, potatoes, onions, and broth among 4 bowls. Sprinkle with parsley and top each serving with a lemon wedge.

LIME-GRILLED FISH WITH FRESH SALSA

Lime-grilled fish is a taste straight from sunny Mexico, and perfect for a backyard summer barbecue. Rum-Baked Black Beans (page 409) and Spanish Rice Picante (page 397) make great accompaniments.

4 servings

1 tablespoon olive oil
1 tablespoon fresh lime juice
4 firm fish fillets such as orange roughy
 or red snapper (1 pound total),
 thawed if frozen
1 cup Fresh Salsa (page 419)
$\frac{1}{2}$ lime, cut into 4 slices

1. Prepare a charcoal grill, or preheat the broiler and prepare the broiler pan with non-stick pan spray.

2. Combine the oil and lime juice; brush over the fish. Grill or broil 4 to 5 inches from the heat source until the fish is opaque, about 6 minutes (depending on the thickness of the fish). Serve immediately, topped with salsa and fresh lime slices.

Nutrition Facts per Serving

Serving size: 1 fish fillet, about 3½ ounces, with ¼ cup salsa

Amount per serving:

Calories 164
Calories from fat 46

Total fat 5 gm
 Saturated fat 1 gm
Cholesterol 42 mg
Sodium 356 mg
Total carbohydrate 5 gm
 Dietary fiber 1 gm
 Sugars 3 gm
Protein 24 gm

Exchange List Approximations

Vegetable 1
Meat, very lean 3
Fat, monounsaturated ½

CRAB CAKES

Traditionally, crab cakes are very rich, made with lots of butter and eggs. This recipe keeps the flavor and texture of the original without all the added fat. The secret to making great crab cakes is to use plenty of high-quality crabmeat. Chilling the crab mixture for an hour or so before shaping the patties also helps them hold together. Serve the crab cakes with lemon wedges and, if you wish, reduced-fat tartar sauce. (Add 1 fat exchange for each tablespoon of tartar sauce used.)

4 servings

½ pound lump crabmeat (fresh, frozen,
          or canned and drained), flaked
1 tablespoon Dijon mustard
1 tablespoon margarine, melted
1 large egg, beaten, or ¼ cup egg substitute
2 teaspoons fresh lemon juice
1 teaspoon Worcestershire sauce
⅛ teaspoon salt
Pinch of cayenne pepper
2 dashes of hot pepper sauce
¾ cup soft bread crumbs, or 1½ pieces
          white bread, finely crumbled
1 small lemon, cut in wedges

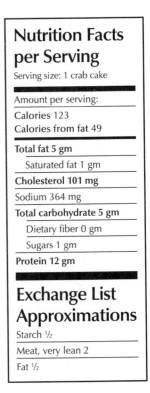

Nutrition Facts per Serving

Serving size: 1 crab cake

Amount per serving:

Calories 123
Calories from fat 49

Total fat 5 gm
   Saturated fat 1 gm
Cholesterol 101 mg
Sodium 364 mg
Total carbohydrate 5 gm
   Dietary fiber 0 gm
   Sugars 1 gm
Protein 12 gm

Exchange List Approximations

Starch ½
Meat, very lean 2
Fat ½

1. Preheat the oven to 400°F. Prepare a cookie sheet with nonstick pan spray.

2. In a medium bowl, combine the crabmeat, mustard, margarine, egg, lemon juice, Worcestershire sauce, salt, pepper, and pepper sauce. Add ¼ cup of the bread crumbs; mix well. If time permits, chill for an hour or more.

3. Shape the crab mixture into 4 patties about ¾ inch thick (use about ½ cup mixture for each). Pat the remaining bread crumbs on all surfaces of the crab cakes; place the cakes on the prepared cookie sheet.

4. Bake for 20 to 25 minutes, or until lightly browned, turning the cakes midway through the cooking time. Serve with lemon wedges.

BROILED LOBSTER TAILS

Save this elegant entrée for a special celebration. Frozen lobster tails are available in most grocery stores, usually labeled "rock lobster." Monkfish, also known as "poor man's lobster," can be substituted for the lobster, if necessary. If using monkfish, modify the directions below by broiling each piece for about 8 minutes total, turning once and adding seasoned crumbs 2 minutes before the fish is completely cooked.

2 servings

2 lobster tails (about 1 pound total)
2 teaspoons margarine, melted
2 teaspoons fresh lemon juice
2 teaspoons chopped shallots, or 1 clove
        garlic, minced
1 teaspoon olive oil
1 tablespoon dried bread crumbs
1 teaspoon chopped fresh thyme,
        or ½ teaspoon dried thyme
1 tablespoon chopped fresh parsley
1 small clove garlic, minced
1 small lemon, cut in wedges

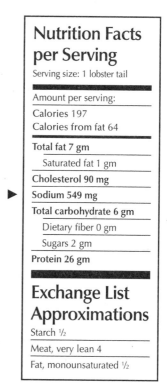

Nutrition Facts per Serving

Serving size: 1 lobster tail

Amount per serving:

Calories 197
Calories from fat 64

Total fat 7 gm
    Saturated fat 1 gm
Cholesterol 90 mg
Sodium 549 mg
Total carbohydrate 6 gm
    Dietary fiber 0 gm
    Sugars 2 gm
Protein 26 gm

Exchange List Approximations

Starch ½
Meat, very lean 4
Fat, monounsaturated ½

1.   Preheat the broiler.

2.   With kitchen shears, cut the top membrane from each lobster tail and discard. Place the tails, shell side up, on the broiler pan. Broil for 8 minutes about 5 inches from the heat source. Turn the tails over and brush with melted margarine and 1 teaspoon of the lemon juice. Broil 4 to 5 minutes longer, or until the lobster meat is opaque.

3.   While the lobster is broiling, prepare the topping. In a small nonstick skillet, sauté the shallots in olive oil until soft. Stir in the bread crumbs and the remaining 1 teaspoon lemon juice. Cook until the crumbs are lightly browned.

4.   Place the topping on the lobster tails; broil for 30 seconds. Serve with lemon wedges.

OYSTER STIR-FRY

The taste of Asia is evident in this unique stir-fry recipe, which pairs oysters and vegetables with a delightful lemon sauce. You can use either canned or freshly shucked oysters. If you use shucked oysters, be sure they are packed in clear, not milky, liquid. This is a clue as to how fresh they really are.

4 servings

1 pint shucked oysters, drained and
     patted dry
1 tablespoon plus 1 teaspoon light
     soy sauce
1 tablespoon dry sherry
2 teaspoons cornstarch
1 teaspoon chopped fresh gingerroot
1 green onion with green top, sliced
1 teaspoon dark-roasted
     sesame oil
1 tablespoon canola or corn oil
1 small red bell pepper, cored, seeded,
     and cubed

LEMON SAUCE

2 teaspoons cornstarch
3 tablespoons fresh lemon juice
1/4 cup Homemade Chicken Broth
     (page 101) or canned reduced-
     sodium chicken broth
1 tablespoon grated lemon zest
1 tablespoon honey
1/4 teaspoon crushed red pepper flakes

8 ounces bok choy, cut into large bite-
     size pieces

Nutrition Facts per Serving

Serving size: 1/4 of recipe

Amount per serving:

Calories 177
Calories from fat 72

Total fat 8 gm
  Saturated fat 1 gm

Cholesterol 62 mg

Sodium 468 mg

Total carbohydrate 17 gm
  Dietary fiber 1 gm
  Sugars 11 gm

Protein 10 gm

Exchange List Approximations

Starch 1

Meat, lean 1

Fat 1

1. In a medium bowl, combine the oysters with the soy sauce, sherry, cornstarch, gingerroot, green onion, and sesame oil.

2. Prepare a large skillet with nonstick pan spray. Heat the canola oil over medium-high heat. Add the oyster mixture and stir-fry for 3 minutes, or until the oysters are just cooked and their edges curl. Remove the oysters with a slotted spoon and set aside in a small bowl. Add the red pepper to the skillet; stir-fry for 1 minute. Add to the oysters.

3. For the sauce, combine the cornstarch, lemon juice, and chicken broth in a small saucepan. Heat over medium heat until thickened, whisking often. Stir in the lemon zest, honey, and red pepper flakes. Allow to cool if to be served at room temperature.

4. At serving time, line a serving bowl with bok choy. Pour the oyster mixture over the bok choy; top with the lemon sauce. Serve warm or cooled to room temperature.

MUSSELS IN BROTH

Mussels are succulent and delicious, releasing their intense flavor into the broth as they cook. Serve the mussels as an appetizer, or over pasta for a main course, if desired. A crusty loaf of French or Italian bread is a must for sopping up the extra broth. Remember to add 1 starch exchange for each ½ cup of pasta or slice of bread.

4 servings

2 pounds mussels in the shell
2 tablespoons margarine
¼ cup chopped shallots or finely
    chopped onion
2 cloves garlic, minced
1 cup dry white wine
1 cup Homemade Chicken Broth
    (page 101) or canned reduced-
    sodium chicken broth
½ teaspoon freshly ground pepper
2 tablespoons chopped fresh parsley,
    preferably flat-leaf (Italian)
    parsley

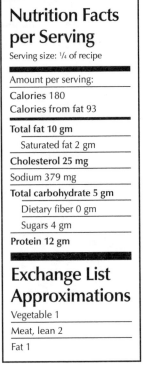

Nutrition Facts per Serving

Serving size: ¼ of recipe

Amount per serving:

Calories 180
Calories from fat 93

Total fat 10 gm
  Saturated fat 2 gm

Cholesterol 25 mg

Sodium 379 mg

Total carbohydrate 5 gm
  Dietary fiber 0 gm
  Sugars 4 gm

Protein 12 gm

Exchange List Approximations

Vegetable 1

Meat, lean 2

Fat 1

1. In a large bowl, soak the mussels in cold salted water for 30 minutes; rinse and scrape off the beards (the hairy tuft protruding from one side of the shell).

2. In a large, deep skillet or sauté pan, melt the margarine. Sauté the shallots and garlic until tender, about 5 minutes. Add the wine, broth, and pepper; bring to a boil. Simmer, uncovered, 5 minutes.

3. Drain the mussels and add to the pan; cover and cook until the mussels are fully open, about 8 minutes, shaking the pan frequently. Discard any mussels that do not open.

4. Divide the mussels and broth among 4 deep soup bowls; sprinkle with parsley.

BROILED SCALLOPS

The naturally sweet and succulent taste of scallops requires a minimum of added ingredients. Scallops cook very quickly, so be careful not to overdo or they'll become rubbery. Sea scallops are better suited for broiling than the smaller bay scallops. If you decide to use bay scallops, sauté them over medium heat in a large nonstick pan sprayed with vegetable cooking spray instead of broiling them; they'll cook in just a minute or two.

4 servings

1 pound sea scallops
1/3 cup seasoned bread crumbs
2 tablespoons fresh lemon juice
1 tablespoon olive oil
1/2 lemon, cut in wedges
1/4 cup light tartar sauce (optional)

1.   Preheat the broiler. Prepare the broiler pan with nonstick pan spray.
2.   Roll the scallops lightly in bread crumbs; place on the prepared pan. Drizzle lemon juice and olive oil over the scallops.
3.   Broil about 2 minutes on each side. Serve immediately with lemon wedges, and light tartar sauce (if desired).

Nutrition Facts per Serving

Serving size: 1/4 of scallops (plus 1 tablespoon light tartar sauce, if desired)

Amount per serving:
Calories 132
Calories from fat 40

Total fat 4 gm
Saturated fat 1 gm
Cholesterol 30 mg
Sodium 416 mg
Total carbohydrate 7 gm
Dietary fiber 0 gm
Sugars 1 gm
Protein 15 gm

Exchange List Approximations

Starch 1/2

Meat, very lean 2

Fat, monounsaturated 1/2

GULF COAST SHRIMP AND VEGETABLES

This sauté is delicious served on its own or as a topping for pasta. The medley of colorful vegetables makes it pretty to look at, too. If you use this recipe to top pasta, remember to add 1 starch exchange for each ½ cup of pasta used.

4 servings

1 tablespoon olive oil
1 large onion, cut into thin wedges
1 small red bell pepper, cored, seeded,
    and cut into thin strips
2 cloves garlic, minced
¼ teaspoon salt (optional)
1 pound medium or large shrimp in
    the shell, peeled and deveined
    (about 12 ounces after peeling)
1 zucchini, cut into thin 2-inch-long
    strips
1 tablespoon chopped fresh thyme,
    or 1 teaspoon dried thyme
¼ teaspoon crushed red pepper flakes

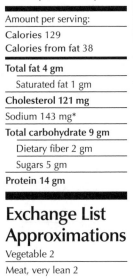

Nutrition Facts per Serving

Serving size:
¼ of recipe, about 1 cup

Amount per serving:

Calories 129
Calories from fat 38

Total fat 4 gm
    Saturated fat 1 gm
Cholesterol 121 mg
Sodium 143 mg*
Total carbohydrate 9 gm
    Dietary fiber 2 gm
    Sugars 5 gm
Protein 14 gm

Exchange List Approximations

Vegetable 2

Meat, very lean 2

1.   Heat the oil in a large nonstick skillet over medium-high heat. Add the onion, red pepper, and garlic. Sauté until limp, about 3 minutes. Sprinkle with salt, if desired.

2.   Push the onion mixture to the edges of the skillet. Add the shrimp and zucchini; sprinkle with thyme and red pepper flakes. Sauté until the shrimp are opaque, 4 to 5 minutes.

3.   Toss to mix well. Serve immediately.

If optional salt is added, add 288 mg sodium per serving.

SHRIMP VERA CRUZ

If you're looking for a taste of Mexico, look no further than this spicy shrimp stew that gets its kick of heat from jalapeño peppers. Served over brown or white rice, this is great for a family meal or for dinner guests. Add 1½ starch exchanges for ½ cup of rice.

4 servings

1 tablespoon olive oil
1 cup chopped onion
2 garlic cloves, minced
One 14- to 15-ounce can stewed
     tomatoes with juice
2 teaspoons chopped fresh jalapeño
     pepper, or 1 tablespoon chopped
     pickled jalapeño pepper
1 small green or red bell pepper, cored,
     seeded, and cut into short, thin
     strips
1 pound medium shrimp in the shell,
     peeled and deveined (about
     12 ounces after peeling)
1 tablespoon cornstarch
¼ cup coarsely chopped cilantro
2 cups hot cooked brown or white rice
1 lime, cut in wedges (optional)

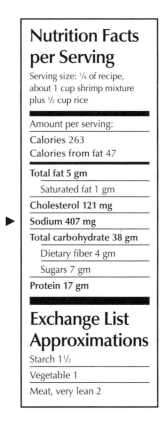

Nutrition Facts per Serving

Serving size: ¼ of recipe, about 1 cup shrimp mixture plus ½ cup rice

Amount per serving:

Calories 263
Calories from fat 47

Total fat 5 gm
  Saturated fat 1 gm
Cholesterol 121 mg
Sodium 407 mg
Total carbohydrate 38 gm
  Dietary fiber 4 gm
  Sugars 7 gm
Protein 17 gm

Exchange List Approximations

Starch 1½
Vegetable 1
Meat, very lean 2

1. Heat the oil in a large nonstick skillet over medium heat. Sauté the onion and garlic until tender, about 5 minutes. Add the tomatoes with their liquid and the jalapeño pepper; simmer 10 minutes.

2. Add the pepper strips and shrimp; cook until the shrimp are opaque, about 5 minutes.

3. Stir the cornstarch into 1 tablespoon water in a small bowl; add to the skillet. Stir and cook until the sauce thickens, about 1 minute. Stir in the cilantro.

4. Divide the hot rice among 4 bowls; pour ¼ of shrimp and vegetables into each bowl. Garnish with lime wedges, if desired.

CURRIED SHRIMP

Curry sauce adds a warm, spicy flavor to shrimp; it tastes creamy without adding a lot of fat. Serve over fragrant basmati or jasmati rice.

4 servings

2 tablespoons margarine
1/4 cup chopped onion
1 small clove garlic, minced
1 cup fat-free milk
2 tablespoons all-purpose flour
1/2 teaspoon salt
1/2 teaspoon curry powder
1/8 teaspoon freshly ground pepper
1 pound raw medium shrimp, peeled
      and deveined (about 12 ounces
      after peeling)

Nutrition Facts per Serving

Serving size:
1/4 of recipe, about 1 cup

Amount per serving:

Calories 154
Calories from fat 59

Total fat 7 gm
   Saturated fat 1 gm
Cholesterol 122 mg
Sodium 528 mg
Total carbohydrate 7 gm
   Dietary fiber 0 gm
   Sugars 4 gm
Protein 16 gm

Exchange List Approximations

Starch 1/2

Meat, lean 2

1. Melt the margarine in a medium nonstick saucepan over medium heat. Sauté the onion and garlic until soft, about 5 minutes. Stir in the milk, flour, salt, curry powder, and pepper. Whisk and simmer until the sauce is thickened, about 5 minutes. Set aside.

2. Bring a pot of water to a boil; drop in the shrimp and return to a boil. Reduce the heat; simmer for 4 minutes, or until the shrimp turn pink and are just cooked through (do not overcook). Drain well.

3. Stir the shrimp into the curry sauce; heat thoroughly. Taste and add more curry powder or pepper, if desired.

SHRIMP AND ASPARAGUS WITH FETTUCCINE IN MUSTARD CREAM SAUCE

Mustard sauce is an unusually tasty and robust topping for this shrimp and asparagus pasta dish. We cut the fat in the "cream" sauce by thickening it with a slurry made from flour and fat-free milk.

About 1 quart (4 servings)

4 ounces uncooked fettuccine noodles

MUSTARD CREAM SAUCE

2 tablespoons margarine
2 tablespoons all-purpose flour
1 cup fat-free milk
$1/4$ teaspoon salt
$1/8$ teaspoon freshly ground pepper
1 tablespoon Dijon mustard
1 tablespoon olive oil
$1/2$ pound raw shrimp, peeled and
    deveined (about 6 ounces after
    peeling)
4 ounces asparagus, cut into 1-inch
    pieces
1 clove garlic, minced

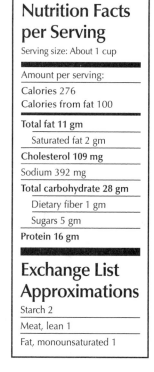

Nutrition Facts per Serving

Serving size: About 1 cup

Amount per serving:

Calories 276
Calories from fat 100

Total fat 11 gm
  Saturated fat 2 gm

Cholesterol 109 mg

Sodium 392 mg

Total carbohydrate 28 gm
  Dietary fiber 1 gm
  Sugars 5 gm

Protein 16 gm

Exchange List Approximations

Starch 2

Meat, lean 1

Fat, monounsaturated 1

1. Cook the fettuccine according to the package directions, omitting salt. Drain.

2. While the pasta is cooking, melt the margarine in a small nonstick saucepan over medium heat. Add the flour; cook until bubbly. Gradually stir in the milk, cooking and stirring until thickened. Add the salt and pepper. Remove from the heat and stir in the mustard.

3. Heat the olive oil in a large nonstick skillet. Sauté the shrimp, asparagus, and garlic over medium heat just until the shrimp are cooked through, about 4 to 5 minutes.

4. In a large warmed bowl, combine the fettuccine, the shrimp mixture, and sauce; toss to mix well. Serve immediately.

9

VEGETABLES

Vegetables are wonderful in so many ways. They're a colorful accompaniment to meat, poultry, and fish dishes, and dazzle in their own right when served as the entrée.

In addition to offering endless variety and great taste, vegetables are a good source of many important vitamins and minerals. Most are high in fiber, a good source of starches, and with few exceptions, low in calories. Unless it is added during preparation, vegetables have very little or no fat and all are naturally cholesterol-free.

NUTRITION

The Dietary Guidelines for Americans recommend eating plenty of vegetables. In fact, health experts recommend eating at least three to five servings each day. Unfortunately, most people get far less than the recommended amount and don't eat a wide enough variety. But it's important to eat many different kinds of vegetables and eat enough of them, because the nutrients found in vegetables vary drastically. For example, deep-yellow, orange, and dark-green leafy vegetables like carrots, sweet potatoes, kale, and spinach are great sources of beta carotene, which helps form vitamin A in the body. Others, like Brussels sprouts, potatoes, bell peppers, and tomatoes, are good sources of vitamin C.

In addition to being rich in vitamins and minerals, most vegetables are also a good source of fiber. Getting enough fiber is important for many reasons—it aids digestion, reduces the danger of intestinal problems, helps you feel full longer, and reduces the risk of certain cancers and heart disease.

Experts recommend eating 20 to 35 grams of fiber per day, but on average, most people consume about 11 grams. Keeping the peels on vegetables is one of the best ways to eat more fiber, as well as many of the vitamins and minerals that are found just under the skin. If you keep the peels on produce, be sure to wash it thoroughly. In fact, all the recipes in this chapter assume vegetables are washed before use.

Frozen vegetables are a good substitute when fresh vegetables aren't available. They're economical, convenient, and equivalent in nutrients to fresh. Canned vegetables are also a good option, but some brands can be high in sodium. If sodium is a concern, look for "no added salt" varieties. Specific information on the nutrient content of fresh fruits and vegetables is available on "Nutrifact" signs and brochures located in the produce sections of most supermarkets. If using frozen or canned vegetables, refer to the Nutrition Facts panel on the food label for information. If you look on the Diabetes Food Guide Pyramid or Exchange Lists, you'll see that vegetables are divided into starchy and nonstarchy categories. Vegetables like potatoes, corn, winter squash, dried peas, and beans have more carbohydrates and calories, so they're considered a starch. Other vegetables, such as leafy greens, mushrooms, peppers, and tomatoes, contain small amounts of carbohydrates and calories and so are categorized under "vegetables." If you follow a carbohydrate-counting plan, make sure you count in the appropriate amount of carbohydrate for whatever vegetables you choose. Remember, you need to eat a variety of both nonstarchy and starchy vegetables for good health.

PREPARATION AND COOKING

To retain nutrients and flavor, cook vegetables as little as possible. Steaming and stir-frying are great quick-cooking methods. Whatever you do, don't overcook them. In addition to diminishing their brilliant color, texture, and flavor, overcooking vegetables also drains them of their nutrients. Watch the amount of fat you add to vegetables, too. While naturally very low in fat, their calorie and fat content expands drastically when excess butter, margarine, oil, sauces, or sour cream is added, so use these toppings sparingly. In the recipes that follow, we've modified our sauces and preparation techniques to use less fat while still enhancing the naturally great taste of the vegetables.

Be adventurous and try a new vegetable that isn't in your current repertoire. Provençal Stuffed Eggplant, Carrot Purée with Dill, Bok Choy with Mirin Stir-Fry, Baked Stuffed Onions with Spinach and Feta, Spaghetti Squash "Carbonara," and Sweet Potatoes with Lemon are just a few examples of ways you can expand your vegetable horizons and turn a ho-hum dinner into wow!

STEAMED ARTICHOKES WITH HERBED MUSTARD SAUCE

Artichokes look exotic but are actually quite easy to prepare, and great fun to eat. Peak globe artichoke season is March through May, and they are best used on the day of purchase. Look for artichokes that are deep green in color and heavy for their size, with tight leaf formation. The leaves should "squeak" when pressed together. The herbed mustard sauce is a delightful accompaniment to this unique vegetable, but you could also try Low-Calorie Hollandaise for dipping (page 417).

2 artichokes (4 servings)

2 large artichokes (1½ pounds total)
2 teaspoons black peppercorns
1 teaspoon fennel seeds
2 tablespoons fresh lemon juice
2 tablespoons plus 1 teaspoon
      extra virgin olive oil
2 teaspoons Dijon mustard
1 teaspoon chopped fresh tarragon
      or fresh thyme leaves, or
      ½ teaspoon dried tarragon
      or dried thyme

1. Trim off ½ of each artichoke stem. Remove the bottom row of tough leaves from each artichoke and snip off the top third of all the other leaves. Cut the artichokes in half from the top to the bottom. With a small knife or melon baller, trim out the inedible prickly choke.

2. Fill a large pot half full of water. Add the peppercorns, fennel seeds, 1 tablespoon of the lemon juice, and 1 teaspoon of the olive oil. Bring to a boil; add the artichokes, reduce the heat, cover, and simmer over low heat, turning once or twice. Cook until the heart is easily pierced with the tip of a knife, about 45 minutes. Drain well.

3. In a small bowl, whisk together the remaining 1 tablespoon of lemon juice, the remaining 2 tablespoons of olive oil, the mustard, and herbs. Serve the sauce with the artichokes for dipping.

Nutrition Facts per Serving
Serving size: ½ large artichoke with 1 tablespoon sauce
Amount per serving:
Calories 96
Calories from fat 63
Total fat 7 gm
Saturated fat 1 gm
Cholesterol 0 mg
Sodium 97 mg
Total carbohydrate 8 gm
Dietary fiber 4 gm
Sugars 1 gm
Protein 2 gm

Exchange List Approximations

Vegetable 1

Fat, monounsaturated 1½

ASPARAGUS WITH DIJON SAUCE

Here's an easy way to serve asparagus that celebrates the advent of spring. The sharp tang of Dijon mustard is all that's needed to enhance the fresh taste of this delightful vegetable. Choose asparagus bunches carefully: spears should be round, straight, and of uniform size and thickness so they'll cook evenly. Remove the woody, bitter bottoms by holding both ends of the spear and bending slightly. They'll snap off naturally where they become tough.

4 servings

3/4 pound (about 9 to 12) fresh asparagus
     spears
1/2 cup Homemade Chicken Broth
     (page 101) or canned reduced-
     sodium chicken broth
1 tablespoon Dijon mustard or tarragon
     Dijon mustard

1. Break the woody ends off the asparagus; place the asparagus spears in a skillet.
2. Pour on the broth; cover and steam over medium heat until crisp-tender, about 4 minutes. Remove the asparagus to a warm serving plate; keep warm.
3. Add the mustard to the skillet; increase the heat to high and bring to a boil, stirring constantly; pour the sauce over the asparagus.

Nutrition Facts per Serving

Serving size: 1/4 of asparagus with about 1 1/2 tablespoons dipping sauce

Amount per serving:

Calories 28
Calories from fat 7

Total fat 1 gm
  Saturated fat 0 gm
Cholesterol 0 mg
Sodium 70 mg
Total carbohydrate 4 gm
  Dietary fiber 2 gm
  Sugars 2 gm
Protein 3 gm

Exchange List Approximation

Vegetable 1

GREEN BEANS WITH SUNFLOWER SEEDS

This recipe is deliberately simple, letting the fresh taste of tender green beans shine through. Sunflower seeds add an unexpected and delightful nutty flavor and crunch.

About 3 cups (6 servings)

1 pound fresh green beans
$1/2$ cup chopped onion
2 cloves garlic, minced
$1/2$ teaspoon salt
$1/8$ teaspoon freshly ground pepper
Pinch of crushed red pepper flakes
2 tablespoons shelled sunflower seeds
1 teaspoon chopped fresh oregano, or
        $1/4$ teaspoon dried oregano

1.   Snap the ends off the beans. If they are very young, leave the beans whole; if large, break the beans into 2-inch lengths. Place the beans in a saucepan; add 1 cup water and the onion, garlic, salt, and pepper.

2.   Cover and bring to a boil; reduce the heat to a simmer, and cook about 8 minutes, until the beans are crisp-tender; drain.

3.   Sprinkle the sunflower seeds and oregano over the beans. Toss lightly to mix.

Nutrition Facts per Serving

Serving size: About $1/2$ cup

Amount per serving:

Calories 38
Calories from fat 14

Total fat 2 gm
  Saturated fat 0 gm

Cholesterol 0 mg

Sodium 37 mg

Total carbohydrate 6 gm
  Dietary fiber 2 gm
  Sugars 1 gm

Protein 2 gm

Exchange List Approximations

Vegetable 1

Fat, polyunsaturated $1/2$

GREEN BEANS IN TARRAGON CREAM

Tarragon has a very distinctive licorice-like flavor that complements the sweet green beans in this recipe. The tarragon sauce is actually a low-fat adaptation of a classic béarnaise sauce. Fat-free evaporated milk helps it taste creamy, but it has only 1 gram of fat per serving.

About 2 cups (4 servings)

$^3/_4$ pound fresh green beans
2 tablespoons fat-free evaporated milk
1 tablespoon Dijon mustard with
      tarragon, or 1 tablespoon Dijon
      mustard plus $^1/_2$ teaspoon dried
      tarragon leaves

1. Snap the ends off the beans. Cut the beans in 1-inch lengths.
2. Simmer the green beans in a small amount of water in a covered medium saucepan until crisp-tender, about 6 minutes; drain.
3. Add the milk and mustard to the saucepan; stir together and heat 1 minute. Return the drained beans to the saucepan; toss with the sauce and serve immediately.

Nutrition Facts per Serving

Serving size: About $^1/_2$ cup

Amount per serving:

Calories 37
Calories from fat 5

Total fat 1 gm
  Saturated fat 0 gm

Cholesterol 0 mg

Sodium 105 mg

Total carbohydrate 7 gm
  Dietary fiber 2 gm
  Sugars 2gm

Protein 2 gm

Exchange List Approximation

Vegetable 1

CARAWAY ROASTED BEETS

Even if you don't consider yourself a beet lover, you'll love the taste of these colorful vegetables roasted. They're intense yet slightly mellow, and the caraway seeds add a delicate nutty anise flavor. Don't pierce or cut into the flesh, and leave at least an inch of stem and root on the beets during preparation. Otherwise, they will bleed out much of their color, flavor, and vitamins during the cooking process.

4 servings

4 beets (1¼ pounds total), greens and all
        but 1 inch of stems removed
2 teaspoons caraway seeds

1.   Preheat the oven to 375°F.

2.   Wash the beets well and place them on a square of heavy-duty aluminum foil. Sprinkle them with the caraway seeds. Fold and pinch the foil to seal the beets in the packet. Put the foil pouch in the oven and bake for 50 minutes.

3.   Remove the packet from the oven, place in the sink, and open. (Be careful; the juice will stain.) Peel the beet skin with a small paring knife and cut the beets in quarters. Dip the beets in the juices from the bottom of the foil packet and sprinkle some caraway seeds from the packet over them. Serve hot.

Nutrition Facts per Serving

Serving size: 4 beet quarters

Amount per serving:

Calories 43
Calories from fat 3

Total fat 0 gm
Saturated fat 0 gm

Cholesterol 0 mg

Sodium 69 mg

Total carbohydrate 9 gm
Dietary fiber 2 gm
Sugars 5 gm

Protein 2 gm

Exchange List Approximation

Vegetable 2

BOK CHOY WITH MIRIN STIR-FRY

Bok choy is a mild, versatile vegetable with a wonderfully crunchy texture. It cooks quickly and is best when served tender-crisp. Mirin, sometimes called rice wine, is available in the gourmet section of most grocery stores and adds sweetness and flavor to many Asian-inspired dishes. To increase the spiciness of this dish, add ¼ teaspoon crushed red pepper flakes when you add the green bok choy leaves.

About 3 cups (4 servings)

1 small head bok choy (1 pound)
1½ teaspoons dark-roasted sesame oil
1½ teaspoons peanut, canola, or corn oil
2 tablespoons light soy sauce
2 tablespoons mirin (sweet rice wine)

1. Slice the large green leaves of the bok choy into thin strips; set aside. Slice the white ribs of the bok choy ½ inch thick.

2. Prepare a large skillet or wok with non-stick pan spray. Heat both oils in the skillet over medium-high heat; add the white bok choy ribs and stir-fry until crisp-tender, 2 to 3 minutes. Add the green leaves; stir-fry 1 minute more.

3. Add the soy sauce and mirin; stir-fry about 1 minute. Serve immediately with the juices from the skillet.

Nutrition Facts per Serving
Serving size: About ¾ cup
Amount per serving:
Calories 55
Calories from fat 31
Total fat 3 gm
Saturated fat 1 gm
Cholesterol 0 mg
Sodium 338 mg
Total carbohydrate 3 gm
Dietary fiber 2 gm
Sugars 2 gm
Protein 2 gm

Exchange List Approximations

Vegetable 1
Fat ½

JADE-GREEN BROCCOLI

This vegetable side dish is equally tasty hot or chilled, and makes a great picnic take-along. Broccoli is a cruciferous vegetable that's part of the cabbage family and is a good source of vitamins A and C, folate, and calcium. Stir-frying the broccoli helps retain nutrients and turns it a beautiful, deep jade-green color.

About 6 cups (8 servings)

1 bunch broccoli (about 2 pounds)
1 tablespoon cornstarch
2 tablespoons light soy sauce
1/2 cup Homemade Chicken Broth (page 101) or canned reduced-sodium chicken broth
1/4 teaspoon salt
2 tablespoons peanut, canola, or corn oil
1 clove garlic, minced
1 teaspoon grated gingerroot
2 tablespoons sherry

Nutrition Facts per Serving	
Serving size: About 3/4 cup	
Amount per serving:	
Calories 66	
Calories from fat 35	
Total fat 4 gm	
Saturated fat 1 gm	
Cholesterol 0 mg	
Sodium 254 mg	
Total carbohydrate 6 gm	
Dietary fiber 3 gm	
Sugars 2 gm	
Protein 3 gm	

Exchange List Approximations

Vegetable 1
Fat 1

1. Peel the broccoli stems only if they are large and tough. Cut the stems diagonally into 1/3-inch slices. Separate the florets.
2. Mix the cornstarch, soy sauce, chicken broth, and salt in a small bowl; set aside.
3. Prepare a large skillet or wok with non-stick pan spray. Heat the oil in the skillet; add the garlic and ginger and cook 2 minutes over medium heat. Add the broccoli. Turn the heat to medium-high and stir-fry for 3 minutes.
4. Add the sherry; cover and cook 2 minutes longer.
5. Add the soy sauce mixture and stir constantly until the sauce thickens. Serve hot or chilled.

CRISP RED CABBAGE

The opposing flavors of sweet and sour in this recipe are just right. Apples, vinegar, and brown sugar balance the slightly peppery taste of cabbage. This is a colorful dish that goes well with Grilled Duck Breast (page 274) or Herb-Roasted Pork Tenderloin (page 212).

About 3 cups (6 servings)

4 cups shredded red cabbage
    (about ¾ pound)
2 medium apples, peeled, cored
    and cut into thin wedges
¼ cup red wine vinegar or apple
    cider vinegar
2 tablespoons brown sugar
½ teaspoon salt
¼ teaspoon ground nutmeg

1. Prepare a medium saucepan with non-stick pan spray. Place the cabbage, apples, ¼ cup water, the vinegar, and brown sugar in the prepared saucepan; mix well.

2. Cover and simmer over medium heat about 10 minutes, until cabbage is crisp-tender. Turn the cabbage several times during cooking and add a bit more water if it starts to stick.

3. Add the salt and nutmeg; mix well. Serve warm.

Nutrition Facts per Serving

Serving size: About ½ cup

Amount per serving:

Calories 62
Calories from fat 3

Total fat 0 gm
    Saturated fat 0 gm

Cholesterol 0 mg

Sodium 202 mg

Total carbohydrate 16 gm
    Dietary fiber 2 gm
    Sugars 13 gm

Protein 1 gm

Exchange List Approximations

Fruit ½

Vegetable 1

CARROT PURÉE WITH DILL

Purées provide very intense, sophisticated flavors and are a nice change of pace from more ordinary side dishes. Served individually in ramekins or piped onto the plate using a pastry bag, this purée goes well with a side dish like sautéed spinach or green beans to accompany Roast Spring Lamb (page 217) or Game Hens with Chutney-Mustard Glaze (page 273).

About 2 cups (4 servings)

6 medium carrots (about ³⁄₄ pound),
    peeled and cut into ¹⁄₂-inch
    pieces
1 tablespoon fat-free milk
1 tablespoon snipped fresh dill, or
    ¹⁄₂ teaspoon dried dill weed
2 teaspoons margarine
¹⁄₂ teaspoon salt
Pinch of nutmeg
Pinch of white pepper

1. Bring a large pot of water to a boil. Add the carrots and cook until tender, about 15 minutes; drain.

2. Place the carrots in a food processor or blender and purée until smooth. Add the remaining ingredients. Process for 1 minute. Taste and adjust the seasoning.

3. Serve hot in individual ramekins, reheated in the oven if necessary.

Nutrition Facts per Serving

Serving size: About ¹⁄₂ cup

Amount per serving:

Calories 44
Calories from fat 18

Total fat 2 gm
    Saturated fat 0 gm
Cholesterol 0 mg
Sodium 352 mg
Total carbohydrate 6 gm
    Dietary fiber 2 gm
    Sugars 2 gm
Protein 1 gm

Exchange List Approximations

Vegetable 1

Fat ¹⁄₂

GINGERED ORANGE CARROTS

Young and old love the delightfully sweet flavor of these orange gems, and they're a terrific source of vitamin A. Slice the carrots into coin shapes, matchsticks, or use sweet baby carrots to cut prep time. They make a great accompaniment to a simple entrée like pork chops or roast chicken.

About 2 cups (4 servings)

6 medium carrots (about ³⁄₄ pound),
    peeled and sliced
¹⁄₂ cup Homemade Chicken Broth
    (page 101) or canned reduced-
    sodium chicken broth
¹⁄₄ cup orange juice
2 teaspoons margarine
1 teaspoon grated fresh gingerroot,
    or ¹⁄₄ teaspoon ground ginger

1. Combine the carrots and broth in a medium saucepan. Cover and simmer over low heat until almost tender, about 10 minutes.

2. Add the orange juice, margarine, and ginger; simmer, uncovered, until almost all the liquid is absorbed. Serve hot.

Nutrition Facts per Serving
Serving size: About ¹⁄₂ cup
Amount per serving:
Calories 52
Calories from fat 20
Total fat 2 gm
Saturated fat 0 gm
Cholesterol 0 mg
Sodium 72 mg
Total carbohydrate 8 gm
Dietary fiber 2 gm
Sugars 4 gm
Protein 1 gm

Exchange List Approximations

Vegetable 1

Fat ¹⁄₂

SCALLOPED CORN

This dish falls somewhere between a pudding and a soufflé and is scrumptious, especially with its toasty brown topping. To make cracker crumbs for the topping, put soda or saltine crackers into a plastic bag and crush them with the bottom of a glass. Or you can whirl the crackers in a food processor using the pulse switch. Scalloped corn is terrific with Low-Fat Oven-Fried Chicken (page 260).

About 3 cups (6 servings)

One 17-ounce can cream-style corn
1 cup fat-free milk
1 large egg, beaten
1 cup soda cracker crumbs
2 tablespoons chopped pimiento
¼ cup chopped onion
½ teaspoon salt
Pinch of freshly ground pepper
2 teaspoons margarine

1. Preheat the oven to 350°F. Prepare a 1-quart casserole with nonstick pan spray.
2. In a medium bowl, combine the corn, milk, and egg; stir to mix well. Add ¾ cup of the crumbs, the pimiento, onion, salt, and pepper. Mix well; pour into the prepared casserole.
3. Melt the margarine in a small skillet. Add the remaining ¼ cup cracker crumbs; stir to distribute the margarine through the crumbs. Sprinkle the crumbs over the corn mixture.
4. Bake for 35 minutes. Serve hot.

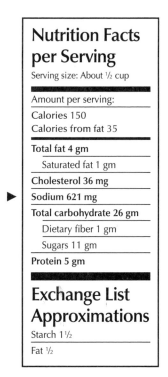

Nutrition Facts per Serving

Serving size: About ½ cup

Amount per serving:

Calories 150
Calories from fat 35

Total fat 4 gm
   Saturated fat 1 gm
Cholesterol 36 mg
Sodium 621 mg
Total carbohydrate 26 gm
   Dietary fiber 1 gm
   Sugars 11 gm
Protein 5 gm

Exchange List Approximations

Starch 1½

Fat ½

INDIAN CORN PUDDING

Vegetable puddings are like, custards, traditionally bound with eggs and cream. We've lightened up this recipe, replacing the cream with fat-free milk and decreasing the amount of eggs used. If you prefer, you can bake this pudding in individual ramekins instead of a casserole dish. Spray the ramekins with cooking spray and pour in the mixture. Decrease the baking time to 45 minutes, or until set. To unmold, run a thin knife around the edge of each custard and invert directly onto dinner plates.

About 3 cups (4 servings)

2 large eggs, beaten, or ½ cup egg
    substitute
2 tablespoons finely chopped onion
2 tablespoons finely chopped green or
    red bell pepper
½ teaspoon salt
¼ teaspoon ground mace
⅛ teaspoon ground white pepper
1 tablespoon margarine
1½ cups fat-free milk
2 cups fresh corn kernels, cut from cobs,
    or one 15-ounce can whole
    kernel corn, drained

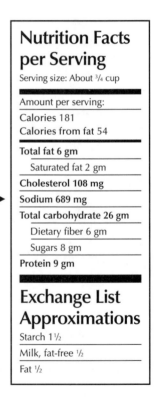

Nutrition Facts per Serving

Serving size: About ¾ cup

Amount per serving:

Calories 181
Calories from fat 54

Total fat 6 gm
   Saturated fat 2 gm
Cholesterol 108 mg
Sodium 689 mg
Total carbohydrate 26 gm
   Dietary fiber 6 gm
   Sugars 8 gm
Protein 9 gm

Exchange List Approximations

Starch 1½

Milk, fat-free ½

Fat ½

1. Preheat the oven to 325°F. Prepare a 1½-quart casserole with nonstick pan spray.
2. Combine the eggs, onion, bell pepper, salt, mace, and white pepper in a medium bowl.
3. Melt the margarine in a large nonstick saucepan; stir in the milk and heat for 5 minutes. Add the egg mixture and corn; stir to mix well.
4. Pour the mixture into the prepared casserole. Bake for 1 hour, or until set.

BRAISED ENDIVE

Braised endive makes a very elegant and unusual side dish. Because endive is bitter, accompanying side dishes should balance its flavor, add texture, and brighten the plate. Try Gingered Orange Carrots (page 320) or Baked Acorn Squash with Apple Stuffing (page 339). Braised endive is delicious with grilled steak, roast chicken, or game.

8 endive halves (4 servings)

4 medium whole Belgian endives
      (1 pound total)
1½ cups Homemade Chicken Broth
      (page 101) or canned reduced-
      sodium chicken broth
2 teaspoons honey
1 teaspoon margarine
⅛ teaspoon freshly ground black pepper

1. Cut the endives in half lengthwise.
2. Combine the broth and honey in a non-stick skillet large enough to hold the endive in one layer. Bring the liquid to a boil. Add the endive, cut side down; reduce the heat. Cover and simmer until tender, about 5 minutes, basting often with the liquid in the skillet.
3. Remove the endive. Simmer the broth to reduce to about ½ cup. Stir in the margarine and pepper. Serve the endive hot, topped with sauce.

Nutrition Facts per Serving

Serving size: 2 endive halves

Amount per serving:

Calories 45
Calories from fat 18

Total fat 2 gm
   Saturated fat 1 gm
Cholesterol 0 mg
Sodium 73 mg
Total carbohydrate 7 gm
   Dietary fiber 3 gm
   Sugars 4 gm
Protein 2 gm

Exchange List Approximations

Vegetable 1

Fat ½

EGGPLANT PARMIGIANA

This recipe is much lower in fat than classic eggplant Parmigiana recipes because it is not breaded and fried. It's terrific as an entrée or a side dish for pasta. We've kept the beautiful deep purple skin on the eggplant for added fiber and color.

1 casserole (4 servings)

1 medium eggplant (1 pound), unpeeled,
    sliced into ½-inch-thick rounds
2 medium tomatoes, sliced
1½ cups garden-style (meatless) pasta
    sauce
½ cup (2 ounces) shredded part-skim
    mozzarella cheese
¼ cup grated Parmesan cheese

1. Preheat the oven to 350°F. Prepare an 8-inch-diameter round pan with olive oil–flavor nonstick pan spray.
2. Layer the eggplant and tomatoes in the prepared pan. Spread the pasta sauce over the vegetables.
3. Cover with foil; bake 20 to 25 minutes, or until the eggplant is fork-tender.
4. Uncover; sprinkle with mozzarella and top with Parmesan cheese. Bake, uncovered, 15 minutes or until the cheese is golden brown. Cut into 4 wedges.

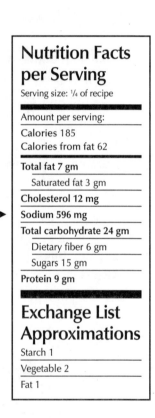

Nutrition Facts per Serving

Serving size: ¼ of recipe

Amount per serving:

Calories 185
Calories from fat 62

Total fat 7 gm
    Saturated fat 3 gm

Cholesterol 12 mg

Sodium 596 mg

Total carbohydrate 24 gm
    Dietary fiber 6 gm
    Sugars 15 gm

Protein 9 gm

Exchange List Approximations

Starch 1

Vegetable 2

Fat 1

PROVENÇAL STUFFED EGGPLANTS

While eggplants are commonly thought of as a vegetable, they are actually a fruit, and more specifically, a berry. There are many varieties of eggplants, ranging in color, shape, and size. Smaller Japanese eggplants, called for in this recipe, tend to be sweeter than the larger ones. The smaller eggplants are also nice because a half is the perfect size for a side dish.

4 stuffed eggplant halves (4 servings)

2 small eggplants 5 to 6 inches long
      (about 1½ pounds total)
1 cup chopped onion
2 cloves garlic, minced
1 tablespoon olive oil
One 14- to 15-ounce can diced tomatoes,
      drained
¼ cup packed chopped fresh basil
      leaves, or 1 teaspoon dried basil
1 tablespoon balsamic vinegar or red
      wine vinegar
¼ teaspoon freshly ground pepper
¼ teaspoon salt

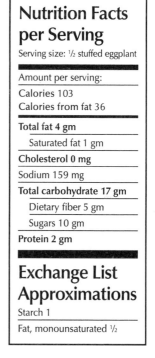

Nutrition Facts per Serving

Serving size: ½ stuffed eggplant

Amount per serving:

Calories 103
Calories from fat 36

Total fat 4 gm
  Saturated fat 1 gm
Cholesterol 0 mg
Sodium 159 mg
Total carbohydrate 17 gm
  Dietary fiber 5 gm
  Sugars 10 gm
Protein 2 gm

Exchange List Approximations

Starch 1

Fat, monounsaturated ½

1. Preheat the oven to 350°F. Prepare a cookie sheet and a medium skillet with nonstick pan spray.

2. Cut the eggplants in half lengthwise. Place them cut side down on the cookie sheet. Bake until tender when pierced with the tip of a knife, about 10 to 15 minutes.

3. Remove the pulp from eggplant, leaving a ¼-inch shell. Coarsely chop the pulp. Reserve the shells.

4. Sauté the onion and garlic in oil in the prepared skillet over medium heat until tender, about 5 minutes. Add the eggplant pulp; continue to sauté 3 to 4 minutes longer. Add the drained tomatoes; cook 2 minutes. Stir in the basil, vinegar, pepper, and salt. Spoon the mixture into the eggplant shells and heat through if serving warm.

5. Serve warm or at room temperature.

FRESH FENNEL MEDLEY

Some people shy away from fennel because of its licorice flavor, but its fragrant taste is sweet and delicate without being overpowering. When fennel is cooked, it's even more complex and mellow. Serve this dish as an accompaniment to roast lamb or pork loin. It's terrific with fish dishes, too. The feathery fennel tops make a pretty and unusual garnish.

About 2²/₃ cups (4 servings)

1 medium bulb fennel (10 ounces), plus
    feathery top
1 tablespoon olive oil
1 sweet onion (Spanish or Vidalia if in
    season), cut into thin wedges
2 ripe plum tomatoes or small tomatoes,
    chopped
¼ teaspoon salt
Pinch of freshly ground pepper

1. Trim the long stalks from the fennel down to the bulb. Chop and reserve 2 tablespoons of the feathery greens from the fennel stalks. Slice the bulb into thin strips.
2. Prepare a medium skillet with nonstick pan spray. Heat the oil in the skillet; sauté the fennel strips and onion until the fennel is crisp-tender, about 8 to 10 minutes. Stir in the tomatoes, salt, and pepper.
3. At serving time, garnish with the chopped fennel greens.

Nutrition Facts per Serving	
Serving size: About ²/₃ cup	
Amount per serving:	
Calories 78	
Calories from fat 34	
Total fat 4 gm	
Saturated fat 0 gm	
Cholesterol 0 mg	
Sodium 187 mg	
Total carbohydrate 11 gm	
Dietary fiber 4 gm	
Sugars 5 gm	
Protein 2 gm	

Exchange List Approximations

Vegetable 2
Fat, monounsaturated ½

BRAISED GARLIC CLOVES

The sharp taste of raw garlic is pleasantly mellowed when it's braised. Serve the cloves with roasted vegetables, meat, or poultry. To eat, squeeze the garlic out of the skin and use as a spread on thick slices of peasant bread in place of butter. It's a deliciously fat-free way to add an abundance of taste.

$1/2$ cup cooked, peeled garlic cloves (4 servings)

2 large bulbs garlic, separated into cloves
      but not peeled
$1/2$ cup Homemade Chicken Broth
      (page 101) or canned reduced-
      sodium chicken broth
2 teaspoons olive oil

1. Combine the garlic, broth, and oil in a small saucepan. Cover and simmer over low heat until the garlic is tender, about 15 minutes.

2. Drain off the liquid and discard.

3. Serve the unpeeled garlic cloves around meat, poultry, or roasted vegetables.

Nutrition Facts per Serving

Serving size: About 6 cloves

Amount per serving:

Calories 27
Calories from fat 0

Total fat 0 gm
  Saturated fat 0 gm
Cholesterol 0 mg
Sodium 3 mg
Total carbohydrate 6 gm
  Dietary fiber 0 gm
  Sugars 5 gm
Protein 1 gm

Exchange List Approximation

Vegetable 1

MUSHROOM DILL SAUTÉ

This is a dazzling side dish, with red or yellow pepper and dill adding brilliant color to the earthy background of mushrooms. Slice the mushrooms lengthwise across the cap and stem; they will fall apart if you cut crosswise. While they cost more, presliced mushrooms are available if you're short on time.

2 cups (4 servings)

1 tablespoon margarine
2 cups sliced white mushrooms
　　　(8 ounces)
1 red or yellow bell pepper, cored,
　　　seeded, and cut in thin strips
1 clove garlic, minced
2 teaspoons Dijon mustard
2 tablespoons snipped fresh dill,
　　　or 1 teaspoon dried dill weed
1/8 teaspoon freshly ground pepper

1. Melt the margarine in a large nonstick skillet over medium heat.
2. Sauté the mushrooms, pepper strips, and garlic until the mushrooms are tender and the liquid has evaporated, about 5 to 7 minutes.
3. Stir in the mustard, dill, and ground pepper; toss to coat. Heat through.

Nutrition Facts per Serving

Serving size: About 1/2 cup

Amount per serving:

Calories 48
Calories from fat 29

Total fat 3 gm
　Saturated fat 1 gm
Cholesterol 0 mg
Sodium 66 mg
Total carbohydrate 5 gm
　Dietary fiber 1 gm
　Sugars 2 gm
Protein 1 gm

Exchange List Approximations

Vegetable 1

Fat 1/2

WILD MUSHROOMS IN COGNAC

Wild mushrooms are not cheap, but you can't match their intense, earthy flavor. Save this recipe for a special occasion. If fresh wild mushrooms are available, use 4 ounces of them instead of 1 ounce of dried mushrooms and add beef broth instead of the soaking water in Step 2. You can also make an Asian variation of this recipe by omitting the cognac and adding 2 chopped green onions with 1 teaspoon grated fresh gingerroot along with the water or broth in Step 2.

About 2 cups (4 servings)

1 ounce dried porcini, shiitake, or other
    dried wild mushrooms
1 clove garlic, minced
1 tablespoon margarine
2 cups sliced white mushrooms
    (8 ounces)
1½ teaspoons chopped fresh thyme,
    or ½ teaspoon dried thyme
2 tablespoons mushroom soaking liquid
    (strained to remove dirt)
1 tablespoon Cognac or brandy
¼ teaspoon salt
Pinch of freshly ground pepper

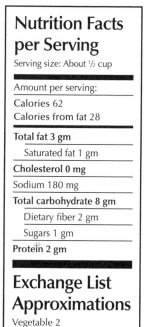

Nutrition Facts per Serving

Serving size: About ½ cup

Amount per serving:

Calories 62
Calories from fat 28

Total fat 3 gm
   Saturated fat 1 gm
Cholesterol 0 mg
Sodium 180 mg
Total carbohydrate 8 gm
   Dietary fiber 2 gm
   Sugars 1 gm
Protein 2 gm

Exchange List Approximations

Vegetable 2

Fat ½

1. Soak the dried mushrooms in enough warm water to cover for 30 minutes. Drain (reserve the soaking liquid) and slice.
2. Sauté the garlic in margarine in a medium nonstick skillet over medium heat for 1 minute. Add the rehydrated and fresh mushrooms and sprinkle with thyme. Sauté until the mushrooms release their liquid and most of the liquid is absorbed, about 5 minutes. Add 2 tablespoons of the soaking liquid, the Cognac, salt, and pepper; continue cooking 2 minutes longer.

GRILLED PORTOBELLO MUSHROOMS

Portobello mushrooms are actually a variation of the commonly cultivated white mushroom. Because the portobello is an older mushroom,
its gills are more exposed, so some of its natural moisture has evaporated. This results in a very concentrated flavor and a dense, meaty texture that makes a wonderful first course, side dish, or main dish. Try one
on a toasted bun in place of a hamburger.

6 mushrooms (6 servings)

6 medium portobello mushrooms
        (1 pound total)
1 tablespoon plus 1 teaspoon
        extra virgin olive oil
2 teaspoons balsamic, wine, or herbed
        vinegar
1 clove garlic, minced
⅛ teaspoon salt
⅛ teaspoon freshly ground pepper

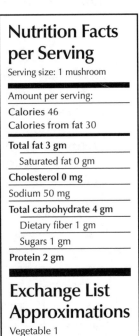

Nutrition Facts per Serving

Serving size: 1 mushroom

Amount per serving:

Calories 46
Calories from fat 30

Total fat 3 gm
    Saturated fat 0 gm
Cholesterol 0 mg
Sodium 50 mg
Total carbohydrate 4 gm
    Dietary fiber 1 gm
    Sugars 1 gm
Protein 2 gm

Exchange List Approximations

Vegetable 1
Fat, monounsaturated ½

1.   Preheat the broiler or prepare a charcoal
grill, spraying the rack with nonstick pan
spray.

2.   Clean the mushrooms well and cut off the
tough bottoms of the stems.

3.   Combine the olive oil, vinegar, and garlic
in a small bowl. Brush all surfaces of the mushrooms with the mixture. Allow to marinate at
least 20 minutes.

4.   Put the mushrooms on the prepared
broiler pan or grill, stem sides up. Broil or grill about 4 inches from the
heat source until the mushrooms are tender, about 4 to 5 minutes on
each side. Sprinkle with salt and pepper.

GRILLED RED ONIONS

This is an easy-to-make side dish that's fabulous with almost any charcoal-grilled entrée. Grilling the onions mellows their sharp flavor and caramelizes their starches into sugars. The balsamic vinaigrette helps add a touch of sweetness to the onions, too.

18 onion wedges (6 servings)

3 medium red onions (about
        1¼ pounds total), peeled
¼ cup Balsamic Vinaigrette (page 176)

1.   Cut each onion into 6 wedges. Try to keep the wedges together by leaving the root ends intact. Place in a shallow dish or pie plate.
2.   Drizzle the wedges with vinaigrette and marinate 30 minutes. Thread the onion wedges onto skewers, reserving any unused vinaigrette.
3.   Prepare a charcoal grill or preheat the broiler. Place the skewers on a rack over medium coals or on the broiler pan 4 to 5 inches from the heat source. Grill or broil until tender, about 5 minutes per side, basting with vinaigrette.

Nutrition Facts per Serving

Serving size:
½ onion, 3 wedges

Amount per serving:

Calories 74
Calories from fat 42

Total fat 5 gm
  Saturated fat 1 gm
Cholesterol 0 mg
Sodium 2 mg
Total carbohydrate 8 gm
  Dietary fiber 1 gm
  Sugars 5 gm
Protein 1 gm

Exchange List Approximations

Vegetable 1

Fat, monounsaturated 1

BAKED STUFFED ONIONS WITH SPINACH AND FETA

Don't limit onions to ingredients in salads, soups, or stews. They make terrific side dishes on their own. This appetizing recipe mixes spinach and feta cheese into a stuffing for sweet onions that's an excellent accompaniment to entrées like Grilled Marinated Sirloin Steak (page 197) or Veal Roast (page 220). For this dish, choose onions that are not too large and are nicely round.

4 servings

2 large sweet or Spanish onions (about
    1½ pounds total), peeled
2 teaspoons olive oil
1 clove garlic, minced
One 10-ounce package frozen chopped
    spinach, thawed and squeezed
    dry
1 teaspoon fresh lemon juice
¼ teaspoon freshly ground pepper
¼ cup bread crumbs
¼ cup (1 ounce) crumbled feta cheese

Nutrition Facts per Serving
Serving size: ½ stuffed onion
Amount per serving:
Calories 141
Calories from fat 40
Total fat 4 gm
Saturated fat 1 gm
Cholesterol 6 mg
Sodium 187 mg
Total carbohydrate 22 gm
Dietary fiber 4 gm
Sugars 9 gm
Protein 5 gm

Exchange List Approximations

Starch 1
Vegetable 1
Fat, monounsaturated 1

1.   Place the onions in a large saucepan and cover with water. Bring to a boil and cook until the onions are partially tender, about 10 to 15 minutes. Drain and cool; cut the onions in half crosswise. Scoop out the center of each onion half, leaving a ½-inch shell. Reserve the centers. If necessary, cut a small piece from the end of each onion shell so the shells will stand upright.

2.   Prepare a shallow baking dish large enough to hold the onion halves in one layer with nonstick pan spray. Place the onions in the prepared dish, hollowed sides up.

3.   Preheat the oven to 350°F.

4.   Chop the reserved centers of the onions. Sauté in oil with the garlic in a medium saucepan until tender, about 5 minutes. Stir in the spinach, lemon juice, and pepper; cook until the liquid evaporates. Remove from the heat; stir in the bread crumbs and cheese.

5.   Fill the onion shells with the spinach mixture. Cover with foil and bake about 25 minutes. Serve hot.

SUGAR SNAP PEAS WITH BASIL AND LEMON

Fresh basil and lemon add just the right touch to sweet sugar snap peas, resulting in a light dish that captures the taste of summer. Remove the strings on both sides of the pods if using fresh peas, but leave the pods whole. Be sure not to overcook the peas; you want them slightly crisp. Fresh sugar snaps are preferable, if they are available.

About 3 cups (4 servings)

2 teaspoons olive oil
1¼ pounds fresh sugar snap peas, or
       two (10-ounce) packages
       thawed frozen sugar snap peas
½ teaspoon salt
¼ teaspoon ground white pepper
⅓ cup coarsely chopped fresh basil
½ teaspoon grated lemon zest
½ lemon, cut in wedges

1. Heat the oil in a large nonstick skillet over medium heat.
2. Add the peas; season with salt and pepper. Stir-fry until the peas are crisp-tender, 3 minutes for fresh or 2 minutes for thawed frozen sugar snaps.
3. Add the basil and lemon zest; stir-fry until the basil is wilted and fragrant. Serve immediately with lemon wedges.

Nutrition Facts per Serving

Serving size: About ¾ cup

Amount per serving:

Calories 83
Calories from fat 24

Total fat 3 gm
    Saturated fat 0 gm
Cholesterol 0 mg
Sodium 301 mg
Total carbohydrate 11 gm
    Dietary fiber 4 gm
    Sugars 6 gm
Protein 4 gm

Exchange List Approximations

Vegetable 2

Fat, monounsaturated ½

SWEET PEPPER AND ONION SAUTÉ

This recipe is a veritable rainbow of colors. All bell peppers, named for their bell shape, have a mild sweet flavor and crisp, very juicy flesh. This sauté is a nice accompaniment to New Mexico–Style Flank Steak (page 202), Steak Fajitas (page 192), or Pork with Green Chile Sauce (page 208).

About 2 cups (4 servings)

1 tablespoon extra virgin olive oil
1 small yellow bell pepper, cored, seeded, and thinly sliced
1 small red bell pepper, cored, seeded, and thinly sliced
1 small green, orange, or purple bell pepper, cored, seeded, and thinly sliced
1 large onion, cut into thin wedges
1 clove garlic, minced
1/4 teaspoon salt

1. Heat the oil in a large nonstick skillet over medium-high heat until very hot. Add the peppers and onion; stir-fry 3 minutes.
2. Add the garlic; continue to stir-fry 2 to 3 minutes longer, or until the vegetables are crisp-tender. Sprinkle with salt.

Nutrition Facts per Serving

Serving size: About 1/2 cup

Amount per serving:

Calories 74
Calories from fat 32

Total fat 4 gm
    Saturated fat 0 gm
Cholesterol 0 mg
Sodium 149 mg
Total carbohydrate 11 gm
    Dietary fiber 2 gm
    Sugars 5 gm
Protein 1 gm

Exchange List Approximations

Vegetable 2
Fat, monounsaturated 1/2

PICKLED SWEET PEPPERS

Peter Piper knew what he was talking about! Pickled sweet peppers can be used as a condiment or an accompaniment for a variety of dishes—including grilled sausages, lamb, beef, or chicken—or as a sandwich topping.

4 servings

1 medium onion, thinly sliced
¼ cup raspberry vinegar or balsamic
    vinegar
2 tablespoons honey
2 cloves garlic, minced
6 whole peppercorns
1 bay leaf
3 small red or yellow bell peppers
    (about 1 pound), cored, seeded,
    and cut into ¾-inch-wide strips

1. Combine 1½ cups water, the onion, vinegar, honey, garlic, peppercorns, and bay leaf in a medium saucepan. Bring to a boil.

2. Add the peppers; simmer, uncovered, 15 minutes, or until the peppers are soft. Cover and refrigerate in their liquid at least 8 hours and up to 1 week before serving.

3. Drain and serve chilled or at room temperature.

Nutrition Facts per Serving

Serving size: ¼ of recipe

Amount per serving:

Calories 47
Calories from fat 1

Total fat 0 gm
    Saturated fat 0 gm
Cholesterol 0 mg
Sodium 3 mg
Total carbohydrate 12 gm
    Dietary fiber 1 gm
    Sugars 8 gm
Protein 1 gm

Exchange List Approximation

Vegetable 2

SPINACH WITH BACON AND MUSHROOMS

Spinach is a delicate green, so it cooks quickly. Sauté the leaves just long enough to wilt them; if you cook them too long, you'll ruin their color and fresh taste. The bacon and mushrooms enhance the slightly bitter flavor of the spinach. Try this dish with Swiss Steak (page 186) or Herb-Roasted Pork Tenderloin (page 212).

About 3 cups (4 servings)

2 slices bacon, diced
$\frac{1}{2}$ cup finely chopped onion
2 cups sliced mushrooms (8 ounces)
1 pound fresh spinach leaves, well
        washed, stems removed
$\frac{1}{8}$ teaspoon freshly ground pepper

1. Cook the bacon in a large nonstick skillet over medium heat until crisp. Remove with a slotted spoon to a paper towel; set aside.
2. In the same skillet, cook the onion in the bacon drippings 1 minute over medium heat. Add the mushrooms; raise the heat to medium-high and cook and stir until the vegetables are tender, about 4 minutes.
3. Add the spinach; cook and stir just until it is wilted, about 1 minute. Sprinkle with the reserved bacon and ground pepper.

Nutrition Facts per Serving

Serving size: About ¾ cup

Amount per serving:

Calories 101
Calories from fat 64

Total fat 7 gm
    Saturated fat 3 gm
Cholesterol 8 mg
Sodium 150 mg
Total carbohydrate 7 gm
    Dietary fiber 3 gm
    Sugars 2 gm
Protein 4 gm

Exchange List Approximations

Vegetable 1

Fat 1½

SPINACH CRÊPES

Crêpes aren't just for dessert. They're also a wonderful enclosure for savory fillings, like this spinach-and-cheese mixture. Try them as an entrée for brunch or a quick dinner. The crêpes can be made ahead of time, frozen, and defrosted as needed, so all you'll need to do is prepare the filling and pop them into the oven.

8 filled crêpes (4 servings)

One 10-ounce package frozen chopped
    spinach, cooked and drained
½ cup low-fat ricotta cheese
2 eggs, slightly beaten, or ½ cup
    egg substitute
3 tablespoons fat-free evaporated milk
¼ teaspoon salt
⅛ teaspoon freshly ground pepper
Pinch of nutmeg
8 Basic Crêpes (page 44)
2 teaspoons margarine, melted
3 tablespoons grated Parmesan cheese

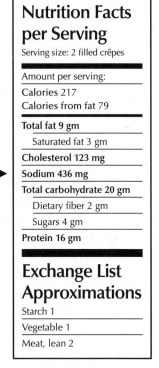

Nutrition Facts per Serving

Serving size: 2 filled crêpes

Amount per serving:

Calories 217
Calories from fat 79

Total fat 9 gm
    Saturated fat 3 gm
Cholesterol 123 mg
Sodium 436 mg
Total carbohydrate 20 gm
    Dietary fiber 2 gm
    Sugars 4 gm
Protein 16 gm

Exchange List Approximations

Starch 1
Vegetable 1
Meat, lean 2

1.   Preheat the oven to 350°F. Prepare a 9 x 13-inch baking pan with nonstick pan spray.
2.   Cook the spinach according to the package directions. Drain thoroughly in a colander, pressing hard on the spinach, or squeeze out the liquid by hand. In a medium bowl, mix the cooked spinach, ricotta, eggs, milk, salt, pepper, and nutmeg.
3.   Put ¼ cup of filling down the center of each crêpe; overlap the sides.
4.   Place the crêpes seam side down in the prepared baking dish. Brush with margarine and sprinkle with Parmesan cheese.
5.   Bake for 20 minutes, until the crêpes are hot and the cheese has melted.

BAKED ACORN SQUASH WITH APPLE STUFFING

Acorn squash is the most common member of the winter squash family. Its bright-orange flesh bakes beautifully, coming out moist, rich, and tender, and its pretty dark green and orange-streaked shell makes a perfect container for the delicious apple stuffing.

4 stuffed squash halves (4 servings)

2 small acorn squash (1½ pounds total),
　　halved and seeded
1 large or 2 small apples, peeled, diced
2 tablespoons diced celery
2 tablespoons finely chopped onion
2 teaspoons margarine, melted
Pinch of salt
Pinch of freshly ground pepper

1.　Preheat the oven to 400°F. Prepare a square baking pan with nonstick pan spray.
2.　Place the squash cut side down in a baking pan. Bake 20 minutes.
3.　While the squash is baking, combine the apples, celery, onion, margarine, and 2 tablespoons water in a medium bowl; mix well.
4.　Turn the squash cut sides up. Sprinkle with salt and pepper. Divide the apple mixture to fill the cavities of the squash. Bake the stuffed squash halves, covered with foil, for 30 minutes more. Serve hot.

Nutrition Facts per Serving

Serving size: ½ squash

Amount per serving:

Calories 87
Calories from fat 19

Total fat 2 gm
　Saturated fat 0 gm
Cholesterol 0 mg
Sodium 63 mg
Total carbohydrate 18 gm
　Dietary fiber 5 gm
　Sugars 10 gm
Protein 1 gm

Exchange List Approximation

Starch 1

GOURMET GOLDEN SQUASH

Choose any one or a combination of winter squashes—such as acorn, buttercup, butternut, golden nugget, Hubbard, pumpkin, or turban—for this luscious mash. It's a pleasant alternative to the usual potato or rice side dishes.

About 3 cups (6 servings)

2 pounds winter squash, peeled and
      cubed, or two 10-ounce packages
      thawed frozen winter squash
$^1\!/_2$ cup finely chopped onion
1 tablespoon margarine
$^1\!/_2$ cup light sour cream
1 teaspoon salt
$^1\!/_4$ teaspoon freshly ground pepper
Pinch of ground nutmeg

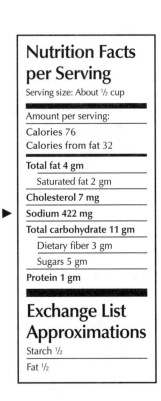

Nutrition Facts per Serving

Serving size: About ½ cup

Amount per serving:

Calories 76
Calories from fat 32

Total fat 4 gm
  Saturated fat 2 gm
Cholesterol 7 mg
Sodium 422 mg
Total carbohydrate 11 gm
  Dietary fiber 3 gm
  Sugars 5 gm
Protein 1 gm

Exchange List Approximations

Starch ½

Fat ½

1.   Cook fresh squash in a pot of boiling water until tender. Drain well and mash or put through a food mill. If you use thawed frozen mashed squash, cook according to the package instructions.

2.   Preheat the oven to 400°F. Prepare a 1-quart casserole with nonstick pan spray.

3.   In a small skillet, sauté the onion in margarine until tender, about 5 minutes. Add the squash, sour cream, salt, and pepper; mix well. Turn into the prepared casserole and sprinkle with nutmeg.

4.   Bake, uncovered, 35 to 45 minutes. Serve hot.

SPAGHETTI SQUASH "CARBONARA"

Spaghetti squash is unique, unlike any other variety of winter squash. Its cooked flesh can be pulled out in strands that resemble orange spaghetti, and its mild taste makes it an ideal partner for pasta sauces. The "carbonara" sauce in this recipe is a low-fat version of the traditional Italian favorite. Using fat-free milk, a small amount of bacon, and egg substitute helps keep fat at just 4 grams per serving. Be sure the spaghetti squash is hot when you add the sauce, and serve immediately.

About 3 cups (6 servings)

1 spaghetti squash (about 2 pounds)
6 strips bacon, cooked crisp, drained,
     and crumbled
¼ cup fat-free evaporated milk
¼ cup egg substitute
2 tablespoons grated Parmesan cheese
½ teaspoon salt
⅛ teaspoon ground white pepper
Pinch of ground nutmeg

1. Preheat the oven to 350°F. Pierce the squash in several places with a fork. Place on a cookie sheet and bake for 50 to 60 minutes, or until soft.

2. Remove from the oven and let stand for 5 minutes. Split the squash lengthwise; remove the seeds. Using a fork, shred the squash strands into a bowl.

3. Add the remaining ingredients to the hot spaghetti squash; toss and serve immediately.

Nutrition Facts per Serving

Serving size: About ½ cup

Amount per serving:

Calories 82
Calories from fat 34

Total fat 4 gm
    Saturated fat 1 gm
Cholesterol 7 mg
Sodium 366 mg
Total carbohydrate 7 gm
    Dietary fiber 1 gm
    Sugars 3 gm
Protein 5 gm

Exchange List Approximations

Starch ½

Fat 1

MEDITERRANEAN STUFFED ZUCCHINI

Abbondanza! Stuffed with rice, raisins, pine nuts, and aromatic mint and cinnamon, this dish is a surefire winner. The most versatile of summer squashes, zucchini has a mild flavor and tender texture that harmonize well with other ingredients. Choose squash about 7 or 8 inches long, since zucchini loses flavor and can be watery when it's overgrown.

6 servings

3 medium zucchini (1½ pounds total),
    ends trimmed
1 tablespoon olive oil
½ cup chopped onion
½ cup finely chopped tomato
½ cup uncooked white rice
¼ cup raisins
2 teaspoons chopped fresh mint leaves,
    or ½ teaspoon dried mint
½ teaspoon salt
½ teaspoon ground cinnamon
1 pinch freshly ground pepper
1 tablespoon pine nuts
¾ cup tomato sauce

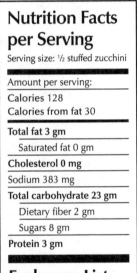

Nutrition Facts per Serving

Serving size: ½ stuffed zucchini

Amount per serving:

Calories 128
Calories from fat 30

Total fat 3 gm
  Saturated fat 0 gm
Cholesterol 0 mg
Sodium 383 mg
Total carbohydrate 23 gm
  Dietary fiber 2 gm
  Sugars 8 gm
Protein 3 gm

Exchange List Approximations

Starch 1
Vegetable 1
Fat, monounsaturated ½

1. Put the zucchini in a medium saucepan. Add enough water to cover and boil about 5 minutes, or just until tender.

2. Preheat the oven to 350°F. Prepare a baking pan with nonstick pan spray.

3. Split the zucchini in half lengthwise; leaving a 1/4-inch shell, scoop out the pulp. Chop the pulp from 1 zucchini; set aside. Save the rest for another use (mixed vegetables, soup, or stew).

4. Heat the olive oil in a nonstick saucepan. Add the onion and sauté over medium heat until tender, about 5 minutes. Add the chopped zucchini pulp and all the other ingredients except the pine nuts and tomato sauce. Cover and simmer over low heat 15 minutes, or until the rice is almost tender.

5. Toast the pine nuts in a small skillet over medium heat for 3 to 5 minutes until light brown and fragrant. Stir them into the rice mixture.

6. Stuff the mixture into the zucchini shells. Arrange the zucchini on the prepared baking pan and pour the tomato sauce over and around the shells. Cover with foil; bake 25 to 30 minutes.

PESTO-FLAVORED SQUASH SAUTÉ

For an easy summer meal, toss this squash sauté into cooked pasta (add 15 grams of carbohydrate or 1 starch exchange for each ½ cup of pasta) and serve with a fresh green salad. Or offer it as a side dish to charcoal-grilled steaks or Lemon Barbecued Chicken (page 229). No matter how you serve it, this sauté is a marvelous way to use up some of your summer squash bounty.

About 3 cups (4 servings)

1 tablespoon pine nuts
1 tablespoon olive oil
1 cup chopped onion
2 cloves garlic, minced
1 medium zucchini, thinly sliced
1 medium yellow squash, thinly sliced
¼ cup packed basil leaves, minced
1 tablespoon freshly grated Parmesan
    cheese
Pinch of freshly ground pepper

1. Toast the pine nuts in a small skillet over medium heat for 3 to 5 minutes, until lightly brown and fragrant. Remove and cool.

2. Heat the oil in a large nonstick skillet over medium heat. Sauté the onion and garlic until tender, about 5 minutes. Add the zucchini and yellow squash; toss. Cover the skillet and cook about 3 minutes, or until the squash is crisp-tender.

3. Stir in the basil; heat through. Sprinkle with the pine nuts, cheese, and pepper. Serve hot or at room temperature.

Nutrition Facts per Serving

Serving size: About ¾ cup

Amount per serving:

Calories 81
Calories from fat 47

Total fat 5 gm
    Saturated fat 1 gm

Cholesterol 1 mg

Sodium 28 mg

Total carbohydrate 8 gm
    Dietary fiber 2 gm
    Sugars 5 gm

Protein 2 gm

Exchange List Approximations

Vegetable 2

Fat, monounsaturated 1

STIR-FRIED ZUCCHINI

This isn't your ordinary stir-fry. Mild zucchini is paired with sweet onions and Asian spices to yield a mouthwatering dish. Choose sweet onions such as Vidalia, Oso-Sweet, Walla Walla, or Texas sweet for optimal flavor.

About 3 cups (4 servings)

1 tablespoon canola or corn oil
1 pound zucchini, cut into 1½- to
      2-inch strips
1 medium sweet onion, peeled and cut
      in thin wedges
½ teaspoon grated fresh gingerroot
1 tablespoon sesame seeds
1 tablespoon light soy sauce
1½ teaspoons dark-roasted sesame oil

1. Heat the canola or corn oil in a large non-stick skillet over medium heat.
2. Add the zucchini, onion, and gingerroot. Stir-fry about 5 to 8 minutes.
3. Sprinkle with sesame seeds, soy sauce, and sesame oil. Toss to blend.

Nutrition Facts per Serving

Serving size: About ¾ cup

Amount per serving:

Calories 90
Calories from fat 58

Total fat 6 gm	
Saturated fat 1 gm	
Cholesterol 0 mg	
Sodium 155 mg	
Total carbohydrate 8 gm	
Dietary fiber 2 gm	
Sugars 5 gm	
Protein 2 gm	

Exchange List Approximations

Vegetable 1

Fat, monounsaturated 1½

GARDEN STIR-FRY

This dish is bursting with color and vitamins. Scrambled egg bits and cashews add some color in addition to protein, but you can boost the protein even more by adding cubed firm tofu when you add the egg mixture. Eight ounces of tofu adds ½ medium fat meat exchange per serving.

About 3 cups (4 servings)

1 tablespoon olive oil
1 large clove garlic, minced
1 cup bite-size pieces broccoli florets
1 cup bite-size cauliflower florets pieces
¼ cup Homemade Chicken Broth (page 101), Vegetable Broth (page 102), or canned reduced-sodium chicken broth
½ cup sliced carrot (½-inch diagonal slices)
¼ cup thinly sliced red bell pepper
2 large eggs, or ½ cup egg substitute
1 tablespoon fat-free milk
½ teaspoon salt
⅛ teaspoon freshly ground pepper
2 teaspoons whole cashews
1 tablespoon light soy sauce (optional)

Nutrition Facts per Serving
Serving size: About ¾ cup
Amount per serving:
Calories 108
Calories from fat 64
Total fat 7 gm
Saturated fat 1 gm
Cholesterol 106 mg
Sodium 358 mg*
Total carbohydrate 7 gm
Dietary fiber 3 gm
Sugars 3 gm
Protein 6 gm

Exchange List Approximations
Vegetable 2
Fat, monounsaturated 1½

*If the optional light soy sauce is used, sodium is **509 mg** per serving.*

1. Place a large nonstick skillet over high heat. Add the oil and garlic and stir-fry for 30 seconds; reduce the heat to medium.

2. Add the broccoli and cauliflower and stir-fry for 1 minute. Add 2 tablespoons of the broth; cover and cook, stirring frequently, for about 3 minutes. Remove the vegetables from the skillet and set aside.

3. Add the remaining 2 tablespoons broth to the skillet; add the carrot and bell pepper. Stir-fry for 2 to 3 minutes, or until the vegetables are crisp-tender.

4. Return the broccoli and cauliflower to the skillet and stir-fry to heat through, about 1 minute more.

5. In a small bowl, combine the eggs, milk, salt, and pepper. Beat until foamy and well blended. Pour the egg mixture over the vegetables. Cook, stirring from the bottom, until the eggs are no longer runny.

6. Serve the vegetables garnished with cashews. Sprinkle with soy sauce, if desired.

BROILED TOMATOES PARMESAN

Here's the perfect accompaniment to a summer meal. The just-ripe tomatoes provide a taste straight from the garden, enhanced by the golden-brown, crunchy Parmesan-crumb topping.

4 servings

2 medium ripe tomatoes (12 to
     14 ounces total)
1 clove garlic, minced
2 teaspoons olive oil
1 tablespoon minced fresh basil,
     or 1 teaspoon dried basil
$1/4$ teaspoon freshly ground pepper
$1/2$ cup fresh soft bread crumbs,
     or 1 slice bread, crumbled
1 tablespoon freshly grated Parmesan
     cheese (preferably imported)

Nutrition Facts per Serving
Serving size: $1/2$ tomato
Amount per serving:
Calories 60
Calories from fat 28
Total fat 3 gm
Saturated fat 1 gm
Cholesterol 1 mg
Sodium 62 mg
Total carbohydrate 7 gm
Dietary fiber 1 gm
Sugars 3 gm
Protein 2 gm

Exchange List Approximations

Vegetable 1

Fat, monounsaturated $1/2$

1.   Cut the tomatoes in half crosswise. Gently squeeze out and discard the seeds. Place the tomatoes cut side up on a broiler pan prepared with nonstick pan spray.

2.   Combine the garlic, oil, basil, and pepper in a small bowl. Brush evenly over the cut surfaces of the tomatoes. Broil 6 inches from the heat source until hot, about 5 minutes.

3.   While the tomatoes are broiling, combine the crumbs and cheese in a small bowl; sprinkle evenly over the tops of the hot tomatoes. Return to the broiler until the crumbs are browned, about 2 minutes. Serve immediately.

MIXED GREENS

If you haven't tried greens before, you don't know what you're missing. Besides being an excellent source of folate and calcium, greens are simply delicious. If you don't like bacon, you can substitute 1 tablespoon of olive oil and boost the seasonings by adding ¼ cup of onion. This substitution does not affect exchange or carbohydrate values.

About 3 cups (6 servings)

1 pound mustard greens
1 pound turnip greens (or any
      combination of greens, such as
      kale or dandelion)
2 slices bacon, diced
1 small hot red pepper, seeded and
      minced, or ¼ teaspoon crushed
      red pepper flakes
1 teaspoon salt

1. Wash the greens well. Cut off and discard the tough stems; slice or coarsely chop the greens.
2. Cook the bacon in a large saucepan or Dutch oven over medium-high heat until crisp. Add the greens to the drippings and bacon bits; toss to mix.
3. Add 2 cups water, the hot pepper, and salt; bring to a boil. Cover and simmer over low heat until the greens are wilted and tender, about 30 to 40 minutes. Uncover and cook 5 minutes more.

Nutrition Facts per Serving
Serving size: About ½ cup
Amount per serving:
Calories 62
Calories from fat 42
Total fat 5 gm
Saturated fat 2 gm
Cholesterol 5 mg
Sodium 465 mg
Total carbohydrate 4 gm
Dietary fiber 2 gm
Sugars 0 gm
Protein 3 gm

Exchange List Approximations
Vegetable 1
Fat 1

VEGETABLE GUMBO

Filé powder is an essential ingredient in gumbo dishes, prized for its thickening power and unique woodsy flavor that's somewhat reminiscent of root beer. Don't stir filé into the gumbo until near the end of the cooking time, since too much heat makes filé tough and stringy. You'll love this vegetable gumbo version as is, but you can also add chicken or shrimp if you want a heartier dish. For shrimp gumbo, add 1 pound fresh or frozen shrimp; for chicken gumbo, add 1 pound cubed raw or cooked chicken. Either addition will increase each serving to 1⅓ cups and add 2 lean meat exchanges.

About 6 cups (6 servings)

2 tablespoons olive oil
2 tablespoons all-purpose flour
One 14- to 15-ounce can diced tomatoes,
　　　with juice
2 cups Homemade Chicken Broth
　　　(page 101), Vegetable Broth
　　　(page 102), or canned reduced-
　　　sodium chicken broth
1 large onion, coarsely chopped
1 cup sliced carrot
1 cup sliced celery
2 cloves garlic, minced
1 bay leaf
1 tablespoon chopped fresh thyme,
　　　or 1 teaspoon dried thyme
¼ teaspoon salt
¼ teaspoon freshly ground pepper
⅛ teaspoon hot pepper sauce
3 cups sliced fresh okra, or one 10-ounce
　　　package frozen sliced okra,
　　　partially thawed to separate
1 large green bell pepper, cored, seeded,
　　　and coarsely chopped
2 teaspoons filé gumbo powder
½ cup chopped fresh parsley

Nutrition Facts per Serving
Serving size: About 1 cup
Amount per serving:
Calories 127
Calories from fat 52
Total fat 6 gm
Saturated fat 1 gm
Cholesterol 0 mg
Sodium 281 mg
Total carbohydrate 18 gm
Dietary fiber 4 gm
Sugars 7 gm
Protein 4 gm

Exchange List Approximations

Starch 1

Fat, monounsaturated 1

1. Heat the oil in a large nonstick saucepan or Dutch oven over medium heat. Add the flour; cook and stir until a reddish brown roux forms, about 5 to 6 minutes.

2. Gradually stir in the tomatoes with their liquid and the broth; bring to a boil. Stir in the onion, carrot, celery, garlic, bay leaf, thyme, salt, ground pepper, and pepper sauce. Reduce the heat; cover and simmer 30 minutes, or until the carrot is almost tender.

3. Add the okra, green pepper, and filé gumbo powder. Cover and simmer 15 minutes more, stirring occasionally. Discard the bay leaf. Sprinkle with parsley at serving time.

VEGETABLE PLATTER WITH PEANUT SAUCE

Rich and creamy Indonesian peanut sauce makes an ideal dip for tender-crisp vegetables. If you like your dip a bit spicier, add a splash of hot pepper sauce. Rinse the vegetables under cold water once you drain them, to stop the cooking process; otherwise, they'll overcook and will be limp.

About 2 quarts vegetables and 1¼ cups dip (8 servings)

2 medium carrots, cut into 2½-inch
    strips
2 cups cauliflower florets
2 cups broccoli florets
1 cup green beans, ends trimmed
1 medium yellow summer squash, cut
    into 2½-inch strips
1 cucumber, cut into rounds
4 radishes, halved

PEANUT SAUCE

2 teaspoons canola or corn oil
¼ cup finely chopped onion
2 cloves garlic, minced
1 cup hot water
½ cup chunky peanut butter
1 teaspoon fresh lemon juice
½ teaspoon hot pepper sauce (optional)
½ teaspoon grated lemon zest
1 teaspoon chopped fresh gingerroot
1 bay leaf
¼ teaspoon salt

Nutrition Facts per Serving

Serving size:
1 cup assorted vegetables
plus 2½ tablespoons dip

Amount per serving:

Calories 145
Calories from fat 86

Total fat 10 gm
    Saturated fat 2 gm
Cholesterol 0 mg
Sodium 175 mg
Total carbohydrate 12 gm
    Dietary fiber 4 gm
    Sugars 6 gm
Protein 6 gm

Exchange List Approximations

Vegetable 2

Fat 2

1.   Bring a large pot of water to a boil; add the carrots and cook 2 minutes. Add the cauliflower and broccoli and cook 2 minutes more. Add the green beans and squash strips; cook 2 minutes longer. Turn all the vegetables into a colander; drain and rinse under cold running water. (This procedure parcooks all the vegetables in 1 pot.) Chill the vegetables, if desired.

2.   For the sauce, heat the oil in a nonstick saucepan. Add the onion and garlic; sauté 5 minutes. Add the remaining ingredients; stir well. (The peanut butter will melt and emulsify the sauce, although it looks strange at first.) Simmer, stirring often, for 10 minutes. Pour the sauce into a serving dish and keep warm.

3.   At serving time, place a bowl of warm dip in the center of a serving platter; arrange all the vegetables, including the cucumbers and radishes, around the bowl.

RATATOUILLE

Eggplant, onion, tomatoes, and peppers are traditional ingredients in ratatouille, but don't be afraid to improvise and add summer squash, scallions, red bell peppers, or other vegetables as desired. Just be sure to include the appropriate exchanges or carbohydrate counts for any substitutions. Essentially a vegetable stew, ratatouille is probably one of the most versatile dishes around: serve it hot, cold, or at room temperature and use it as a side dish, main dish, or appetizer with bread or crackers.

6 servings

2 tablespoons olive oil
1 large onion, sliced
2 cloves garlic, minced
1 medium eggplant, peeled and diced
2 small zucchini, sliced
3/4 cup thinly sliced green bell pepper
2 medium tomatoes, chopped
2 tablespoons chopped fresh basil,
    or 1 teaspoon dried basil
1/2 teaspoon salt
1/4 teaspoon freshly ground pepper
1 tablespoon drained capers

1. Heat the oil in a large nonstick skillet. Add the onions and garlic; stir-fry over medium-high heat about 2 minutes.
2. Add the eggplant and stir-fry about 2 minutes. Add the zucchini, green pepper, and tomatoes; stir-fry 3 minutes more.
3. Add the basil, salt, and pepper. Cover and simmer 30 minutes over low heat.
4. Uncover, stir gently, and simmer 10 minutes more. Add the drained capers. Serve hot or chilled.

Nutrition Facts per Serving

Serving size: About 2/3 cup

Amount per serving:

Calories 91
Calories from fat 44

Total fat 5 gm
  Saturated fat 1 gm
Cholesterol 0 mg
Sodium 203 mg
Total carbohydrate 12 gm
  Dietary fiber 3 gm
  Sugars 7 gm
Protein 2 gm

Exchange List Approximations

Vegetable 2

Fat, monounsaturated 1

NEW POTATOES WITH OLIVE OIL AND GARLIC

These new potatoes are simply divine and perfect with almost any entrée.

12 new potatoes (4 servings)

12 small new potatoes
     (1 pound total)
1 tablespoon plus 1 teaspoon
     extra virgin olive oil
1 large clove garlic, minced
1/4 teaspoon salt
Pinch of freshly ground pepper

1. Peel off a 1/2-inch strip of skin around the center of each potato.
2. Place the potatoes in a steamer set over simmering water. Cover and steam until tender, 15 to 20 minutes. Drain and reserve.
3. Heat the oil and garlic in a nonstick skillet large enough to hold the potatoes in one layer. Cook over medium heat until the garlic is fragrant, about 2 minutes. Add the potatoes and roll them in the oil mixture. Season with salt and pepper.

Nutrition Facts per Serving

Serving size:
About 3 small potatoes

Amount per serving:

Calories 123
Calories from fat 41

Total fat 5 gm
  Saturated fat 1 gm

Cholesterol 0 mg

Sodium 153 mg

Total carbohydrate 19 gm
  Dietary fiber 3 gm
  Sugars 2 gm

Protein 3 gm

Exchange List Approximations

Starch 1

Fat, monounsaturated 1

POTATOES AU GRATIN

We've trimmed the fat but not the flavor in this rich and creamy favorite by using reduced-fat cheese and fat-free milk and decreasing the amount of margarine.

About 2 cups (4 servings)

½ cup fat-free milk
2 tablespoons all-purpose flour
½ teaspoon salt
⅛ teaspoon celery seeds
2 cups thinly sliced peeled potatoes
¾ cup (3 ounces) shredded reduced-fat
       Cheddar cheese
2 teaspoons margarine
¼ teaspoon paprika

1. Preheat the oven to 350°F. Prepare an 8-inch-square pan with nonstick pan spray.

2. Heat the milk in a small saucepan over medium-low heat for 3 minutes. Combine the flour, salt, and celery seeds in a small bowl. Add to the milk and stir well.

3. Place half the potatoes in the prepared pan. Sprinkle on half the cheese. Repeat the layers. Pour the hot milk mixture over all. Dot with margarine and sprinkle with paprika.

4. Cover the pan with foil; bake for 15 to 20 minutes. Uncover and bake for 10 minutes longer, or until the potatoes are tender when pierced with a fork.

Nutrition Facts per Serving

Serving size: About ½ cup

Amount per serving:

Calories 171
Calories from fat 45

Total fat 5 gm
   Saturated fat 2 gm
Cholesterol 12 mg
Sodium 455 mg
Total carbohydrate 20 gm
   Dietary fiber 2 gm
   Sugars 3 gm
Protein 10 gm

Exchange List Approximations

Starch 1½

Meat, lean 1

MASHED POTATO PUFF

Yukon Gold potatoes are the spuds of choice in this recipe, since they make the creamiest mashed potatoes. Separating the eggs and folding in the whites just prior to baking helps keep the potatoes light and rich-tasting without a lot of added fat.

About 6 cups (6 servings)

4 medium potatoes (1¼ pounds total),
    Yukon Gold if available
⅔ cup fat-free milk
2 teaspoons margarine
¼ teaspoon salt
3 large eggs, separated
1 tablespoon grated onion
1 tablespoon chopped fresh parsley,
    or 1 teaspoon dried parsley flakes
¾ cup (about 3 ounces) grated or finely
    shredded reduced-fat Cheddar
    cheese

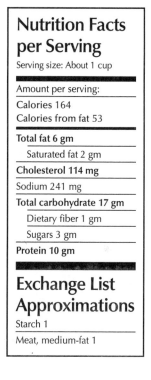

Nutrition Facts per Serving

Serving size: About 1 cup

Amount per serving:

Calories 164
Calories from fat 53

Total fat 6 gm
    Saturated fat 2 gm

Cholesterol 114 mg

Sodium 241 mg

Total carbohydrate 17 gm
    Dietary fiber 1 gm
    Sugars 3 gm

Protein 10 gm

Exchange List Approximations

Starch 1

Meat, medium-fat 1

1. Preheat the oven to 375°F. Prepare a 1½-quart casserole with nonstick pan spray.
2. Peel, quarter, and boil the potatoes until tender. Drain and mash with ⅓ cup of the milk, the margarine, and salt.
3. In a small bowl, beat the egg yolks with the remaining ⅓ cup milk. Add the egg mixture, onion, parsley, and cheese to the potatoes; mix well.
4. In another bowl, beat the egg whites until stiff and fold them into the potatoes. Turn into the prepared casserole.
5. Bake for 35 to 40 minutes, or until a knife inserted in the center comes out clean. Serve immediately.

WHIPPED POTATOES WITH HORSERADISH

You only need a touch of horseradish to give a pungently spicy kick to these potatoes. Whatever you do, don't use a food processor to whip potatoes. Food processors don't whip in air the way an electric mixer does, so the potatoes turn out sticky instead of fluffy.

About 2¹/₂ cups (5 servings)

2 large baking potatoes (about
　　　1¹/₄ pounds total), peeled and
　　　cut into 2-inch chunks
2 tablespoons margarine
¹/₄ cup fat-free evaporated milk
1 tablespoon freshly grated horseradish
　　　or drained prepared horseradish
¹/₂ teaspoon salt
¹/₄ teaspoon freshly ground pepper

1.　Boil the potatoes in a large pot until tender, about 15 minutes. Drain well.
2.　Whip the hot potatoes, margarine, and milk with an electric mixer until light and fluffy.
3.　Add the horseradish, salt, and pepper; mix well. Serve immediately.

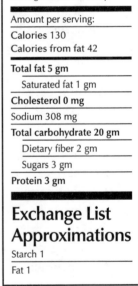

Nutrition Facts per Serving

Serving size: About ¹/₂ cup

Amount per serving:

Calories 130
Calories from fat 42

Total fat 5 gm
　　Saturated fat 1 gm
Cholesterol 0 mg
Sodium 308 mg
Total carbohydrate 20 gm
　　Dietary fiber 2 gm
　　Sugars 3 gm
Protein 3 gm

Exchange List Approximations

Starch 1

Fat 1

SPEEDY CHIVE POTATOES

Here's a quick way to make boxed potato buds taste more like home-made when you don't have time to make them from scratch. Buttermilk adds creaminess sans the fat, and a sprinkle of chives makes even a pack-aged mix seem special.

About 2 cups (4 servings)

1⅓ cups instant mashed potato flakes
½ cup low-fat (1 percent fat) buttermilk
2 tablespoons chopped fresh chives, or
      finely chopped green onion tops
¼ teaspoon freshly ground pepper

1. Bring 1 cup water to a boil in a small saucepan.
2. Stir in the remaining ingredients; remove from the heat. Cover and let stand 2 minutes; stir with a fork.

Nutrition Facts per Serving
Serving size: About ½ cup
Amount per serving:
Calories 81
Calories from fat 3
Total fat 0 gm
Saturated fat 0 gm
Cholesterol 1 mg
Sodium 53 mg
Total carbohydrate 17 gm
Dietary fiber 1 gm
Sugars 2 gm
Protein 3 gm

Exchange List Approximation
Starch 1

POTATO PANCAKES

Potato pancakes are also known by their Yiddish name, latkes. To cut down on the amount of fat absorbed by the pancakes while cooking, be sure the pan is very hot before adding the potato batter. Also, place the cooked pancakes on paper towels to help drain off any excess fat. Serve potato pancakes the traditional way, topped with unsweetened applesauce. Each ½ cup of applesauce counts as 1 fruit exchange or 15 grams of carbohydrate.

10 pancakes (5 servings)

2 large baking potatoes (about
    1¼ pounds), peeled and
    coarsely grated
1 small onion, grated
¼ cup egg substitute, or 1 large egg
¼ cup all-purpose flour
½ teaspoon salt
4 teaspoons margarine

1. Preheat the oven to 250°F.
2. Combine the potatoes, onion, egg substitute, flour, and salt in a large bowl; mix well.
3. Heat a large nonstick skillet over high heat. Melt 2 teaspoons of the margarine in the skillet. Drop the potato mixture by scant ¼ cupfuls into the skillet; flatten with the back of a spatula or pancake turner. Cook the pancakes until browned, about 4 to 5 minutes per side.
4. Cook the potatoes in batches, adding the remaining margarine as necessary. Keep the pancakes warm in a 250°F oven while cooking the remaining mixture. Serve immediately.

Nutrition Facts per Serving

Serving size: 2 pancakes

Amount per serving:

Calories 141
Calories from fat 29

Total fat 3 gm
  Saturated fat 1 gm
Cholesterol 0 mg
Sodium 295 mg
Total carbohydrate 25 gm
  Dietary fiber 2 gm
  Sugars 3 gm
Protein 4 gm

Exchange List Approximations

Starch 1½

Fat ½

ROASTED POTATOES WITH GARLIC AND ROSEMARY

Roasting really brings out the flavor of these potatoes tossed with garlic and sprinkled with a touch of rosemary. Use a heavy preheated pan (such as a cast-iron skillet) to prepare this dish and be careful not to crowd the potatoes. If necessary, you can make the potatoes ahead of time and pop them back into the oven for 10 minutes to reheat and re-crisp before serving.

8 to 12 wedges (4 servings)

2 large baking potatoes or 3 medium
      potatoes (1¼ pounds total), each
      cut in 4 wedges
1 tablespoon olive oil
2 cloves garlic, minced
½ teaspoon crushed rosemary
¼ teaspoon salt

1.   Preheat the oven to 350°F. Prepare a shallow dish or pan with nonstick pan spray.

2.   Arrange the potato wedges in the prepared pan. Combine the oil, garlic, rosemary, and salt in a small bowl. Brush the potatoes lightly with the oil mixture.

3.   Bake until tender and golden brown, about 1 hour, basting with oil from the pan every 15 minutes.

Nutrition Facts per Serving
Serving size: 2 to 3 wedges
Amount per serving:
Calories 136
Calories from fat 31
Total fat 3 gm
Saturated fat 0 gm
Cholesterol 0 mg
Sodium 155 mg
Total carbohydrate 24 gm
Dietary fiber 4 gm
Sugars 3 gm
Protein 3 gm

Exchange List Approximations

Starch 1½

Fat, monounsaturated ½

BAKED POTATO SKINS

No one can resist these potato skins, excellent as an appetizer or party snack. Potato skins are often loaded with fat and calories, since the skins are fried. To slim down our version, we baked the potatoes, scooped on an array of lean, tempting toppings, and then baked them again. Try all three variations—Mexican-Style, Pizza-Style, or Bacon and Sour Cream. Any way you fix them, they're a definite crowd pleaser.

4 potato skins (4 servings)

2 medium baking potatoes
    (1 pound total)

Toppings (choose one)

MEXICAN-STYLE

2 tablespoons green chiles or salsa
1/4 cup (1 ounce) shredded reduced-fat
    Cheddar cheese

PIZZA-STYLE

1/4 cup pizza sauce
1/4 cup (1 ounce) shredded part-skim
    mozzarella cheese

BACON AND SOUR CREAM

1 tablespoon bacon bits or chopped
    crisp bacon
2 tablespoons light sour cream
1 green onion with green top, finely
    chopped

1. Preheat the oven to 400°F.
2. Bake the potatoes for 1 hour, or until soft. Split lengthwise and scoop out the pulp; reserve it for mashed potatoes.
3. Divide the Mexican or pizza topping to top the skins. Reheat 5 to 10 minutes until the topping melts. If using bacon and sour cream, serve the hot potato skins topped with room-temperature bacon bits, sour cream, and green onion. Do not reheat this combination.

MEXICAN-STYLE

Nutrition Facts per Serving

Serving size:
1 potato skin (with topping)

Amount per serving:

Calories 86
Calories from fat 10

Total fat 1 gm
    Saturated fat 1 gm

Cholesterol 4 mg

Sodium 67 mg

Total carbohydrate 15 gm
    Dietary fiber 1 gm
    Sugars 1 gm

Protein 4 gm

Exchange List Approximation

Starch 1

PIZZA-STYLE

Nutrition Facts
per Serving

Serving size:
1 potato skin (with topping)

Amount per serving:

Calories 91
Calories from fat 13

Total fat 1 gm
   Saturated fat 1 gm

Cholesterol 4 mg

Sodium 157 mg

Total carbohydrate 16 gm
   Dietary fiber 1 gm
   Sugars 1 gm

Protein 3 gm

Exchange List
Approximation

Starch 1

BACON AND SOUR CREAM

Nutrition Facts
per Serving

Serving size:
1 potato skin (with topping)

Amount per serving:

Calories 81
Calories from fat 8

Total fat 1 gm
   Saturated fat 0 gm

Cholesterol 3 mg

Sodium 41 mg

Total carbohydrate 16 gm
   Dietary fiber 1 gm
   Sugars 1 gm

Protein 2 gm

Exchange List
Approximation

Starch 1

TWICE-BAKED POTATOES

Some people swear these potatoes are twice as good as regular baked potatoes—and they may be right! Twice-baked potatoes are typically quite high in fat and calories, but we have adapted this recipe by using low-fat buttermilk and reduced-fat Cheddar cheese in place of their full-fat counterparts.

4 servings

2 medium baking potatoes
    (about 1 pound)
½ cup (2 ounces) shredded reduced-fat
    Cheddar cheese
¼ cup low-fat (1 percent fat) buttermilk
    or fat-free milk
2 green onions with green tops, finely
    chopped
¼ teaspoon salt
1 clove garlic, minced
⅛ teaspoon freshly ground pepper
Pinch of hot or sweet Hungarian paprika
    (optional)

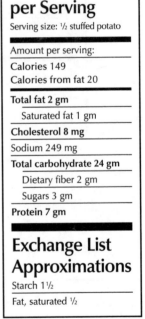

Nutrition Facts per Serving

Serving size: ½ stuffed potato

Amount per serving:
Calories 149
Calories from fat 20

Total fat 2 gm
Saturated fat 1 gm

Cholesterol 8 mg

Sodium 249 mg

Total carbohydrate 24 gm
Dietary fiber 2 gm
Sugars 3 gm

Protein 7 gm

Exchange List Approximations

Starch 1½

Fat, saturated ½

1.   Preheat the oven to 400°F. Scrub the potatoes and prick in several places with a sharp knife. Bake until tender, about 50 to 60 minutes.

2.   Slice the potatoes in half lengthwise. Scoop out the pulp, leaving ¼-inch shells.

3.   Combine the potato pulp, cheese, buttermilk, green onions, salt, garlic, and pepper in medium bowl. Whip with an electric mixer to blend well. Fill the potato shells with the potato mixture.

4.   Place the potatoes in a baking pan. If desired, sprinkle with paprika. Bake 20 minutes, or until the potatoes are heated through and the tops are slightly browned.

SWEET POTATOES WITH LEMON

Sweet potatoes are bursting with beta carotene and are one of the best food sources of this important nutrient. In general, the darker the skin of the potato, the sweeter its flesh. Lemon zest and a sprinkle of nutmeg add an intriguing taste.

4 sweet potatoes (4 servings)

4 small to medium sweet potatoes
    (1¼ pounds total)
1 tablespoon plus 1 teaspoon margarine
2 tablespoons fresh lemon juice
1 teaspoon grated lemon zest
¼ teaspoon salt
⅛ teaspoon nutmeg, preferably freshly
    grated

1. Preheat the oven to 375°F.
2. Scrub the potatoes, pierce them with the tip of a sharp knife in several places, and place them in the oven. Bake until the potatoes are tender, about 50 minutes.
3. Slit the tops of the potatoes lengthwise with a knife. Press the ends to open the slits. Top each potato with 1 teaspoon margarine. Sprinkle each with lemon juice, zest, salt, and nutmeg. Serve immediately while hot.

Nutrition Facts per Serving

Serving size: 1 potato

Amount per serving:

Calories 181
Calories from fat 35

Total fat 4 gm
  Saturated fat 1 gm
Cholesterol 0 mg
Sodium 205 mg
Total carbohydrate 35 gm
  Dietary fiber 4 gm
  Sugars 16 gm
Protein 3 gm

Exchange List Approximations

Starch 2

Fat ½

STOVETOP YAMS AND APPLES

Here's a quick and easy one-pot side dish that's wonderful with roast pork. The apples lend just the right tartness to balance the sweet taste of the yams and cinnamon.

About 4 cups (6 servings)

3 to 4 yams or sweet potatoes
　　　(1½ pounds total), peeled and
　　　cut into ¼-inch slices
2 tablespoons margarine
1 tablespoon brown sugar
⅛ teaspoon salt
3 tart apples, peeled, cored, and sliced
¼ teaspoon ground cinnamon

1. Place the potato slices in a large nonstick skillet. Pour 1½ cups water over the potatoes. Dot with margarine; sprinkle with brown sugar and salt. Cover, bring to boil, and cook over moderate heat 20 minutes.

2. Spread the apple slices over the potatoes. Sprinkle with cinnamon; cover and cook 10 minutes longer. Stir gently.

3. Remove the cover and simmer until the liquid is absorbed, about 5 minutes.

Nutrition Facts per Serving

Serving size: About ⅔ cup

Amount per serving:

Calories 173
Calories from fat 37

Total fat 4 gm
　Saturated fat 1 gm
Cholesterol 0 mg
Sodium 100 mg
Total carbohydrate 34 gm
　Dietary fiber 4 gm
　Sugars 21 gm
Protein 2 gm

Exchange List Approximations

Starch 1

Fruit 1

Fat ½

VERMONT-STYLE SWEET POTATOES

Pure maple syrup has a rich, subtle flavor that's far superior to its maple-flavored imitators. You need only a small amount for sweetness and color.

About 2 cups (4 servings)

2 large sweet potatoes (1 pound total),
    peeled and quartered
1 tablespoon margarine
2 tablespoons pure maple syrup
2 teaspoons finely grated orange zest
⅛ teaspoon freshly grated nutmeg

1. Place the potatoes in a skillet large enough to hold them in one layer. Add water to cover. Bring to a boil; reduce the heat. Cover and simmer until tender, about 15 minutes.
2. Drain, reserving 2 tablespoons of the water. Using a potato masher or fork, mash the potatoes with the reserved water, the margarine, syrup, orange zest, and nutmeg. Serve hot.

Nutrition Facts per Serving
Serving size: About ½ cup
Amount per serving:
Calories 143
Calories from fat 26
Total fat 3 gm
Saturated fat 1 gm
Cholesterol 0 mg
Sodium 43 mg
Total carbohydrate 28 gm
Dietary fiber 3 gm
Sugars 16 gm
Protein 2 gm

Exchange List Approximation
Starch 2

10

PASTA, GRAINS, PIZZA, AND LEGUMES

Pasta, grains, beans, and their assorted variations are a great way to add pizzazz and dress up a simple meal. If you're following a vegetarian diet, or simply in the mood for some vegetarian fare, you can use many of the recipes in this chapter as entrées. Whether your meal is simple or elaborate, the possibilities are endless for creating delicious dishes using these staple ingredients.

All these foods provide vitamins, minerals, carbohydrate (starch and dietary fiber), and other substances important for good health. All of them are naturally low in fat—it's the toppings you add that contribute most of the fat and calories. Pasta, grains, and beans contain a fair amount of carbohydrate and as a result can affect blood glucose levels. We've provided exchanges and grams of carbohydrate for each recipe so you can figure out how to fit the recipe into your own meal plan.

PASTA AND NOODLES

From angel hair to ziti, a wide variety of pasta shapes can add texture, color, and interest to a meal. In addition to shapes, you can also choose from a rainbow of colors. Try herb- and vegetable-flavored pastas, such as spinach, lemon and peppercorn, tomato basil, or garlic. These flavored pastas don't count in the vegetable group because they don't contain enough vegetables, but they're tasty and pretty all the same. Whole wheat pasta, like all pastas, is high in starch. But its fiber content is almost three times as high! One-half cup of whole wheat pasta has 3 grams of fiber, compared with 1 gram in regular pastas.

The most important tip for cooking pasta? Don't over- or under-cook. Pasta should be cooked to the *al dente* stage, tender yet firm to the bite. One of the biggest mistakes people make is not using enough water in the pot. You need at least 8 quarts per pound of pasta to help prevent it from sticking. And contrary to popular opinion, don't add oil to the water in an attempt to keep the pasta from clinging. Oil makes the pasta slippery and can prevent the sauce from taking hold. Immediately after draining, toss pasta with a bit of sauce as a low-fat means to prevent it from sticking together. By the way, it's not necessary to add salt to the water, either. Salt is used only for flavoring, which you'll get from the sauce or topping anyway. Speaking of toppings, they're usually the downfall of pasta dishes, from a fat and calories standpoint. All the toppings we've included are focused on reducing both without compromising taste.

Noodles are also used in a variety of favorite dishes, like macaroni and cheese, and in salads. Egg noodles may have small amounts of cholesterol and a bit more fat than pasta, but they are still considered to be low in fat and cholesterol. If you prefer, you can also buy yolk-free egg noodles. They have no cholesterol and very little fat.

Ziti with Eggplant, Asian Noodle Salad, Macaroni and Two-Cheese Casserole, Pasta Primavera, and North African Couscous are just a few of our favorite pasta dishes.

RICE

There are many varieties of rice in addition to the plain white rice with which most of us are familiar. All types are a good source of B vitamins. But when it comes to nutritional value, brown rice is the hands-down winner, with 1½ grams of fiber per serving—three times the amount found in white rice. Brown rice has a distinct nutty flavor and can be a delicious substitute for white rice in many dishes, but it takes longer to cook. If serving white rice as a side dish, add herbs to enhance the flavor. A bit of ground ginger and a bay leaf tossed into the rice as it cooks add a nice taste. Chopped vegetables are also a welcome addition. Other types of rice, such as arborio rice (used to make risotto) and basmati or Texmati rice (with a slightly fruity and nutty flavor) are widely available.

Wild rice, contrary to its name, is not really rice at all, but a long-grain marsh grass. Its fiber content is a bit higher than that of white rice but not anywhere near that of brown rice, with just ½ gram per ½-cup serving. Wild rice also has a wonderful nutty flavor and a chewy texture. Try it in salads, stuffing, and soups and as a side dish.

Mushroom Risotto, Apple Wild Rice, and Brown Rice with Chiles are just a few of the delicious rice-based recipes you'll find in this chapter.

GRAINS

Whole grains are good sources of fiber, B vitamins, and vitamin E and are low in fat. And they make very interesting side or main dishes, as you'll see in the following recipes. If you aren't familiar with the wide variety of grains available, like barley, couscous, millet, bulgur, or quinoa, you're in for a taste treat. Experiment with them in salads, as side dishes, and mixed with fruits and vegetables. Each grain has its own unique taste and can be a terrific change of pace from rice or noodles. Try Golden Currant Pilaf with Cinnamon, Grits and Cheese Chile Pie, and Creamy Polenta as a side dish to brighten up a meal.

LEGUMES

Legumes are the general category that encompasses dried beans, peas, and lentils. Black beans, navy beans, lima beans, red lentils, Great Northern beans, and chick-peas are just a few examples of the many varieties of legumes available. Packed with nutrients like protein, starches, B vitamins, and fiber (½ cup of legumes has between 4 and 10 grams of fiber), each type of legume has a distinct appearance and flavor. Whether spiced up as the star of the dish or combined with other foods, legumes are nothing short of delicious. Try them in soups, in place of meat in recipes like tacos or sauces, on salads, as a topping for pastas, and in mixed dishes like chili, meat loaf, meatballs, and stews.

You can buy beans either canned or dried. Dried beans have firmer texture than canned and so are sometimes preferred, but they require soaking before use. There are two options: you can soak the beans overnight or use the quick method, by bringing the beans to a boil in water, turning off the heat, and soaking 1 or more hours, depending on the variety.

Some people avoid eating beans because of their unpleasant side effects. To help reduce gas problems, rinse the beans, discard their soaking water, and cook them in fresh water. You'll need about 6 cups of water for each pound of beans. You can add seasonings to the pot, but not salt, since it can make the beans tough. To keep the liquid from foaming as you cook them, you can add a drop of cooking oil to the water. Simmer the beans until tender, then add them to your favorite dish.

Canned beans are a much more convenient alternative to preparing dried beans, but they are higher in sodium. Simply rinsing them under water before use helps wash away some of the sodium.

Chick-peas and Green Peppers, Rum-Baked Black Beans, and Lentils Italiano make great side dishes or entrées.

ASIAN NOODLE SALAD

A tasty twist on pasta dishes, this salad is brimming with bright, colorful vegetables and the earthy flavor of mushrooms. It's delicious hot, as a dinner entrée, or as a cold salad for lunch. Udon noodles are Japanese noodles that look like spaghetti and are available in the specialty sections of many grocery stores or in Asian markets, but you can also substitute vermicelli, a very thin spaghetti, if desired.

6 cups (6 servings)

8 ounces uncooked Japanese udon
    noodles or vermicelli
4 ounces fresh pea pods, cut into
    thin strips
2 tablespoons oriental dark-roasted
    sesame oil
1 tablespoon peanut oil
2 tablespoons light soy sauce
2 tablespoons rice wine vinegar or
    white wine vinegar
1/2 ounce dried shiitake, porcini, or tree
    ear mushrooms, soaked in warm
    water for 15 minutes, drained
    and sliced
1 carrot, sliced with a vegetable peeler
    into thin strips
2 or 3 green onions with green tops,
    cut diagonally into 1/4-inch slices
1 cup fresh bean sprouts, or 1 cup
    drained canned bean sprouts
2 tablespoons chopped dry-roasted
    peanuts or cashews

Nutrition Facts per Serving

Serving size: 1 cup

Amount per serving:

Calories 243
Calories from fat 81

Total fat 9 gm
    Saturated fat 1 gm

Cholesterol 0 mg

Sodium 213 mg

Total carbohydrate 35 gm
    Dietary fiber 4 gm
    Sugars 5 gm

Protein 7 gm

Exchange List Approximations

Starch 2

Vegetable 1

Fat 1 1/2

1. Cook the noodles according to the package directions, omitting salt. Thirty seconds before the noodles are cooked, add the pea pods to blanch. Drain the pasta and pea pods.

2. Mix the sesame oil and peanut oil in a small bowl.

3. In another small bowl, combine the soy sauce and vinegar. Whisk in 2 tablespoons of the oil mixture.

4. Put the hot noodles in a large bowl. Mix the remaining tablespoon of oil mixture into the noodles. Add the mushrooms, pea pods, carrot, onions, and bean sprouts. Add the soy dressing; toss well. Sprinkle with chopped nuts. Serve hot or cold.

MACARONI AND TWO-CHEESE CASSEROLE

We've updated this old favorite with a winning combination of Cheddar and Parmesan cheeses and covered the casserole with browned bread crumbs to add a toasty topping. Paprika is used for both color and flavor in this recipe, so be sure to buy a good Hungarian paprika.

3 cups (4 servings)

1 cup (4 ounces) uncooked elbow, small shell, or ziti macaroni
2 tablespoons margarine
2 tablespoons finely chopped shallots or onion
1 tablespoon all-purpose flour
1 cup fat-free milk
3/4 cup (3 ounces) shredded reduced-fat sharp Cheddar cheese
1 slice whole wheat bread, crumbled into soft crumbs
1/4 teaspoon paprika, preferably hot Hungarian
2 tablespoons grated Parmesan or Asiago cheese

Nutrition Facts per Serving

Serving size: 3/4 cup

Amount per serving:

Calories 270
Calories from fat 93

Total fat 10 gm
 Saturated fat 3 gm
Cholesterol 14 mg
Sodium 303 mg
Total carbohydrate 28 gm
 Dietary fiber 2 gm
 Sugars 4 gm
Protein 14 gm

Exchange List Approximations

Starch 2

Meat, lean 1

Fat 1

1.   Cook the macaroni according to the package directions, omitting salt; drain well.

2.   While the macaroni is cooking, melt 1 tablespoon of the margarine in a medium saucepan over medium heat. Sauté the shallots until tender, about 3 minutes. Add the flour; cook and stir 1 minute. Add the milk; cook until the sauce thickens, about 4 minutes, stirring often.

3.   Stir in the Cheddar cheese until melted. Add the cooked macaroni and mix well. Prepare a gratin dish or shallow ovenproof baking dish with nonstick pan spray. Transfer the macaroni and cheese to the dish. Preheat the broiler.

4.   Melt the remaining margarine; combine it with the bread crumbs and Parmesan cheese. Sprinkle over the macaroni.

5.   Broil 4 to 5 inches from the heat source until the top is lightly browned, about 2 minutes.

CREAMY MACARONI AND CHEESE

The ultimate in comfort foods, this rendition of "mac and cheese" is as cheesy and good as you remember but with half the fat.

4 cups (4 servings)

1 cup (4 ounces) uncooked elbow
    macaroni
2 tablespoons grated onion
1½ cups (6 ounces) shredded reduced-
    fat Cheddar cheese
1 tablespoon margarine
1 tablespoon all-purpose flour
2 cups fat-free milk
½ teaspoon salt
¼ teaspoon freshly ground pepper

Nutrition Facts per Serving
Serving size: About 1 cup
Amount per serving:
Calories 297
Calories from fat 86
Total fat 10 gm
Saturated fat 4 gm
Cholesterol 25 mg
Sodium 628 mg
Total carbohydrate 28 gm
Dietary fiber 1 gm
Sugars 7 gm
Protein 21 gm

Exchange List Approximations
Starch 2
Meat, lean 2
Fat ½

1.	Preheat the oven to 375°F. Cook the macaroni according to the package directions, omitting salt. Drain.

2.	Place half of the cooked macaroni in a 1½-quart casserole sprayed with nonstick pan spray. Sprinkle with half of the onion and cheese. Repeat the layers.

3.	Melt the margarine in a small saucepan. Remove from the heat and stir in the flour. Add the milk slowly, stirring until smooth. Add salt and pepper. Return the pan to the heat and cook over medium heat, stirring constantly, until the sauce thickens. (The sauce will be thin.)

4.	Pour the sauce over the macaroni. Cover and bake for 30 minutes. Uncover and bake 15 minutes longer.

LASAGNA

Lasagna is always a popular choice for hearty family suppers. To help speed cooking time, use no-cook lasagna noodles instead of regular noodles. They work equally well and don't require any advance cooking—simply line the pan with raw noodles, layer with filling ingredients, cover, and bake.

12 pieces (12 servings)

1 pound 90 percent lean ground beef
³/₄ cup chopped onion
1 clove garlic, minced
One 16-ounce can tomatoes with juice
Two 6-ounce cans tomato paste
2 teaspoons dried basil
1 teaspoon dried oregano
1¹/₂ teaspoons salt
8 ounces uncooked lasagna noodles
3 cups low-fat ricotta cheese
¹/₄ cup chopped fresh parsley,
        or 1 tablespoon dried parsley flakes
2 large eggs, beaten, or ¹/₂ cup egg
        substitute
2 cups (8 ounces) shredded part-skim
        mozzarella cheese
¹/₃ cup grated Parmesan cheese

Nutrition Facts per Serving
Serving size: 3 x 4-inch piece
Amount per serving:
Calories 303
Calories from fat 96
Total fat 11 gm
Saturated fat 5 gm
Cholesterol 100 mg
Sodium 620 mg
Total carbohydrate 26 gm
Dietary fiber 3 gm
Sugars 5 gm
Protein 28 gm

Exchange List Approximations

Starch 1¹/₂
Meat, lean 3

1.   In a large skillet, brown the beef with the onion and garlic; drain well. Return the mixture to the skillet and add the tomatoes with liquid, the tomato paste, basil, oregano, and salt. Simmer, uncovered, for 30 minutes, stirring occasionally.

2.   Preheat the oven to 350°F.

3.   Cook the lasagna noodles according to the package instructions.

4.   In a small bowl, mix the ricotta cheese, parsley, and eggs.

5.   Spray a 9 x 13-inch baking pan with nonstick olive oil–flavored pan spray. Layer in half the noodles and half the cheese mixture, then the meat sauce, and then the mozzarella. Repeat the layers with the remaining ingredients. Sprinkle the top with Parmesan cheese.

6.   Bake for 35 to 45 minutes. Let stand 10 minutes before cutting into 12 rectangles (each about 3 x 3 inches).

CHEESE MANICOTTI

An old Italian favorite that uses crêpes instead of pasta tubes to encase a mouthwatering cheese stuffing.

12 filled crêpes (6 servings)

CRÊPES

¾ cup all-purpose flour
⅛ teaspoon salt
2 large eggs

FILLING

3 large eggs, or ¾ cup egg substitute
2 cups low-fat ricotta cheese
1¾ cups (7 ounces) shredded part-skim
    mozzarella cheese
3 tablespoons chopped fresh parsley, or
    2 teaspoons dried parsley flakes
One 15-ounce jar prepared pasta sauce,
    garden-style or with mushrooms
⅓ cup grated Parmesan cheese

Nutrition Facts per Serving

Serving size: 2 crêpes

Amount per serving:

Calories 366
Calories from fat 143

Total fat 16 gm
  Saturated fat 8 gm
Cholesterol 233 mg
Sodium 743 mg
Total carbohydrate 28 gm
  Dietary fiber 3 gm
  Sugars 5 gm
Protein 30 gm

Exchange List Approximations

Starch 1½
Vegetable 1
Meat, medium-fat 3

1.   Preheat the oven to 350°F. Spray a 9 x 13-inch baking dish with nonstick pan spray.

2.   To make the crêpes, combine ¾ cup cold water with the crêpe ingredients in a food processor or blender and process until smooth.

3.   Heat a 5- or 6-inch skillet or crêpe pan until moderately hot. Prepare the pan with nonstick pan spray.

4.   Pour 1 ounce (2 tablespoons) of batter into the pan; tilt quickly to cover the pan with the thinnest possible layer.

5.   Cook until the bottom is lightly browned and the edges lift easily. Turn and cook on the other side for a few minutes. Remove each crêpe to a sheet of wax paper and repeat the process until all the batter is used. There should be 12 crêpes.

6.   To make the filling, beat the eggs and combine them with the ricotta and mozzarella cheeses and the parsley. Spoon the filling down the center of each crêpe and roll the crêpes.

7.   Cover the bottom of the prepared baking dish with about half of the pasta sauce. Arrange filled crêpes in the dish seam side down. Cover the top of the crêpes with the remaining pasta sauce. Sprinkle Parmesan cheese on top.

8.   Bake for 30 minutes.

LINGUINE WITH CLAM SAUCE

An Italian classic that's a cinch to make using canned clams. Red pepper flakes add a little spice to the dish. Use as much (or as little) as you like, depending on your heat tolerance.

5 cups (4 servings)

8 ounces uncooked linguine or
      other pasta
2 tablespoons olive oil
1/2 cup chopped onion
4 cloves garlic, minced
3/4 cup packed chopped fresh parsley
1 teaspoon dried oregano
1/2 teaspoon crushed red pepper flakes
Two 6 1/2-ounce cans minced clams,
      drained, juice reserved
1/4 cup white wine or water

Nutrition Facts per Serving

Serving size: 1 1/4 cups

Amount per serving:

Calories 357
Calories from fat 79

Total fat 9 gm
   Saturated fat 1 gm
Cholesterol 29 mg
Sodium 164 mg
Total carbohydrate 48 gm
   Dietary fiber 3 gm
   Sugars 6 gm
Protein 19 gm

Exchange List Approximations

Starch 3
Meat, lean 2

1.   Cook the linguine according to the package directions, omitting salt; drain well.

2.   While the pasta is cooking, prepare the sauce. In a medium skillet, sauté the onion and garlic about 2 minutes. Add 1/2 cup of the parsley, the oregano, pepper flakes, and the juice saved from the clams. Add the wine and simmer about 5 minutes. Add the clams and heat about 1 minute.

3.   Add the pasta to the sauce; toss until mixed. Sprinkle the remaining chopped parsley on top of the pasta.

PASTA PRIMAVERA

Primavera means "spring-style," and the bright, festive colors of the fresh vegetables used in this dish certainly reflect the season. If you're in a time crunch, consider buying precut vegetables from the salad bar. They're more expensive but can be worth it from a time perspective.

9 cups (6 servings)

8 ounces uncooked spaghetti
2 tablespoons margarine
1 onion, cut into thin wedges
2 cups broccoli florets
2 carrots, thinly sliced
1 zucchini, thinly sliced
1 yellow summer squash, diced
¾ cup Homemade Chicken Broth
      (page 101) or canned reduced-
      sodium chicken broth
⅓ cup chopped fresh parsley
⅓ cup chopped fresh basil
3 tablespoons fresh lemon juice
½ teaspoon salt
¼ teaspoon freshly ground pepper
3 tablespoons grated Parmesan cheese

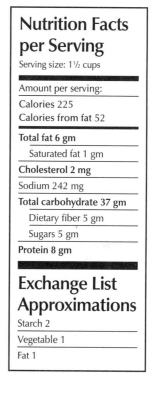

Nutrition Facts per Serving

Serving size: 1½ cups

Amount per serving:

Calories 225
Calories from fat 52

Total fat 6 gm
  Saturated fat 1 gm

Cholesterol 2 mg

Sodium 242 mg

Total carbohydrate 37 gm
  Dietary fiber 5 gm
  Sugars 5 gm

Protein 8 gm

Exchange List Approximations

Starch 2

Vegetable 1

Fat 1

1. Cook the spaghetti according to the package directions, omitting salt; drain well.
2. While the pasta is cooking, heat the margarine in a large skillet. Add the onion and sauté about 1 minute.
3. Add the vegetables and chicken broth; stir. Cover and simmer about 6 minutes. Add the parsley, basil, lemon juice, salt, and pepper. Stir and cook 1 minute more.
4. Add the spaghetti to the vegetables; toss well.
5. Sprinkle with Parmesan cheese at serving time.

ZITI WITH EGGPLANT

This eggplant preparation is robust and more like a vegetable topping than a sauce, so it's perfect for a sturdy pasta like ziti. Although fresh basil is definitely preferred in this recipe, it's not always available or affordable during the winter months. If you need to substitute dried basil, use only 2 teaspoons and mix it in when you add the tomato paste. Top the dish with some chopped parsley for color.

About 1 quart (4 servings)

8 ounces uncooked ziti or mostaccioli
      pasta
½ pound Japanese or other small
      eggplant, unpeeled
1 tablespoon olive oil
2 cloves garlic, minced
¾ cup reduced-sodium beef broth
2 tablespoons tomato paste
¼ teaspoon crushed red pepper flakes
¼ cup packed chopped fresh basil,
      or 2 teaspoons dried basil
¼ cup (1 ounce) grated Romano cheese

1. Cook the pasta according to the package directions, omitting salt. While the pasta is cooking, cut the eggplant into bite-size pieces.
2. Heat the oil in a large nonstick skillet. Sauté the eggplant with the garlic over medium-low heat until lightly browned. Add the broth, tomato paste, and pepper flakes; simmer, uncovered, about 5 minutes.
3. Drain the pasta; divide it among 4 shallow bowls. Spoon the eggplant mixture over the pasta; sprinkle with basil and cheese.

Nutrition Facts per Serving
Serving size: About 1 cup
Amount per serving:
Calories 278
Calories from fat 56
Total fat 6 gm
Saturated fat 2 gm
Cholesterol 4 mg
Sodium 220 mg
Total carbohydrate 45 gm
Dietary fiber 4 gm
Sugars 5 gm
Protein 10 gm

Exchange List Approximations

Starch 3

Fat, monounsaturated ½

NORTH AFRICAN COUSCOUS

Couscous is a wheat pasta and a staple in Middle Eastern stews and side dishes. Try it in place of rice or noodles alongside grilled chicken, lamb, or pork. If you're looking for a vegetarian option for a main course, this recipe also makes a tasty base for grilled vegetables.

2 cups (4 servings)

1 tablespoon margarine
1 cup quick-cooking couscous
1 cup Homemade Chicken Broth
      (page 101) or 1 cup canned
      reduced-sodium chicken broth
1 small carrot, thinly sliced
1 small onion, thinly sliced
¼ cup dark seedless raisins
Pinch of cayenne pepper

1. Melt the margarine in a medium saucepan. Add the couscous and mix to coat the grains with margarine. Add the chicken broth and bring to a boil. Cover and remove from the heat; let stand for 15 minutes.

2. Meanwhile, prepare a skillet with nonstick pan spray; add the carrot and onion. Cook for about 5 minutes, or until the onion is tender.

3. Stir the onions, carrots, and raisins into the couscous. Add the cayenne.

Nutrition Facts per Serving
Serving size: ½ cup
Amount per serving:
Calories 245
Calories from fat 34
Total fat 4 gm
Saturated fat 1 gm
Cholesterol 0 mg
Sodium 76 mg
Total carbohydrate 46 gm
Dietary fiber 3 gm
Sugars 9 gm
Protein 7 gm

Exchange List Approximation

Starch 3

GRITS AND CHEESE CHILE PIE

A true Southern favorite, grits are often eaten as a hot cereal, but they can also serve as an ingredient in side or main dishes, as this savory pie recipe demonstrates. Try it as a side dish for barbecued chicken or as an entrée at Sunday brunch.

1 pie (8 servings)

¾ cup quick-cooking hominy grits
1 cup (4 ounces) shredded reduced-fat
    Monterey Jack cheese
3 green onions with green tops,
    thinly sliced
1 large egg, beaten, or
    ¼ cup egg substitute
¼ teaspoon hot pepper sauce
Two 4-ounce cans whole green chiles,
    drained and patted dry

1. Preheat the oven to 350°F. Bring 3 cups water to a boil in a medium saucepan. Slowly stir in the grits; simmer until thickened, about 3 to 5 minutes, stirring frequently.
2. Remove from the heat; stir in the cheese, onions, eggs or egg substitute, and pepper sauce.
3. Arrange the chiles in a 9-inch pie plate in spoke fashion, with the larger ends against the edges of the plate and the tips toward the center. Pour the grits mixture evenly over the chiles. Bake 30 minutes or until set. Let stand 5 minutes. Cut into wedges and serve warm.

Nutrition Facts per Serving

Serving size: 1 wedge of pie

Amount per serving:

Calories 87
Calories from fat 21

Total fat 2 gm
   Saturated fat 1 gm

Cholesterol 32 mg

Sodium 126 mg

Total carbohydrate 12 gm
   Dietary fiber 1 gm
   Sugars 1 gm

Protein 5 gm

Exchange List Approximation

Starch 1

SOUTHERN SPOON BREAD

Spoon bread is a puddinglike bread mixture that's generally served as a side dish. This reduced-fat version is sure to please even the truest Southerner.

3 cups (6 servings)

$\frac{1}{2}$ cup yellow cornmeal
1 cup boiling water
$\frac{1}{2}$ cup fat-free milk
$\frac{1}{2}$ teaspoon salt
$1\frac{1}{2}$ teaspoons baking powder
1 tablespoon canola or corn oil
2 large eggs, separated

1. Preheat the oven to 375°F. Prepare a $1\frac{1}{2}$-quart casserole with nonstick pan spray.
2. Put the cornmeal in a medium bowl and pour on the boiling water; stir until smooth. Beat in the remaining ingredients except the egg whites.
3. In another bowl, beat the egg whites until stiff; fold into the cornmeal mixture. Turn into the prepared casserole.
4. Bake for 25 to 30 minutes, or until set. Spoon into serving dishes. Serve hot.

Nutrition Facts per Serving
Serving size: $\frac{1}{2}$ cup
Amount per serving:
Calories 96
Calories from fat 38
Total fat 4 gm
Saturated fat 1 gm
Cholesterol 71 mg
Sodium 316 mg
Total carbohydrate 10 gm
Dietary fiber 1 gm
Sugars 1 gm
Protein 4 gm

Exchange List Approximations

Starch 1

Fat, monounsaturated $\frac{1}{2}$

BAKED POLENTA WITH MUSHROOM SAUCE

This polenta recipe is a bit different from the creamy version on page 388. The mushroom sauce provides a deep, intense, earthy flavor that complements the taste and texture of the polenta. For variety, try different shapes of cookie cutters instead of cutting the polenta into squares.

12 servings

POLENTA

2 cups fat-free milk
1 tablespoon margarine
$\frac{1}{2}$ teaspoon salt
1 cup quick-cooking yellow cornmeal
$\frac{1}{4}$ cup (1 ounce) shredded part-skim
    mozzarella cheese
2 tablespoons grated Parmesan cheese
$\frac{1}{8}$ teaspoon ground white pepper

MUSHROOM SAUCE

2 shallots, sliced, or 2 cloves garlic,
    minced
1 tablespoon olive oil
1 cup sliced portobello, brown, or other
    full-flavored mushrooms
1 cup sliced white mushrooms
1 cup beef broth or reduced-sodium
    beef broth
$\frac{1}{4}$ teaspoon seasoned salt (optional)
Pinch of freshly ground pepper

Nutrition Facts per Serving

Serving size:
One 3-inch square with about 2 tablespoons sauce

Amount per serving:

Calories 99
Calories from fat 27

Total fat 3 gm
    Saturated fat 1 gm
Cholesterol 3 mg
Sodium 306 mg
Total carbohydrate 14 gm
    Dietary fiber 2 gm
    Sugars 2 gm
Protein 4 gm

Exchange List Approximations

Starch 1

Fat, monounsaturated $\frac{1}{2}$

1.   Make the polenta. In a medium saucepan, heat the milk, 2 cups water, the margarine, and salt to boiling. Reduce the heat and whisk in the cornmeal. Continue stirring and cooking until the mixture pulls away from the sides of the pan, about 10 minutes. Stir in the cheeses and pepper.

2.   Prepare a jelly roll pan or large cookie sheet with nonstick pan spray. Pour the polenta mixture on the pan and spread to a 9 x 12-inch rectangle. Let cool to room temperature.

3.   Preheat the oven to 350°F.

4.   Bake the polenta for 15 to 20 minutes, or until the edges are browned.

5.   Meanwhile, prepare the sauce. In a medium skillet, sauté the shallots in olive oil until soft. Stir in all the mushrooms and sauté over medium-high heat for 5 minutes. Add the beef broth and simmer for 5 minutes. Add salt, if desired, and pepper.

6.   Slice the polenta in twelve 3-inch squares. Serve some mushroom sauce on each square.

CREAMY POLENTA

Polenta, a mush made from cornmeal, is an Italian favorite. It's delicious served plain as a side dish or topped with a favorite tomato sauce. You can also use it as a base ingredient in casseroles instead of noodles. If you add other ingredients to the polenta, be sure to include the appropriate exchanges.

2 cups (4 servings)

2 cups Homemade Chicken Broth
      (page 101) or canned reduced-
      sodium chicken broth
½ cup yellow or white cornmeal
½ teaspoon salt (optional)
¼ cup freshly grated Parmesan cheese

1. Combine the broth and cornmeal in a medium saucepan. Bring to a boil, stirring frequently. Reduce the heat and simmer over low heat until thickened but creamy, about 12 to 15 minutes. Stir often to prevent sticking. Taste and add salt, if desired.

2. Remove from the heat. Sprinkle with cheese.

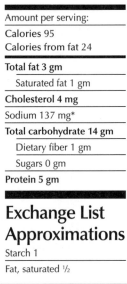

Nutrition Facts per Serving

Serving size: ½ cup

Amount per serving:

Calories 95
Calories from fat 24

Total fat 3 gm
   Saturated fat 1 gm

Cholesterol 4 mg

Sodium 137 mg*

Total carbohydrate 14 gm
   Dietary fiber 1 gm
   Sugars 0 gm

Protein 5 gm

Exchange List Approximations

Starch 1

Fat, saturated ½

If the optional salt is used, sodium is 428 mg per serving.

BROWN RICE WITH CHILES

You can serve this casserole as either a main or a side dish. Brown rice adds a distinctive nutty flavor that goes well with the flavor of the cheese and chiles.

**2 cups (2 servings as a main course,
4 servings as a side dish)**

½ cup uncooked brown rice
1 cup plain low-fat yogurt
¼ teaspoon salt
⅛ teaspoon freshly ground pepper
2 ounces (½ of a 4-ounce can) green
      chiles, drained and chopped
¼ cup (1 ounce) shredded reduced-fat
      Monterey Jack/Colby blend
      cheese

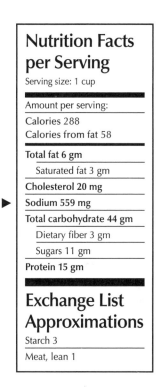

**Nutrition Facts
per Serving**

Serving size: 1 cup

Amount per serving:

Calories 288
Calories from fat 58

Total fat 6 gm
   Saturated fat 3 gm

Cholesterol 20 mg

Sodium 559 mg

Total carbohydrate 44 gm
   Dietary fiber 3 gm
   Sugars 11 gm

Protein 15 gm

**Exchange List
Approximations**

Starch 3

Meat, lean 1

1. Cook the brown rice according to the package directions, omitting salt. While the rice is cooking, preheat the oven to 350°F. Prepare a 1½-quart casserole with nonstick pan spray.
2. Add the yogurt, salt, and pepper to the cooked rice; mix well.
3. Place half of the mixture in the bottom of the casserole. Top with half the chiles and half the cheese. Repeat the layers, topping with the remaining cheese.
4. Bake, uncovered, about 25 to 30 minutes, or until the top is lightly browned.

CHEESE- AND RICE-STUFFED PEPPERS

Stuffed peppers are a delicious way to use up leftover white or brown rice, and they make an attractive side dish for almost any entrée. To keep the peppers from tipping over, bake them in large cupcake tins so they stand upright.

4 peppers (4 servings)

4 medium green bell peppers
2 cups cooked rice
1 cup (4 ounces) shredded reduced-fat
       Cheddar cheese
2 tablespoons chopped fresh parsley
½ teaspoon salt
⅛ teaspoon freshly ground pepper

1. Preheat the oven to 300°F.
2. Slice off the tops of the peppers. Wash the peppers and remove the cores and seeds. Stand the pepper cups upright in a saucepan containing ½ cup boiling water. Cover tightly and allow to steam 5 minutes. Remove and drain.
3. In a large bowl, mix together the rice, cheese, parsley, salt, and ground pepper. Divide the mixture and stuff each pepper.
4. Stand the peppers in a loaf pan or cupcake tins. Bake for about 15 minutes, until the filling is hot and the cheese melts.

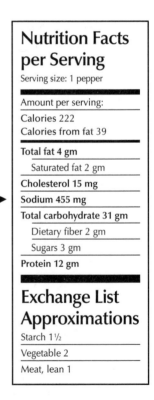

Nutrition Facts per Serving

Serving size: 1 pepper

Amount per serving:

Calories 222
Calories from fat 39

Total fat 4 gm
   Saturated fat 2 gm
Cholesterol 15 mg
Sodium 455 mg
Total carbohydrate 31 gm
   Dietary fiber 2 gm
   Sugars 3 gm
Protein 12 gm

Exchange List Approximations

Starch 1½
Vegetable 2
Meat, lean 1

VEGETABLE FRIED RICE

Chinese five-spice powder is a key ingredient in this colorful recipe. A pungent mix of ground spices (usually consisting of equal parts cinnamon, cloves, fennel seed, star anise, and Szechwan peppercorns), it's available in most grocery stores and Asian markets. Serve this rice as an entrée or side dish.

6 servings

1 tablespoon canola or corn oil
3 tablespoons light soy sauce
2 teaspoons cider vinegar or lemon juice
2 teaspoons brown sugar
½ teaspoon Chinese five-spice powder
¼ teaspoon crushed red pepper flakes
3 cloves garlic, minced
1½ cups chopped fresh broccoli
½ cup thinly sliced carrot
1½ cups diced cooked chicken
    (about 9 ounces)
1 large egg, lightly beaten, or
    ¼ cup egg substitute
4 green onions with green tops, sliced
    diagonally
3 cups cooked white rice

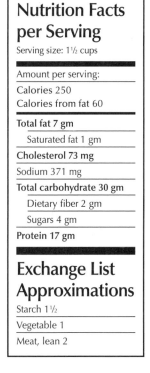

Nutrition Facts per Serving

Serving size: 1½ cups

Amount per serving:

Calories 250
Calories from fat 60

Total fat 7 gm
  Saturated fat 1 gm
Cholesterol 73 mg
Sodium 371 mg
Total carbohydrate 30 gm
  Dietary fiber 2 gm
  Sugars 4 gm
Protein 17 gm

Exchange List Approximations

Starch 1½
Vegetable 1
Meat, lean 2

1. Heat a nonstick wok or large skillet; add the oil and coat the surface. Add the soy sauce, vinegar, sugar, five-spice powder, garlic, and red pepper flakes. Cook over medium heat for 1 minute.

2. Add the broccoli and carrot; stir-fry 2 to 3 minutes.

3. Add the chicken, egg, and green onions; stir-fry until the egg is cooked.

4. Add the rice and toss to mix well; cook until the rice is heated through.

JAMBALAYA

A hallmark of Creole cooking, jambalaya is a versatile dish that combines cooked rice with a variety of vegetables—like tomatoes, onions, and green peppers—and almost any kind of meat, poultry, and shellfish. Jambalaya recipes vary from cook to cook and ingredients are often added depending upon what's at hand. Here's one of our favorite versions that's sure to become a favorite with you, too.

About 10 cups (8 servings)

1 tablespoon canola or corn oil
2 medium onions, chopped
1 small green bell pepper, cored, seeded, and chopped
2 ribs celery, chopped
2 cloves garlic, minced
One 16-ounce can diced tomatoes in purée, undrained
2 cups Homemade Chicken Broth (page 101) or canned reduced-sodium chicken broth
2 tablespoons tomato paste
1 teaspoon salt
1½ teaspoons chopped fresh thyme, or ½ teaspoon dried thyme
¼ teaspoon freshly ground pepper
¼ teaspoon cayenne pepper
1 bay leaf
8 drops hot pepper sauce
1½ cups uncooked converted rice
¼ pound diced cooked ham (1 cup)
1 whole chicken breast, boneless and skinless, cooked and cubed, or 1 cup diced cooked chicken or turkey
6 ounces medium shrimp, peeled and deveined (about 4 or 5 ounces after peeling)

> **Nutrition Facts per Serving**
>
> Serving size: 1¼ cups
>
> Amount per serving:
>
> Calories 263
> Calories from fat 40
>
> Total fat 4 gm
>   Saturated fat 1 gm
> Cholesterol 56 mg
> Sodium 658 mg
> Total carbohydrate 37 gm
>   Dietary fiber 2 gm
>   Sugars 5 gm
> Protein 18 gm
>
> **Exchange List Approximations**
>
> Starch 2
> Vegetable 2
> Meat, lean 1

1. Heat the oil in a large heavy pot. Add the onions, green pepper, celery, and garlic and sauté over medium heat until softened.

2. Add the tomatoes and liquid, the chicken broth, tomato paste, and seasonings; simmer, uncovered, for 10 minutes.

3. Add the rice; cover and simmer for 10 minutes. Add the ham and chicken. Continue cooking, covered, for 10 to 15 minutes, or until the rice absorbs the liquid. Stir to mix well. Add the shrimp for the last 3 minutes of cooking. Remove the bay leaf before serving.

NASI GORENG

Nasi goreng is a quick and easy rice-and-beef preparation from Indonesia. Spicy curry powder and red pepper flakes are balanced with the flavors of tart apples, tomatoes, and green peppers for a one-of-a-kind dish. Serve hot or at room temperature, accompanied by chutney, banana slices, mango, raisins, peanuts, and/or shredded coconut. Serve with Indian flat bread for an authentic Indonesian meal. Remember to add in the appropriate exchanges for any accompaniments you include.

About 1 quart (4 servings)

1 pound (90 percent lean) ground beef
2 onions, thinly sliced
³/₄ cup diced green bell pepper
1 tomato, seeded and diced
1 tart apple, peeled, cored, and diced
1½ teaspoons curry powder or to taste
½ teaspoon salt
¼ teaspoon crushed red pepper flakes
1½ cups cooked white rice

1. Prepare a large skillet with nonstick pan spray; brown the ground beef over medium-high heat. Drain the fat.

2. Add the onions, green pepper, tomato, and apple. Continue cooking until the vegetables are crisp-tender.

3. Stir in the curry powder, salt, and crushed red pepper flakes. Lower the heat and cook for 5 minutes. Stir in the rice and cook 5 minutes longer.

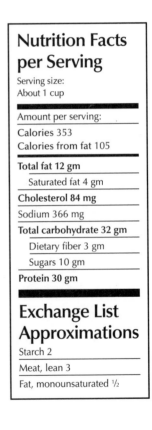

Nutrition Facts per Serving

Serving size:
About 1 cup

Amount per serving:

Calories 353
Calories from fat 105

Total fat 12 gm
  Saturated fat 4 gm
Cholesterol 84 mg
Sodium 366 mg
Total carbohydrate 32 gm
  Dietary fiber 3 gm
  Sugars 10 gm
Protein 30 gm

Exchange List Approximations

Starch 2

Meat, lean 3

Fat, monounsaturated ½

GOLDEN CURRANT PILAF WITH CINNAMON

This aromatic side dish is especially good when made with basmati rice, a fragrant rice that has a slightly nutty flavor and rich aroma. Turmeric, with its bitter, pungent taste and intense yellow-orange color is very popular in East Indian cooking. If you don't have dried currants on hand, you can use raisins or chopped dried apricots instead.

3 cups (6 servings)

¾ cup chopped onion
2 teaspoons olive oil
1 cup uncooked long-grain white rice
2 cups Homemade Chicken Broth
       (page 101) or canned reduced-
       sodium chicken broth
½ cup dried currants
1 teaspoon ground turmeric
½ teaspoon ground cinnamon
½ teaspoon salt (optional)
¼ cup packed chopped fresh parsley

1.   Sauté the onion in the oil in a medium saucepan over medium-low heat until tender, about 5 minutes. Add the rice; cook 1 minute. Stir in the broth, currants, turmeric, cinnamon, and salt (if desired).
2.   Bring to a boil. Reduce the heat; cover and simmer until most of the liquid is absorbed, about 20 minutes. Remove from the heat; let stand, covered, 5 minutes. Stir in the parsley.

Nutrition Facts per Serving	
Serving size: ½ cup	
Amount per serving:	
Calories 179	
Calories from fat 22	
Total fat 2 gm	
Saturated fat 0 gm	
Cholesterol 0 mg	
Sodium 35 mg*	
Total carbohydrate 37 gm	
Dietary fiber 1 gm	
Sugars 10 gm	
Protein 4 gm	

Exchange List Approximations

Starch 1½

Fruit 1

If the optional salt is added, sodium is 229 mg per serving.

MUSHROOM RISOTTO

Arborio rice is a special Italian short-grain rice used to make risotto. Its higher starch content gives a rich, creamy texture unlike that of other rice varieties. Wild mushrooms imbue the dish with a rich, earthy flavor.

2½ cups (5 servings)

2¼ cups Homemade Chicken Broth
      (page 101), or 1 can condensed
      reduced-sodium chicken broth
      plus 1 cup water
¼ cup (¼ ounce) dried mushrooms
      such as Chinese tree ear, shiitake,
      porcini, or morels
1 tablespoon olive oil
1 cup finely chopped onion
1 clove garlic, minced
¾ cup uncooked arborio rice
¼ cup dry white wine
¼ cup freshly grated Parmesan or
      Romano cheese

Nutrition Facts per Serving	
Serving size: ½ cup	
Amount per serving:	
Calories 160	
Calories from fat 42	
Total fat 5 gm	
Saturated fat 1 gm	
Cholesterol 3 mg	
Sodium 104 mg	
Total carbohydrate 25 gm	
Dietary fiber 1 gm	
Sugars 3 gm	
Protein 5 gm	

Exchange List Approximations

Starch 1½

Fat, monounsaturated 1

1. Combine the broth and mushrooms in a saucepan. Bring to a boil; reduce the heat and simmer uncovered 10 minutes, or until the mushrooms have softened.

2. Remove the mushrooms with a slotted spoon; chop and reserve. Keep the broth warm over low heat.

3. Heat the oil in a large skillet over medium heat. Sauté the onion and garlic until tender, about 5 minutes. Add the rice; sauté 1 minute.

4. Add the wine to the rice mixture and simmer until the wine is absorbed. Add the reserved broth, ½ cup at a time, maintaining a simmer so that the rice absorbs the broth mixture slowly. Stir often.

5. When the rice has absorbed most of the broth (about 25 minutes), stir in the mushrooms and heat through. Continue to add the remaining broth ¼ cup at a time, stirring often, until the rice is creamy and the grains are slightly firm in the center.

6. Sprinkle with cheese and serve immediately.

SPANISH RICE PICANTE

Nothing could be easier than this recipe for spicing up plain old white rice. Use hot or mild picante sauce or salsa, depending on your taste for spiciness. This is a terrific accompaniment to Mexican favorites like tacos and enchiladas.

3 cups (4 servings)

1 cup chopped onion
2 cloves garlic, minced
2 teaspoons olive oil
1 cup uncooked converted rice
2 cups Homemade Chicken Broth
      (page 101) or canned reduced-
      sodium chicken broth
1/3 cup prepared picante sauce or salsa
1/2 cup chopped fresh tomato
2 tablespoons coarsely chopped cilantro

1. Sauté the onion and garlic in the oil in a small saucepan until tender, about 5 minutes.
2. Stir in the rice; cook 1 minute. Add the broth and picante sauce; bring to a boil. Reduce to a simmer; cover and cook 20 minutes, until the rice has absorbed the liquid.
3. Add the tomato and stir to mix; cover and let stand 5 minutes. Add the cilantro and mix again.

Nutrition Facts per Serving

Serving size: 3/4 cup

Amount per serving:

Calories 228
Calories from fat 33

Total fat 4 gm
    Saturated fat 1 gm

Cholesterol 0 mg

Sodium 105 mg

Total carbohydrate 44 gm
    Dietary fiber 2 gm
    Sugars 5 gm

Protein 6 gm

Exchange List Approximation

Starch 3

APPLE-PECAN WILD RICE

Wild rice is not really a rice at all, but a long-grain grass with a nutty flavor and chewy texture. Bits of apple and apple juice add a slightly sweet flavor and interesting texture to this dish. If you add the pecans, toast them first in a skillet before adding them to the rice mixture to help intensify their flavor.

2 cups (4 servings)

½ cup uncooked wild rice
1 small onion, very thinly sliced
2 teaspoons margarine
1 cup unsweetened apple juice
1 cup Homemade Chicken Broth
      (page 101) or canned reduced-
      sodium chicken broth
¼ teaspoon salt (optional)
¼ teaspoon ground cinnamon
1 apple, cored and cut in ¼-inch dice
1 tablespoon chopped pecans (optional)

1. Wash the rice in cold water and drain well. Sauté the onion in the margarine in a medium saucepan until tender, about 5 minutes.

2. Add the rice; cook and stir 1 minute. Add the juice, broth, salt if desired, and cinnamon. Bring to a boil; reduce the heat. Cover and simmer until the rice is tender and most of the liquid is absorbed, about 45 minutes.

3. Stir in the apple; cover and let stand 5 minutes. Drain off any excess liquid before serving. Sprinkle with chopped pecans, if desired.

Nutrition Facts per Serving

Serving size: ½ cup

Amount per serving:

Calories 154
Calories from fat 26

Total fat 3 gm
    Saturated fat 1 gm

Cholesterol 0 mg

Sodium 53 mg*

Total carbohydrate 30 gm
    Dietary fiber 3 gm
    Sugars 13 gm

Protein 4 gm

Exchange List Approximations

Starch 1
Fruit 1

If the optional salt is added, sodium is 198 mg per serving.

PIZZA

Why order takeout when you can fix pizza at home for less than half the price? Mix and match your favorite vegetables and meats to create a masterpiece of your own. Here are a few of our favorite renditions.

CHEESE PIZZA

One 12-inch pizza (4 servings)

One 8-ounce can pizza sauce
1 prepared 12-inch pizza crust
    (about 9 ounces)
2 cups (4 ounces) shredded part-skim
    mozzarella cheese
1/2 teaspoon dried oregano
1/4 teaspoon freshly ground pepper

1. Preheat the oven to 400°F for at least 10 minutes. Put a cookie sheet or pizza pan on the center oven rack. (Preheating the pan makes a crisper crust.)
2. Spread pizza sauce evenly over the prepared crust; arrange the mozzarella evenly over the top; sprinkle with oregano and pepper.
3. Transfer the pizza to the hot cookie sheet. Bake 12 to 15 minutes, or until the cheese is melted and the crust is crisp. Cut in 8 equal slices.

Nutrition Facts per Serving

Serving size: 2 slices

Amount per serving:

Calories 348
Calories from fat 89

Total fat 10 gm
  Saturated fat 6 gm
Cholesterol 32 mg
Sodium 787 mg
Total carbohydrate 43 gm
  Dietary fiber 3 gm
  Sugars 5 gm
Protein 19 gm

Exchange List Approximations

Starch 3

Meat, lean 2

SAUSAGE PIZZA

One 12-inch pizza (4 servings)

One 8-ounce can pizza sauce
1 prepared 12-inch pizza crust
     (about 9 ounces)
2 cups (8 ounces) shredded part-skim
     mozzarella cheese
1/2 teaspoon dried oregano
1/4 teaspoon freshly ground pepper
6 ounces (2 links) lean fresh hot or
     sweet Italian turkey sausage

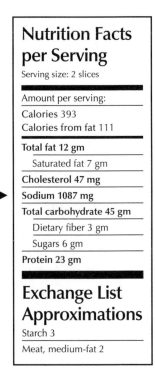

Nutrition Facts per Serving

Serving size: 2 slices

Amount per serving:

Calories 393
Calories from fat 111

Total fat 12 gm
   Saturated fat 7 gm
Cholesterol 47 mg
Sodium 1087 mg
Total carbohydrate 45 gm
   Dietary fiber 3 gm
   Sugars 6 gm
Protein 23 gm

Exchange List Approximations

Starch 3

Meat, medium-fat 2

1. Preheat the oven to 400°F for at least 10 minutes. Put a cookie sheet or pizza pan on the center oven rack. (Preheating the pan makes a crisper crust.)

2. Spread the pizza sauce evenly over the prepared crust; arrange the mozzarella evenly over the top; sprinkle with oregano and pepper.

3. Arrange small bits of sausage over the top of the pizza. (Squeeze the sausage from the casings if links are used.) If small bits are used, precooking is unnecessary, but if you want to reduce the fat, sauté the crumbled sausage for 2 minutes and drain.

4. Transfer the pizza to the hot cookie sheet. Bake 12 to 15 minutes, or until the cheese is melted, the sausage is cooked, and the crust is crisp. Cut in 8 equal slices.

VEGETABLE PIZZA

One 12-inch pizza (4 servings)

1 onion, thinly sliced, rings separated
1 small green bell pepper, cored, seeded,
    and sliced in rings
8 mushrooms, sliced
1 prepared 12-inch pizza crust
    (about 9 ounces)
One 8-ounce can pizza sauce
2 cups (8 ounces) shredded part-skim
    mozzarella cheese
2 cloves garlic, minced
$\frac{1}{2}$ teaspoon dried oregano
$\frac{1}{4}$ teaspoon crushed red pepper flakes
    (if spicier pizza desired)

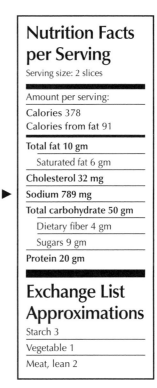

Nutrition Facts per Serving

Serving size: 2 slices

Amount per serving:

Calories 378
Calories from fat 91

Total fat 10 gm
  Saturated fat 6 gm
Cholesterol 32 mg
Sodium 789 mg
Total carbohydrate 50 gm
  Dietary fiber 4 gm
  Sugars 9 gm
Protein 20 gm

Exchange List Approximations

Starch 3
Vegetable 1
Meat, lean 2

1.   Preheat the oven to 400°F. Put a cookie sheet or pizza pan on the center oven rack. (Preheating the pan makes a crisper crust.)

2.   Prepare a large nonstick skillet with olive oil–flavored nonstick pan spray. Heat the skillet and sauté the onion, pepper, and mushrooms just until limp, about 3 minutes.

3.   Spread the pizza sauce evenly over the prepared crust; arrange the mozzarella evenly over the top.

4.   Arrange the sautéed vegetables over the pizza. Sprinkle with garlic and oregano, and crushed red pepper flakes, if desired.

5.   Transfer the pizza to the hot cookie sheet. Bake 10 minutes, or until the cheese is melted and the vegetables are cooked. Cut in 8 equal slices.

THIN-CRUST SPA PIZZA

A homemade crust makes this pizza special, and it's very easy to prepare. Topped with an assortment of thinly sliced vegetables and bubbly with cheese, it is sure to be a hit with your family.

4 pizzas (4 servings)

½ package (1½ teaspoons) active dry
    quick-rising yeast
1 teaspoon sugar
¾ cup warm water (110° to 115°F)
1 cup all-purpose flour
1 cup whole wheat flour
1 tablespoon olive oil
2 teaspoons cornmeal
½ cup no-salt-added tomato sauce
1 tablespoon chopped fresh basil leaves,
    or 1 teaspoon dried basil
1½ cups (6 ounces) shredded part-skim
    mozzarella cheese
1 medium red bell pepper, cored,
    seeded, and thinly sliced into
    rings
4 thin slices red or sweet white onion,
    separated into rings

Nutrition Facts per Serving	
Serving size: 1 pizza	
Amount per serving:	
Calories 389	
Calories from fat 100	
Total fat 11 gm	
Saturated fat 5 gm	
Cholesterol 24 mg	
Sodium 206 mg	
Total carbohydrate 55 gm	
Dietary fiber 6 gm	
Sugars 5 gm	
Protein 19 gm	

Exchange List Approximations

Starch 3	
Vegetable 2	
Meat, lean 1	
Fat 1	

1. Stir the yeast and sugar into the warm water; let stand 5 minutes, until the yeast is activated and bubbles form.

2. Combine the flours in a large bowl. Add the yeast mixture and the oil, stirring until a dough forms. Knead by hand, in a food processor fitted with the plastic blade, or in a mixer fitted with a dough hook, until smooth and elastic. Transfer the dough to a bowl that has been prepared with nonstick pan spray and let the dough rise in a warm place until double in bulk, 20 to 30 minutes.

3. Preheat the oven to 450°F. Punch down the dough and transfer it to a lightly floured surface. Divide the dough into 4 balls. Roll and stretch each portion of dough into a circle about 8 inches in diameter. Transfer the crusts to cookie sheets that has been prepared with nonstick pan spray and sprinkled with cornmeal.

4. Combine the tomato sauce and basil. Divide the sauce among the 4 pizzas and spread evenly over the dough, leaving a ½-inch border. Sprinkle each pizza with 3 tablespoons of the cheese. Add the bell pepper and onion slices; then top with the remaining cheese.

5. Bake 10 to 12 minutes, or until the crust is golden brown and the cheese is melted and bubbly.

CHICK-PEAS AND GREEN PEPPERS

Chick-peas, sometimes called garbanzo beans, are a great source of protein, especially for vegetarians. Ginger, cumin, and ground coriander are the main spices added to this stew, providing a sweet, peppery taste. Serve the chick-peas hot on a flour tortilla or in half a pita pocket with shredded lettuce (add 1 starch exchange for either).

3 cups (4 servings)

½ cup chopped onion
½ teaspoon chopped fresh gingerroot
1 tablespoon canola, corn, or olive oil
1 teaspoon cumin seeds
1 teaspoon ground coriander
¼ teaspoon freshly ground pepper
⅛ teaspoon salt (optional)
1 cup chopped green bell pepper
One 15-ounce can chick-peas (garbanzo
    beans), drained
2 fresh tomatoes, seeded, chopped, and
    drained
2 tablespoons fresh lemon juice

1. In a skillet, sauté the onion and ginger in the oil. Add the cumin, coriander, ground pepper, and salt, if desired; stir for 1 minute.
2. Add the green pepper and chick-peas. Cook about 5 minutes. Add the tomatoes and lemon juice. Cook about 2 minutes, stirring frequently.

Nutrition Facts per Serving

Serving size: ¾ cup

Amount per serving:

Calories 168
Calories from fat 49

Total fat 5 gm
    Saturated fat 0 gm
Cholesterol 0 mg
Sodium 99 mg*
Total carbohydrate 25 gm
    Dietary fiber 5 gm
    Sugars 7 gm
Protein 7 gm

Exchange List Approximations

Starch 1

Vegetable 2

Fat, monounsaturated 1

If the optional salt is used, sodium is 171 mg per serving.

BEAN AND SAUSAGE CASSEROLE

Although this meal takes a little longer than usual to cook, the hands-on preparation time is less than 20 minutes. Lean sausage made from beef, pork, chicken, or turkey is widely available in supermarkets. Use any type and intensity of flavor you like—hot, mild, or Italian-style. If lean bulk sausage is not available, buy lean or low-fat link sausages and cut them into 1-inch pieces as a substitute for the sausage balls.

About 6 cups (6 servings)

One 14- to 15-ounce can pinto beans, drained
One 14- to 15-ounce can navy, kidney, or Great Northern beans, drained
One 10-ounce package frozen lima beans
³⁄₄ pound (90 percent lean) ground sausage
¹⁄₄ cup beef broth (homemade, canned, or bouillon)
One 8-ounce can tomato sauce
1 teaspoon ground cumin (optional)
3 tablespoons dry red wine
¹⁄₂ teaspoon salt
¹⁄₂ teaspoon freshly ground pepper
2 cloves garlic, minced
1 cup finely chopped onion

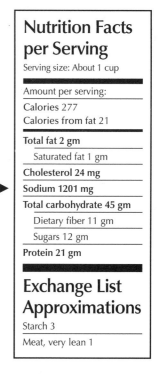

Nutrition Facts per Serving

Serving size: About 1 cup

Amount per serving:

Calories 277
Calories from fat 21

Total fat 2 gm
    Saturated fat 1 gm
Cholesterol 24 mg
Sodium 1201 mg
Total carbohydrate 45 gm
    Dietary fiber 11 gm
    Sugars 12 gm
Protein 21 gm

Exchange List Approximations

Starch 3

Meat, very lean 1

1.   Preheat the oven to 325°F. Prepare a 2¹⁄₂-quart casserole with nonstick pan spray.
2.   Combine the beans in the casserole and set aside.
3.   Shape the sausage into about 24 small balls and brown in a nonstick skillet. Drain the fat.
4.   While the sausage browns, add the beef broth, tomato sauce, cumin, wine, salt, and pepper to the beans. Add the browned sausage.
5.   Put the onions and garlic in the skillet used to cook the sausage; sauté 5 minutes. Add to the ingredients in the casserole; mix well.
6.   Cover the casserole and bake for 1 hour.

RED BEANS AND BROWN RICE

This Caribbean favorite is wonderful as a side dish or as an entrée. We used brown instead of white rice to help increase the fiber content and provide a heartier, nuttier taste. For a flavorful change, substitute pinto beans or black-eyed peas for the kidney beans and add as much picante or hot pepper sauce as you wish to increase the heat quotient. None of these changes add any additional exchanges.

1 quart (6 servings)

½ cup uncooked brown rice
1 slice bacon, diced
1 cup chopped onion
½ cup diced celery
½ cup diced green bell pepper
One 15-ounce can dark red kidney
      beans, undrained
¼ to ½ teaspoon hot pepper sauce
⅛ teaspoon freshly ground pepper

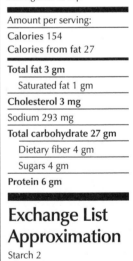

Nutrition Facts per Serving

Serving size: ⅔ cup

Amount per serving:

Calories 154
Calories from fat 27

Total fat 3 gm
  Saturated fat 1 gm
Cholesterol 3 mg
Sodium 293 mg
Total carbohydrate 27 gm
  Dietary fiber 4 gm
  Sugars 4 gm
Protein 6 gm

Exchange List Approximation

Starch 2

1.   In a small pot, bring the rice and 1½ cups water to a boil; cover and simmer until the water is absorbed, about 45 minutes. Set aside.
2.   In a large skillet, cook the diced bacon, onion, celery, and green pepper over low heat, about 10 minutes.
3.   Add the undrained canned beans, pepper sauce, and ground pepper. Bring to a boil; cover and simmer 5 minutes.
4.   Add the cooked rice and mix lightly, adding a little water if the mixture is too dry.

TWO-BEAN CHILI

This "pantry food" recipe is quick to fix using canned beans and other pantry ingredients you probably already have on hand. Prep-to-plate time is a mere 45 minutes. Chili freezes well in tightly covered plastic containers, so make an extra batch to have on hand when unexpected football company arrives.

About 7 cups (7 servings)

2 onions, coarsely chopped
2 cloves garlic, minced
2 teaspoons canola, corn, or olive oil
One 14- to 15-ounce can stewed
        tomatoes with juice
1 can or bottle beer (12 ounces)
1 tablespoon chili powder
1 teaspoon ground cumin
1 teaspoon hot pepper sauce, or
        1 tablespoon hot salsa or picante
        sauce
¼ teaspoon salt (optional)
One 15-ounce can pinto beans, rinsed
        and drained
One 15-ounce can dark red kidney
        beans, rinsed and drained
1 large green bell pepper, cored, seeded,
        and coarsely chopped

Nutrition Facts per Serving	
Serving size: About 1 cup	
Amount per serving:	
Calories 173	
Calories from fat 19	
Total fat 2 gm	
Saturated fat 0 gm	
Cholesterol 0 mg	
Sodium 238 mg*	
Total carbohydrate 32 gm	
Dietary fiber 8 gm	
Sugars 9 gm	
Protein 9 gm	

Exchange List Approximations

Starch 1½
Vegetable 2

1. Sauté the onions and garlic in oil in a large saucepan or Dutch oven until tender, about 5 minutes. Stir in the tomatoes with their liquid, the beer, chili powder, cumin, hot sauce, and salt (if desired).
2. Simmer, uncovered, 15 minutes. Stir in the beans and green pepper; simmer, uncovered, 15 minutes longer.

If the optional salt is used, sodium is 321 mg per serving.

WESTERN-STYLE BEANS

These beans have a bit of a kick and make a great side dish for enchiladas or backyard barbecue fare like grilled chicken or ribs. Feel free to substitute green chile salsa or tomatillo salsa for the canned green chili sauce if you prefer. We recommend using dried beans in this recipe, since they have a firmer bite than canned beans. If you're short on time; however, canned varieties work just fine. You'll need about three 15-ounce cans, drained and rinsed, to equal 1 pound of dried beans when cooked.

6 cups (9 servings)

1 pound dried beans (pinto, red, pink,
    or navy)
1 teaspoon canola or corn oil
1 cup chopped onion
1 tablespoon chili powder, hot or mild as
    you prefer
1/2 teaspoon salt
1 cup green chili sauce

1. Wash and pick over the beans. Cover with water and soak overnight; drain.
2. Heat the oil in a large pot. Add the onion and sauté until tender, about 5 minutes. Add the chili powder, salt, beans, and 5 cups water. Bring to a boil. Reduce the heat, cover, and simmer until the beans are tender, 1 to 1 1/2 hours.
3. Add the green chili sauce; stir and simmer, uncovered, 30 minutes longer. If the mixture is too soupy, simmer a few minutes longer to reduce the liquid.

Nutrition Facts per Serving

Serving size: 2/3 cup

Amount per serving:

Calories 190
Calories from fat 12

Total fat 1 gm
    Saturated fat 0 gm
Cholesterol 0 mg
Sodium 218 mg
Total carbohydrate 35 gm
    Dietary fiber 13 gm
    Sugars 4 gm
Protein 11 gm

Exchange List Approximations

Starch 2
Vegetable 1

RUM-BAKED BLACK BEANS

Rum adds a rich, fragrant flavor to these beans, and the orange wedge garnishes add a bright accent to their deep color. Try them with Steak Fajitas (page 192) or New Mexico–Style Flank Steak (page 202).

4 cups (6 servings)

1¼ cups dried black beans
      (½ pound)
¾ cup chopped onion
1 cup finely chopped celery
⅔ cup chopped carrot
2 cloves garlic, minced
1 small bay leaf
2 tablespoons chopped fresh parsley
¾ teaspoon dried thyme
¼ teaspoon salt
½ teaspoon freshly ground pepper
1 tablespoon margarine
2 tablespoons dark rum
1 orange, cut into 6 wedges

Nutrition Facts per Serving

Serving size: ⅔ cup

Amount per serving:

Calories 187
Calories from fat 23

Total fat 3 gm
  Saturated fat 1 gm
Cholesterol 0 mg
Sodium 147 mg
Total carbohydrate 33 gm
  Dietary fiber 8 gm
  Sugars 6 gm
Protein 10 gm

Exchange List Approximations

Starch 2
Vegetable 1

1. Rinse the beans. Cover with water and soak overnight; drain.

2. Place the beans, 3 cups water, the onion, celery, carrot, garlic, bay leaf, parsley, thyme, salt, and pepper in a large pot. Bring to a boil; cover and simmer 1 hour.

3. Preheat the oven to 325°F.

4. Transfer the beans and the liquid in the pot to a bean pot or a 1½-quart casserole prepared with nonstick pan spray. Stir in the margarine and rum. Cover and bake for 2 hours. Remove the cover and bake 30 minutes longer.

5. Serve topped with orange wedges.

SPICY BLACK BEANS

These beans are delicious hot, spooned over rice, or chilled, as a main dish or side salad. To prepare the chilled beans, simply mix all the ingredients together, cover, and refrigerate for several hours to allow the flavors to blend.

2 cups (4 servings)

2 teaspoons olive oil
1 clove garlic, minced
One 16-ounce can black beans, rinsed
    and drained
1/3 cup prepared hot salsa or picante
    sauce
1 tablespoon fresh lime juice
1 tomato, seeded and chopped
1/4 cup coarsely chopped cilantro

1. Heat the oil in a medium saucepan. Sauté the garlic until tender, about 2 minutes. Add the beans, salsa, and lime juice. Simmer until heated through, about 5 minutes, stirring occasionally.
2. Stir in the tomato; sprinkle with cilantro.

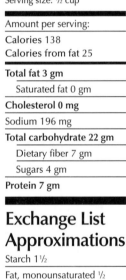

Nutrition Facts per Serving

Serving size: 1/2 cup

Amount per serving:

Calories 138
Calories from fat 25

Total fat 3 gm
  Saturated fat 0 gm

Cholesterol 0 mg

Sodium 196 mg

Total carbohydrate 22 gm
  Dietary fiber 7 gm
  Sugars 4 gm

Protein 7 gm

Exchange List Approximations

Starch 1 1/2

Fat, monounsaturated 1/2

BARBECUED LIMA BEANS

These beans are a nice twist on classic New England baked beans. Serve them with hamburgers, frankfurters, or grilled chicken at summer barbecues, along with other picnic salads. To impart a gentle, smoky flavor, add 4 ounces of diced lean ham or diced smoked turkey when you uncover the beans during the last 30 minutes of cooking time. The ham adds 1 lean meat exchange per serving.

3 cups (6 servings)

1¼ cups dried lima beans (¼ pound)
½ onion, thinly sliced
½ teaspoon salt
¼ teaspoon dry mustard
½ teaspoon vinegar
2 tablespoons molasses
3 tablespoons chili sauce

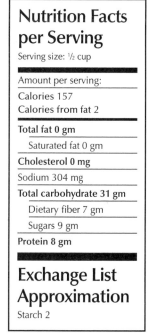

Nutrition Facts per Serving

Serving size: ½ cup

Amount per serving:

Calories 157
Calories from fat 2

Total fat 0 gm
  Saturated fat 0 gm
Cholesterol 0 mg
Sodium 304 mg
Total carbohydrate 31 gm
  Dietary fiber 7 gm
  Sugars 9 gm
Protein 8 gm

Exchange List Approximation

Starch 2

1. Place the beans in a soup pot. Cover with water; boil 2 minutes. Remove from the heat, cover, and let stand 1 hour.

2. Preheat the oven to 300°F. Prepare a 1½-quart casserole with nonstick pan spray.

3. Drain the beans, reserving 1 cup liquid. Combine the beans and the reserved liquid with the remaining ingredients and put in the casserole.

4. Cover and bake 1¾ hours. Uncover and bake 30 minutes longer, adding liquid if the beans seem dry.

FRIJOLES COCIDOS

These Mexican-style mashed beans are great all by themselves, or can be served on top of tostadas, in hollowed-out green peppers, or with steamed tortillas or pita bread. Remember to add the appropriate exchange for any items you add to the beans.

4½ cups (6 servings)

1¾ cups dried pinto beans
     (12 ounces)
1¼ cups chopped onion
3 cloves garlic, minced
2 teaspoons ground cumin
1 tablespoon olive oil
½ cup chopped green bell pepper
½ teaspoon ground coriander
1 teaspoon salt
¼ teaspoon freshly ground pepper

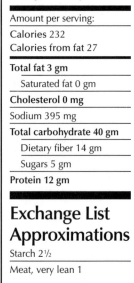

Nutrition Facts per Serving

Serving size: ¾ cup

Amount per serving:

Calories 232
Calories from fat 27

Total fat 3 gm
    Saturated fat 0 gm
Cholesterol 0 mg
Sodium 395 mg
Total carbohydrate 40 gm
    Dietary fiber 14 gm
    Sugars 5 gm
Protein 12 gm

Exchange List Approximations

Starch 2½

Meat, very lean 1

1. Wash and pick over the beans. Cover them with water and soak for 4 hours or overnight; drain.

2. Cover the beans with fresh water in a large saucepan. Bring to a boil; reduce the heat. Cover and simmer for 1 to 1½ hours, or until the beans are tender.

3. In a medium skillet, sauté the onion, garlic, and cumin in the oil for 4 minutes. Add the green pepper and sauté 5 minutes longer.

4. Drain the beans; reserve ½ cup liquid. Mash the beans with the reserved liquid; add the sautéed vegetables, the coriander, salt, and pepper. Mix well.

LENTILS ITALIANO

Beans, including lentils, are often used in Italian cooking as a substitute for meat. In addition to being a good source of protein, lentils also provide a fair amount of calcium and iron.

3¾ cups (6 servings)

¾ cup chopped onion
1 clove garlic, minced
1 tablespoon olive oil
2 cups Vegetable Broth (page 102),
      or one 14-ounce can beef or
      vegetable broth
¾ cup dried lentils, washed
One 16-ounce can diced tomatoes with
      juice
¼ to ½ teaspoon crushed red pepper
      flakes
½ teaspoon salt
1 tablespoon chopped fresh basil,
      or 1 teaspoon dried basil
1 tablespoon chopped fresh oregano,
      or 1 teaspoon dried oregano
¼ teaspoon freshly ground pepper

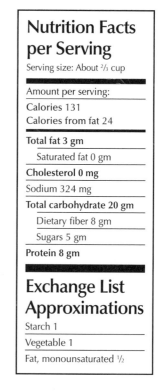

Nutrition Facts per Serving

Serving size: About ⅔ cup

Amount per serving:

Calories 131
Calories from fat 24

Total fat 3 gm
   Saturated fat 0 gm
Cholesterol 0 mg
Sodium 324 mg
Total carbohydrate 20 gm
   Dietary fiber 8 gm
   Sugars 5 gm
Protein 8 gm

Exchange List Approximations

Starch 1
Vegetable 1
Fat, monounsaturated ½

1. In a heavy saucepan, sauté the onion and garlic in the olive oil for 5 minutes, until the onion is tender.

2. Add the broth and lentils. Cover and simmer for 30 minutes.

3. Add the tomatoes with their liquid, ½ cup water, and the remaining ingredients; simmer over low heat, uncovered, for about 45 minutes, stirring occasionally. Add water if the mixture becomes too dry.

11

SAUCES, RELISHES, AND CONDIMENTS

Sauces, relishes, and condiments are the finishing touches that enhance the appearance and great taste of food, from entrées to desserts. They can complement or add contrast in flavor, color, and texture and help turn an ordinary dish into one that's extraordinary.

Slenderized versions of your favorite toppings are the stars of this chapter. Traditionally quite high in fat and calories, toppings have been adapted here to cut out the excess but keep the flavor. Several of the recipes for dessert sauces include sugar as an ingredient. Recent nutrition guidelines for diabetes management allow sugar in moderation and count it as part of the total amount of carbohydrate in your meal plan. We've provided a complete breakdown of exchanges and carbohydrate counts for each recipe to make it easier to figure them into your plan.

Try Low-Calorie Hollandaise, Pesto Sauce, Bolognese Sauce, and Spicy Salsa to top off meat, eggs, fish, and vegetable dishes. Gingered Peach Sauce, Blueberry Chutney, and Bittersweet Chocolate Sauce are delicious toppings for desserts and in some cases for entrées as well. No matter your selection, our sauces, relishes, and condiments are certain to embellish your favorite dishes without overwhelming them with fat or calories.

BOLOGNESE SAUCE

This traditional Italian meat sauce is a snap to make and freezes well. Make a big batch so you always have some on hand. Use it as a base sauce for Lasagna (page 377) or ladle some over any shape of pasta, from angel hair to ziti.

3 cups (4 servings)

¾ pound (90 percent lean) ground beef
½ cup chopped onion
1 clove garlic, minced
¼ cup chopped carrot
One 16-ounce can chopped tomatoes
 with juice
¼ cup dry red wine
1 tablespoon chopped fresh basil,
 or ½ teaspoon dried basil
2 teaspoons chopped fresh oregano, or
 ½ teaspoon dried oregano
¾ teaspoon salt
⅛ teaspoon freshly ground pepper
1 tablespoon tomato paste

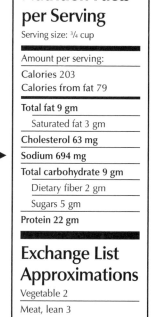

Nutrition Facts per Serving

Serving size: ¾ cup

Amount per serving:

Calories 203
Calories from fat 79

Total fat 9 gm
 Saturated fat 3 gm
Cholesterol 63 mg
Sodium 694 mg
Total carbohydrate 9 gm
 Dietary fiber 2 gm
 Sugars 5 gm
Protein 22 gm

Exchange List Approximations

Vegetable 2
Meat, lean 3

1. Brown the ground beef in a large non-stick skillet with the onion, garlic, and carrot over medium heat; drain off the fat and return the beef and vegetables to the skillet.

2. Add the tomatoes with their liquid, the wine, and the seasonings and herbs. Cover and simmer for 40 to 45 minutes, stirring occasionally.

3. Stir in the tomato paste; simmer, uncovered, for 5 to 10 minutes, until slightly thickened.

CUCUMBER SAUCE

Cucumber sauce is delightful served with poached, broiled, or grilled fish, Provençal Stuffed Eggplants (page 325), or as a topping on gyros, Greek pita sandwiches stuffed with lamb.

1 cup (8 servings)

1 small cucumber
½ cup plain low-fat yogurt
1 tablespoon grated onion
1 tablespoon fresh lemon juice
1 teaspoon prepared yellow mustard
1 teaspoon snipped fresh dill,
     or ½ teaspoon dried dill weed
¼ teaspoon salt
Pinch of white pepper

1. Peel the cucumber, slice lengthwise, and scoop out the seeds. Shred or coarsely grate the cucumber. Put the shredded cucumber in a strainer and press out as much liquid as possible.

2. Combine all the other ingredients in a small bowl; mix well. Add the cucumber and stir to mix. Cover and chill at least 1 hour for the flavors to blend.

Nutrition Facts per Serving

Serving size: 2 tablespoons

Amount per serving:

Calories 12
Calories from fat 3

Total fat 0 gm
  Saturated fat 0 gm
Cholesterol 1 mg
Sodium 92 mg
Total carbohydrate 2 gm
  Dietary fiber 0 gm
  Sugars 1 gm
Protein 1 gm

Exchange List Approximation

Free food

LOW-CALORIE HOLLANDAISE

Traditional hollandaise sauce recipes use plenty of butter and egg yolks. This version slashes the fat and calories, but not its rich, smooth taste. Try it spooned over eggs Benedict, drizzled on asparagus spears and other vegetables, or as a topping for fish.

³/₄ cup (6 servings)

1 tablespoon cornstarch
2 tablespoons fat-free dry milk solids
1 egg yolk
¹/₄ teaspoon salt
¹/₈ teaspoon dry mustard
2 to 3 tablespoons fresh lemon juice

1. Combine ¹/₂ cup water and all the ingredients except the lemon juice in a food processor or blender. Blend for 10 seconds or until smooth.

2. Pour the mixture into a small nonstick saucepan. Set over low heat and whisk constantly until thickened, about 5 to 8 minutes. Whisk in the lemon juice. Serve hot or warm.

Nutrition Facts per Serving

Serving size: 2 tablespoons

Amount per serving:

Calories 21
Calories from fat 8

Total fat 1 gm
  Saturated fat 0 gm

Cholesterol 36 mg

Sodium 107 mg

Total carbohydrate 2 gm
  Dietary fiber 0 gm
  Sugars 1 gm

Protein 1 gm

Exchange List Approximation

Free food

PESTO SAUCE

Pesto sauce has so many wonderful uses. It is always terrific tossed with pasta, but you can also use it as a dressing for mozzarella and tomato salad, mix it with chicken and vegetables for chicken salad, or serve it as a topping for poached fish or grilled chicken breasts, or as a spread instead of garlic butter on bread. A little bit of pesto goes a long way—use this "green gold" sparingly. Pesto freezes well, so make an extra batch to enjoy later. For convenient ready-to-use portions, freeze the pesto in ice cube trays. Just pop out the amount you need and bring it to room temperature before serving.

About 1/2 cup (8 servings)

1 cup loosely packed fresh basil leaves
2 cloves garlic
2 tablespoons pine nuts
2 tablespoons grated Parmesan cheese
1/4 teaspoon freshly ground pepper
2 tablespoons extra virgin olive oil

1.   Combine all the ingredients except the oil in a food processor or blender. Process until almost smooth.

2.   Pour the oil through the feed tube with the food processor or blender running at the slowest speed, and process until blended.

Nutrition Facts per Serving
Serving size: 1 tablespoon
Amount per serving:
Calories 52
Calories from fat 46
Total fat 5 gm
Saturated fat 1 gm
Cholesterol 1 mg
Sodium 28 mg
Total carbohydrate 1 gm
Dietary fiber 0 gm
Sugars 0 gm
Protein 1 gm

Exchange List Approximation

Fat, monounsaturated 1

FRESH SALSA

Fresh homemade salsa captures the essence and flavor of summer and is a far cry from its bottled counterpart. Salsa is sensational over grilled fish or poultry, and makes a tasty fat-free topping for baked potatoes, too. Of course, it's a natural with Mexican favorites, like baked tortilla chips and quesadillas.

About 1 cup (4 servings)

1 large tomato (8 ounces), seeded and
    chopped
3 green onions with green tops,
    chopped
1/3 cup packed chopped fresh cilantro
1 tablespoon fresh lime juice
1 tablespoon seeded and chopped
    jalapeño
2 cloves garlic, minced
1/2 teaspoon salt

1. Combine all the ingredients in a bowl; mix well.

2. Leave at room temperature for 30 to 60 minutes for flavors to mingle.

Nutrition Facts per Serving
Serving size: 1/4 cup
Amount per serving:
Calories 20
Calories from fat 2
Total fat 0 gm
Saturated fat 0 gm
Cholesterol 0 mg
Sodium 306 mg
Total carbohydrate 4 gm
Dietary fiber 1 gm
Sugars 3 gm
Protein 1 gm

Exchange List Approximation

Free food

SPICY SALSA

The longer you let this salsa sit, the better it tastes. Make it the day before a party to give the flavors enough time to blend. This thick and chunky salsa recipe calls for canned tomatoes, so it's especially easy to make. You can pump up the heat to your liking by adding more green chiles.

2½ cups (5 servings)

One 14- to 15-ounce can diced tomatoes
    with liquid
⅔ cup chopped green bell pepper
⅓ cup chopped radishes
⅓ cup chopped onion
One 4-ounce can chopped green chiles
    or jalapeño peppers, drained
2 green onions with green tops,
    chopped
3 tablespoons chopped fresh cilantro
2 cloves garlic, minced

1. Combine all the ingredients; mix well.
2. Leave at room temperature for 30 to 60 minutes for flavors to mingle.

Nutrition Facts per Serving
Serving size: ½ cup
Amount per serving:
Calories 19
Calories from fat 2
Total fat 0 gm
Saturated fat 0 gm
Cholesterol 0 mg
Sodium 90 mg
Total carbohydrate 4 gm
Dietary fiber 1 gm
Sugars 3 gm
Protein 1 gm

Exchange List Approximation

Free food

WHITE SAUCE

Classic white sauce, also known as béchamel, is often used as a topping or binder for cooked vegetables, poultry, and seafood dishes. White sauce is considered a "mother sauce" because so many sauces (such as Cheddar cheese sauce, mustard sauce, and cream sauce) use it as a base. Here are a few other variations to try: Sauté ¼ cup of chopped onion or celery in the margarine before you add the flour, then proceed with the recipe. Or add 1 teaspoon of dry mustard to each cup of sauce for a zippy tang that's terrific with broiled fish steaks. Both variations have the same calorie and exchange values as the basic white sauce recipe.

1 cup (8 servings)

2 tablespoons margarine
2 tablespoons all-purpose or instant flour
¼ teaspoon salt
⅛ teaspoon freshly ground pepper
1 cup fat-free milk

1.   Melt the margarine in a small nonstick saucepan over low heat. Blend in the flour, salt, and pepper.
2.   Add the milk, stirring constantly. Remove from the heat when the sauce thickens and reaches a rolling boil.

Nutrition Facts per Serving
Serving size: 2 tablespoons
Amount per serving:
Calories 43
Calories from fat 26
Total fat 3 gm
Saturated fat 1 gm
Cholesterol 1 mg
Sodium 122 mg
Total carbohydrate 3 gm
Dietary fiber 0 gm
Sugars 1 gm
Protein 1 gm

Exchange List Approximation

Fat 1

WASHINGTON STATE APPLE BUTTER

Apple butter isn't really "butter" at all, but more like a thick preserve. It makes a luscious spread on toast, muffins, crêpes, and waffles.

3 cups (24 servings)

2½ pounds Golden Delicious apples,
    cored and cut into eighths
2 tablespoons fresh lemon juice
¾ teaspoon ground cinnamon
⅛ teaspoon ground cloves
⅛ teaspoon ground mace
1 tablespoon brown sugar

1. Combine the apples, ¾ cup water, and the lemon juice in a large nonstick pot. Bring to a boil over medium-high heat. Cover and simmer for 30 minutes. Drain.

2. Push the apples through a food mill or strainer to purée and remove skin. Return the applesauce to the pot of water; add the cinnamon, cloves, mace, and brown sugar. Simmer, uncovered, over low heat until the mixture thickens, about 45 to 60 minutes, stirring often.

3. Cover and refrigerate. Apple butter keeps in the refrigerator for 1 week. Freeze for longer storage.

Nutrition Facts per Serving

Serving size: 2 tablespoons

Amount per serving:

Calories 26
Calories from fat 1

Total fat 0 gm
    Saturated fat 0 gm
Cholesterol 0 mg
Sodium 0 mg
Total carbohydrate 7 gm
    Dietary fiber 1 gm
    Sugars 6 gm
Protein 0 gm

Exchange List Approximation

Fruit ½

BLUEBERRY CHUTNEY

An unusual chutney that's sweet but not overly so, and delightful with pork, poultry, or cottage cheese.

2½ cups (20 servings)

1 pound thawed frozen or 3 cups
      (1½ pints) fresh blueberries
½ cup chopped onion
½ cup sugar
⅓ cup cider vinegar
3 tablespoons golden raisins
2 teaspoons chopped peeled gingerroot
1 teaspoon ground cinnamon
½ teaspoon mustard seeds
¼ teaspoon ground cloves
⅛ teaspoon cayenne pepper

1. Combine all the ingredients with 1 cup water in a large nonaluminum saucepan. Bring to a boil over medium heat. Lower the heat and simmer, uncovered, for 1 hour, or until thick.
2. Cover and chill to use within 1 week, or freeze for up to 6 months.

Nutrition Facts per Serving

Serving size: 2 tablespoons

Amount per serving:

Calories 38
Calories from fat 1

Total fat 0 gm
   Saturated fat 0 gm
Cholesterol 0 mg
Sodium 2 mg
Total carbohydrate 10 gm
   Dietary fiber 1 gm
   Sugars 8 gm
Protein 0 gm

Exchange List Approximation

Other carbohydrate ½

BITTERSWEET CHOCOLATE SAUCE

For chocolate lovers only! Serve this luscious sauce over frozen yogurt, on cream puffs or crêpes, or as a dip for strawberries and other fruit. Chocolate melts most easily if it's chopped into smaller pieces. Be sure to use a double boiler to melt the chocolate, so it doesn't scorch; keep the water below a simmer so no steam or water gets into the chocolate, which could cause it to stiffen.

1 cup (8 servings)

Three 1-ounce squares unsweetened
      chocolate, coarsely chopped
$\frac{1}{3}$ cup fat-free milk
1 tablespoon cornstarch
$\frac{1}{2}$ cup unsweetened pineapple juice
$\frac{1}{3}$ cup sugar
1 teaspoon pure vanilla extract

1. In a double boiler over low heat, melt the chocolate with the milk.
2. In a small bowl, combine the cornstarch with the pineapple juice; stir to dissolve the cornstarch. Stir the pineapple juice mixture, the sugar, and vanilla into the melted chocolate in the top of the double boiler. Stir constantly, still over low heat, until the sauce thickens and is smooth. Serve warm.

Nutrition Facts per Serving
Serving size: 2 tablespoons
Amount per serving:
Calories 109
Calories from fat 53
Total fat 6 gm
Saturated fat 3 gm
Cholesterol 0 mg
Sodium 14 mg
Total carbohydrate 16 gm
Dietary fiber 2 gm
Sugars 11 gm
Protein 2 gm

Exchange List Approximations
Other carbohydrate 1
Saturated fat 1

STRAWBERRY SAUCE

Here's a deliciously fat-free way to celebrate the bounty of this favorite summer fruit. Serve with Coeur à la Crème (page 447), or over low-fat ice cream, frozen yogurt, cake, or pudding. Strawberry sauce takes just minutes to make and doesn't require any cooking, so it's nice for a hot summer day.

1 cup (8 servings)

½ pound thawed frozen strawberries, unsweetened
1 tablespoon sugar
1 teaspoon fresh lemon juice

1.   Purée all the ingredients plus 2 tablespoons water in a food processor or blender until the berries are crushed and their liquid is released.

2.   Chill well. Shake or stir before serving.

Nutrition Facts per Serving
Serving size: 2 tablespoons
Amount per serving:
Calories 14
Calories from fat 1
Total fat 0 gm
Saturated fat 0 gm
Cholesterol 0 mg
Sodium 0 mg
Total carbohydrate 3 gm
Dietary fiber 1 gm
Sugars 3 gm
Protein 0 gm

Exchange List Approximation
Free food

GINGERED PEACH SAUCE

The possibilities of this versatile sauce are endless. It's scrumptious on slices of angel food cake, over low-fat frozen yogurt, or even with grilled chicken or fish. A delicious peak-of-summer treat exploding with peach flavor.

1½ cups (6 servings)

2 large very ripe peaches, peeled and
    pitted
2 tablespoons almond-flavored liqueur
2 teaspoons finely chopped fresh
    gingerroot

1. Cut the peaches into chunks; place in a blender or food processor.

2. Add the liqueur and ginger; blend or process until smooth, scraping down the sides as necessary. Chill the sauce.

Nutrition Facts per Serving
Serving size: ¼ cup
Amount per serving:
Calories 42
Calories from fat 1
Total fat 0 gm
Saturated fat 0 gm
Cholesterol 0 mg
Sodium 1 mg
Total carbohydrate 8 gm
Dietary fiber 1 gm
Sugars 7 gm
Protein 0 gm

Exchange List Approximation

Other carbohydrate ½

SOFT CUSTARD SAUCE

You may know this sauce as crème Anglaise. It's delectable drizzled over sliced ripe nectarines, fresh blueberries, raspberries, or blackberries. Be sure to use a double boiler when making this sauce, since this will result in a much better texture than cooking it over direct heat.

About 2 cups (8 servings)

2 large eggs, slightly beaten
2 tablespoons sugar
1/4 teaspoon salt
1 1/2 cups fat-free milk
1 teaspoon pure vanilla extract

1. Combine all the ingredients except the vanilla in the top of a double boiler or in a small saucepan.

2. Cook over hot (not boiling) water, stirring constantly. If using a saucepan, cook over the lowest possible heat, stirring constantly. When the custard is thick enough to coat a spoon, remove from the heat.

3. Cool quickly by placing the pan in a bowl of ice water. Stir in the vanilla. Serve while warm, or let cool to room temperature and serve immediately.

Nutrition Facts per Serving
Serving size: 1/4 cup
Amount per serving:
Calories 47
Calories from fat 12
Total fat 1 gm
Saturated fat 0 gm
Cholesterol 54 mg
Sodium 112 mg
Total carbohydrate 6 gm
Dietary fiber 0 gm
Sugars 5 gm
Protein 3 gm

Exchange List Approximation

Other carbohydrate 1/2

12

DESSERTS

Who doesn't love dessert? For many people, it's the best part of the meal. Fortunately, recent guidelines for people with diabetes allow sugar as part of a healthful eating plan, good news for dessert lovers! But desserts often provide more carbohydrates than other starch-based foods, fewer vitamins and minerals, and more fat, so you need to work them into your meal plan carefully. The amount of carbohydrate in food is what affects blood sugar, so if you're planning dessert, the dessert must take the place of other carbohydrate-containing foods (like starch, fruit, or milk) in your meal plan. Desserts can be a part of but not an *addition* to your regular meal plan.

Along with fats and sugars, desserts can also add a significant amount of calories, important to keep in mind if you're trying to watch your waistline. In the following recipes, we've cut fat and calories from favorites like Strawberry Shortcake, Blueberry Crumble or Fresh Peach Crumble, and Raisin Rice Pudding but kept their characteristic taste and texture. Part of our strategy focuses on using fruits as the base ingredient in the majority of our recipes. We also used margarine instead of butter to cut saturated fat, decreased the total amount of margarine we used, and substituted reduced-fat or fat-free ingredients for their full-fat counterparts, like cream cheese, milk, sour cream, and evaporated milk. If you're watching cholesterol, you can also use egg whites or egg substitutes instead of whole eggs in most of these recipes.

Above all, moderation is key when it comes to dessert. You *can* "have your cake," as long as you account for it in your meal plan.

BAKED APPLES

Think of this dessert treat as apple pie without all the fat and calories. Firm fruit makes the best baked apples: Rome, Winesap, and Cortland are ideal choices, since they hold their shape well during baking.

4 apples (4 servings)

4 medium baking apples
1/4 cup raisins
1/2 cup unsweetened apple juice

1.   Preheat the oven to 375°F.
2.   Wash and core the apples. Pare a strip from around the top of each apple and discard. Place the apples in an 8-inch-round or 8-inch-square baking pan.
3.   Put 1 tablespoon of raisins in each apple. Pour the apple juice over the apples and cover the apples with foil.
4.   Bake for 20 minutes. Remove the foil; baste the apples with the juice. Bake another 20 minutes, or until apples are fork-tender.
5.   Serve baked apples warm or chilled.

Nutrition Facts per Serving

Serving size: 1 apple

Amount per serving:

Calories 124
Calories from fat 5

Total fat 1 gm
  Saturated fat 0 gm
Cholesterol 0 mg
Sodium 2 mg
Total carbohydrate 32 gm
  Dietary fiber 4 gm
  Sugars 27 gm
Protein 1 gm

Exchange List Approximation

Fruit 2

APPLE RASPBERRY CRISP

Simple to make and scrumptious to eat, fruit crisps are always crowd pleasers. But traditional recipes are usually pretty high in fat because of their toppings. In this mouthwatering revision, we've significantly reduced the amount of fat and let the sweet and tart flavors of the fruit take center stage.

4 servings

¼ cup margarine
¼ cup quick-cooking oats
¼ cup all-purpose flour
1 tablespoon brown sugar
½ pint fresh raspberries
1 large Granny Smith or other tart
        cooking apple, peeled, cored,
        and cut into ¼-inch slices
2 teaspoons fresh lemon juice
½ teaspoon ground cinnamon
½ teaspoon grated lemon zest
½ teaspoon pure vanilla extract

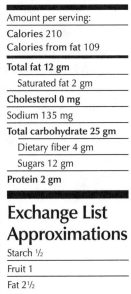

Nutrition Facts per Serving

Serving size: ¼ of crisp

Amount per serving:
Calories 210
Calories from fat 109

Total fat 12 gm
Saturated fat 2 gm
Cholesterol 0 mg
Sodium 135 mg
Total carbohydrate 25 gm
Dietary fiber 4 gm
Sugars 12 gm
Protein 2 gm

Exchange List Approximations

Starch ½
Fruit 1
Fat 2½

1.   Preheat the oven to 400°F. Prepare an 8-inch-round baking dish or 4 small ovenproof ramekins with nonstick pan spray.

2.   Combine the margarine, oats, flour, and brown sugar in a small bowl until crumbly; set aside.

3.   Combine the remaining ingredients, tossing gently to coat the fruit. Pour into the prepared dish. Top with the oats mixture.

4.   Bake for 15 to 20 minutes, or until the top is slightly browned and crisp.

KEY LARGO BANANAS FLAMBÉ

Here's a delicious interpretation of the classic Bananas Foster dessert created at Commander's Palace in New Orleans many years ago, but ours has just 3 grams of fat per serving! This makes a very impressive presentation, so if you have a portable burner or an open kitchen where guests can view the preparation, by all means invite them to watch. If you like, you can also serve the bananas over low-fat or nonfat vanilla frozen yogurt (add 1 carbohydrate exchange and 0 to 1 fat exchange per ⅓ cup serving).

4 servings

2 medium bananas, ripe but firm
½ lime
1 tablespoon margarine
1 tablespoon dark brown sugar
2 tablespoons rum

1. Peel the bananas and slice in half both lengthwise and crosswise. (Each banana will be quartered.) Squeeze the juice from the lime over the bananas.

2. Melt the margarine in a large nonstick skillet over medium heat. Sauté the bananas for 2 minutes per side. Sprinkle with brown sugar; cook 1 minute more per side.

3. Drizzle with rum. Remove from the stove and carefully ignite. Shake the skillet until the flames are extinguished. Serve immediately on warmed dessert plates.

Nutrition Facts per Serving

Serving size:
½ banana (2 slices)

Amount per serving:

Calories 103
Calories from fat 28

Total fat 3 gm
  Saturated fat 1 gm

Cholesterol 0 mg

Sodium 35 mg

Total carbohydrate 17 gm
  Dietary fiber 1 gm
  Sugars 12 gm

Protein 1 gm

Exchange List Approximations

Fruit 1

Fat 1

BLUEBERRY CRUMBLE

Fresh blueberries make this a berry dessert your whole family will love.

2¹/₂ cups (5 servings)

²/₃ cup graham cracker crumbs
2 tablespoons sugar
¹/₂ teaspoon ground cinnamon
2 tablespoons margarine
2 cups fresh blueberries

1. Preheat the oven to 350°F. Prepare an 8-inch-round baking dish with butter-flavored nonstick pan spray.
2. In a small bowl, combine the crumbs, sugar, and cinnamon. Cut in the margarine with a fork or pastry blender until the mixture is crumbly.
3. Place the berries in a prepared baking dish. Cover with the crumb mixture.
4. Bake 30 minutes. Serve warm.

Nutrition Facts per Serving

Serving size: ¹/₂ cup

Amount per serving:

Calories 164
Calories from fat 58

Total fat 6 gm
  Saturated fat 1 gm
Cholesterol 0 mg
Sodium 159 mg
Total carbohydrate 26 gm
  Dietary fiber 2 gm
  Sugars 13 gm
Protein 2 gm

Exchange List Approximations

Starch 1
Fruit ¹/₂
Fat 1

MELON BALLS WITH MINT

This is a refreshingly light dessert that's a sweet ending to a hot summer day. Be sure both the honeydew melon and the cantaloupe are ripe when you choose them; the blossom end of the melon should be slightly soft and smell sweet when pressed.

1 quart (4 servings)

¹/₄ medium honeydew melon, cut in balls
      or chunks (about 2 cups)
¹/₂ medium to large cantaloupe, cut in
      balls or chunks (about 2 cups)
2 tablespoons chopped fresh mint leaves
Mint sprigs (optional)

1. Combine the melon balls in a medium bowl.
2. Toss gently with the chopped mint leaves; cover and chill at least 1 hour or up to 6 hours. Toss again before serving. Garnish with mint sprigs, if desired.

Nutrition Facts per Serving

Serving size: 1 cup

Amount per serving:

Calories 58
Calories from fat 3

Total fat 0 gm
   Saturated fat 0 gm
Cholesterol 0 mg
Sodium 16 mg
Total carbohydrate 14 gm
   Dietary fiber 1 gm
   Sugars 13 gm
Protein 1 gm

Exchange List Approximation

Fruit 1

ORANGES WITH SOUTHERN-STYLE BOURBON SYRUP

Don't count on leftovers with this impressive yet deceptively simple dessert. Navel orange segments are marinated with sweet bourbon syrup, providing a special finale to a memorable meal.

4 servings

2 large navel oranges (1 pound total)
3 tablespoons sugar
1 tablespoon bourbon or Irish whiskey

1. Cut wide, thin strips of zest (colored part only) from 1 orange, using a vegetable peeler. Cut the zest into long, thin strips.
2. Combine ½ cup water and the sugar in a small saucepan. Cook, uncovered, over low heat until the sugar dissolves. Add the zest; simmer, uncovered, 4 minutes. Add the bourbon; simmer 1 minute more. Cool.
3. Cut all the peel and white pith from the oranges. Cut the oranges in ¼-inch slices and place them in a shallow serving bowl. Pour the syrup over the oranges. Chill at least 2 hours for the sauce to permeate the orange slices.

Nutrition Facts per Serving
Serving size: ¼ of recipe
Amount per serving:
Calories 68
Calories from fat 1
Total fat 0 gm
Saturated fat 0 gm
Cholesterol 0 mg
Sodium 0 mg
Total carbohydrate 16 gm
Dietary fiber 2 gm
Sugars 13 gm
Protein 1 gm

Exchange List Approximation

Fruit 1

BAKED PAPAYA WITH CINNAMON

A papaya is a pear-shaped fruit with beautiful golden-yellow skin and flesh and a sweet-tart flavor. Papayas are a great source of vitamin A and vitamin C in the diet. Choose fruit that yields slightly to pressure. Slightly green papayas will ripen quickly at room temperature, or you can hasten the ripening process by placing them in a paper bag. Once ripe, the fruit should be refrigerated and used as quickly as possible for the best flavor.

1 papaya (2 servings)

1 ripe papaya (about 1 pound)
1 teaspoon margarine, melted,
         or 1 teaspoon almond or walnut oil
2 teaspoons brown sugar
1/8 teaspoon ground cinnamon

1. Preheat the oven to 350°F.
2. Cut the papaya in half lengthwise; scoop out and discard the seeds. Place the halves cut side up in a shallow baking dish. Brush the top with margarine or oil. Sprinkle sugar and cinnamon over the papaya.
3. Bake 15 to 20 minutes, or until heated through. Serve warm or at room temperature.

Nutrition Facts per Serving
Serving size: 1/2 papaya
Amount per serving:
Calories 94
Calories from fat 19
Total fat 2 gm
Saturated fat 0 gm
Cholesterol 0 mg
Sodium 29 mg
Total carbohydrate 19 gm
Dietary fiber 3 gm
Sugars 13 gm
Protein 1 gm

Exchange List Approximations
Fruit 1
Fat 1/2

PORT-POACHED PEARS

Port wine syrup adds a rich, slightly fruity flavor to pears in this elegant fat-free dessert.

4 pear halves (4 servings)

2 large firm but ripe pears (1 pound
          total), peeled, cored, and halved
¾ cup port wine
¼ cup apple juice
Pinch of freshly ground pepper
          (optional)

1. Preheat the oven to 350°F.
2. Place the pear halves, cut side down, in a glass pie plate or ovenproof casserole. Pour the wine and juice over the pears.
3. Cover and bake 20 to 30 minutes, basting every 10 minutes, or until the pears are tender when pierced with the tip of knife. Cooking time will vary depending on the ripeness of the pears. Let stand in the pie plate until cooled to room temperature, spooning port syrup over the pears several times.
4. Transfer the pear halves to dessert dishes; spoon 1 tablespoon port syrup over each pear half, discarding the remaining syrup. Sprinkle with pepper, if desired.

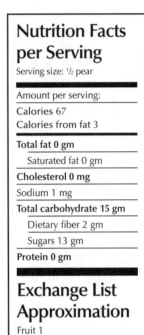

Nutrition Facts per Serving

Serving size: ½ pear

Amount per serving:

Calories 67
Calories from fat 3

Total fat 0 gm
  Saturated fat 0 gm
Cholesterol 0 mg
Sodium 1 mg
Total carbohydrate 15 gm
  Dietary fiber 2 gm
  Sugars 13 gm
Protein 0 gm

Exchange List Approximation

Fruit 1

QUICK RASPBERRY ICE

Here's a cool and refreshing dessert that's perfect any season. You can either buy frozen unsweetened berries in your supermarket or freeze the raspberries yourself in the summer when they're at their peak. Make sure the raspberry mixture doesn't get too thin during processing—you want it to be slightly chunky and definitely thick. If it gets too thin, place it in the freezer for a few minutes to solidify.

1 cup (2 servings)

2 cups frozen unsweetened raspberries
1 tablespoon raspberry or cassis liqueur
Mint sprigs (optional)

1. Place the frozen raspberries and liqueur in a blender or food processor.
2. Process until thick and slightly chunky, scraping down sides as necessary. Serve immediately while still frosty. Garnish with mint sprigs, if desired.

Nutrition Facts per Serving

Serving size: 1/2 cup

Amount per serving:

Calories 89
Calories from fat 7

Total fat 1 gm
　Saturated fat 0 gm
Cholesterol 0 mg
Sodium 1 mg
Total carbohydrate 18 gm
　Dietary fiber 8 gm
　Sugars 10 gm
Protein 1 gm

Exchange List Approximation

Fruit 1 1/2

STRAWBERRY BANANA SORBET

This sorbet packs a burst of fresh strawberry and banana flavor in every bite. The consistency of a sorbet should be very smooth, not chunky, so using an electric mixer in Step 3 is critical to provide smoothness and fluffiness.

5 cups (10 servings)

1 pound frozen unsweetened
    strawberries
2 ripe medium bananas, peeled
One 16-ounce container plain low-fat
    yogurt
1 tablespoon sugar

1. Purée the strawberries and bananas in a blender or food processor. Blend until smooth. Add the yogurt and sugar. Blend until smooth.
2. Pour into an 8-inch-square pan. Freeze for 2 to 3 hours, or until firm. Break the frozen mixture into chunks and place in a chilled mixer bowl.
3. Beat with an electric mixer on medium speed until fluffy. Return to the pan; cover and freeze for at least 6 hours, or until firm.

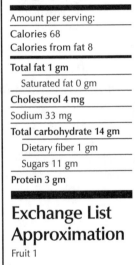

Nutrition Facts per Serving

Serving size: ½ cup

Amount per serving:

Calories 68
Calories from fat 8

Total fat 1 gm
   Saturated fat 0 gm
Cholesterol 4 mg
Sodium 33 mg
Total carbohydrate 14 gm
   Dietary fiber 1 gm
   Sugars 11 gm
Protein 3 gm

Exchange List Approximation

Fruit 1

TROPICAL FRUIT CUP

Papaya, pineapple, and mango are mixed with a light dressing of orange liqueur and lime juice in this exotic fruit cup. It's an especially good dessert choice to follow a spicy meal.

2 cups (4 servings)

$1/2$ ripe papaya, peeled, seeded, and cut
　　　into chunks (about 4 ounces)
$1/6$ ripe pineapple, peeled, cored, and cut
　　　into cubes (about 4 ounces)
$1/2$ ripe mango, peeled, seeded, and cut
　　　into chunks (about 3 ounces)
1 tablespoon orange-flavored liqueur
1 teaspoon fresh lime juice
$1/2$ lime, cut in wedges

1.　Combine the fruit in a serving bowl.
2.　Pour the liqueur and lime juice over the fruit; toss lightly to coat. Serve immediately or cover and chill up to 6 hours. Serve garnished with lime wedges.

Nutrition Facts per Serving

Serving size: $1/2$ cup

Amount per serving:

Calories 55
Calories from fat 2

Total fat 0 gm
　Saturated fat 0 gm
Cholesterol 0 mg
Sodium 2 mg
Total carbohydrate 12 gm
　Dietary fiber 1 gm
　Sugars 10 gm
Protein 0 gm

Exchange List Approximation

Fruit 1

AMBROSIA

A classic American dessert, ambrosia is ideal for winter brunches or as a dessert when fruit selection is limited. Tossing the banana slices with the orange juice helps keep them from discoloring.

2 cups (4 servings)

1¼ cups orange segments
1 small banana (about 4 ounces),
    peeled and sliced
¼ cup orange juice
2 tablespoons shredded coconut
    (sweetened or unsweetened
    as available)

1. Combine the fruits and juice.
2. Sprinkle with coconut at serving time.

Nutrition Facts per Serving
Serving size: ½ cup
Amount per serving:
Calories 72
Calories from fat 10
Total fat 1 gm
Saturated fat 1 gm
Cholesterol 0 mg
Sodium 7 mg
Total carbohydrate 16 gm
Dietary fiber 2 gm
Sugars 12 gm
Protein 1 gm

Exchange List Approximation

Fruit 1

POACHED DRIED FRUIT COMPOTE

Serve the compote on its own as a dessert or spoon some over waffles, pancakes, or frozen yogurt as a topping. It will keep up to five days if refrigerated. This recipe can also be made using 8 ounces of a single type of dried fruit, such as prunes, figs, or apricots, instead of a mix of dried fruits, if desired. You can substitute water for the wine as a poaching liquid, but keep in mind that the wine provides a bit of flavor that the water doesn't.

2 cups (6 servings)

One 8-ounce package mixed dried fruit
1 cup sweet white wine, such as Riesling
2 teaspoons grated fresh lemon zest
1 cinnamon stick
4 whole cloves
4 allspice or juniper berries (optional)

1. Combine all the ingredients plus 1 cup water in a medium saucepan. Bring to a boil. Reduce the heat, cover, and simmer until the fruit is tender, about 15 to 20 minutes. Chill.
2. Discard the spices; serve the fruit with its liquid in small shallow bowls.

Nutrition Facts per Serving	
Serving size: ⅓ cup	
Amount per serving:	
Calories 121	
Calories from fat 2	
Total fat 0 gm	
Saturated fat 0 gm	
Cholesterol 0 mg	
Sodium 56 mg	
Total carbohydrate 26 gm	
Dietary fiber 3 gm	
Sugars 15 gm	
Protein 1 gm	

Exchange List Approximation
Fruit 2

STRAWBERRY SHORTCAKE

Classic strawberry shortcake uses biscuits, but you can substitute packaged sponge shortcake shells or slices of angel food cake if you're in a hurry. A slice of angel food cake ($^1/_{12}$ of a cake) equals 2 carbohydrate exchanges; a sponge cake shell equals 1 carbohydrate and 1 fat. Light whipped cream has only 20 calories and $1^1/_2$ grams of fat in a 2-tablespoon serving, and counts as a free food.

6 shortcakes (6 servings)

1 quart fresh, ripe strawberries, washed,
    drained, and hulled
2 tablespoons sugar
6 Baking Powder Biscuits, 2 inches
    in diameter (page 59)
1 cup whipped light cream (homemade
    or from a pressurized can)

1. Cut the strawberries in halves or quarters. Place in a medium bowl and add the sugar and 1 tablespoon water. Chill 2 hours.

2. Split the biscuits. Put the bottoms on individual dessert plates. Allowing $^1/_2$ cup of berries per serving, layer half ($^1/_4$ cup) the berries over the bottom of each biscuit. Add the biscuit tops and the remaining berries.

3. Top each shortcake with a generous dollop (or squirt) of whipped cream.

Nutrition Facts per Serving

Serving size: 1 biscuit, $^1/_2$ cup berries, $2^1/_2$ tablespoons whipped cream

Amount per serving:

Calories 207
Calories from fat 77

Total fat 9 gm
    Saturated fat 2 gm
Cholesterol 8 mg
Sodium 383 mg
Total carbohydrate 30 gm
    Dietary fiber 3 gm
    Sugars 12 gm
Protein 3 gm

Exchange List Approximations

Starch 1

Fruit 1

Fat $1^1/_2$

BREAD PUDDING WITH RAISINS

A classic English dessert, bread pudding will never go out of style. Stale or dry bread is best to use, since its moisture has evaporated, allowing the flavored custard to saturate the bread more easily.

3 cups (6 servings)

3 slices day-old white bread, cubed
½ cup raisins
2 cups fat-free milk
2 large eggs, slightly beaten, or
      ½ cup egg substitute
2 tablespoons sugar
1 teaspoon ground cinnamon
1 teaspoon pure vanilla extract
¼ teaspoon salt

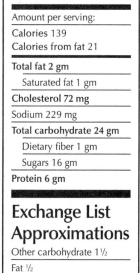

Nutrition Facts per Serving

Serving size: ½ cup

Amount per serving:
Calories 139
Calories from fat 21

Total fat 2 gm
Saturated fat 1 gm
Cholesterol 72 mg
Sodium 229 mg
Total carbohydrate 24 gm
Dietary fiber 1 gm
Sugars 16 gm
Protein 6 gm

Exchange List Approximations

Other carbohydrate 1½

Fat ½

1. Preheat the oven to 350°F. Prepare a 1½-quart baking dish with nonstick pan spray.
2. Mix the bread cubes and raisins in the prepared dish.
3. Combine the remaining ingredients in a medium bowl; pour the mixture over the bread and raisins; stir to blend.
4. Set the filled baking dish in a shallow pan on the middle rack of the oven. Pour hot water into the shallow pan to a depth of 1 inch around the baking dish. This creates a water bath to cook the pudding slowly.
5. Bake 45 to 55 minutes, or until a knife inserted in the pudding comes out clean. Remove the pan from the water bath and serve warm or chilled.

RAISIN RICE PUDDING

Rice pudding is a delightfully sweet and creamy way to use up leftover rice. Our version, with just 1 gram of fat and 126 calories per serving, is a definite winner.

4 cups (8 servings)

2 large eggs, slightly beaten, or
      ½ cup egg substitute
2 cups cooked rice
1½ cups fat-free milk
2 tablespoons sugar
½ cup golden raisins
1 teaspoon pure vanilla extract
½ teaspoon ground cinnamon or
      nutmeg
¼ teaspoon salt

Nutrition Facts per Serving

Serving size: ½ cup

Amount per serving:	
Calories 126	
Calories from fat 13	
Total fat 1 gm	
Saturated fat 0 gm	
Cholesterol 54 mg	
Sodium 114 mg	
Total carbohydrate 24 gm	
Dietary fiber 1 gm	
Sugars 11 gm	
Protein 5 gm	

Exchange List Approximation

Other carbohydrate 1½

1.　Preheat the oven to 350°F. Prepare a 1½-quart baking dish with nonstick pan spray.
2.　In the prepared dish, combine all the ingredients. Stir gently to mix.
3.　Set the filled dish in a shallow pan on the middle oven rack. Pour hot water into the outer pan to a depth of 1 inch around the baking dish. This makes a water bath to cook the pudding slowly.
4.　Bake for 45 minutes, or until a knife inserted in the pudding comes out clean. Remove the dish from the water bath. Serve the pudding warm or chilled.

ORANGE TAPIOCA

We've updated this childhood dessert with oranges to add flavor and texture, and trimmed the fat by using fat-free milk and fewer eggs than called for in traditional tapioca pudding recipes.

2 cups (4 servings)

1½ cups fat-free milk
3 tablespoons quick-cooking tapioca
1 large egg, beaten, or ¼ cup egg
        substitute
1 tablespoon sugar
Pinch of salt
½ cup orange juice
½ teaspoon pure vanilla extract
1 orange, peeled, seeded, and diced

Nutrition Facts per Serving

Serving size: ½ cup

Amount per serving:

Calories 117
Calories from fat 13

Total fat 1 gm
   Saturated fat 1 gm
Cholesterol 55 mg
Sodium 98 mg
Total carbohydrate 21 gm
   Dietary fiber 1 gm
   Sugars 13 gm
Protein 5 gm

Exchange List Approximation

Other carbohydrate 1½

1.   Combine the milk, tapioca, egg, sugar, and salt in a small nonstick saucepan. Cook over medium heat, stirring constantly, until the mixture comes to a boil.

2.   Remove from the heat. Add the orange juice slowly, stirring constantly. Return to the heat, stirring until the mixture boils again. Remove from the heat.

3.   Let cool 10 to 15 minutes, stirring occasionally. Mix in the vanilla and diced orange. Chill well before serving, at least 2 hours.

NOODLE KUGEL

Often served on Jewish holidays, kugel is a baked pudding that can be either sweet or savory. This sweet dessert version uses egg noodles as a base and is plump with raisins, tart apple chunks, and spice.

12 servings

8 ounces uncooked broad egg noodles
3 large eggs, beaten, or ¾ cup egg substitute
¾ cup low-fat small-curd cottage cheese
1 tablespoon brown sugar
1 teaspoon ground cinnamon
1 teaspoon pure vanilla extract
1 large tart apple, peeled, cored, and
     diced in ¼-inch pieces
¼ cup raisins, soaked in hot water for
     10 minutes and drained
¼ cup margarine, melted

1. Cook the noodles according to the package directions, omitting salt; drain well. (There should be 4 cups of cooked noodles.)
2. Preheat the oven to 350°F. Prepare an 8-inch-square pan with nonstick pan spray.
3. Combine the eggs, cottage cheese, brown sugar, cinnamon, and vanilla in a large bowl. Stir in the noodles, apple, and raisins. Pour into the prepared dish.
4. Drizzle the margarine evenly over the top of the casserole. Bake, uncovered, for 45 to 55 minutes, or until lightly browned. Cut the kugel into 12 equal pieces (about 2 x 2 inches). Serve hot or chilled.

Nutrition Facts per Serving

Serving size:
One 2 x 2½-inch square

Amount per serving:

Calories 156
Calories from fat 55

Total fat 6 gm
  Saturated fat 1 gm
Cholesterol 71 mg
Sodium 122 mg
Total carbohydrate 20 gm
  Dietary fiber 1 gm
  Sugars 6 gm
Protein 6 gm

Exchange List Approximations

Starch 1½
Fat 1

COEUR À LA CRÈME

This classic French dessert (meaning "heart of cream") is usually made in a special heart-shaped basket or mold. The cream cheese mixture is drained of its whey to yield a richer, creamier mixture using low-fat Neufchâtel cheese to reduce fat content. We molded our cheese into a round ball, but you can use any shape tin or mold you like. Just line the dish with plastic wrap to make removal easier, spread the cream cheese mixture to the top of the mold, and cover with more plastic wrap. Chill for several hours. To unmold, remove the top sheet of plastic wrap, place a plate on top of the mold, invert the dish, and remove the mold and bottom plastic wrap. Garnish the dessert with plump fresh strawberries and strawberry sauce.

6 servings

1½ packages (12 ounces total) reduced-
      fat cream cheese or Neufchâtel
      cheese
1 teaspoon fresh lemon juice
¼ cup fat-free evaporated milk, chilled
1 tablespoon brown sugar
½ teaspoon maple-flavored extract
1 cup Strawberry Sauce (page 425)
6 fresh strawberries, to garnish
      (optional)

1. In a food processor or blender, purée the cream cheese with the lemon juice, evaporated milk, brown sugar, and maple extract. Blend until smooth.

2. Place the cheese mixture in a strainer and set over a bowl. Chill for 8 hours to allow the liquid to drain. Discard the liquid.

3. Shape the cheese into a ball and place in the center of a small serving dish. Surround with ¼ cup strawberry sauce, and fresh berries if desired. Pass the remaining sauce.

Nutrition Facts per Serving	
Serving size: ⅙ of recipe	
Amount per serving:	
Calories 178	
Calories from fat 109	
Total fat 12 gm	
Saturated fat 8 gm	
Cholesterol 40 mg	
Sodium 234 mg	
Total carbohydrate 12 gm	
Dietary fiber 1 gm	
Sugars 11 gm	
Protein 6 gm	

Exchange List Approximations

Other carbohydrate 1

Fat, saturated 2

OLD-FASHIONED BAKED CUSTARD

Baked custards are always a familiar and comforting treat, and this recipe is no exception. Custard is traditionally made from a base of eggs and cream, but we've modified our recipe to use fat-free milk and fewer eggs to trim fat. Old-fashioned baked custard can be served hot, warm, or chilled.

3 cups (6 servings)

3 large eggs, slightly beaten, or ³⁄₄ cup
     egg substitute
2 tablespoons sugar
¹⁄₄ teaspoon salt
¹⁄₈ teaspoon ground nutmeg
2 cups fat-free milk
¹⁄₂ teaspoon pure vanilla extract
Pinch of ground cinnamon

1. Preheat the oven to 325°F.
2. In a large bowl, combine the eggs, sugar, salt, and nutmeg. Slowly stir in the milk and vanilla.
3. Pour ¹⁄₂ cup of custard into each of six 5-ounce custard cups. Sprinkle with cinnamon.
4. Set the filled custard cups in a shallow pan. Pour about 1 inch of hot water in the pan around the custard cups. Bake on the center rack of the oven for 35 minutes, or until a knife inserted in the custard comes out clean.
5. Serve hot, warm, or chilled.

Nutrition Facts per Serving

Serving size: ¹⁄₂ cup

Amount per serving:

Calories 82
Calories from fat 24

Total fat 3 gm
   Saturated fat 1 gm
Cholesterol 108 mg
Sodium 171 mg
Total carbohydrate 8 gm
   Dietary fiber 0 gm
   Sugars 8 gm
Protein 6 gm

Exchange List Approximations

Other carbohydrate ¹⁄₂
Meat, medium-fat ¹⁄₂

HAWAIIAN SOUFFLÉ PUDDING

This dessert provides a taste of the tropics and is a hit with young and old alike. Many people fear making soufflés, but don't let that prevent you from trying this. The one essential piece of equipment is a soufflé dish—its straight sides are crucial to getting the soufflé to rise. Soufflés always fall once they are removed from the oven, because the hot air trapped in the soufflé starts to escape immediately, causing the mixture to deflate. This dessert keeps well if refrigerated.

1 soufflé (8 servings)

2 cups orange juice
1 cup white cornmeal
¼ teaspoon salt
2 tablespoons margarine
1 cup fat-free evaporated milk
1 teaspoon pure vanilla extract
3 tablespoons sugar
1 cup (2 ounces) flaked sweetened
    coconut
4 large egg whites

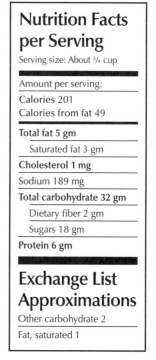

Nutrition Facts per Serving

Serving size: About ¾ cup

Amount per serving:

Calories 201
Calories from fat 49

Total fat 5 gm
  Saturated fat 3 gm
Cholesterol 1 mg
Sodium 189 mg
Total carbohydrate 32 gm
  Dietary fiber 2 gm
  Sugars 18 gm
Protein 6 gm

Exchange List Approximations

Other carbohydrate 2
Fat, saturated 1

1. Preheat the oven to 400°F. Prepare a 1½-quart soufflé dish with nonstick pan spray.
2. Combine the orange juice, cornmeal, and salt in a medium nonstick saucepan. Bring to a boil, whisking constantly. Reduce the heat; add the margarine. Cook and stir until thickened, about 5 minutes.
3. Remove from the heat. Slowly whisk in the milk and vanilla. Stir in the sugar and coconut; mix well.
4. Beat the egg whites to stiff peaks and fold them into the pudding.
5. Pour the mixture into the soufflé dish; bake 30 minutes. Reduce the oven temperature to 325°F and continue baking 15 minutes more, or until the soufflé is puffed and golden brown. Cool 15 minutes. (The soufflé will fall as it cools.) Serve warm or chilled.

FRESH FRUIT CLAFOUTI

A clafouti is a country-French dessert that's made by topping a layer of fresh, ripe fruit with a cakelike batter and baking it. It makes a great addition to a brunch menu.

1 cake (6 servings)

1½ cups sliced ripe nectarines, plums,
      peaches, or pitted cherries
      (about 10 ounces cut fruit)
⅔ cup fat-free evaporated milk
1 large egg, beaten, or ¼ cup egg substitute
2 tablespoons all-purpose flour
2 tablespoons sugar
½ teaspoon pure vanilla extract
⅛ teaspoon nutmeg, preferably freshly
      grated
⅛ teaspoon salt
1 tablespoon sifted powdered sugar

1. Preheat the oven to 375°F. Prepare an 8-inch glass pie plate with nonstick pan spray. Layer the fruit in the pie plate.
2. Combine the milk, egg, flour, sugar, vanilla, nutmeg, and salt in a food processor. Process until smooth; pour over the fruit.
3. Bake 35 to 40 minutes, or until puffed and golden brown. Serve warm or at room temperature. At serving time, sprinkle with powdered sugar and cut into 6 slices.

Nutrition Facts per Serving	
Serving size: 1 slice	
Amount per serving:	
Calories 92	
Calories from fat 11	
Total fat 1 gm	
Saturated fat 0 gm	
Cholesterol 36 mg	
Sodium 92 mg	
Total carbohydrate 17 gm	
Dietary fiber 1 gm	
Sugars 13 gm	
Protein 4 gm	

Exchange List Approximation

Other carbohydrate 1

CHERRY CHOCOLATE PIE

For an extra-special presentation, garnish the edges of the pie with light whipped topping, or add a 2-tablespoon dollop on top of each slice. Either garnish adds about 20 calories per serving and is considered a free food.

1 pie (8 servings)

CHERRY TOPPING

1³/₄ cups thawed frozen pitted tart
      cherries (¹/₂ of a 1-pound bag)
¹/₂ cup sugar
1 tablespoon cornstarch
¹/₂ teaspoon almond extract

CHOCOLATE FILLING

6 ounces soft fat-free cream cheese
¹/₂ cup semisweet chocolate chips
3 tablespoons fat-free milk

1 prepared 9-inch pie shell, baked

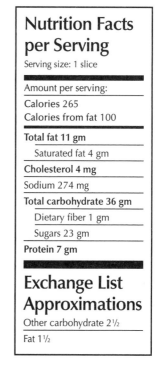

Nutrition Facts per Serving

Serving size: 1 slice

Amount per serving:

Calories 265
Calories from fat 100

Total fat 11 gm
   Saturated fat 4 gm
Cholesterol 4 mg
Sodium 274 mg
Total carbohydrate 36 gm
   Dietary fiber 1 gm
   Sugars 23 gm
Protein 7 gm

Exchange List Approximations

Other carbohydrate 2¹/₂

Fat 1¹/₂

1. For the topping, combine the cherries, sugar, ¹/₄ cup water, and the cornstarch in a medium saucepan. Stir well to dissolve the cornstarch. Cook over medium heat, stirring often, until the sauce is thickened and clear. Add the almond extract and stir to blend. Refrigerate the sauce to chill and firm.

2. For the filling, combine the cream cheese and chocolate chips in a small pan or in the top of a double boiler. Cook over very low heat, stirring constantly, until the chips are melted; add the milk and stir until the mixture is smooth.

3. Pour the chocolate filling into the baked pie crust. Let cool at least 10 minutes, or until the pudding sets. Gently spread the cooled cherry topping over the chocolate layer. Chill the pie at least 2 hours before serving.

4. At serving time, cut into 8 equal pieces.

SWEET POTATO PIE

Delicious at Thanksgiving or any other time, this not-too-sweet version of sweet potato pie mixes sweet potatoes with cinnamon and lemon zest and encases the mixture in a flaky, golden crust. Separating the eggs is an important step in this recipe, because the whipped egg whites help add volume to the pie.

1 pie (8 servings)

3 tablespoons margarine
1/4 cup sugar
1/4 teaspoon salt
1 large egg yolk
3 tablespoons fresh lemon juice
1 teaspoon grated lemon zest
1/2 teaspoon ground cinnamon
3 large sweet potatoes (1 1/2 pounds
    total), cooked, peeled, and
    mashed
1 cup fat-free evaporated milk
3 large egg whites
1 prepared 9-inch pie shell, unbaked

Nutrition Facts per Serving
Serving size: 1 slice
Amount per serving:
Calories 291
Calories from fat 117
Total fat 13 gm
Saturated fat 3 gm
Cholesterol 28 mg
Sodium 313 mg
Total carbohydrate 38 gm
Dietary fiber 3 gm
Sugars 17 gm
Protein 7 gm

Exchange List Approximations
Other carbohydrate 2 1/2
Fat 2

1. Preheat the oven to 350°F. Beat together the margarine, sugar, and salt in a large bowl. Add the egg yolk, lemon juice, lemon zest, and cinnamon; mix well. Stir in the sweet potatoes and milk; mix again.

2. Beat the egg whites to stiff peaks and fold them into the sweet potato mixture; pour into the pie shell. Bake for about 40 to 50 minutes, or until a knife inserted in the center comes out clean. Cool and cut the pie in 8 equal slices.

GRANNY SMITH APPLE TART

Refrigerated folded pie crusts make pies and tarts simple, and are more tender and flexible than frozen pie crusts. Dough hearts add a pretty decorative touch, but feel free to use any other shape cookie cutter, such as leaves, apples, or stars, for variety.

1 tart (8 servings)

1 refrigerated fill-and-bake pie crust
    (7 to 7½ ounces)
3 large Granny Smith apples (about
    1½ pounds total), peeled,
    cored, and thinly sliced
2 teaspoons fresh lemon juice
¼ cup packed brown sugar
¼ cup sour half-and-half, or ¼ cup
    nonfat sour cream
1 tablespoon quick-cooking tapioca
1½ teaspoons ground cinnamon
2 teaspoons granulated sugar

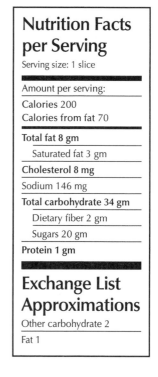

Nutrition Facts per Serving

Serving size: 1 slice

Amount per serving:

Calories 200
Calories from fat 70

Total fat 8 gm
   Saturated fat 3 gm
Cholesterol 8 mg
Sodium 146 mg
Total carbohydrate 34 gm
   Dietary fiber 2 gm
   Sugars 20 gm
Protein 1 gm

Exchange List Approximations

Other carbohydrate 2

Fat 1

1.   Preheat the oven to 350°F.

2.   Put the pie crust into a 9-inch-diameter tart pan with a removable bottom; press the crust against the fluted edge and trim off any pastry that extends over the top. Roll the trimmed dough into a ball; flatten to ¼ inch and cut 2 or 3 shapes with a cookie cutter. Prick the tart shell in several places with the tines of a fork.

3.   Put the sliced apples in a large bowl; drizzle them with lemon juice and toss to mix.

4.   In a small bowl, blend the brown sugar, sour half-and-half, tapioca, and cinnamon.

5.   Fold the brown sugar mixture into the apples until all the fruit is coated. Spoon the apples into the tart shell; arrange the dough shapes on top of the apples. Sprinkle granulated sugar over the top.

6.   Bake for 35 minutes, or until the apples are tender. Cut in 8 equal slices. Serve hot or at room temperature.

FRESH PLUM TART

This plum tart requires perfectly ripe fruit for optimal flavor. Peak plum season is in June, but you can also make this delicious recipe using nectarines (use 3 nectarines in place of the plums) or peeled pears (2 large or 3 small) if plums are out of season.

1 tart (8 servings)

1 refrigerated fill-and-bake pie crust
      (7 to 7½ ounces)
4 ripe plums (about 1 pound total),
      peeled and thinly sliced
2 large eggs, or ½ cup egg substitute
⅓ cup sugar
¼ cup fat-free sour cream
3 tablespoons all-purpose flour

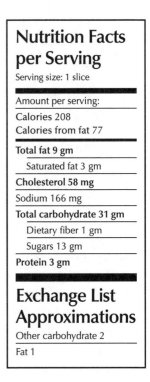

Nutrition Facts per Serving

Serving size: 1 slice

Amount per serving:

Calories 208
Calories from fat 77

Total fat 9 gm
   Saturated fat 3 gm

Cholesterol 58 mg

Sodium 166 mg

Total carbohydrate 31 gm
   Dietary fiber 1 gm
   Sugars 13 gm

Protein 3 gm

Exchange List Approximations

Other carbohydrate 2

Fat 1

1.   Preheat the oven to 350°F.

2.   Press the prepared pie crust into a 9-inch-diameter tart pan with a removable bottom. Press the crust against the fluted edge and trim off any pastry that extends over the top. Discard any extra dough and the trimmings (about 1 ounce).

3.   Bake the crust only 5 minutes, until it is set but not brown. Cool on a rack.

4.   Arrange the plum slices in overlapping circles to cover the bottom of the tart shell.

5.   In a small bowl, whisk together the eggs, sugar, fat-free sour cream, and flour until smooth. Pour the custard over the plums; it should fill the spaces between the plums.

6.   Bake at 350°F for 18 to 20 minutes, until the custard is set and the edges are slightly browned. Cool and cut into 8 equal slices.

FRESH PEACH CRUMBLE

Nothing says summer like this "peachy keen" recipe. Serve it fresh out of the oven topped with a scoop of low-fat frozen yogurt or a dollop of whipped topping. One-third cup of low-fat or fat-free frozen yogurt adds 1 carbohydrate and 0 to 1 fat exchange; 2 tablespoons of whipped topping adds 20 calories and is considered a free food.

1 crumble (8 servings)

6 medium ripe peaches (about 2 pounds total)
2 tablespoons almond-flavored liqueur
1/2 teaspoon ground cinnamon
Pinch of freshly grated nutmeg
3/4 cup quick-cooking oats, uncooked
1/4 cup all-purpose flour
1/3 cup packed light brown sugar
3 tablespoons margarine, chilled and cut into small pieces

Nutrition Facts per Serving
Serving size: About 2/3 cup
Amount per serving:
Calories 161
Calories from fat 44
Total fat 5 gm
Saturated fat 1 gm
Cholesterol 0 mg
Sodium 54 mg
Total carbohydrate 29 gm
Dietary fiber 3 gm
Sugars 19 gm
Protein 2 gm

Exchange List Approximations
Other carbohydrate 2
Fat 1/2

1. Preheat the oven to 375°F. Prepare an 8-inch-square baking dish or deep glass pie pan with butter-flavored nonstick pan spray.
2. Peel, pit, and slice the peaches and put them in a large bowl. There should be about 6 cups. Add the liqueur, cinnamon, and nutmeg. Spoon the mixture into the prepared dish.
3. In a small bowl, combine the oats, flour, and brown sugar. Cut in the margarine until crumbly; sprinkle over the peaches. Bake 30 minutes, or until the peaches are tender and the topping is golden brown. Serve warm or at room temperature.

ANGEL FOOD CAKE WITH COCOA WHIPPED CREAM

This heavenly dessert takes just minutes to make—especially if you purchase an angel food cake at the supermarket and just make the cocoa whipped topping. You can also make the cake from scratch or buy a box mix. Try a flavored cake—orange, cherry, or chocolate—in place of plain angel food cake for a bit of variety.

1 frosted cake (12 servings)

1½ cups whipping cream, chilled
¼ cup Dutch-process cocoa
½ cup sifted powdered sugar
1 teaspoon pure vanilla extract
One 8-inch-diameter angel food cake
        (about 10 ounces)

1. In a chilled medium bowl, whip the cream until it stands in peaks.
2. Combine the cocoa and sugar in a small bowl. Beat into the whipped cream; add the vanilla just before finishing the beating.
3. Cut the cake horizontally into 2 layers. Spread ¼ of the cream mixture on the bottom layer. Replace the top layer. Frost the top and sides with the remaining whipped cream. Refrigerate until serving time.
4. Cut the cake in 12 equal slices.

Nutrition Facts per Serving

Serving size: 1 slice

Amount per serving:

Calories 196
Calories from fat 103

Total fat 11 gm
  Saturated fat 7 gm
Cholesterol 41 mg
Sodium 58 mg
Total carbohydrate 22 gm
  Dietary fiber 1 gm
  Sugars 15 gm
Protein 3 gm

Exchange List Approximations

Other carbohydrate 1½
Fat, saturated 2

CINNAMON APPLE COFFEE CAKE

The perfect accompaniment for a leisurely morning cup of coffee or tea, this coffee cake spiced with cinnamon and apple chunks is sure to become standard weekend fare in your house. It has only 5 grams of fat per serving!

1 coffee cake (9 servings)

½ cup packed brown sugar
¼ cup margarine, softened
2 large egg whites
½ cup low-fat (1 percent fat) buttermilk
2 cups all-purpose flour
2 teaspoons baking powder
½ teaspoon baking soda
2 teaspoons ground cinnamon
¼ teaspoon salt
1 medium apple, unpeeled, cored and
      finely chopped

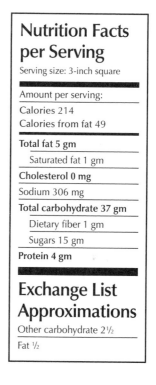

Nutrition Facts per Serving

Serving size: 3-inch square

Amount per serving:

Calories 214
Calories from fat 49

Total fat 5 gm
   Saturated fat 1 gm
Cholesterol 0 mg
Sodium 306 mg
Total carbohydrate 37 gm
   Dietary fiber 1 gm
   Sugars 15 gm
Protein 4 gm

Exchange List Approximations

Other carbohydrate 2½
Fat ½

1. Preheat the oven to 375°F. Prepare a 9-inch-square baking pan with nonstick pan spray.

2. In a large bowl, beat together the sugar, margarine, and egg whites until smooth. Stir in the buttermilk. Add the flour, baking powder, baking soda, cinnamon, and salt and mix just until the ingredients are moistened. (The batter will be stiff.) Fold in the apple.

3. Spread the batter in the prepared pan. Bake 25 to 30 minutes, or until a toothpick inserted in the center comes out clean. Cut into nine 3-inch squares. Serve warm or at room temperature.

LEMON POPPY SEED CAKE

This cake, with its tart pucker of lemon and scattering of poppy seeds, is ideal for afternoon tea or as a dessert. Serve with a dollop of vanilla or lemon nonfat yogurt. One tablespoon of yogurt is considered a free food.

1 cake (9 servings)

1 cup all-purpose flour
1/2 cup sugar
1/3 cup poppy seeds
1 1/2 teaspoons baking powder
1/2 teaspoon baking soda
1/8 teaspoon salt
1/4 cup margarine, melted
2 large egg whites, or 1/4 cup egg substitute
1/2 cup fat-free milk
3 tablespoons fresh lemon juice
1 teaspoon finely grated lemon zest
1 teaspoon pure vanilla extract
2 tablespoons powdered sugar

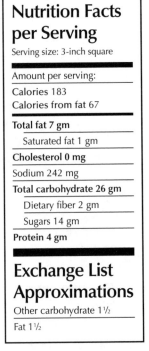

Nutrition Facts per Serving

Serving size: 3-inch square

Amount per serving:

Calories 183
Calories from fat 67

Total fat 7 gm
   Saturated fat 1 gm

Cholesterol 0 mg

Sodium 242 mg

Total carbohydrate 26 gm
   Dietary fiber 2 gm
   Sugars 14 gm

Protein 4 gm

Exchange List Approximations

Other carbohydrate 1 1/2

Fat 1 1/2

1. Preheat the oven to 350°F. Prepare a 9-inch-square baking pan with nonstick pan spray.

2. Combine the flour, sugar, poppy seeds, baking powder, baking soda, and salt in a large bowl.

3. Add the margarine, egg whites, milk, lemon juice, zest, and vanilla. Mix just until the dry ingredients are moistened. Pour into the prepared pan. Bake 30 minutes, or until the cake springs back when the center is lightly pressed.

4. Cool on a wire rack. Sift powdered sugar over the cake. Cut into 3-inch squares to serve.

CLASSIC SPONGE CAKE

Serve this tasty cake plain or dress it up with a topping of fresh peaches, berries, Gingered Peach Sauce (page 426), Strawberry Sauce (page 425), or Bittersweet Chocolate Sauce (page 424). Remember to add the appropriate exchanges for whichever topping you choose.

1 cake (16 servings)

6 large eggs, separated
½ teaspoon cream of tartar
½ cup cold fat-free milk
1½ cups sugar
½ teaspoon pure vanilla extract
½ teaspoon lemon extract
1½ cups sifted cake flour
¼ teaspoon salt

Nutrition Facts per Serving
Serving size: 1 slice
Amount per serving:
Calories 140
Calories from fat 18
Total fat 2 gm
Saturated fat 1 gm
Cholesterol 80 mg
Sodium 64 mg
Total carbohydrate 27 gm
Dietary fiber 0 gm
Sugars 19 gm
Protein 3 gm

Exchange List Approximation
Other carbohydrate 2

1. Preheat the oven to 325°F.
2. In a chilled mixer bowl, beat the egg whites until foamy. Add the cream of tartar and beat until stiff peaks form. Reserve.
3. In a large bowl, beat the egg yolks until thick and light. Add the milk and stir to mix. Beat in the sugar gradually. Add the vanilla and lemon extract. Set aside.
4. Sift the flour with the salt. Fold into the egg yolk mixture ½ cup at a time. Gently fold the beaten egg whites into the batter.
5. Bake in an ungreased 10-inch tube pan for 1 hour, or until the top springs back when touched lightly. Place on a wire rack for 10 minutes; invert to remove the cake. Allow the cake to cool completely.
6. At serving time, cut the cake in 16 equal wedges.

NEW YORK CHEESECAKE

This special "do ahead" cake takes a bit of time to cook, cool, and chill, but it's well worth the effort. It has just 9 grams of fat per slice, compared with 13 to 16 grams in a regular, full-fat version, but it's equally delicious. You won't go back to your old cheesecake recipe! Garnish the chilled cake with fresh blueberries or strawberries, if desired. Just be sure to add in the appropriate fruit exchanges.

1 cake (12 servings)

CRUST

2 teaspoons margarine
⅓ cup graham cracker crumbs
    (about 2 to 3 crackers)

FILLING

One 12-ounce container soft fat-free
    cream cheese
One 8-ounce container fat-free sour
    cream
3 large eggs
One 8-ounce container whipped cream
    cheese
⅔ cup sugar
1 tablespoon cornstarch
1¼ teaspoons pure vanilla extract
2 teaspoons fresh lemon juice

Nutrition Facts per Serving
Serving size: 1 slice (¹⁄₁₂ of cake)
Amount per serving:
Calories 196
Calories from fat 77
Total fat 9 gm
Saturated fat 5 gm
Cholesterol 78 mg
Sodium 301 mg
Total carbohydrate 19 gm
Dietary fiber 0 gm
Sugars 16 gm
Protein 10 gm

Exchange List Approximations

Other carbohydrate 1½

Fat, saturated 1½

1. Let the margarine, cream cheeses, eggs, and sour cream come to room temperature.

2. Rub all the interior surfaces of an 8½-inch-diameter springform pan with margarine. Press the graham cracker crumbs onto the sides of the springform pan, using all the crumbs. Preheat the oven to 375°F.

3. Whip the fat-free cream cheese in the food processor until soft and creamy.

4. Transfer the whipped fat-free cheese to the bowl of an electric mixer. Add the fat-free sour cream and the regular whipped cream cheese; mix about 1 minute. Add the sugar, cornstarch, vanilla, and lemon juice. Beat until well blended.

5. Beat in 1 egg at a time until each is very well blended and the mixture is smooth.

6. Pour the mixture into the prepared springform pan. Set the pan in a roasting pan. Pour hot water around the springform pan up to the level of the batter. (Do not overfill; simmering water could splash into the cake.)

7. Bake 45 minutes, until the edges are golden brown and the cheesecake is set. Remove the pans from the oven and let the cake (still in its water bath) cool 30 minutes. Remove the springform pan from the water bath and set on a cooling rack to cool 30 minutes more.

8. Cover the pan lightly with foil and refrigerate at least 6 hours or overnight. To serve, remove the sides of the springform pan and cut into 12 equal wedges.

CRANBERRY NUT TEA CAKE

Cranberries add a pleasant tartness to this sweet cake. It's a perfect choice for a coffee break, afternoon tea, or after-dinner dessert. Make it in the fall, when fresh cranberries are plentiful.

1 cake (9 servings)

1³/₄ cups all-purpose flour
¹/₂ cup sugar
2 teaspoons baking powder
¹/₂ teaspoon salt
¹/₂ teaspoon ground cinnamon
³/₄ cup orange juice
¹/₃ cup plus 2 tablespoons canola or
    corn oil
1 large egg
¹/₂ cup fresh or thawed frozen
    cranberries, chopped
¹/₂ cup chopped walnuts
1 teaspoon grated orange zest
1 tablespoon powdered sugar

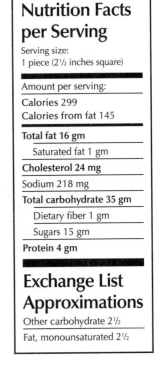

Nutrition Facts per Serving

Serving size:
1 piece (2½ inches square)

Amount per serving:

Calories 299
Calories from fat 145

Total fat 16 gm
  Saturated fat 1 gm

Cholesterol 24 mg

Sodium 218 mg

Total carbohydrate 35 gm
  Dietary fiber 1 gm
  Sugars 15 gm

Protein 4 gm

Exchange List Approximations

Other carbohydrate 2½

Fat, monounsaturated 2½

1.   Preheat the oven to 375°F. Prepare an 8-inch-square baking pan with nonstick pan spray.

2.   Combine the flour, sugar, baking powder, salt, and cinnamon in a medium bowl; mix to blend. Stir in the orange juice, oil, and egg. Fold in the cranberries, walnuts, and orange zest.

3.   Pour the batter into the prepared pan. Bake for 25 to 30 minutes, until the top is firm and an inserted toothpick or knife comes out clean. Cool on a wire rack.

4.   Before serving, sift powdered sugar on top of the cake and cut it into nine 2¹/₂-inch squares.

MERINGUE COOKIES

These irresistible cookies are a melt-in-your-mouth treat, with only 2 grams of fat for a serving of three cookies. Meringues should be light, dry, and airy, so don't attempt to make them in damp weather. Too much moisture in the air ruins their texture.

3½ dozen (14 servings)

2 large egg whites
¼ teaspoon fresh lemon juice
¾ cup powdered sugar
Pinch of salt
⅓ cup finely chopped pecans or
     almonds

Nutrition Facts per Serving

Serving size: 3 cookies

Amount per serving:

Calories 46
Calories from fat 16

Total fat 2 gm
  Saturated fat 0 gm
Cholesterol 0 mg
Sodium 18 mg
Total carbohydrate 7 gm
  Dietary fiber 0 gm
  Sugars 6 gm
Protein 1 gm

Exchange List Approximation

Other carbohydrate ½

1.   Preheat the oven to 250°F. Line 2 cookie sheets with parchment paper or nonstick oven liner film.

2.   Put the egg whites and lemon juice in a chilled bowl. Beat with an electric mixer to a soft foam. Slowly beat in the sugar, mixing well after each addition. Continue beating at medium-high speed until stiff peaks form. Add the vanilla and salt. Gently fold in the nuts.

3.   Drop the batter by heaping teaspoons onto the cookie sheets. Shape with the back of a spoon into 1-inch circles. Bake until set and firm, about 1 hour. Turn off the oven but leave the cookies there until the oven is completely cool. Remove the cookies from the oven and store in an airtight container at room temperature.

ALMOST SHORTBREAD COOKIES

While not quite traditional shortbread, these cookies are delicious nonetheless, and low only in fat, not flavor. Refrigerating the dough helps make rolling out and cutting the cookies much easier.

2 dozen cookies (24 servings)

2 cups all-purpose flour
1½ teaspoons baking powder
½ cup corn or canola oil
1 large egg
2 tablespoons sugar
1 teaspoon pure vanilla extract

1.   Preheat the oven to 350°F. Prepare a cookie sheet with nonstick pan spray.
2.   Combine all the ingredients and ¼ cup water in a large bowl to form a soft dough. Refrigerate the dough 1 hour to chill. Roll or pat out ¼ inch thick on a floured board.
3.   Cut 2-inch rounds and place them 1 inch apart on the prepared cookie sheet. Bake for 15 to 20 minutes, until the edges are a light golden brown. Cool and store in an airtight container.

Nutrition Facts per Serving

Serving size: 1 cookie

Amount per serving:

Calories 90
Calories from fat 48

Total fat 5 gm
 Saturated fat 1 gm
Cholesterol 9 mg
Sodium 26 mg
Total carbohydrate 9 gm
 Dietary fiber 0 gm
 Sugars 1 gm
Protein 1 gm

Exchange List Approximations

Starch ½

Fat, polyunsaturated 1

OATMEAL RAISIN COOKIES

These cookies are perfectly chewy and just sweet enough. Soaking the raisins helps keep them moist and plump during baking. Drain them well before adding to the batter, though, so you don't add extra moisture. Be sure to use regular margarine. While fine for use as a spread, light or reduced-fat margarines don't work well for baking. These products have added water and/or air in them to reduce the fat content, so the cookies turn out flat and runny.

About 54 cookies (27 servings)

³⁄₄ cup (1½ sticks) margarine, at room
     temperature
½ cup packed brown sugar
½ cup granulated sugar
1 large egg, or ¼ cup egg substitute
1 teaspoon pure vanilla extract
1 cup all-purpose flour
1 teaspoon salt
½ teaspoon baking soda
½ cup raisins, soaked in water and
     well drained
3 cups rolled oats, quick-cooking
     or regular

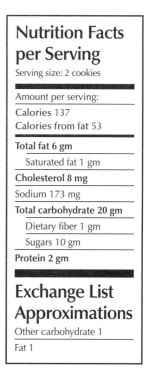

**Nutrition Facts
per Serving**

Serving size: 2 cookies

Amount per serving:

Calories 137
Calories from fat 53

Total fat 6 gm
  Saturated fat 1 gm

Cholesterol 8 mg

Sodium 173 mg

Total carbohydrate 20 gm
  Dietary fiber 1 gm
  Sugars 10 gm

Protein 2 gm

**Exchange List
Approximations**

Other carbohydrate 1

Fat 1

1. Preheat the oven to 350°F.
2. In a large bowl, beat together the margarine, sugars, egg, ¼ cup water, and vanilla until creamy.
3. Combine the flour, salt, and soda in a medium bowl. Add to the creamed mixture. Add the raisins and rolled oats. Mix well.
4. Drop by rounded teaspoonfuls on ungreased cookie sheets. Bake the cookies 12 to 15 minutes, or until set. Remove the cookies to wire cooling racks while still warm or they will stick to the pan. When they cool, store them in an airtight container.

CHOCOLATE CREAM PUFFS

A guaranteed crowd pleaser, these puffs may be made up to three days in advance if you store them in an airtight container. We've filled them with chocolate frozen yogurt and drizzled Bittersweet Chocolate Sauce on top, but you can fill them with just about anything you want. Try ripe berries, creamy custard, or pudding, and top with a dessert or fruit sauce of your choice. Just be sure to add in the appropriate exchanges for whatever filling you use.

4 puffs (4 servings)

PUFF SHELLS

2 tablespoons unsalted margarine
2 teaspoons sugar
Pinch of salt
¼ cup all-purpose flour
1 large egg

FILLING

1 cup chocolate low-fat frozen yogurt or
    chocolate ice cream

TOPPING

½ cup (½ recipe) Bittersweet Chocolate
    Sauce (page 424)

Nutrition Facts per Serving

Serving size: 1 filled puff with 2 tablespoons sauce

Amount per serving:

Calories 269
Calories from fat 123

Total fat 14 gm
  Saturated fat 5 gm
Cholesterol 58 mg
Sodium 85 mg
Total carbohydrate 34 gm
  Dietary fiber 2 gm
  Sugars 20 gm
Protein 6 gm

Exchange List Approximations

Other carbohydrate 2

Fat 2½

1.   Preheat the oven to 425°F. In a small saucepan, bring ¼ cup water, the margarine, sugar, and salt to a boil.

2.   Add the flour all at once, stirring vigorously over medium heat until the dough leaves the sides of the pan and forms a ball.

3.   Remove from the heat; allow to cool for 3 minutes. Beat in the egg.

4.   Drop the batter in 4 small mounds, about 1 rounded tablespoon each, on an ungreased cookie sheet. Bake for 12 minutes. Reduce the heat to 350°F. Continue baking for 10 to 12 minutes longer, or until the puffs are golden brown. Cool on a wire rack.

5.   Slice a thin cap off the top of each puff; remove any doughy filling if present. Fill each puff with ¼ cup frozen yogurt or ice cream. Replace the caps and drizzle 2 tablespoons of chocolate sauce over each puff. Serve immediately.

13

BEVERAGES

Beverages certainly help quench thirst, but whether ice cold or steaming hot, they can also serve as snacks, desserts, and accompaniments to meals. Except for water, coffee, tea, and diet sodas, you need to count the appropriate exchange or grams of carbohydrate for anything you drink, including juices, milk, and the beverages in this chapter. Like other foods, they contain ingredients that can affect blood glucose levels, so they need to be counted into meal plans.

All of the beverage recipes we've included are quick to fix. Kids and adults alike will love the frappes, shakes, and coolers, like fruity Strawberry Slush, Mango Frappe, and Root Beer Frosty. Breakfast on the Run is a liquid meal in itself, and perfect for the weekday morning rush. Or try Hot Mocha Dream or Spiced Tea to cap off an evening meal. Both are delicious alternatives to coffee. We think you'll agree—beverages can be much more than just a drink!

HOT MOCHA DREAM

Coffee and chocolate make a delicious combination, and this drink is perfect for an after-dinner treat. It's especially impressive served in tall glass mugs, each topped with a dollop of light whipped topping (2 tablespoons is considered a fat-free food). We used sugar-free cocoa mix in this recipe because sweetened mixes have varying amounts—and usually quite a lot—of sugar. If you prefer presweetened cocoa, add the carbohydrate listed on the ingredient label.

2 cups (2 servings)

1½ teaspoons instant coffee, regular or
    decaffeinated
1 tablespoon sugar-free cocoa mix
½ cinnamon stick
1 cup hot water
1 cup fat-free milk
1½ teaspoons pure vanilla extract
¼ cup light whipped cream or light
    whipped topping

1. In a small pot, combine the coffee, cocoa mix, cinnamon stick, and ¼ cup of the hot water. Bring to boil; cook for 1 minute.

2. Add the remaining hot water and the milk. Reheat to a simmer. Remove from the heat and stir in the vanilla extract. Remove the cinnamon stick.

3. Divide the hot mocha between 2 cups. Top each with 2 tablespoons light whipped cream or light whipped topping.

Nutrition Facts per Serving

Serving size: 1 cup

Amount per serving:

Calories 95
Calories from fat 20

Total fat 2 gm
   Saturated fat 1 gm

Cholesterol 9 mg

Sodium 162 mg

Total carbohydrate 12 gm
   Dietary fiber 0 gm
   Sugars 10 gm

Protein 6 gm

Exchange List Approximation

Milk, fat-free 1

SPICED TEA

Touches of cinnamon, cloves, nutmeg, and citrus perk up this tea, giving it a delightful spicy flavor. Serve hot or cold.

1 quart (4 servings)

1 cinnamon stick
2 whole cloves
1 long strip (4 inches) lemon peel
1 long strip (6 inches) orange peel
Pinch of nutmeg
3 tea bags

1. In a saucepan combine 1 quart water and all the ingredients except the tea. Simmer for 5 to 10 minutes.

2. Add the tea bags. Let steep to desired strength.

3. Serve hot, or chill for iced tea. Remove the cinnamon stick, cloves, and peels before serving.

Nutrition Facts per Serving
Serving size: 1 cup
Amount per serving:
Calories 3
Calories from fat 0
Total fat 0 gm
Saturated fat 0 gm
Cholesterol 0 mg
Sodium 7 mg
Total carbohydrate 1 gm
Dietary fiber 0 gm
Sugars 0 gm
Protein 0 gm

Exchange List Approximation

Free food

APPLE TEA COOLER

Apple juice adds a sweet, fruity flavor to tea, resulting in a refreshing drink that hits the spot on a warm summer day.

1 quart (4 servings)

2 cups unsweetened apple juice
2 cups strong tea
4 lemon wedges (optional)

1. In a quart pitcher, mix the apple juice and tea.
2. Serve over ice. Garnish each glass with a lemon wedge, if desired.

Nutrition Facts per Serving

Serving size: 1 cup

Amount per serving:

Calories 59
Calories from fat 1

Total fat 0 gm
  Saturated fat 0 gm
Cholesterol 0 mg
Sodium 7 mg
Total carbohydrate 15 gm
  Dietary fiber 0 gm
  Sugars 14 gm
Protein 0 gm

Exchange List Approximation

Fruit 1

BANANA SHAKE

This creamy shake takes just minutes to make and is ideal for a quick on-the-go breakfast or afternoon pick-me-up—with just 1 gram of fat. Experiment with other fruits for a change of flavor, substituting 1 cup of another fresh or frozen (no sugar added) fruit in place of the banana. Try pitted sweet Bing cherries, raspberries, strawberries, peaches, mango, or a combination of fruits.

2 cups (2 servings)

1 cup fat-free milk
½ cup vanilla low-fat frozen yogurt
1 small ripe banana, peeled
¼ teaspoon pure vanilla extract

1. Blend the milk and frozen yogurt in a blender or food processor about 1 minute.
2. Add the banana and vanilla; blend a few seconds longer.

Nutrition Facts per Serving

Serving size: 1 cup

Amount per serving:

Calories 130
Calories from fat 10

Total fat 1 gm
    Saturated fat 1 gm
Cholesterol 7 mg
Sodium 83 mg
Total carbohydrate 24 gm
    Dietary fiber 1 gm
    Sugars 17 gm
Protein 6 gm

Exchange List Approximations

Fruit 1

Milk, low-fat ½

BREAKFAST ON THE RUN

There's no excuse for not eating breakfast when a shake like this is so easy to fix. The yogurt and fat-free milk are great sources of calcium, while the wheat germ adds a delicate nutty flavor as well as some vitamin E, folate, zinc, and iron.

About 2½ cups (2 servings)

2 medium-size ripe bananas, peeled
1 cup fat-free milk
½ cup plain low-fat yogurt
¼ cup wheat germ
2 teaspoons pure vanilla extract
2 teaspoons sugar
Pinch of ground nutmeg (optional)

1. Slice the bananas and freeze overnight. (There should be about 1⅓ cups sliced bananas.)
2. Place the bananas and remaining ingredients in a blender and blend until smooth.

Nutrition Facts per Serving
Serving size: About 1¼ cups
Amount per serving:
Calories 241
Calories from fat 28
Total fat 3 gm
Saturated fat 1 gm
Cholesterol 7 mg
Sodium 108 mg
Total carbohydrate 45 gm
Dietary fiber 4 gm
Sugars 31 gm
Protein 13 gm

Exchange List Approximations
Starch 1
Fruit 1
Milk, skim 1

ROOT BEER FROSTY

Always a childhood favorite, this adult version of a root beer float is just as delicious as you remember—and fat-free!

2 cups (2 servings)

½ cup fat-free milk
6 ounces diet root beer
¼ cup vanilla low-fat frozen yogurt
¾ cup ice cubes
½ teaspoon pure vanilla extract

1. Place all the ingredients in a blender or food processor.
2. Blend 30 seconds, or until smooth.

Nutrition Facts per Serving

Serving size: 1 cup

Amount per serving:

Calories 49
Calories from fat 4

Total fat 0 gm
  Saturated fat 0 gm
Cholesterol 4 mg
Sodium 58 mg
Total carbohydrate 8 gm
  Dietary fiber 0 gm
  Sugars 6 gm
Protein 3 gm

Exchange List Approximation

Milk, fat-free ½

MANGO FRAPPE

Mangos are the star in this wonderfully sweet and fizzy frappe. Serve over ice in tall glasses and garnish each with a sprig of mint for a bit of color. If fresh mangos are not available, look for frozen mangos (no sugar added), available in some grocery stores.

3 cups (3 servings)

1 medium whole ripe mango
      (12 ounces), peeled and pitted
¾ cup orange juice
¼ cup lime juice
1¼ cups club soda
2 ice cubes

1. Purée the mango in a food processor or blender. Add the orange and lime juices; process until smooth.
2. Add the club soda and ice cubes; process just to blend and crush the ice. Serve at once.

Nutrition Facts per Serving

Serving size: 1 cup

Amount per serving:

Calories 83
Calories from fat 2

Total fat 0 gm
  Saturated fat 0 gm

Cholesterol 0 mg

Sodium 27 mg

Total carbohydrate 22 gm
  Dietary fiber 2 gm
  Sugars 18 gm

Protein 1 gm

Exchange List Approximation

Fruit 1½

GEORGIA PEACH COOLER

Make this sparkling cooler at the height of summer when plump ripe peaches are at their peak. If fresh peaches aren't available, you can substitute ½ to ¾ cup frozen peaches or a 6-ounce can of juice-packed sliced peaches, drained. Try fresh, ripe nectarines for variety, too.

2 cups (3 servings)

2 very ripe fresh peaches, peeled, pitted,
    and diced
¾ cup diet lemon/lime soda or diet
    ginger ale
½ cup ice cubes
1 teaspoon sugar
¼ teaspoon pure vanilla extract
3 sprigs fresh mint (optional)

1. Purée the peaches in a blender.

2. Add the remaining ingredients except the mint sprigs; blend until the ice is crushed.

3. Serve each portion garnished with a mint sprig, if desired.

Nutrition Facts per Serving

Serving size: ⅔ cup

Amount per serving:
Calories 43
Calories from fat 1

Total fat 0 gm
Saturated fat 0 gm
Cholesterol 0 mg
Sodium 11 mg
Total carbohydrate 11 gm
Dietary fiber 2 gm
Sugars 9 gm
Protein 1 gm

Exchange List Approximation

Fruit ½

STRAWBERRY SLUSH

Strawberry slush is a great afternoon refresher. Fresh strawberries are best, but you can also use unsweetened frozen berries, if necessary.

2 cups (3 servings)

1 pint ripe fresh strawberries, washed
     and hulled
2 tablespoons fresh lemon juice
2 tablespoons fresh lime juice
1 tablespoon sugar
$\frac{1}{4}$ cup club soda
$\frac{1}{2}$ to 1 cup ice cubes

1. Reserve 3 strawberries for garnish. Purée the remaining strawberries in a food processor or blender.

2. Add the remaining ingredients. Blend well until smooth and foamy.

3. Garnish each serving with a fresh strawberry.

Nutrition Facts per Serving

Serving size: $\frac{2}{3}$ cup

Amount per serving:

Calories 54
Calories from fat 4

Total fat 0 gm
   Saturated fat 0 gm

Cholesterol 0 mg

Sodium 8 mg

Total carbohydrate 13 gm
   Dietary fiber 3 gm
   Sugars 10 gm

Protein 1 gm

Exchange List Approximation

Fruit 1

STRAWBERRY-GRAPEFRUIT PUNCH

This punch is perfect for a summer afternoon gathering. The taste of ripe, sweet strawberries is balanced by tart grapefruit juice to create a refreshing beverage young and old alike will love.

2 quarts (8 servings)

One 10-ounce package frozen
     unsweetened strawberries
3 cups unsweetened grapefruit juice
1 liter (4¼ cups) club soda

1. Blend the strawberries and juice in a blender or food processor until smooth. Pour into a pitcher or punch bowl.
2. Slowly pour the club soda down the side of the container. Stir gently to mix. Serve immediately.

Nutrition Facts per Serving
Serving size: 1 cup
Amount per serving:
Calories 48
Calories from fat 1
Total fat 0 gm
Saturated fat 0 gm
Cholesterol 0 mg
Sodium 30 mg
Total carbohydrate 12 gm
Dietary fiber 1 gm
Sugars 8 gm
Protein 1 gm

Exchange List Approximation

Fruit 1

TOMATO COCKTAIL

Worcestershire sauce, celery seeds, and lemon juice add a well-seasoned kick that spices up plain tomato juice.

3 cups (4 servings)

3 cups tomato juice
2 tablespoons fresh lemon juice
$\frac{1}{2}$ teaspoon sugar
$\frac{1}{4}$ teaspoon seasoned salt
$\frac{1}{2}$ teaspoon Worcestershire sauce
$\frac{1}{8}$ teaspoon celery seeds
1 rib celery

1. Combine the juice and seasonings. Chill.
2. Slice the celery ribs into 4 sticks. Serve a celery stick as a "stirrer" in each tomato cocktail.

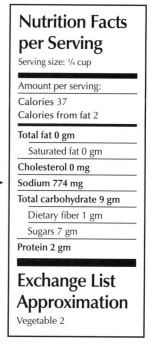

Nutrition Facts per Serving

Serving size: $\frac{3}{4}$ cup

Amount per serving:

Calories 37
Calories from fat 2

Total fat 0 gm
  Saturated fat 0 gm
Cholesterol 0 mg
Sodium 774 mg
Total carbohydrate 9 gm
  Dietary fiber 1 gm
  Sugars 7 gm
Protein 2 gm

Exchange List Approximation

Vegetable 2

14

Appendix: Exchange Lists for Meal Planning

What Are Exchange Lists?

Exchange lists are foods listed together because they are alike. Each serving of a food has about the same amount of carbohydrate, protein, fat, and calories as the other foods on that list. That is why any food on a list can be "exchanged" or traded for any other food on the same list. For example, you can trade the slice of bread you might eat for breakfast for one-half cup of cooked cereal. Each of these foods equals one starch choice. The charts that follow show the amount of nutrients in one serving from each list.

The lists are organized in three main groups—the Carbohydrate group, the Meat and Meat Substitute group (protein), and the Fat group. Starch, fruit, milk, other carbohydrates, and vegetables are in the Carbohydrate group. The Meat and Meat Substitute group is divided into very lean, lean, medium-fat, and high-fat foods. You can see at a glance which are the lower-fat choices. Foods in the Fat group—monounsaturated, polyunsaturated, and saturated—have very small serving sizes.

The exchange lists provide you with a lot of food choices (foods from the basic food groups, foods with added sugars, free foods, combination foods, and fast foods). This gives you variety in your meals. Several foods, such as dried beans and peas, bacon, and peanut butter, are on two lists. This gives you flexibility in putting your meals together. Whenever you choose new foods or vary your meal plan, monitor your blood glucose to see how these different foods affect your blood glucose level.

Most foods in the Carbohydrate group have about the same amount of carbohydrate per serving. You can exchange starch, fruit, or milk choices in your meal plan. Vegetables are in this group, but contain only about 5 grams of carbohydrate.

GROUPS/LISTS	CARB (grams)	PROTEIN (grams)	FAT (grams)	Calories
CARBOHYDRATE GROUP				
Starch	15	3	1 or less	80
Fruit	15	—	—	60
Milk				
Fat-free/low-fat	12	8	0–3	90
Reduced-fat	12	8	5	120
Whole	12	8	8	150
Other carbohydrates	15	varies	varies	varies
Vegetables	5	2	—	25
MEAT AND MEAT SUBSTITUTE GROUP				
Very lean	—	7	0–1	35
Lean	—	7	3	55
Medium-fat	—	7	5	75
High-fat	—	7	8	100
FAT GROUP	—	—	5	45
(Monounsaturated)				
(Polyunsaturated)				
(Saturated)				

Carbohydrate Group

Starch List

Cereals, grains, pasta, breads, crackers, snacks, starchy vegetables, and cooked dried beans, peas, and lentils are starches. In general, one starch is:

- ½ cup of cereal, grain, pasta, or starchy vegetable
- 1 ounce of a bread product, such as 1 slice of bread
- ¾ to 1 ounce of most snack foods (Some snack foods may also have added fat.)

Nutrition Tips

1. Most starch choices are good sources of B vitamins.
2. Foods made from whole grains are good sources of fiber.
3. Dried beans and peas are a good source of protein and fiber.

Selection Tips

1. Choose starches made with little fat as often as you can.
2. Starchy vegetables prepared with fat count as one starch and one fat.
3. Bagels or muffins can be 2, 3, or 4 ounces in size, and can, therefore, count as 2, 3, or 4 starch choices. Check the size you eat.
4. Dried beans, peas, and lentils are also found on the Meat and Meat Substitutes list.
5. Regular potato chips and tortilla chips are found on the Other Carbohydrates list.
6. Most of the serving sizes are measured after cooking.
7. Always check Nutrition Facts on the food label.

Some food you buy uncooked will weigh less after you cook it. Starches often swell in cooking, so a small amount of uncooked starch will become a much larger amount of cooked food. The following table shows some of the changes.

FOOD (STARCHES)	Uncooked	Cooked
Oatmeal	3 tbsp	½ cup
Cream of Wheat	2 tbsp	½ cup
Grits	3 tbsp	½ cup
Rice	2 tbsp	⅓ cup
Spaghetti	¼ cup	½ cup
Noodles	⅓ cup	½ cup
Macaroni	¼ cup	½ cup
Dried beans	¼ cup	½ cup
Dried peas	¼ cup	½ cup
Lentils	3 tbsp	½ cup

One starch exchange equals 15 grams carbohydrate,
3 grams protein, 0–1 grams fat, and 80 calories.

BREAD

Bagel	½ bagel (1 oz)
Bread, reduced-calorie	2 slices (1½ oz)
Bread, white, whole-wheat, pumpernickel, rye	1 slice (1 oz)
Bread sticks, crisp, 4 x ½ in.	2 (⅔ oz)
English muffin	½
Hot dog or hamburger bun	½ (1 oz)
Pita, 6 in. across	½
Raisin bread, unfrosted	1 slice (1 oz)
Roll, plain, small	1 (1 oz)
Tortilla, corn, 6 in. across	1
Tortilla, flour, 6 in. across	1
Waffle, 4½ in. square, reduced-fat	1

CEREALS AND GRAINS

Bran cereals	½ cup
Bulgur	½ cup
Cereals	½ cup
Cereals, unsweetened, ready-to-eat	¾ cup
Cornmeal (dry)	3 tbsp
Couscous	⅓ cup
Flour (dry)	3 tbsp
Granola, low-fat	¼ cup
Grape-Nuts	¼ cup
Grits	½ cup
Kasha	½ cup
Millet	¼ cup
Muesli	¼ cup
Oats	½ cup
Pasta	½ cup
Puffed cereal	1½ cups

CEREALS AND GRAINS *(cont.)*

Rice milk	½ cup
Rice, white or brown	⅓ cup
Shredded Wheat	½ cup
Sugar-frosted cereal	½ cup
Wheat germ	3 tbsp

STARCHY VEGETABLES

Baked beans	⅓ cup
Corn	½ cup
Corn on cob, medium	1 (5 oz)
Mixed vegetables with corn, peas, or pasta	1 cup
Peas, green	½ cup
Plantain	½ cup
Potato, baked or boiled, small	1 (3 oz)
Potato, mashed	½ cup
Squash, winter (acorn, butternut)	1 cup
Yam, sweet potato, plain	½ cup

CRACKERS AND SNACKS

Animal crackers	8
Graham crackers, 2½ in. square	3
Matzoh	¾ oz
Melba toast	4 slices
Oyster crackers	24
Popcorn (popped, no fat added or low-fat microwave)	3 cups
Pretzels	¾ oz
Rice cakes, 4 in. across	2
Saltine-type crackers	6
Snack chips, fat-free (tortilla, potato)	15–20 (¾ oz)
Whole wheat crackers, no fat added	2–5 (¾ oz)

BEANS, PEAS, AND LENTILS

Count as 1 starch exchange, plus 1 very lean meat exchange

Beans and peas (garbanzo, pinto, kidney, white, split, black-eyed)	½ cup
Lima beans	⅔ cup
Lentils	½ cup
Miso*	3 tbsp

* = 400 mg or more of sodium per exchange.

STARCHY FOODS PREPARED WITH FAT

Count as 1 starch exchange, plus 1 fat exchange

Biscuit, 2½ in. across	1
Chow mein noodles	½ cup
Corn bread, 2 in. cube	1 (2 oz)
Crackers, round butter type	6
Croutons	1 cup
French-fried potatoes	16–25 (3 oz)
Granola	¼ cup
Muffin, small	1 (1½ oz)
Pancake, 4 in. across	2
Popcorn, microwave	3 cups
Sandwich crackers, cheese or peanut butter filling	3
Stuffing, bread (prepared)	⅓ cup
Taco shell, 6 in. across	2
Waffle, 4½ in. square	1
Whole wheat crackers, fat added	4–6 (1 oz)

Fruit List

Fresh, frozen, canned, and dried fruits and fruit juices are on this list. In general, one fruit exchange is:
- 1 small to medium fresh fruit
- ½ cup of canned or fresh fruit or fruit juice
- ¼ cup of dried fruit

Nutrition Tips

1. Fresh, frozen, and dried fruits have about 2 grams of fiber per choice. Fruit juices contain very little fiber.
2. Citrus fruits, berries, and melons are good sources of vitamin C.

Selection Tips

1. Count ½ cup cranberries or rhubarb sweetened with sugar substitutes as free foods.
2. Read the Nutrition Facts on the food label. If one serving has more than 15 grams of carbohydrate, you will need to adjust the size of the serving you eat or drink.
3. Portion sizes for canned fruits are for the fruit and a small amount of juice.
4. Whole fruit is more filling than fruit juice and may be a better choice.
5. Food labels for fruits may contain the words "no sugar added" or "unsweetened." This means that no sucrose (table sugar) has been added.
6. Generally, fruit canned in extra-light syrup has the same amount of carbohydrate per serving as the "no sugar added" or the juice pack. All canned fruits on the fruit list are based on one of these three types of pack.

One fruit exchange equals 15 grams carbohydrate and 60 calories.
The weight includes skin, core, seeds, and rind.

FRUIT

Apple, unpeeled, small	1 (4 oz)
Applesauce, unsweetened	½ cup
Apples, dried	4 rings
Apricots, fresh	4 whole (5½ oz)
Apricots, dried	8 halves
Apricots, canned	½ cup
Banana, small	1 (4 oz)
Blackberries	¾ cup
Blueberries	¾ cup
Cantaloupe, small	⅓ melon (11 oz) or 1 cup cubes

Cherries, sweet, fresh	12 (3 oz)
Cherries, sweet, canned	½ cup
Dates	3
Figs, dried	1½
Figs, fresh	2 medium or 1½ large (3½ oz)
Fruit cocktail	½ cup
Grapefruit, large	½ (11 oz)
Grapefruit sections, canned	¾ cup
Grapes, small	17 (3 oz)
Honeydew melon	1 slice (10 oz) or 1 cup cubes
Kiwi	1 (3½ oz)
Mandarin oranges, canned	¾ cup
Mango, small	½ fruit (5½ oz) or ½ cup cubes
Nectarine, small	1 (5 oz)
Orange, small	1 (6½ oz)
Papaya	½ fruit (8 oz) or 1 cup cubes
Peach, medium, fresh	1 (6 oz)
Peaches, canned	½ cup
Pear, large, fresh	½ (4 oz)
Pears, canned	½ cup
Pineapple, canned	½ cup
Pineapple, fresh	¾ cup
Plums, canned	½ cup
Plums, small	2 (5 oz)
Prunes, dried	3
Raisins	2 tbsp
Raspberries	1 cup
Strawberries	1¼ cups whole berries
Tangerines, small	2 (8 oz)
Watermelon	1 slice (13½ oz) or 1¼ cups cubes

FRUIT JUICE

Apple juice/cider	½ cup
Cranberry juice cocktail	⅓ cup
Cranberry juice cocktail, reduced-calorie	1 cup
Fruit juice blends, 100% juice	⅓ cup
Grape juice	⅓ cup
Grapefruit juice	½ cup
Orange juice	½ cup
Pineapple juice	½ cup
Prune juice	⅓ cup

Milk List

Different types of milk and milk products are on this list. Cheeses are on the Meat list, and cream and other dairy fats are on the Fat list. Based on the amount of fat they contain, milks are divided into fat-free/low-fat milk, reduced-fat milk, and whole milk. One choice of these includes:

	CARB (grams)	PROTEIN (grams)	FAT (grams)	Calories
Fat-free/low-fat	12	8	0–3	90
Reduced-fat	12	8	5	120
Whole	12	8	8	150

Nutrition Tips

1. Milk and yogurt are good sources of calcium and protein. Check the food label.
2. The higher the fat content of milk and yogurt, the greater the amount of saturated fat and cholesterol. Choose lower-fat varieties.
3. Those who are lactose-intolerant should look for lactose-reduced or lactose-free varieties of milk.

Selection Tips

1. One cup equals 8 fluid ounces or ½ pint.
2. Look for chocolate milk, frozen yogurt, and ice cream on the Other Carbohydrates list.
3. Nondairy creamers are on the Free Foods list.
4. Look for rice milk on the Starch list.
5. Look for soy milk on the Medium-fat Meat list.

One milk exchange equals 12 grams carbohydrate
and 8 grams protein.

FAT-FREE AND LOW-FAT MILK

(0–3 grams fat per serving)

Fat-free milk	1 cup
Low-fat (½%) milk	1 cup
Low-fat (1%) milk	1 cup
Nonfat or low-fat buttermilk	1 cup
Fat-free evaporated milk	½ cup
Nonfat dry milk	⅓ cup dry
Plain nonfat yogurt	¾ cup
Nonfat or low-fat fruit-flavored yogurt sweetened with aspartame or with a nonnutritive sweetener	1 cup

REDUCED-FAT MILK

(5 grams fat per serving)

Reduced-fat (2%) milk	1 cup
Plain low-fat yogurt	¾ cup
Sweet acidophilus milk	1 cup

WHOLE MILK

(8 grams fat per serving)

Whole milk	1 cup
Whole evaporated milk	½ cup
Goat's milk	1 cup
Kefir	1 cup

Other Carbohydrates List

You can substitute food choices from this list for a starch, fruit, or milk choice on your meal plan. Some choices will also count as one or more fat choices.

Nutrition Tips

1. These foods can be substituted in your meal plan even though they contain added sugars or fat. However, they do not contain as many important vitamins and minerals as the choices on the Starch, Fruit, and Milk lists.
2. When planning to include these foods in your meal, be sure to include foods from all the lists to eat a balanced meal.

Selection Tips

1. Because many of these foods are concentrated sources of carbohydrate and fat, the portion sizes are often very small.
2. Always check Nutrition Facts on the food label. It will be your most accurate source of information.
3. Many fat-free or reduced-fat products made with fat replacers contain carbohydrate. When eaten in large amounts, they may need to be counted. Talk with your dietitian to determine how to count these in your meal plan.
4. Look for fat-free salad dressings in smaller amounts on the Free Foods list.

One other-carbohydrates exchange equals 15 grams carbohydrate, or 1 starch, or 1 fruit, or 1 milk.

OTHER CARBOHYDRATES

Angel food cake, unfrosted
  Serving size: 1/12 cake
  Exchanges per serving: 2 carb
Brownie, small, unfrosted
  Serving size: 2 in. square
  Exchanges per serving: 1 carb, 1 fat
Cake, unfrosted
  Serving size: 2 in. square
  Exchanges per serving: 1 carb, 1 fat
Cake, frosted
  Serving size: 2 in. square
  Exchanges per serving: 2 carb, 1 fat
Cookie, fat-free
  Serving size: 2 small
  Exchanges per serving: 1 carb
Cookie or sandwich cookie with cream filling
  Serving size: 2 small
  Exchanges per serving: 1 carb, 1 fat
Cranberry sauce, jellied
  Serving size: 1/4 cup
  Exchanges per serving: 1 1/2 carb
Cupcake, frosted
  Serving size: 1 small
  Exchanges per serving: 2 carb, 1 fat
Doughnut, plain cake
  Serving size: 1 medium (1 1/2 oz)
  Exchanges per serving: 1 1/2 carb, 2 fat
Doughnut, glazed
  Serving size: 3 3/4 in. across (2 oz)
  Exchanges per serving: 2 carb, 2 fat
Fruit juice bars, frozen, 100% juice
  Serving size: 1 bar (3 oz)
  Exchanges per serving: 1 carb

Fruit snacks, chewy (puréed fruit concentrate)
Serving size: 1 roll (³/₄ oz)
Exchanges per serving: 1 carb

Fruit spreads, 100% fruit
Serving size: 1 tbsp
Exchanges per serving: 1 carb

Gelatin, regular
Serving size: ¹/₂ cup
Exchanges per serving: 1 carb

Gingersnaps
Serving size: 3
Exchanges per serving: 1 carb

Granola bar
Serving size: 1 bar
Exchanges per serving: 1 carb, 1 fat

Granola bar, fat-free
Serving size: 1 bar
Exchanges per serving: 2 carb

Honey
Serving size: 1 tbsp
Exchanges per serving: 1 carb

Hummus
Serving size: ¹/₃ cup
Exchanges per serving: 1 carb, 1 fat

Ice cream
Serving size: ¹/₂ cup
Exchanges per serving: 1 carb, 2 fat

Ice cream, light
Serving size: ¹/₂ cup
Exchanges per serving: 1 carb, 1 fat

Ice cream, fat-free, no sugar added
Serving size: ¹/₂ cup
Exchanges per serving: 1 carb

Jam or jelly, regular
Serving size: 1 tbsp
Exchanges per serving: 1 carb

Milk, chocolate, whole
Serving size: 1 cup
Exchanges per serving: 2 carb, 1 fat

Pie, fruit, 2 crusts
  Serving size: 1/6 pie
  Exchanges per serving: 3 carb, 2 fat
Pie, pumpkin or custard
  Serving size: 1/8 pie
  Exchanges per serving: 2 carb, 2 fat
Potato chips
  Serving size: 12–18 (1 oz)
  Exchanges per serving: 1 carb, 2 fat
Pudding, regular (made with low-fat milk)
  Serving size: 1/2 cup
  Exchanges per serving: 2 carb
Pudding, sugar-free (made with low-fat milk)
  Serving size: 1/2 cup
  Exchanges per serving: 1 carb
Salad dressing, fat-free*
  Serving size: 1/4 cup
  Exchanges per serving: 1 carb
Sherbet, sorbet
  Serving size: 1/2 cup
  Exchanges per serving: 2 carb
Spaghetti or pasta sauce, canned*
  Serving size: 1/2 cup
  Exchanges per serving: 1 carb, 1 fat
Sugar
  Serving size: 1 tbsp
  Exchanges per serving: 1 carb
Sweet roll or Danish
  Serving size: 1 (2 1/2 oz)
  Exchanges per serving: 2 1/2 carb, 2 fat
Syrup, light
  Serving size: 2 tbsp
  Exchanges per serving: 1 carb
Syrup, regular
  Serving size: 1 tbsp
  Exchanges per serving: 1 carb
Syrup, regular
  Serving size: 1/4 cup
  Exchanges per serving: 4 carb

Tortilla chips
  Serving size: 6–12 (1 oz)
  Exchanges per serving: 1 carb, 2 fat
Vanilla wafers
  Serving size: 5
  Exchanges per serving: 1 carb, 1 fat
Yogurt, frozen, low-fat, fat-free
  Serving size: 1/3 cup
  Exchanges per serving: 1 carb, 0–1 fat
Yogurt, frozen, fat-free, no sugar added
  Serving size: 1/2 cup
  Exchanges per serving: 1 carb
Yogurt, low-fat with fruit
  Serving size: 1 cup
  Exchanges per serving: 3 carb, 0–1 fat

* = 400 mg or more of sodium per exchange.

Vegetable Group

Vegetables that contain small amounts of carbohydrates and calories are on this list. Vegetables contain important nutrients. Try to eat at least 2 or 3 vegetable choices each day. In general, one vegetable exchange is:

- ½ cup of cooked vegetables or vegetable juice
- 1 cup of raw vegetables.

If you eat 1 or 2 vegetable choices at a meal or snack, you do not have to count the calories or carbohydrates because they contain small amounts of these nutrients.

Nutrition Tips
1. Fresh and frozen vegetables have less added salt than canned vegetables. Drain and rinse canned vegetables if you want to remove some salt.
2. Choose more dark green and dark yellow vegetables, such as spinach, broccoli, romaine, carrots, chiles, and peppers.
3. Broccoli, Brussels sprouts, cauliflower, greens, peppers, spinach, and tomatoes are good sources of vitamin C.
4. Vegetables contain 1 to 4 grams of fiber per serving.

Selection Tips

1. A 1-cup portion of broccoli is a portion about the size of a light bulb.
2. Tomato sauce is different from spaghetti sauce, which is on the Other Carbohydrates list.
3. Canned vegetables and juices are available without added salt.
4. If you eat more than 4 cups of raw vegetables or 2 cups of cooked vegetables at one meal, count them as 1 carbohydrate choice.
5. Starchy vegetables such as corn, peas, winter squash, and potatoes that contain larger amounts of calories and carbohydrates are on the Starch list.

One vegetable exchange equals 5 grams carbohydrate, 2 grams protein, 0 grams fat, and 25 calories.

Artichoke

Artichoke hearts

Asparagus

Beans (green, wax, Italian)

Bean sprouts

Beets

Broccoli

Brussels sprouts

Cabbage

Carrots

Cauliflower

Celery

Cucumber

Eggplant

Green onions, or scallions

Greens (collard, kale, mustard, turnip)

Kohlrabi

Leeks

Mixed vegetables (without corn, peas, or pasta)

Mushrooms

Okra

Onions

Pea pods

Peppers (all varieties)

Radishes

Salad greens (endive, escarole, lettuce, romaine, spinach)

Sauerkraut*

Spinach

Summer squash

Tomato

Tomatoes, canned

Tomato sauce*

Tomato/vegetable juice*

Turnips

Water chestnuts

Watercress

Zucchini

* = 400 mg or more sodium per exchange.

Meat and Meat Substitutes Group

Meat and meat substitutes that contain both protein and fat are on this list. In general, one meat exchange is:

- 1 oz meat, fish, poultry, or cheese
- 1/2 cup beans, peas, or lentils

Based on the amount of fat they contain, meats are divided into very lean, lean, medium-fat, and high-fat lists. This is done so you can see which ones contain the least fat. One ounce (one exchange) of each of these includes:

	CARB (grams)	PROTEIN (grams)	FAT (grams)	Calories
Very lean	0	7	0–1	35
Lean	0	7	3	55
Medium-fat	0	7	5	75
High-fat	0	7	8	100

Nutrition Tips

1. Choose very lean and lean meat choices whenever possible. Items from the high-fat group are high in saturated fat, cholesterol, and calories and can raise blood cholesterol levels.
2. Meats do not have any fiber.
3. Dried beans, peas, and lentils are good sources of fiber.
4. Some processed meats, seafood, and soy products may contain carbohydrate when consumed in large amounts. Check the Nutrition Facts on the label to see if the amount is close to 15 grams. If so, count it as a carbohydrate choice as well as a meat choice.

Selection Tips

1. Weigh meat after cooking and removing bones and fat. Four ounces of raw meat is equal to 3 ounces of cooked meat. Some examples of meat portions are:

- 1 ounce cheese = 1 meat choice and is about the size of a 1-inch cube
- 12 ounces meat = 2 meat choices, such as
    1 small chicken leg or thigh
    1/2 cup cottage cheese or tuna

- 3 ounces meat = 3 meat choices and is about the size of a deck of cards, such as

    1 medium pork chop

    1 small hamburger

    ½ of a whole chicken breast

    1 unbreaded fish fillet

2. Limit your choices from the high-fat group to three times per week or less.

3. Most grocery stores stock Select and Choice grades of meat. Select grades of meat are the leanest. Choice grades contain a moderate amount of fat, and Prime cuts of meat have the highest amount of fat.

4. Restaurants usually serve Prime cuts of meat.

5. "Hamburger" may contain added seasoning and fat, but ground beef does not.

6. Read labels to find products that are low in fat and cholesterol (5 grams or less of fat per serving).

7. Dried beans, peas, and lentils are also found on the Starch list.

8. Peanut butter, in smaller amounts, is also found on the Fats list.

9. Bacon, in smaller amounts, is also found on the Fats list.

Meal-Planning Tips

1. Bake, roast, broil, grill, poach, steam, or boil these foods rather than frying them.

2. Place meat on a rack so the fat will drain off during cooking.

3. Use nonstick spray and a nonstick pan to brown or fry foods.

4. Trim off visible fat before or after cooking.

5. If you add flour, bread crumbs, coating mixes, fat, or marinades when cooking, ask your dietitian how to count them in your meal plan.

Very Lean Meat and Substitutes List

One very-lean-meat exchange equals 0 grams carbohydrate,
7 grams protein, 0–1 grams fat, and 35 calories.

One very lean meat exchange is equal to any one of the following items.

Poultry: Chicken or turkey (white meat, no skin), Cornish hen (no skin)	1 oz
Fish: Fresh or frozen cod, flounder, haddock, halibut, trout; tuna, fresh or canned in water	1 oz
Shellfish: Clams, crab, lobster, scallops, shrimp, imitation shellfish	1 oz
Game: Duck or pheasant (no skin), venison, buffalo, ostrich	1 oz
Cheese with 1 gram or less fat per ounce:	
Nonfat or low-fat cottage cheese	¼ cup
Fat-free cheese	1 oz
Other:	
Processed sandwich meats with 1 gram or less fat per ounce, such as deli thin, shaved meats, chipped beef,* turkey ham	1 oz
Egg whites	2
Egg substitutes, plain	¼ cup
Hot dogs with 1 gram or less fat per ounce[z]	1 oz
Kidney (high in cholesterol)	1 oz
Sausage with 1 gram or less fat per ounce	1 oz

Count the following as one very lean meat and one starch exchange:

Beans, peas, lentils (cooked)	½ cup

* = 400 mg or more sodium per exchange.

Lean Meat and Substitutes List

One lean-meat exchange equals 0 grams carbohydrate,
7 grams protein, 3 grams fat, and 55 calories.

One lean meat exchange is equal to any one of the following items.

Beef: USDA Select or Choice grades of lean beef trimmed of fat, such as round, sirloin, and flank steak; tenderloin; roast (rib, chuck, rump); steak (T-bone, porterhouse, cubed), ground round	1 oz
Pork: Lean pork, such as fresh ham; canned, cured, or boiled ham; Canadian bacon;* tenderloin, center loin chop	1 oz
Lamb: Roast, chop, leg	1 oz
Veal: Lean chop, roast	1 oz
Poultry: Chicken, turkey (dark meat, no skin), chicken white meat (with skin), domestic duck or goose (well-drained of fat, no skin)	1 oz
Fish:	
Herring (uncreamed or smoked)	1 oz
Oysters	6 medium
Salmon (fresh or canned), catfish	1 oz
Sardines (canned)	2 medium
Tuna (canned in oil, drained)	1 oz
Game: Goose (no skin), rabbit	1 oz
Cheese:	
4.5%-fat cottage cheese	¼ cup
Grated Parmesan	2 tbsp
Cheeses with 3 grams or less fat per ounce	1 oz
Other:	
Hot dogs with 3 grams or less fat per ounce*	1½ oz
Processed sandwich meat with 3 grams or less fat per ounce, such as turkey pastrami or kielbasa	1 oz
Liver, heart (high in cholesterol)	1 oz

* = 400 mg or more sodium per exchange.

Medium-Fat Meat and Substitutes List

**One medium-fat-meat exchange equals 0 grams carbohydrate,
7 grams protein, 5 grams fat, and 75 calories.**

One medium-fat meat exchange is equal to any one of the following items.

Beef: Most beef products fall into this category (ground beef, meat loaf, corned beef, short ribs, Prime grades of meat trimmed of fat, such as prime rib)	1 oz
Pork: Top loin, chop, Boston butt, cutlet	1 oz
Lamb: Rib roast, ground	1 oz
Veal: Cutlet (ground or cubed, unbreaded)	1 oz
Poultry: Chicken (dark meat, with skin), ground turkey or ground chicken, fried chicken (with skin)	1 oz
Fish: Any fried fish product	1 oz
Cheese with 5 grams or less fat per ounce:	
Feta	1 oz
Mozzarella	1 oz
Ricotta	1/4 cup (2 oz)
Other:	
Egg (high in cholesterol, limit to 3 per week)	1
Sausage with 5 grams or less fat per ounce	1 oz
Soy milk	1 cup
Tempeh	1/4 cup
Tofu	4 oz or 1/2 cup

High-Fat Meat and Substitutes List

One high-fat-meat exchange equals 0 grams carbohydrate,
7 grams protein, 8 grams fat, and 100 calories.

Remember, these items are high in saturated fat, cholesterol, and calories and may raise blood cholesterol levels if eaten on a regular basis. One high-fat meat exchange is equal to any one of the following items.

Pork: Spareribs, ground pork, pork sausage	1 oz
Cheese: All regular cheeses, such as American,* Cheddar, Monterey Jack, Swiss	1 oz
Other:	
Processed sandwich meats with 8 grams or less fat per ounce, such as bologna, pimiento loaf, salami	1 oz
Sausage, such as bratwurst, Italian, knockwurst, Polish, smoked	1 oz
Hot dog (turkey or chicken)*	1 (10/lb)
Bacon	3 slices (20 slices/lb)

Count the following as one high-fat meat plus one fat exchange:

Hot dog (beef, pork, or combination)*	1 (10/lb)

Count the following as one high-fat meat plus two fat exchanges.

Peanut butter (contains unsaturated fat)	2 tbsp

* = 400 mg or more sodium per exchange.

Fat Group

Fats are divided into three groups, based on the main type of fat they contain: monounsaturated, polyunsaturated, and saturated. Small amounts of monounsaturated and polyunsaturated fats in the foods we eat are linked with good health benefits. Saturated fats are linked with heart disease and cancer. In general, one fat exchange is:

- 1 teaspoon of regular margarine or vegetable oil
- 1 tablespoon of regular salad dressings

Nutrition Tips

1. All fats are high in calories. Limit serving sizes for good nutrition and health.
2. Nuts and seeds contain small amounts of fiber, protein, and magnesium.
3. If blood pressure is a concern, choose fats in the unsalted form to help lower sodium intake, such as unsalted peanuts.

Selection Tips

1. Check the Nutrition Facts on food labels for serving sizes. One fat exchange is based on a serving size containing 5 grams of fat.
2. When selecting regular margarine, choose those with liquid vegetable oil as the first ingredient. Soft margarines are not as saturated as stick margarines, so they are healthier choices. Avoid those listing hydrogenated or partially hydrogenated fat as the first ingredient.
3. When selecting low-fat margarines, look for liquid vegetable oil as the second ingredient. Water is usually the first ingredient.
4. When used in smaller amounts, bacon and peanut butter are counted as fat choices. When used in larger amounts, they are counted as high-fat meat choices.
5. Fat-free salad dressings are on the Other Carbohydrates list and the Free Foods list.
6. See the Free Foods list for nondairy coffee creamers, whipped topping, and fat-free products such as margarines, salad dressings, mayonnaise, sour cream, cream cheese, and nonstick cooking spray.

Monounsaturated Fats List

One fat exchange equals 5 grams fat and 45 calories.

Avocado, medium	1/8 (1 oz)
Oil (canola, olive, peanut)	1 tsp
Olives:	
Ripe (black)	8 large
Green, stuffed*	10 large
Nuts:	
Almonds, cashews	6 nuts
Mixed (50% peanuts)	6 nuts
Peanuts	10 nuts
Pecans	4 halves
Peanut butter, smooth or crunchy	2 tsp
Sesame seeds	1 tbsp
Tahini paste	2 tsp

Polyunsaturated Fats List

One fat exchange equals 5 grams fat and 45 calories.

Margarine:	
Stick, tub, or squeeze	1 tsp
Lower-fat (30% to 50% vegetable oil)	1 tbsp
Mayonnaise:	
Regular	1 tsp
Reduced-fat	1 tbsp
Nuts, walnuts, English	4 halves
Oil (corn, safflower, soybean)	1 tsp
Salad dressing:	
Regular*	1 tbsp
Reduced-fat	2 tbsp
Miracle Whip salad dressing:	
Regular	2 tsp
Reduced-fat	1 tbsp
Seeds (pumpkin, sunflower)	1 tbsp

* = 400 mg or more sodium per exchange.

Saturated-Fats List
One fat exchange equals 5 grams fat and 45 calories.

Remember that these items are high in saturated fat and may raise blood cholesterol levels if eaten on a regular basis.

Bacon, cooked	1 slice (20 slices/lb)
Bacon, grease	1 tsp
Butter:	
Stick	1 tsp
Whipped	2 tsp
Reduced-fat	1 tbsp
Chitterlings, boiled	2 tbsp (½ oz)
Coconut, sweetened, shredded	2 tbsp
Cream, half-and-half	2 tbsp
Cream cheese:	
Regular	1 tbsp (½ oz)
Reduced-fat	2 tbsp (1 oz)
Fatback or salt pork, see below*	
Shortening or lard	1 tsp
Sour cream:	
Regular	2 tbsp
Reduced-fat	3 tbsp

*Use a piece 1 x 1 x ¼ in. if you plan to eat the fatback cooked with vegetables. Use a piece 2 x 1 x ½ in. when eating only the vegetables with the fatback removed.

Free-Foods List

A free food is any food or drink that contains less than 20 calories or less than 5 grams of carbohydrate per serving. Foods with a serving size listed should be limited to three servings per day. Be sure to spread them out throughout the day. If you eat all three servings at one time, it could affect your blood glucose level. Foods listed without a serving size can be eaten as often as you like.

Fat-Free or Reduced-Fat Foods

Cream cheese, fat-free	1 tbsp
Creamers, nondairy, liquid	1 tbsp
Creamers, nondairy, powdered	2 tsp
Margarine, fat-free	4 tbsp
Margarine, reduced-fat	1 tsp
Mayonnaise, fat-free	1 tbsp
Mayonnaise, reduced-fat	1 tsp
Miracle Whip, nonfat	1 tbsp
Miracle Whip, reduced-fat	1 tsp
Nonstick cooking spray	
Salad dressing, fat-free	1 tbsp
Salad dressing, fat-free, Italian	2 tbsp
Salsa	1/4 cup
Sour cream, fat-free, reduced-fat	1 tbsp
Whipped topping, regular or light	2 tbsp

Sugar-Free or Low-Sugar Foods

Candy, hard, sugar-free	1 candy
Gelatin dessert, sugar-free	
Gelatin, unflavored	
Gum, sugar-free	
Jam or jelly, low-sugar or light	2 tsp
Sugar substitutes*	
Syrup, sugar-free	2 tbsp

* Sugar substitutes, alternatives, or replacements that are approved by the Food and Drug Administration (FDA) are safe to use. Common brand names include: Equal (aspartame), Sprinkle Sweet (saccharin), Sweet One (acesulfame K), Sweet-10 (saccharin), Sugar Twin (saccharin), or Sweet 'n Low (saccharin).

Drinks

Bouillon, broth, consommé*	
Bouillon or broth, low-sodium	
Carbonated or mineral water	
Club soda	
Cocoa powder, unsweetened	1 tbsp
Coffee	
Diet soft drinks, sugar-free	
Drink mixes, sugar-free	
Tea	
Tonic water, sugar-free	

* = 400 mg or more of sodium per choice.

Condiments

Catsup	1 tbsp
Horseradish	
Lemon juice	
Lime juice	
Mustard	
Pickles, dill*	1½ large
Soy sauce, regular or light*	
Taco sauce	1 tbsp
Vinegar	

* = 400 mg or more of sodium per choice.

Seasonings

Be careful with seasonings that contain sodium or are salts, such as garlic or celery salt and lemon pepper.

Flavoring extracts
Garlic
Herbs, fresh or dried
Pimiento
Spices
Tabasco or hot pepper sauce
Wine, used in cooking
Worcestershire sauce

Combination Foods List

Many of the foods we eat are mixed together in various combinations. These combination foods do not fit into any one exchange list. Often it is hard to tell what is in a casserole dish or prepared food item. This is a list of exchanges for some typical combination foods to help you fit these foods into your meal plan. Ask your dietitian for information about any other combination foods you would like to eat.

Entrées

Tuna noodle casserole, lasagna, spaghetti with meatballs, chili with beans, macaroni and cheese*
   Serving size: 1 cup (8 oz)
   Exchanges per serving: 2 carb, 2 med-fat meat
Chow mein (without noodles or rice)*
   Serving size: 2 cups (16 oz)
   Exchanges per serving: 1 carb, 2 lean meat
Pizza, cheese, thin crust*
   Serving size: ¼ of 10 in. (5 oz)
   Exchanges per serving: 2 carb, 2 med-fat meat, 1 fat
Pizza, meat topping, thin crust*
   Serving size: ¼ of 10 in. (5 oz)
   Exchanges per serving: 2 carb, 2 med-fat meat, 2 fat
Pot pie*
   Serving size: 1 (7 oz)
   Exchanges per serving: 2 carb, 1 med-fat meat, 4 fat

* = 400 mg or more sodium per exchange.

Frozen Entrées

Salisbury steak with gravy, mashed potato*
Serving size: 1 (11 oz)
Exchanges per serving: 2 carb, 3 med-fat meat, 3–4 fat
Turkey with gravy, mashed potato, dressing*
Serving size: 1 (11 oz)
Exchanges per serving: 2 carb, 2 med-fat meat, 2 fat
Entrée with less than 300 calories*
Serving size: 1 (8 oz)
Exchanges per serving: 2 carb, 3 lean meat

* = 400 mg or more sodium per exchange.

Soups

Bean*
Serving size: 1 cup
Exchanges per serving: 1 carb, 1 very lean meat
Cream (made with water)*
Serving size: 1 cup (8 oz)
Exchanges per serving: 1 carb, 1 fat
Split pea (made with water)*
Serving size: ½ cup (4 oz)
Exchanges per serving: 1 carb
Tomato (made with water)*
Serving size: 1 cup (8 oz)
Exchanges per serving: 1 carb
Vegetable beef, chicken noodle, or other broth-type*
Serving size: 1 cup (8 oz)
Exchanges per serving: 1 carb

* = 400 mg or more sodium per exchange.

Fast Foods

Ask at your fast-food restaurant for nutrition information about your favorite fast foods.

Burritos with beef*
Serving size: 2
Exchanges per serving: 4 carb, 2 med-fat meat, 2 fat

Chicken nuggets*
> *Serving size: 6 nuggets*
> *Exchanges per serving: 1 carb, 2 med-fat meat, 1 fat*

Chicken breast and wing, breaded and fried*
> *Serving size: 1 each (breast, wing)*
> *Exchanges per serving: 1 carb, 4 med-fat meat, 2 fat*

Fish sandwich/tartar sauce*
> *Serving size: 1*
> *Exchanges per serving: 3 carb, 1 med-fat meat, 3 fat*

French fries, thin*
> *Serving size: 20–25*
> *Exchanges per serving: 2 carb, 2 fat*

Hamburger, regular
> *Serving size: 1*
> *Exchanges per serving: 2 carb, 2 med-fat meat*

Hamburger, large*
> *Serving size: 1*
> *Exchanges per serving: 2 carb, 3 med-fat meat, 1 fat*

Hot dog with bun*
> *Serving size: 1*
> *Exchanges per serving: 1 carb, 1 high-fat meat, 1 fat*

Individual pan pizza*
> *Serving size: 1*
> *Exchanges per serving: 5 carb, 3 med-fat meat, 3 fat*

Soft-serve cone
> *Serving size: 1 medium*
> *Exchanges per serving: 2 carb, 1 fat*

Submarine sandwich*
> *Serving size: 1 sub (6 in.)*
> *Exchanges per serving: 3 carb, 1 veg, 2 med-fat meat, 1 fat*

Taco, hard shell*
> *Serving size: 1 (6 oz)*
> *Exchanges per serving: 2 carb, 2 med-fat meat, 2 fat*

Taco, soft shell*
> *Serving size: 1 (3 oz)*
> *Exchanges per serving: 1 carb, 1 med-fat meat, 1 fat*

* = 400 mg or more of sodium per serving.

Recipe Index

General Index

About the Associations

The American Diabetes Association is the nation's leading voluntary health organization dedicated to improving the lives of all people affected by diabetes. Equally important is its unceasing support for research to prevent and cure this chronic disease that affects some 16 million Americans. The association carries out this important mission through the efforts of thousands of volunteers working in more than 800 communities throughout the United States.

Membership in the American Diabetes Association puts you in contact with a network of more than 35,000 caring people. We can provide access to support groups, educational programs, counseling, and other special services. Membership also brings twelve issues of our healthy lifestyle magazine, *Diabetes Forecast*.

In addition, the association publishes an array of materials for every age group on topics important not just to the individual with diabetes but to the entire family. For the latest catalogue featuring cookbooks and self-care guides, call 1-800-ADA-ORDER. Considerable effort is also devoted to educating health care professionals and to building public awareness about diabetes, and advocating on behalf of people with diabetes.

Contact the American Diabetes Association for information on membership and programs at 1660 Duke Street, Alexandria, VA 22314, by calling 800-DIABETES, or by visiting our website at www.diabetes.org.

The American Dietetic Association is the world's largest organization of food and nutrition professionals. Founded in 1917, The American Dietetic Association promotes optimal nutrition to improve public health and well-being. The association has nearly 70,000 members, of whom approximately 75 percent are registered dietitians (RD). The membership also includes dietetic technicians (DTR) and others holding advanced degrees in nutrition and dietetics. As the public education center of the association, the National Center for Nutrition and Dietetics provides programs and services to inform and educate the public about food and nutrition issues. The center and The American Dietetic Association are located at 216 W. Jackson Boulevard, Chicago, IL 60606.

Registered dietitians offer preventive and therapeutic nutrition services in a variety of settings, including health care, business, research, and educational organizations, as well as private practice. Registered dietitians working in the health care field serve as vital members of medical teams, providing medical nutrition therapy to treat illnesses, injuries, and chronic conditions such as diabetes.

An RD (registered dietician) has completed a rigorous program of education and training. The registered dietitian must have at least a baccalaureate degree in an approved program of dietetics or a related field from an accredited U.S. college or university. In addition, he or she must complete an internship or similar experience and pass a national credentialing exam. To retain RD status, dietitians must fulfill continuing education requirements to update and enhance their knowledge and skills.

To find a registered dietitian—the expert in diet, health, and nutrition—ask your physician or call your local hospital. You can also access The American Dietetic Association's toll-free dietitian referral service by calling 800-366-1655 or visiting the web site at www.eatright.org.

COMMON MEASUREMENTS

Volume to Volume

3 tsp	=	1 tbsp
4 tbsp	=	¼ cup
5⅓ tbsp	=	⅓ cup
4 ounces	=	½ cup
8 ounces	=	1 cup
1 cup	=	½ pint

Volume to Weight

¼ cup liquid or fat	=	2 ounces
½ cup liquid or fat	=	4 ounces
1 cup liquid or fat	=	8 ounces
2 cups liquid or fat	=	1 pound
1 cup sugar	=	7 ounces
1 cup flour	=	5 ounces

METRIC EQUIVALENCIES

Liquid and Dry Measure Equivalencies

CUSTOMARY	METRIC
¼ teaspoon	1.25 milliliters
½ teaspoon	2.5 milliliters
1 teaspoon	5 milliliters
1 tablespoon	15 milliliters
1 fluid ounce	30 milliliters
¼ cup	60 milliliters
⅓ cup	80 milliliters
½ cup	120 milliliters
1 cup	240 milliliters
1 pint (2 cups)	480 milliliters
1 quart (4 cups)	960 milliliters (.96 liter)
1 gallon (4 quarts)	3.84 liters
1 ounce (by weight)	28 grams
¼ pound (4 ounces)	114 grams
1 pound (16 ounces)	454 grams
2.2 pounds	1 kilogram (1000 grams)

OVEN-TEMPERATURE EQUIVALENCIES

DESCRIPTION	°FAHRENHEIT	°CELSIUS
Cool	200	90
Very slow	250	120
Slow	300–325	150–160
Moderately slow	325–350	160–180
Moderate	350–375	180–190
Moderately hot	375–400	190–200
Hot	400–450	200–230
Very hot	450–500	230–260